The Uncounted Irish

ALSO BY JOSEPH A. KING:

The Irish Lumberman-Farmer (1982)
Lithuanian Families of Luzerne County, Pennsylvania (1986)

The Uncounted Irish

in Canada and the
United States

_____

by

Margaret E. Fitzgerald

and

Joseph A. King

_____

P. D. MEANY PUBLISHERS
Toronto

Canadian Cataloguing in Publishing Data:
Fitzgerald, Margaret E.
The Uncounted Irish in Canada and the United States
Bibliography: p.
Includes index
ISBN 0-88835-024-4 (bound)
1, Irish - United States - History. 2. Irish - United States - Genealogy. 3. Irish Americans - History. 4. Irish Americans - Genealogy. 5. Irish - Canada - History. 6. Irish - Canada - Genealogy. 7. Irish Canadians - History.* 8. Irish Canadians - Genealogy.* 9. Ireland - Genealogy. I. King, Joseph A., 1925- II. Title.
E184.I6F58 1988 973'049162 C88-094397-1

ISBN 0-88835-024-4

Cover by Jeffrey W. Brain

Although the authors are responsible, individually and distinctively, for their own chapters, the editor and publisher takes responsibility for grouping and sequence. The authors are indebted to each other for information that was indispensable in writing their respective chapters. Each author, however, does not necessarily subscribe to opinions expressed by the other.

Printed and bound in Canada by
Hignell Printing Limited
Willowdale, Ontario
for
P. D. Meany Company, Inc., Publishers
Box 534, Port Credit, Ontario, Canada L5G 4M2

TABLE OF CONTENTS

By Margaret E. Fitzgerald: Chapters 2, 7, 8, 10, 11, 14, 16.
By Joseph A. King: Chapters 1, 3, 4, 5, 6, 9, 12, 15, 17, 18, 19, 20, preface, illustrations, indexes.
Co-authored: Chapter 13.

IN MEMORIAM

All of our great-grandparents were born in Ireland. One great-grandmother died in Kensington, London, England, after bearing ten children, and is buried in common ground at the huge Catholic cemetery at Kensal Green. The other seven arrived in the New World between the years 1830 and 1880. They settled in the Colony of New Brunswick, now a province of Canada, and in Wisconsin, Illinois, Minnesota, and Brooklyn, New York. They had large families; they worked hard and suffered much, but they lived with hope as they tried to pass on to their children and children's children the best and most enduring values of their Irish culture.

Their descendants owe them a debt of gratitude for the softer life for which they laid the foundation. This book, therefore, is dedicated to them: Patrick King, hod-carrier and publican, and Catherine Lawless, washerwoman, of County Mayo, St. Marylebone (London), and Brooklyn, New York; Timothy Lenehan, laborer, and Ellen Callaghan, washerwoman, of County Cork, Kensington (London), and Brooklyn, New York; James Tyrrell, farmer, and Margaret O'Leary, farm-manager, of Counties Wexford and Dublin, Evanston (Illinois), and the St. Croix River Valley, Minnesota; Maurice Fitzgerald, lumberman and farmer, and Johanna Cassin, homemaker, of Counties Cork and Laois, New Brunswick (Canada), and Oshkosh, Wisconsin.

It is also dedicated in appreciation to our beloved grandparents, John Anthony King and Elizabeth Lenehan, and Charles Martin Fitzgerald and Elizabeth Tyrrell; to our parents, the late Joseph Anthony King and Margaret Mary Fitzgerald, who loved words and people, and especially their children; and to the late Professor Gerald E. Fitzgerald of St. John's University, New York, fine scholar and gentleman, loving husband of Margaret E. Fitzgerald, née King.

MEF
JAK

List of Illustrations

FOREWORD

The Irish diaspora in America has been chronicled a number of times through a variety of approaches ranging from filiopietistic to scientific. Many studies exhibit an eastern urban bias in their attempt to characterize the Irish American experience.

In recent decades a number of influential syntheses have been published. Lawrence McCaffrey in his *Irish Diaspora in America* attempts to consider the ideological basis of the Irish American experience, with Irish Americans as the pioneers of the urban ghetto. *The American Irish: A Political and Social Portrait* by William Shannon takes a who's who approach, emphasizing the contributions of notable Irish American political and cultural personalities. In *The Irish Americans: The Rise to Money and Power*, Andrew Greeley emphasizes the accommodation of Irish Catholics to urban America in terms of upward social mobility and loss of ethnic identity. More recently, an award-winning book by Kerby Miller, *Emigrants and Exiles: Ireland and the Irish Exodus to America*, consists of, in many ways, a pejorative account of the Irish in America. It views the Irish, especially the Irish Catholics, as the products of social pathology due to the misfortune of history and archaic socio-cultural baggage from Ireland. Although widely acclaimed and well reviewed, it is not without its methodological flaws, especially with regard to the representativeness of Miller's sample and the subjective interpretation of the real versus ideal meaning of his sources. Further, the work smacks of WASP-ish superiority and academic smugness.

Dennis Clark has most recently attempted to rectify the eastern bias in his *Hibernia America: The Irish and Regional Cultures.* Clark, through his regional approach, confronts the Irish-American experience from a broader perspective. He discusses the Irish American farmer, rancher, and miner of the West, South and Midwest as well as the urban proletariat of the eastern cities. He illustrates the full range of the varieties of Irish America, an Irish America that is not, and never was, monolithic.

Donald Akenson, basing his conclusions primarily on his Canadian research, has recently criticized scholarly activity on the Irish American experience in his book *Being Had: Historians, Evidence, and the Irish in North America.* He feels that the historians have overemphasized the urban experience of the Irish Americans because of their reliance on flawed United States census data. Although Akenson's own work in Canada has been criticized by scholars such as Nicolson, his critique of Irish American studies should not go unnoticed. His correctives may not solve the problems he suggests, but his views could serve to temper conclusions and assumptions based on a limited sample of socio-historical reality.

Most studies of the Irish in America begin by accepting two conclusions: (1) that the early Irish emigration to America was overwhelmingly that of the so-called "Scotch-Irish" Presbyterians; and (2) that the onset of the potato famine of the 1840s changed the emigration pattern to one that was predominantly Catholic with settlement in the eastern seaboard cities. These assumptions ignore the facts that the early Irish Presbyterian immigrants called themselves Irish, not Scotch-Irish, and that Irish Catholic immigration was considerable in pre-Revolutionary times. Further ignored is the fact that a large number of Irish settled in rural areas.

Though Irish Catholics and Irish Presbyterians differed from each other, they both differed even more from the possessors of the dominant Anglo-American cultural-religious heritage of early America. Both groups of Irish were subjected to similar stereotypes and prejudices and were considered threats to Anglo-American institutions. The differentiation of the categories Scotch-Irish and Irish is really an artifact of the 19th century, when Anglophiles wanted to separate the most threatening and despised Irish Catholics from the less threatening and more acceptable Irish Protestants.

In this work the authors recognize the necessity to present a more balanced story of the Irish experience in America. They feel that the rural aspects of the experience have been largely ignored. It is their conclusion that before the Civil War most Irish immigrants settled in rural areas rather than cities. Therefore, they are attempting to fill a serious void in socio-historical scholarship by reconstructing the role of the "uncounted" Irish.

A study of the geographic distribution of the Irish, especially in the United States, presents difficult methodological problems. As pointed out by Akenson, by Houston and Smythe (and by J. A. King in *Canadian Journal of Irish Studies,* June 1984, and *The Irish Lumberman-Farmer,* 1982), American census data regarding ethnicity leave much to be desired. Census figures recorded before the Civil War are not very useful. It was not until the 1850 census that country of birth was recorded. Most quantitative studies of the Irish in America limit their analysis to those identified as Irish born. They omit large numbers of American born Irish who were an integral part of the Irish American experience. It is also important to keep in mind that, given the liability of being Irish in Anglo-Saxon America, many chose to disguise their ethnicity for socio-economic reasons. The

Anglicization of Irish names has been commonplace in America as the O's and Mc's were dropped and spellings changed in an effort to avoid prejudice and discrimination.

Margaret E. Fitzgerald and Joseph A. King contend that during the period 1815-1860 the Irish settlement in the United States was predominantly rural. Reliable quantitative data for these years are unavailable, however. It has been suggested by other scholars that by 1860, 44 percent of the Irish-born lived in forty-three cities and that all but 500,000 were located in urban areas. (The authors question the usefulness of such figures, since they include only the Irish born in Ireland.) We must also question whether the Irish living in the mill villages of the Northeast, the smelting towns of Pennsylvania and the coal towns of northern Illinois were rural or urban in their socio-cultural configuration. In the 19th century United States, rural and urban as polar opposites were not very useful structural concepts. American cities of this period were small and had gardens, goats, pigs, chickens and horses, while rural areas included mill hands, miners, smelters, mechanics and domestics. Traditionally, urban states such as New York, New Jersey and Massachusetts also had the largest numbers of Irish.

In the more sparsely settled western states, the Irish made a statistically greater impact even though their absolute numbers were not large. In the midwestern grain belt significant clusters of Irish farmers existed and continue to exist in Ohio, Illinois, Indiana, Iowa, and Wisconsin. Enclaves of rural Irish are still found in the northern areas of New York, Michigan and Wisconsin, from Malone, New York, to Beaver Island, Michigan. What accounts for the large number of Texans claiming Irish ancestry from a state that is predominantly rural, or for the inordinate number of Irish names on the tombstones in the rural southeast and mountain west? What of the American-born Irish, how many settled in rural areas after an initial sojourn in the city?

There are many more questions than answers with respect to the rural Irish. Who were they? How did they differ from their urban counterparts? How did they accommodate to the American way of life? How numerous were they, and what happened to them and their descendants? The authors of this work have begun the complicated task of unraveling some of the mysteries concerning the rural Irish in America.

Through the use of genealogical and historical research, they have uncovered many previously forgotten aspects of Irish American social history. They have posed a challenge for scholars to prove or disprove their contentions. This work not only presents us with new material and suggests new areas for future research, but it also illustrates a new approach to ethnic history. It reveals the potential of genealogical methods as a tool in historical research. Even those historians who disagree with the authors' conclusions on the rurality of the Irish must admire the meticulous detail of their work.

For too long the Irish American story has been clouded by a combination of overzealous apologists and braggarts, smug and unsympathetic academics, and hostile Anglophiles. We need new perspectives based on new material, fresh analysis free of both popular stereotypes and pseudo-scientific academic license. Dennis Clark has presented us with a new direction in *Hibernia America*. Now, Professor King and Dr. Fitzgerald challenge what are almost axiomatic ideas on the Irish experience. Let us hope it is the first of many such challenges that will contribute to a dynamic re-examination of the Irish diaspora in America.

Seamus P. Metress
University of Toledo
Toledo, Ohio
1989

PREFACE

The genealogist looks for the who, the where, and the when. The historian seeks also the how and the why. These historical questions also occur to the genealogist, if he has normal human curiosity. If he pursues the answers using his genealogical data to support his hypotheses, he finds himself in the realm of the historian, writing history. Similarly, the historian often finds it difficult to function without accurate genealogical data and, if the data has not been published, he must learn the techniques of the genealogist, arduous though they may be, unless he is satisfied with reporting the work of prior historians, some of whom may not have done their homework and may be repeating the errors of historians who preceded them.

The book is intended to represent a reasonably balanced blend of history and genealogy. The unifying theme is that the rural Irish in America and Canada have been largely "uncounted" by major historians in the past. They have been both ignored and denied by historians focusing on the "city-Irish." The fact is that the majority of Irish immigrants in the period before the Civil War, 1815 to 1860, settled not in the cities but in rural America. True, two or three generations of American historians and even an Irish President of the United States (Kennedy, *A Nation of Immigrants*) have told us just the opposite, but they have been wrong for reasons this book tries to explain. The city-Irish were actually part of a general movement, a consequence of the commercial and industrial revolution, into cities. The greatest Irish movement into the cities occurred after the peak years of Irish emigration in the early 1850s. Even in 1870, according to United States census figures, 55 percent of the Irish-born lived outside of cities with populations of 25,000 or more.

The book is in no way an attempt to record the whole range of the Irish presence in America and Canada, even in the rural areas. But it is a contribution, it is hoped, to dispelling some of the half-truths about that presence.

Much appreciation is due to the following scholars, archivists, and clergymen for their personal help with various chapters: Professor W.D. Hamilton of the University of New Brunswick at Fredericton, for critiqueing the New Brunswick chapters; Tim Cadogan of the Cork County Library, historians Father James Coombes of Skibbereen, Father Patrick Hickey of Cork City, and Professor Patrick Corish of Maynooth, for their critiques of the West Cork chapter; Fathers Diarmuid O'Connor and the late John Deasy, parish priests of Goleen and Schull, County Cork, for searches of their parish registers; Kitty

Hobson of the Oshkosh Public Museum and Sister Marie Laurence Kortendick, archivist for the Sinsinawa Dominicans, for Wisconsin records; and Ronald E. Whealan, Head Librarian of the John Fitzgerald Kennedy Library, Boston, Massachusetts, for providing several score of documents on Kennedy family lineage. Gary Boyd Roberts of the New England Historic Genealogical Society carefully read the chapter on United States Presidents, recommending a number of thoughtful corrections and additions. The Alameda County section of the California chapter owes much to Virginia Bennett of Hayward, California; to Herbert Hagemann and James Concannon of Livermore; and to genealogist Dr. Donald F. Foxworthy of Baltimore, Maryland. Yvonne Bodle contributed much to the McGrath family section of that chapter. Professor Robert Ryal Miller of Berkeley, California, was generous in sharing his own immense research on Mexican and California history. Peter Berresford Ellis of London, England, provided helpful items of information on the Fenians. Professor Samuel J. Fanning of St. John's University in New York, prior to his death in 1988, was a constant source of encouragement and a helpful adviser to my sister and co-author.

Many courtesies were also extended by the staffs of the Rare Books and Manuscripts Division of the New York Public Library; the Library of Congress; the National Library and the National Archives of Canada in Ottawa; the Provincial Archives of New Brunswick; the National Library of Ireland; the Genealogical Department of the Church of Jesus Christ of Latter-day Saints in Salt Lake City; the Bancroft Library at Berkeley, California; and the National Archives and Records Center at San Bruno, California. Kevin McEneany of the American Irish Historical Society in New York City provided access to the society's fine collection. Dr. Jeffrey M. Burns helped with the resources of the Archdiocese of San Francisco archives at Colma. Cathi Boronkay and Betty Bortz of the Diablo Valley College library staff obtained much material through interlibrary loan. Dan Downey of the Dublin (California) Historical Preservation Society provided access to that society's manuscript collection. Publisher Patrick Meany improved the manuscript beyond measure by laborious editing and wise suggestions. Betty Wayne King provided ever-patient instruction in the mysteries of computers and word-processing, translated Spanish sources for Chapters 11 and 12, and edited the final manuscript.

Joseph A. King
Lafayette, California

1990

I
OLD WORLD ROOTS: THE IRISH HERITAGE

Chapter 1

GENEALOGY, HISTORY, AND IRISH IMMIGRATION

By 1870, most ethnic Irish in states such as Wisconsin and Minnesota were of Canadian or United States birth, but they have been largely ignored by historians who have depended on misleading United States census statistics which reveal only the Irish-born. Historians need to study surname and genealogical data if the influence of the Irish on the rural and western economy of 19th century America is to be correctly and adequately assessed.

History and genealogy are separate disciplines, but they frequently overlap and inform each other. Historians, however, often dismiss the genealogists, who they think are engaged in a lesser craft, akin to collecting stamps or old bottles. For that reason I propose to tell a small story to illustrate how the historian can sometimes learn something about history from the genealogist.

For a number of years, as a genealogist, I have been inspecting census returns; tax lists; land, church and cemetery records; and old newspapers for Wisconsin, Minnesota, other states, and parts of Canada, for the years 1825 to 1900. In the course of this research I was astonished to learn that my own pioneer ancestors were not isolated Irish in a sea of Germans and Scandinavians and Scots and English. They were part of an Irish involvement in the western and rural economy of the United States and Canada that was much greater, and earlier, than I had formerly believed.

"Most of those (Irish) who entered...into the United States before the Civil War...flocked to the cities," I had been told by Grace McDonald in her study, *History of the Irish in Wisconsin in the Nineteenth Century.* "The Irish congregated mainly in the cities along the Eastern seaboard for they did not have the money to travel after reaching shore," I was told by John F. Kennedy in *A Nation of Immigrants.* "The Irishman chose to fight it out in the dangerous city

1

rather than turn to the West," wrote John B. Duff in *The Irish in the United States.*

That is the way the story was told to me by a score of historians, major and minor. The Irish did not arrive, they believed, in significant numbers until mid-19th century, after the Great Hunger of 1845-1848. They settled mainly in the big cities, or went to work on the railroads or the canals or in the mines; but, in any case, they largely avoided the farms and the forests and the prairies of the truly rural West. I was even told that the Irish were fearful of leaving their priests for the priestless wilderness.

I now believe that such conclusions are less than half-truths. Although the Irish did indeed settle in the big cities in large numbers, they also settled in the rural West in perhaps greater numbers. They were not counted as Irish on the United States censuses for 1850 to 1880, by which time many Irish heads of household in states like Wisconsin and Minnesota were United States or Canadian born.

I also had to re-examine the other cherished notion: that Irish, and especially Irish Catholic, immigration was of little consequence until the Great Hunger. That had to be abandoned after the study of thousands of enumerations for families on the United States censuses for 1850, 1860, and 1870 for Wisconsin and Maine, and on the census of the Colony of New Brunswick for 1851, which lists the year of entry into the Colony for every family member. I received an explanation for the arrival of so many Irish in New Brunswick and elsewhere in the 1820s and 1830s from historian William Forbes Adams in *Ireland and Irish Emigration to the New World: From 1815 to the Famine.* Adams concluded that the first great emigration of the Irish poor actually began about 1830, when the rates from Irish ports to Canada dropped dramatically from about five pounds, which only strong tenant farmers and hardy tradesmen could afford, to thirty shillings and less.

A typical Irish laborer earned no more than eight pence per day, which meant two shillings for three days labor, one pound for thirty days labor. Prior to 1830, a man, wife, and five children needed a total of 35 pounds for passage. That amounted to 1,050 days of labor, over three years if the man found work on every day but the Sabbath. When the rates were lowered the same family needed only 210 shillings, the earnings from 315 days of labor, about one year of work excluding Sundays, if one were among the fortunate few that got steady work. This saving for passage money by the poor, who meantime had to eat and pay rent, indicates the strength and determination that they would carry to the New World.

In the years 1831 and 1832, according to Adams' estimate, more than 65,000 sailed each year from Ireland to North America, and between 1825 and 1844 at least 672,000 emigrated. Among these were the Harrigans and Fitzgeralds, maternal ancestors of the authors, who sailed from Southwest Cork to New Brunswick in 1830 and 1831.

It was timber into Ireland, passengers out, with Ireland hungry for timber and Irishmen hungry to get out of a land where there were serious failures of the potato crop in 1821 and again in 1831. There was also an exploitative system of land ownership and leasing. It was quite usual to have three layers of middle-men between the head landlord, frequently an absentee, and the smallest cottier or rack renter. This situation helped to make the lot of the Irish peasant worse than that of any other peasantry in Europe, according to some contemporary travellers. After the Peace of 1815 and the growth of the timber trade between Ireland and British North America, Irishmen with sufficient funds were quick to board the timber ships for the return journey. Ships sailed from many a tiny port such as Ballyshannon, Baltimore, and Bantry, for Quebec and the Maritimes, especially for New Brunswick ports such as Saint John, Newcastle, Chatham, and St. Andrews. These Irish joined earlier-arriving Scots. In the 1830s and 1840s they learned or invented the lumbering skills in the woods and on the rivers of New Brunswick and Maine that they or their children and grandchildren would one day take farther west.

By mid-century many of them had fallen victim to "Michigan Fever" or "Wisconsin Fever." The Erie Canal boats were full of westward-bound Irish, many from Maine and New Brunswick. The tow horses pulling the canal boats were driven by more Irish. They made their way by train and boat to ports on Lake Michigan, then overland by horse and wagon to communities on the river systems of Wisconsin and Minnesota. They were reported on the censuses under "occupation" mostly as farmers and laborers, but almost all were engaged during some months of the year in some aspect of the lumber industry. They felled the pines in the winter and drove them down the rivers in the spring. They taught their skills to the later-arriving Germans and Scandinavians and Poles. They worked in the sawmills and they farmed in the summer. They were not counted as "Irish" in the statistics, being largely United States or Canadian born. Many of the Irish, like the Scots, English, and Welsh, ceased to be statistically identifiable even as early as 1850 or 1860.

Judging from the official summary statistics for the 1850 to 1870 United States censuses, one would have to conclude that the Irish component of the population of the western states was relatively insignificant, about five percent of a Wisconsin population, for example, of 1,054,670 in 1870, and about the same percentage for a Minnesota population of 439,706. Such statistics badly distort the ethnic reality. Cited below are eleven Winnebago County, Wisconsin, families whose genealogical histories are known to the author. Of sixty-seven people in eleven households, only sixteen are reported as Irish-born on the 1870 census. That is accurate enough as far as it goes. But genealogical evidence reveals that all sixty-seven were of Irish parentage or grandparentage, a fact that did not become part of the statistics. Here are the families as listed on this census:

1870 UNITED STATES CENSUS - Winnebago County, Wisconsin
Sample of 11 families
Column (A) age, column (B) occupation,
column (C) country of birth

		(A)	(B)	(C)
1.	NEKIMI TOWN(SHIP)			
	Morris Fitzgerald	50	farmer	Ireland
	Johanna	26		"
	Mary	6		Wisconsin
	Charles	4		"
	Agnes	1		"
2.	NEKIMI TOWN(SHIP)			
	James Fitzgerald	53	farmer	Ireland
	Mary	40		"
	William	17		Maine
	Mary	15		"
	Maurice	13		"
	Cornelius	11		Wisconsin
	Albert	8		"
3.	OSHKOSH CITY			
	John Lucy	37	lumberman	Ireland
	Maggie	34		"
	Mary E.	5		Maine
	Clara	3		"
	Alice M.	1		Wisconsin
4.	OSHKOSH CITY			
	Charles McPartlin	30	laborer	New Brunswick
	Mary	28		Ireland
	Kate	3		California
	Charles J.	5/12		Wisconsin
5.	OSHKOSH CITY			
	John McPartlin	28	lumberman	New Brunswick
	Elizabeth	23		"
6.	OSHKOSH CITY			
	Daniel Fitzgerald	40	retail grocer	New Brunswick
	Elizabeth	29		Maine
	Josephine	12		Wisconsin
	Henry	10		"
	Laura	8		"
	Franklin	2		"
7.	OSHKOSH CITY			
	James Blake	45	drayman	Ireland

Mary A.	45		Ireland
Mary	18		Canada
Katherine	16		"
Thomas	15		"
Elizabeth	12		Wisconsin
Matilda	10		"
Margaretha	9		"

8. OSHKOSH CITY

Patrick McPartlin	40	lumberman	New Brunswick
Kate	35		"
Agnes	9		Wisconsin
William	7		"
Mary	5		"
Francis	3		"
John	2		"
James	3/12		"
William Fitzgerald	78		Ireland
Ann Fitzgerald	78		"
Kate Desmond	20	servant	New Brunswick

9. OSHKOSH CITY

Patrick Desmond	47	lumberman	Ireland
Elizabeth	44		"
William	18		New Brunswick
Elizabeth	14		"
Thomas	12		"
Jennie	10		"

10. OSHKOSH CITY

Patrick Fitzgerald	60	farmer	Ireland
Catherine	65		"
James	26	laborer	New Brunswick
William	28	laborer	"
Patrick	20	laborer	"
Honora	15		"

11. POYGAN TOWN(SHIP)

Joseph Kavanagh	40	farmer	Ireland
Ellen	21		New Brunswick
Mary	3		Wisconsin
Elizabeth	2		"
James	4/12		"
Ellen Kavanagh	26		Ireland

The census information reveals no Irish connection for four of the eleven household heads. Every person in these households, nevertheless, was Irish-born or had Irish-born parents or grandparents. Household heads Patrick, Charles, and John McPartlin were the sons of Charles McPartlin and Margaret McGee who emigrated from Ireland to Miramichi, New Brunswick, about 1825. Patrick's spouse was Kate Fitzgerald, herself New Brunswick-born but daughter of Irish-born William Fitzgerald and Ann Harrigan in the same household. The servant Kate Desmond was the daughter of neighbors

Patrick and Elizabeth Desmond, both Irish-born. Daniel Fitzgerald, whose birthplace is given erroneously as New Brunswick (he was brought there from Ireland as an infant), had a Maine-born spouse, Elizabeth, herself the daughter of Irish-born Samuel Casey and Margaret McNab.

This was a great Irish *derbfine* (or *cineadh*), the Irish kin-group down to second cousins having common great-grandparents, that managed to transport itself from Ireland to the Maritimes to Wisconsin over the course of two generations. An even larger segment of the *derbfine*, the Harrigans and other Luceys, would also settle in Oshkosh, and in Stillwater, Minnesota. This suggests the need to re-examine another notion, fostered by some New Brunswick historians, that the typical Irish immigrant in the early years of the century was a rootless male forever separated from his kinsmen.

These eleven Winnebago County families are a very small sample, but sufficient to suggest that the number of ethnic Irish is far, far greater than the following official statistics reveal:

WISCONSIN - UNITED STATES CENSUS OF 1870

TOTAL POPULATION	1,054,670
TOTAL NATIVE BORN	690,171
Ireland	48,500
Germany	162,500
Other foreign born	153,499
TOTAL FOREIGN BORN	364,499

The uncounted ethnic Irish are buried in the 690,171 figure for native born and in the 153,499 figure for non-German foreign born which includes many thousands of Irish born in England or in British North America.

That the emigration of ethnic Irish from British North America to Michigan, Wisconsin, and Minnesota was substantial has been brilliantly documented by Professor W.D. Hamilton of the University of New Brunswick at Fredericton in *Old North Esk on the Miramichi*, a model for genealogical studies. Hamilton meticulously gathered genealogical and other data on almost three hundred pioneering Miramichi families, a majority of them Irish. He traced the movement westward of many of these families, identifying the communities where they re-settled. Their driving forces were the white pine, the timber industry, and land.

A further clue that the United States census figures badly understate the Irish presence is suggested by data from the Canadian censuses for 1851, 1861, and 1871. These censuses indicate the "race" (i.e., country of birth of paternal grandparents) of each person enumerated, the country of birth, and, for the 1861 and 1871 censuses, the religion. According to the category of race, the Irish in 1871 were the most numerous people in Canada save for the French:

1871 CENSUS FOR CANADA (%)
French racial origin   31.07
Irish   24.28
English   20.26
Scottish   15.78
All others (mostly German)   8.61

It is evident that, if one were to use only country of birth data, the Irish in Canada would have been as badly undercounted as were the Irish in the United States. Researchers Houston and Smyth in their piece in *Irish Geography* (vol. 13, 1980) have pointed out, among other examples, that the Irish-born in Ontario were a meager 11 percent of the population in 1871, whereas those of the Irish "race" represented 34 percent, making them the largest of the eighteen ethnic groups officially recognized by the census.

How is one to rectify the misleading statistics on the Irish in America a century ago? The historian will have to study the genealogical data, often arduous work but not unduly complicated. Attention has to be given to surnames. Take, for example, the boarding house of Richard and Hannah Sutton in Stillwater, Minnesota. Of the thirty-one residents in the Sutton house, according to the 1875 Minnesota State Census, only Hannah, age sixty-one, was Irish-born. All of the others, with the single exception of Theodore Swanson of Sweden, have easily identifiable Irish surnames, and the birthplace of most of them, including Hannah's spouse, is given as New Brunswick or Maine. (The official statistics would lead one to think there were as many Swedes as Irish in this household!)

Take another example, on the 1880 United States census for the same community: the boarding house of carpenter Dennis Harrigan and his spouse, Kate (Ahearn). Both were New Brunswick-born, of Irish-born parents, although that is not revealed in the census data. The fifty-two boarders in this household, mostly New Brunswick-born, have, in most cases, identifiable Irish surnames.

The intention of this chapter is not to magnify chauvinistically the merits and contributions of the Irish. It is only to suggest that the quantity and quality of the Irish contributions to rural America have not been reported adequately by historians. There are at least two reasons for the bad reporting. One is that the equally great Irish involvement in big city life has been perhaps more immediately newsworthy and even easier to research and write about, studded as it is with an all-star cast of sparkling characters including the Ed Curleys, Boss Prendergasts, Jimmy Walkers, Honey Fitzgeralds, Richard

Daleys, and Boss Crokers. Another reason, the one that is underscored in this chapter, is that statisticians and historians have
depended too much on United States census figures which hide more
than they reveal in the matter of ethnicity. Certainly they hide great
numbers of ethnic Irish born in the New World who married other
ethnic Irish, bringing their Irish and usually Catholic culture with
them to the rural West in the mid-19th century, and who had children
and grandchildren who moved farther westward in the last quarter of
the century to the Pacific Northwest. It is a great pattern of migration
that has not been much studied.

The Irish on this northern migration path made a permanent
mark, felling the timber, tilling the soil, building schools and churches
and hospitals and great universities in the riverports and on the
prairies. They were quieter than their city cousins but their legacy is
at least as enduring in states such as Wisconsin and Minnesota, which
were indeed settled by Celtic as well as by Nordic Giants in the Earth.
The ethnic Irish in Wisconsin and Minnesota in, say, the year 1870
represented perhaps 25 percent of the total population, about the
same percentage as recorded for ethnic Irish by the Canadians in the
census for 1871, and perhaps even as much as the 34 percent recorded
for Ontario in that year. Professor Donald Akenson of Queen's
University, Kingston, Ontario, has reached a similar conclusion (*Being
Had: Historians, Evidence, and the Irish in North America*), calling on
historians to study the genealogical literature and to learn the genealogist's skills. Some of them, in the process, will doubtless have to eat
a portion of their lecture notes, as the author sometimes has had to
eat his own.

JAK

Chapter 2

A LONG INHERITANCE:
THE GAEL AND GENEALOGY

Before we consider further the uncounted Irish in Canada and the United States, we should turn to the Old World roots influencing and shaping the New World branches. Set deep in the past, these roots were developed in pagan Ireland, were watered by the coming of St. Patrick, budded with the founding of great scholastic houses, and flowered with the exploits of the missionaries. In turn, they were starved by English colonization and subjugation, by the suppression of the monasteries, and by centuries of persecution of religion. Yet much of the ancient culture survived.

THE SEARCH FOR IRISH ROOTS

Genealogy has always been important to the Irish, from ancient times to modern, from cottage to castle. In the days of the earliest chiefs, kings, and clans in pagan Ireland, kinship determined a man's loyalty, inheritance, and obligations. There was, however, a period in the 19th century when Irish American immigrants broke with tradition and ignored their roots.

In Ireland, they had needed the bards and village story-tellers (the *seanachies or seanchaithe)* to trace the greatness of the past in order to remember that their ancestors had the oldest vernacular literature and traditions in Western Europe and had kept the lamp of learning aglow when barbarians overran the European mainland and England. Without those reminders, they would have degenerated into the role their English conquerors set for them: that of tip-the-forelock people at best, with a slave mentality; a sub-human race; a degraded species; a role described so well in *A Modest Proposal,* Jonathan Swift's bitter satire on the English rule in Ireland.

9

In the New World, the Irish saw themselves as founders of families who could hold their heads up with pride and freedom. The exiles did not want to look back upon centuries of oppression, persecution, and unsuccessful rebellions, with martyrs making the "blood sacrifice." What inspiration could their children receive from that?

As the immigrant generations passed from first to second to third, the horrors from which they had fled dimmed. The later generations were several memory-steps removed from the nightmares of starving evictees huddled in ditches; skeleton women dying of green-mouth as they delivered dead babies; plague-ridden bodies tossed from "coffin ships"; men hanged, cut down, and disembowelled alive in the garrison towns. They imagined instead a romantic Ireland through popular ballads such as "Galway Bay" and "I'll Take You Home Again, Kathleen."

Diverse reasons have been ascribed to the increasing number of Irish Americans interested in tracing their roots. Some may be looking for a title, a coat-of-arms, a famous or infamous ancestor. Some may be investigating a bit of family folklore about a little farm in County Roscommon that belonged by right to their emigrating ancestor. But most of us just have an inborn need to go back and find out exactly where our ancestors came from and what they were like. Why and how did they leave? What happened to them in the United States or Canada? How did we descendants get where we are? How do we find the links in the chain that connects us to our emigrating ancestors, and even beyond to their ancestors in Ireland? There seems to be a deeply implanted human need to understand something of our roots in the past as we grow in the present and move into the future.

There are at least two other satisfactions that come from genealogical research. One comes when we stand on that spot in the Old Country where our ancestors walked and tilled the soil. We feel a mystical union with them. The other comes from the discovery of and meeting with distant cousins with whom we share a common heritage.

There is still another delight when we recognize on our family tree the names of the Old Gaelic Order. The Irish, perhaps more than any people except the Welsh and Scots, who are fellow Celts, have legends of being descended from kings and chieftains, who, in turn, were descended from Moses and Adam.

Until the 19th century the Irish laborer with a Gaelic name could tell his children of the time when their family of O'Sullivans, O'Donnells, O'Mahoneys, or MacCarthys were rulers of the land. The father or the *seanchaí* could trace a family's Gaelic origins via genealogies back through the centuries to the chiefs of Ireland before the Norman invasion in the 12th century.

Likewise, if the peasant family bore a Norse, Norman, or gallowglass (foreign mercenary serving an Irish chief) name, such as Coppinger, Fitzgerald, or Sweeney, the father could trace back to the 16th and 17th centuries, when their ancestors' loyalty to Ireland and the Catholic Church had cost them the land and titles that had been taken from the Gaelic Irish in preceding centuries. The Old Norse and Norman families had become "more Irish than the Irish themselves."

Nobody in Ireland is "pure Irish," but a little arithmetic or geometric progression makes it likely that anyone with an old Gaelic surname in his heritage has some strain of chieftain's blood running in his veins, for whatever that is worth. For someone born in 1925, for instance, going back and allowing for twenty-five years in each generation (two parents, four grandparents, eight great-grandparents, and so on), we would find 1,073,741,824 direct ancestors living in 1175 A.D., just after the Norman invasion.

That is a mathematical exercise, not allowing for intermarriage nor for the fact that the population of Ireland in 1175 A.D. has been estimated at little more than half a million. However, it is not the height of the ridiculous, although it might be if one were too serious about it, for a person with all Irish roots to assume that one of his million forebears was a chief or a king. Indeed the odds are in favor of this claim, since Gaelic Ireland did not lack for kings. There were always one hundred to two hundred small kingdoms and many more chieftainships. So, if one has Irish roots, one may consider them royal roots.

ANCIENT IRELAND

The Irish are the longest settled people in Europe on their own soil and have traditions that are the oldest of any people north or west of the Alps. This is not a claim that there was a single isolated race of Irish people from neolithic times until the Norman invasions, but it is a claim that the earliest Irish absorbed new settlers from the continent and that these settlers became Irish because there seemed to be no further place westward to venture.

Until recently, very little was known about the earliest inhabitants of Ireland, the Stone Age hunters who settled in 6000 B.C., or possibly some four thousand years before that. Now archaeologists are learning more about these long-ago people, especially at the rich sites of Coleraine in County Derry and Tullamore in County Offaly. More is known about the colonizers expanding from the continent in 3000 B.C. because these tillers of the soil left behind many artifacts that have been dug up by archaeologists. One of the most rewarding sites is the area around Lough Gur in County Limerick. Even more is known about the prospectors and metallurgists who reached Ireland around 2000 B.C., because evidence of their industry and life has been found everywhere later-day miners have worked.

There is evidence that the prehistoric people of Ireland had chieftains, small kin groups, and settlements of larger kin groups. However, their religion, language, institutions, and traditions were absorbed by the later-arriving Celts, coming in waves after 1000 B.C. The Celts would give Ireland its lasting genealogical and historical culture and traditions. Genealogy and history were basic to Celtic society, since that society was founded on family relationships. Kinship decided a man's or woman's place in the social structure.

The Celts were genealogists and historians of the first class, and were thorough record-keepers in oral, artistic, and written tradition. Their coming to Ireland and their history before arriving is carefully recorded. The ancient *Lebor Gabála* or *An Leabhar Gabhála* (Book of Invasions) of the Celts traces the coming of the sons of Mil (Mileadh) from Spain and tells how three of these sons became ancestors to all the royal clans of later Ireland. As the Milesian Celts, who invaded from 1000 B.C. to 600 B.C., were joined by continental Celts around 350 B.C., they blended the memories of the ancients, the Firbolgs and the Tuatha Dé Danann, with those of their own.

The ancients had already divided Ireland into fifths, or five kingdoms, and the Celts kept that division. They took over the monarchy form of government of the ancients, although they had been republican on the continent. In religion, Celtic druidism blended with much of the earlier paganism.

Although many names were given to them by contemporary geographers, historians, and travelers of Europe, the Irish Celts called themselves Gaels and they called their country Ériu (Erin, Éire). The Celts traced their ancestry back to persons named in the Old Testament.

Since the Celtic genealogists recognized the difference, sometimes shadowy, between myth and legend, it is helpful to pause and do the same. Celtic druids drew upon mythological, superhuman figures, frequently using parables or allegories. Although the stories were ostensibly historical, they could have only an imaginary and unverifiable existence. Celtic genealogists drew upon legendary human figures in stories coming down from the past, with possible exaggeration of heroic but still human actions. These stories were regarded by the people as historical, but probably not verifiable by methods available and known at the time.

The continental druids, as perceived and reported by Julius Caesar, may have traced all ancestry to a common deity, *Dis Pater* (Irish *Donn*), and may have developed cults worshipping ancestral gods such as the equivalent of the Gaulish and Roman Mercury (Irish *Lugh*) and Minerva (Irish *Brighid*). The Irish *filí* genealogists, however, did not confuse these mythological religious tales with the legendary historical tales of the race. The ancestry-tracing by the *filí* through human rather than divine figures gives some credence to the generalities of the stories of the Gaelic wanderings before coming to Ireland, even though the specifics are unlikely to be exact.

Before discussing the *filí*, it is interesting to note the opinion of linguist-historian Thomas O'Rahilly. Writing from the viewpoint of philology, he attacked the credibility of all annals, manuscripts, monastic copyings, and oral histories. His criticism of Celtic translators and modern scholars was caustic and destructive. He upheld the "worthiness" and veracity of the ancient traditions up to the story of the Milesian invasions. That story he considered a "sheer fabrication" by which genealogists tried to give a common ancestor, Mil, to the Irish people. Although admitting he was mindful of the Irish saying *dall cách I gceard ar-oile*, freely translated as one generally makes a fool of one's self if one intrudes into subjects other than his own, O'Rahilly failed to see the opposing folly of eliminating from consideration disciplines other than his own. By frequently stating that his conclusions were in no way dependent on archaeological or genealogical "speculations," by not trying to understand the philosophy and mechanics of archaeologists and genealogists, and by not distinguishing between heroic and human genealogies, he suffered a severe handicap in his voluminous Celtic studies. His referring to other great Celtic scholars as "pseudo-historians" who persisted in pure fiction, sheer fantasy, pious frauds, self-serving delusions, and constant blunders, showed that he never understood the very important institution of the *filí*. O'Rahilly may have contributed nothing other than admirable and valuable philological theories to ancient Irish history, but yet one could say he also made a backhand contribution in promoting a wealth of dissent and additional research buoying up that dissent.

THE FILI

A remarkable institution of the Irish Celts was their learned class, the *filí*, who were responsible for preserving traditions, history, epics, laws, and pedigrees of the race. As we shall see later, the *filí* were most likely to be careful and accurate about the recording of what unfolded before them in Ireland. Their recording of the pre-Ireland days is second-hand, but the general story fits in with new historical and archaeological evidence.

According to the *filí*, the origins of the Irish Celts or Gaels were in Scythia or Egypt where their common ancestor Gaodhal Glas was cured by Moses of a serpent's bite. Moses then promised Gaodhal that no serpents would infest the Island of Destiny that his Gaedhal (Gael) descendants would someday inhabit. Gaodhal's grandson, Niul, married Scota, daughter of the Pharaoh, but the descendants of Niul and Scota were driven from Egypt. Later descendants reached Spain, where they heard that their Island of Destiny was to the north. Eight sons of Mileadh or Milesius (who also married a daughter of the Pharaoh named Scota in the *fili's* recordings) set forth for Ireland.

Ancient manuscripts preserve the prayer composed by the poet Amergin for their safe arrival in Ireland and for their successful subjugation of the natives. Despite Amergin's prayer, all did not go well, since five brothers were lost at sea, and their mother, Queen Scota, was lost in battle. Another brother, Ir, was lost in landing. The two remaining brothers, Eber and Eremon, fought each other for the high kingship. Fighting continued for generations, not only among the Milesian Celts, but in alliances both with and against the natives. Variant spellings are given for Eremon, Ir, and Eber, even in the same manuscript.

The genealogies of the *fili* give us a long list of Irish kings, from Eremon on, with many important events in their lives. Some historians who cannot accept the thesis that the Irish could have lists of kings more ancient than those recorded in any other country of modern western Europe strangely accept with unquestioning faith the traditional oral genealogies and lore of Polynesians and American Indians. Other historians, accepting the general authenticity of the lists, call attention to the singularly compact and remote situation of Ireland. It was free from Roman conquest and from the effects of the fall of the Roman Empire. This made it quite possible for the Irish to have more accurate lists than their British and continental contemporaries. The shorter antiquities of memory of other western European peoples puts their history in a kind of infancy compared to that of the Irish.

The best argument for accepting the popular tradition of Milesian royalty in pre-Christian Ireland, if not accepting the details of the Gaels' wanderings from Scythia and Egypt, is the nature of the institution of the *fili*. The Irish *file* was carefully trained and he knew that he had a sacred trust, unlike the bard, who was a poet and a versifier, a member of the learned aristocracy, superior to the freeman harper but inferior to the *file*. The *file* was a scholar who was required to study for twelve years under masters. Recent studies of archives and excavations, as well as analysis of some tall epic tales, indicate that the *fili* did not deviate from the truth in important things, especially in history and genealogy. They might use imagery, imagination, literary devices, and elaboration, especially to praise kings and heroes, but the *fili* had to guard traditional knowledge and truth. Stories of greater imagination and exaggeration were left to the bards and harpers, who were not bound by the limits of the *filí.*

The people reverenced the *filí*, but their reverence for the truth took precedence.   Under Brehon Law, a *file* who falsified was degraded to the lowest class and disgraced.   At the annual *Feis* at Tara, as well as at smaller fairs, the ancient history of the land was recited.   If it was recited by the High King's *seanchaí*, who was himself a *file*, he was in the presence of many other critical *seanchaithe* and *filí* and, therefore, did not dare distort or lie, else another would gladly take his place.

Every chief or petty king (Celtic society had many chieftains who had the title "king") had his own skilled *seanchaí* or *file*, who, at large assemblies or small gatherings, would be asked to recite passages of local and national history.   He would tell each little kin group, even if they already knew it by heart, the history of the deeds of their forefathers.   Thus all people, even the lowest classes, had pride in race, family, and clan, the pride that comes from familiarity with the achievements of one's kinfolk.

The continued telling of the ever-lengthening history of Ireland fixed the stories in the minds of the people.   There may have been much poetic coloring, but the basic truths were preserved.   In some ways the *filí* and their oral records gave way to the great books of the Christian monasteries with their bilingual writing in Irish and Latin in magnificent illuminated manuscripts.   In other ways, the *seanchaí* remained through the coming of Christianity because the oral recitation and repetition provided the most practical way of keeping all the people familiar with their country's history and leaders and with their own place in history.   In the dark days of the penal codes, the *seanchaí* and the *file*, as well as the bard, played a most important role again.

FAMILY RELATIONSHIPS

In Gaelic Ireland, overlapping from pagan to Christian times, society was strictly classified.   There was a layer of kings over a larger layer of nobles above a mass of commoners.   Within these three classes, there were further distinctions in status.   These distinctions provided for a person's obligations and rights under Brehon Law.   So important was status and honor in early Irish society that it is difficult to exaggerate it.   Every person had his "honor price," which set the limits of what he could legally do and what could be legally done to him, and for what price.

Each person had his place within the *tuath*, the basic political unit.   The *tuath* was a cluster of families, all freemen, ruled by a king elected from those eligible.   The actual bond was the acceptance of common rule by a king, who himself was subject to one of the kings of the Five Provinces.

The *filí*, as genealogists, were responsible for keeping records of all relationships within the *tuath*, for just as the *tuath* was the basic political unit, the family was the basic social unit. The legal Irish family was defined in a special way that is best described by the Irish word *fine*, later translated as *cineadh*, or kin-group. The obligations and responsibilities of a *fine* were so far-reaching that its actions could increase or decrease the power of a *tuath*.

It required a good genealogical mind to keep track of the *fine* because the Brehon lawyers drew a very elaborate system of different degrees of relationship. The *derbfine (deirbfhine)*, sometimes called *gelfine (geilfhine or cineadh)*, consisted of all male members of the family for five generations. Basically the relationship between a man and his brothers, it extended to include his own sons, his father and his father's brothers, his grandfather and his brothers, his great-grandfather and his brothers. Some historians see each man as belonging for practical purposes only to a four generation unit since the fifth generation might be either too young or too old for obligations. Unlikely as it might seem for all five generations to be alive and active at one time, the lawyers had to provide for this contingency.

It may be practical to consider the *derbfine* as a four generation group of all males with a common great-grandfather, thus allowing for the fifth generation being minor children. This, however, is a simplification of the careful delineations of Brehon Law because, however one sees it, the *derbfine* were "certain kin" who had responsibilities that they could not avoid.

There were infrequent circumstances in which the responsibilities of the *derbfine* might be taken over by a wider group, the *iarfine*, a five or six generation group according to the way minors are counted, or by the *indfine*, which went one generation further. Outside the actual sixth generation there would be no responsibilities of kinship. To put this in perspective, one must think of fourth cousins, people with sibling great-great-grandparents. How many people today can name their fourth cousins? Can one imagine being responsible for the actions of even second cousins?

In Brehon Law the basic *fine* relationship went upward and downward from a man's great-grandparents and his brothers to his great-grandchildren and his brothers' great-grandchildren, the last being third cousins to each other. Obviously only a genealogist could keep track of *fine* relationships, and just as obviously, every man in ancient Ireland had to be a genealogist or have a *file* available to keep track for him. Since each generation gave rise to a new *fine* when there were male descendants, there was a constant spinning off and rearranging process.

In practice, in the classical period in ancient Ireland, a smaller kinship group emerged, a three generation group with a common grandfather which was adequate to take on all obligations if enough heirs were produced. This did not supersede the *derbfine* in law, but it helped keep responsibility under control.

RIGHTS AND RESPONSIBILITIES OF THE *FINE*

Before the coming of the Normans, the Gaelic Irish did not have the same land-ownership practices or feudal system that was developing in England and on the continent, where inheritance by primogeniture (everything to the oldest son) or inheritance by designation (paternal bestowal to several sons of lands to be held in their own right) prevailed. In Ireland, all freemen were considered landowners, but within the *fine* land was shared equally by brothers. The head of the senior line was the *cenn fine,* who represented the family in its affairs. He could not make decisions that would affect the *fine* without consulting its most responsible members. If he or any member of the *fine* accepted a fief (grant of cattle, horses, land-use) from a lord, the whole *fine* would be concerned since all would be responsible for default and all would be assessed according to the degree of relationship to the defaulter.

Loyalty to the *fine* meant that buying, selling, and contracting should be arranged with fellow members of the *fine.* It meant joint plowing and cattle-driving if an individual member was unable to work his land because of poor health or lack of a good team of oxen. It meant that the *fine* bore the duty of blood vengeance if any member were slain. In practice, they accepted the payment of an *éraic,* blood money, from the slayer or his kin. In the same way, the *fine* was responsible for wrongs committed by its members and would pay blood money or honor price to the victim's *fine.*

In royal families, each member of the king's *derbfine* was eligible to be elected king. Sometimes one branch of the family monopolized the kingship for three or four generations, and as each new *fine* spun off, some were in danger of falling outside the kingly *derbfine* and losing royal status. In reality, many eligibles to kingship were ruled out at an early stage because of age, physical defects, lack of ambition, poor fighting strength, or inability to take leadership and inspire confidence in followers. However, enough contenders in the *derbfine* usually remained to keep them constantly fighting among themselves and to tempt those on the outer edge to slay their own kin (the serious crime of *fingal*) in order to stay within the royal relationship.

To prevent kin-slaying, a *tanaiste ríg*, or heir apparent, would be elected during the king's lifetime. Since this would be the member of the *derbfine* who had the largest number of followers or vassals to support him, the heir-apparent solution led to another temptation, that of being too impatient to wait for the king's natural death. If the heir-apparent died before the king or died in warfare at the same time as the king and other members of the *derbfine*, the *filí* would be responsible for identifying whatever eligible claimants remained. This limited the fighting for the kingship to those truly eligible, since vassals would withdraw support from pretenders with no chance for success.

All the laws and ramifications of the Brehon system for the *fine* make it easy to understand why Irish nobles were careful to preserve their genealogies and why they delegated this function to a trusted *seanchaí* or *file*. Since there was a possibility of commoners, both freemen and those made free by education, moving upward into the ranks of the nobility, it was important too for the lower classes to preserve their genealogies. In addition, there was the chance of downward movement among the nobility. Nobility was measured in part by the number of vassals a man had. If a noble who had many sons by a first wife took a second wife and had many sons by her, the great number of heirs would cut deeply into the inheritance; some of the sons or grandsons would have so few vassals that they would become commoners.

WOMEN

A woman at marriage passed into her husband's *fine* and was accorded half his worth in honor-price, but she also had status in her own right. Some historians believe that the high status of women in ancient Ireland was part of the pre-Celtic culture that was absorbed by the invading Celts. One thesis is based on the fact that invaders of all countries were accustomed to taking as booty the women of the land they conquered. The pre-Celtic women, having been accustomed to comparative liberty, would not accept marriages that took away their freedom. The Celtic men realized that rape and force might subdue a woman, but would not make her a good wife. Thus, a man who wanted a permanent wife, booty or not, to rear his heirs, to protect his home and property in his absence, and to live congenially and loyally with him, had to accept the woman's conditions.

Another explanation of the position of women comes from the 14th century *Book of Ballymote*, which cites as its reference the *Book of Leinster*, which in turn takes as its source the pre-Patrician *Cin Droma Snechta*. This story begins when the sons of Milesius found in *Ériu*, their Island of Destiny, female Hebrew exiles. These far-from-home but independent women had been driven by a fierce tempest from the Tirrén (Mediterranean) Sea into the ocean and thence to the shores of Ireland. In response to proposals by the Milesian leaders, the ladies agreed to marriage on the condition that the men recognize their worth by pairing only those of equal status and by giving them a dowry. From this came the ancient Irish custom, rare among the world's cultures, of the husbands' providing the price or dowry to purchase the wives.

From the *Táin Bo Cuailnge* (Cattle Raid of Cooley) comes another tale of a woman's insistence that her personal status be recognized. Queen Maeve (*Medb, Medhbh*) represents the liberated, outspoken, free-spirited, free-minded heroine of the ancient Irish people. The story has elements of the mythical, but modern historical research has indicated a legendary base which brings it close to what is now known as historical fiction. Maeve became angry with her third husband, Ailill, because he boasted that it was his status that gave honor and worth to her. She presented arguments to prove that she had her own status that was as good as, if not better than, his. She reminded him that she was Queen of Connaught not through him, but through her father, the High King, who selected her because she was the best warrior of his four daughters (although she may have acquired her solid title to queenship through her second husband). She enumerated her victorious battles and the fighting men that she had in her own right. She also claimed freedom to do as men did and take lovers, something Ailill should have understood clearly when she chose him as her husband on the basis of his lack of jealousy.

The inheritance or allotment of the land for use or sharing was tied to the military duty necessary to protect one's *fine, tuath*, or a greater kingdom. Since men were considered physically stronger than women, they were given preference in inheriting land-use and also given responsibility for military service. If there were no son, however, a daughter could inherit or be assigned the use of land and the corresponding requirement of going into battle if there was a military levy. In the 1st Century A.D., Bridget Brethra of the Judgments, a great woman lawmaker, had the law revised so that an exemption was granted by which any female land inheritor could provide and pay a substitute male warrior to fulfill her military obligation. Some women, nevertheless, felt duty-bound to fight their own battles or to fight alongside their husbands, brothers, and sons.

In the earliest records of Ireland, mythological, legendary, and historical, freeborn women are portrayed as emancipated individuals and slave women are portrayed as more valuable than male slaves. Women were warriors, druids, physicians, poets, lawgivers, and scholars. Brehon law gave women equal standing with men, although it is likely that only firm and powerful women could enforce the law. Women, like men, were subject to the decisions of their *fine* and the male *cenn fine.*

Marriage was a voluntary contract in which, for purpose of order, the man was made head of the household. His wife, nevertheless, retained rights sufficient to prevent her husband from ever owning her. She could not be a chattel as in other ancient societies. She received part of the marriage portion (*coibche*) that her husband paid to her father. She retained sole ownership of any property that she had acquired before her marriage. She could pass on her property by will. She had equal rights with her husband in joint ownership of properties; both had to consent to sale or leasing. A wife could appear and appeal in Brehon courts on equal terms with her husband. She could go to court as an individual to collect a debt or ask for a judgment. If she had a legal separation for good cause, she was entitled to the marriage portion, to the marriage gifts from friends, and to the homemaking articles that she had brought with her to the union.

The coming of Christianity confirmed the high position of Irish women. The pre-Christian Irish had a mythological goddess, Bridget, patron of wisdom and poetry, and a human Bridget, expounder of law and judgments. The Christian Irish had St. Bridget, founder of the famous school, church, and monastery at Kildare. St. Bridget was no cloistered mystic, but was an active trail-blazer who journeyed throughout Ireland to teach, to counsel, to spread the faith, and to direct about thirty religious houses. Such a role could have been possible only in a country in which women had long commanded the respect that made them eligible for rank, education, leadership, and the professions.

Christianity is credited with influencing one change, although this might have resulted anyway from an evolving culture. The pedestal on which Christianity placed women was not that of Maeve, sexual adventuress and ruthless warrior, but that of Mary, chaste virgin and merciful refuge of sinners. Women, despite lawgiver Bridget's exemption, were still taking up arms and marching into battle. Not only queens, princesses, and landowners, but women of all ranks appear in poetry and verse as victors or victims in bloody contests. This became a major concern of St. Adamnán (Eunan).

Donegal-born Adamnán was the elected head of the great abbey of Iona. Too much of a leader to be allowed to remain in holy and studious retirement, he was called to represent and negotiate for the Irish, the English, the Northumbrians, the Pope, and competing kings and princes. He is known for his voluminous scholarly writings, especially his *Life of St. Columba (Columcille)* and for his unflagging and eventually successful attempts to get the church in Ireland and Scotland to accept Roman customs, in particular the dating of the Easter feast. More important, he is remembered for his successful attempts to remove women and children from warfare.

At the Council of Birr in present-day County Offaly, Adamnán convinced the assembly to recommend exemption of women from all military engagements. In 697 A.D., at the Synod of Tara, he succeeded in having legislation passed that became known variously as the Canon of Adamnán, Adamnán's Law, Law of the Innocents, and the "law not to kill women." Women were not to take up arms. Women were not to participate in warfare. Neither women nor their children were to be killed or taken prisoner. Whether all the ladies who followed their lords and their lords' liegemen into battle appreciated their exclusion from demonstrating their superiority on the field is not known, but one can be certain that all appreciated the ban on their being carried off as prisoners after attacks on their homes and settlements.

St. Adamnán won for women the status and privilege of being classified as non-combatants. Women were still prey, however, to the pagan Viking raiders, who were not party to the "Adamnán Convention" until they were Christianized. They also may have been prey to their own passions or preferences, as in the case of the beautiful Devorgilla, wife of One-Eyed Tiernan O'Rourke, King of the Bréifne.

According to both Irish and Norman accounts, Devorgilla invited ambitious Dermot MacMurrough, King of Leinster, to carry her off, along with her jewels, cattle, and marriage portion. Some minority accounts do say that Devorgilla, age forty-plus, was forcibly abducted by MacMurrough in a power play. All accounts admit that she and her serving women cried and screamed during the capture, but some versions, such as that of historian Geoffrey Keating, claim the protests were a pretense. Devorgilla later was forcibly re-abducted or happily rescued (depending on which version is to be believed) by the High King and returned to her husband.

Whether Devorgilla was a willing collaborator or a reluctant victim is not as significant as the after-effect of this breaking of the laws of Adamnán and the Church. Several years of struggle between the sub-kings of Ireland resulted in MacMurrough's banishment. One charge brought against him was that he had broken the law of God and man by abducting Devorgilla.

Ironically, MacMurrough subsequently made a similar accusation, at the court of Henry II, against the Irish. They were, he claimed, breaking church law. Reform was needed. This was welcome news for Henry, although no serious historian believes that either Henry or Dermot was interested in religion. Henry, constantly at odds with the Popes over rights in his own dominions, now had an excuse to appear as a defender of the rights of Rome while he was satisfying his acquisitive and marauding instincts. Dermot's true objective is expressed well in the "Song of Dermot and the Earl":

> *Hear, noble King Henry...*
> *Wrongfully my own people*
> *Have cast me out of my kingdom...*
> *Your liege man I shall become*
> *Henceforth all the days of my life*
> *On condition that you be my helper,*
> *So that I do not lose everything...*

MacMurrough hoped to gain more than he had lost and Henry hoped to help himself to the whole of Ireland.

Although Devorgilla entered the convent at Mellifont, she has no pedestal or altar in Ireland. She is the symbol and the scapegoat for the beginning of centuries of English subjugation, misrule, and persecution. Perhaps Adamnán's Law, set in place five centuries before the Norman invasion, should have removed women not only from warfare but from being used as reasons for war.

GENEALOGY

Genealogy was a natural and essential part of the lives of all classes in pagan and early Christian Ireland. For those untraceable ancient Irish ancestors of ours, genealogy was a matter of status and honor that dominated their lives. For us, it is a pleasant hobby. Who knows, however, whether or not there may be deep in our inherited memories the sense of importance and survival that spurred our Irish ancestor to know his place and the place of every third cousin in the *derbfine* or *cineadh*.

MEF

Chapter 3

HARRIGAN'S ROCKS

In BEING HAD: HISTORIANS, EVIDENCE, AND THE IRISH IN NORTH AMERICA, *historian D.H. Akenson of Queens's University, Ontario, accuses historians of doing a poor and often inaccurate job in counting the Irish presence in America, especially in the 18th and early 19th centuries. As a corrective strategy, historians should pay more attention, he thinks, to the genealogical literature. These include the "thousands of individual family histories" where linkages are shown to the Old Country. The following narrative by one of the authors of this volume describes his personal quest for his maternal Irish roots. It reveals, it is hoped, the kind of research in establishing linkages that Professor Akenson says is required for describing the Irish presence in America and Canada. One product of that research is the genealogical data on the Fitzgerald and Harrigan and other families woven into the fabric of the basically historical chapters "A Parish in West Cork" and "The Miramichi Irish" in this volume.*

GRANDFATHER FITZGERALD

My grandfather Charles Martin Fitzgerald was born in Oshkosh, Wisconsin, in 1866, and raised on a farm south of the city. While employed on the ore docks at Ashland, he met and marrried Elizabeth Tyrrell in 1894. Her parents, like her husband's, were Irish-born. Charles was a smart and witty man, a major in the Army during World War I, after which he worked as a civilian in the Army Supply Corps. Elizabeth was an equally wise and witty farm girl from Minnesota. The fortunes or misfortunes of government service brought them to Brooklyn, New York, where their daughter married Joseph Anthony King, also of totally Irish forebears. They had five children, of whom I was the third.

My grandparents lived to great age. Charles passed away at 88, Elizabeth at 92. I knew them well and loved them much. I sometimes questioned them about their forebears. Charles knew that his father was Maurice Fitzgerald, who died in the early 1880s near Oshkosh.

23

He thought he knew that his father's father was also Maurice whose spouse was Mary Lucey (he was wrong on both counts). He vaguely remembered their deaths when he was a child. He did know the names of several of his aunts and uncles who also settled in or near Oshkosh, and thought they had all been born in County Cork and had all spent some time in New Brunswick before moving on to Wisconsin long before he was born. He knew no more. No folklore, no records, no Bible, no keepsakes of the New Brunswick or Ireland periods of his ancestors. He did have some old photos, including one of four children, perhaps relatives, taken in Stillwater, Minnesota, but he did not know how they fitted into the family.

ACUTE GENEALOGIA

With this information and misinformation, I began my quest. It was a genealogical project of consuming interest for several years. It involved much travel to archives in the United States, Canada, and Ireland, and the writing of hundreds of letters to distant cousins, librarians, record keepers, local historians, and others. It was also very expensive. In the process I learned, among many other things perhaps interesting only to me, that I was a third-cousin (once-removed) of Bing Crosby, and a potential claimant to a forelorn out-cropping known as Harrigan's Rocks in a little bay on the coast of the Mizen Peninsula in southwest Cork. But that is getting a bit ahead of the story of my quest for the genealogical Holy Grail, the exact spot, the townland in Ireland from whence my ancestors sprang.

WISCONSIN RECORDS

I began by obtaining the Winnebago County, Wisconsin, death certificate of Charles' father, Maurice. It indicated his death date in 1884, and the names of his parents, William Fitzgerald and Ann Harrigan. That was when I first learned that Harrigan was a family name. County Cork was given as Maurice's place of birth, no specifics as to parish.

I also was able to obtain the death records of William and Ann, who passed away in 1873 and 1880 in Oshkosh. No parents' names were given.

I proceeded to search all sorts of other records: obituaries, cemetery records, probate papers, United States censuses from 1850 to 1900 and more, all devoid of information on the New Brunswick and Ireland years. I learned that William and Ann emigrated from Ireland in 1830. I located the obituaries of several uncles and aunts of my grandfather Charles. They also settled in Oshkosh and raised large families. Uncle Mike and his sister, Aunt Mary (Blake), died in Oshkosh in 1927 and 1926, both over 100 years of age. Obituaries and articles about them in the Oshkosh newspaper indicated that the family spent a number of years in New Brunswick before they and other members of the family moved on to Maine and to Wisconsin, where they began arriving in the early 1850s.

One interesting bit of information was that Ann Harrigan Fitzgerald, my great-great grandmother, had a sister named "Mrs. Ellen Lucey" who passed away in Oshkosh "some years ago" at the age of 112, "the oldest woman in the state." I obtained Ellen's death certificate. It indicated that she died in 1891, age 112, birthyear 1779, County Cork, Ireland. Her parents' names, alas, were not recorded. But Ellen Lucey's brief obituary in the local paper indicated that she was survived by a son John Lucey, a policeman. John Lucey's own obituary indicated he was born in County Cork in June 1833, the son of Timothy Lucey and Ellen Harrigan. After much sleuthing and letter writing, I located descendants in Wisconsin and Minnesota, but they had less information than I had. I also located many descendants of Great-grandfather Maurice's siblings, score upon score of them. They were equally uninformed about New Brunswick and the Old Ireland years.

NEW BRUNSWICK RECORDS

There was no relief for my curiosity without getting into the New Brunswick records. I started with the entire 1851 census for the Colony of New Brunswick, the first census to give genealogical data of value. It was on microfilm at the great Mormon archives in Salt Lake City. The local Mormon library obtained it for me on loan. It consisted of about a dozen reels of film. I turned the crank of the film reader for many hours, many evenings, county by county, eleven of them. Finally, I got to Northumberland County, the last one to be searched. The county is popularly referred to as "Miramichi," after the great bay and river system. There, in Nelson Parish (northside), were William and Ann Fitzgerald and several of their youngest children. In the same log cabin were their daughter Mary and her husband, James Blake, and their young family. In neighboring North Esk Parish were the families of Patrick, William Jr., and John Fitzgerald, all siblings of Great-grandfather Maurice, listed consecutively with the families of Dennis and Catherine Harrigan and families with surnames O'Brien, Regan, Sullivan, Kingston. These census records indicated that the Fitzgeralds and Harrigans had come over during the spring and summer months of 1830 and 1831.

Passenger lists are not available for the Miramichi ports of Newcastle and Chatham for this period, but there are many other fascinating records on which my ancestors and their relatives made their marks. The tax lists indicate that the Luceys lived for a time in the

1840s with the Fitzgeralds in North Nelson, now Derby Parish. I learned that Ann Harrigan Fitzgerald had a brother named Cornelius Harrigan and that he raised a large family. I learned from the register at the Catholic church at South Nelson that Ann Harrigan Fitzgerald's two youngest children were born in the New World in 1832 and 1835; and that her brother Dennis Harrigan's youngest child, Dennis Jr, was also born in New Brunswick. Dennis Jr. will play a role in this story, of which more later.

The school rosters for the 1830s and 1840s were a valuable source of confirming evidence. They indicated that these families placed great value on education.

The marriage and baptismal records for these large families, invariably citing the names of witnesses and godparents, pointed to the closeness of the Harrigans, Fitzgeralds, O'Briens, and Sauntrys. The absence of cross-marriages between members of these families suggested that they were indeed close kin. In the one instance where Michael Sauntry, whose grandfather was Dennis Harrigan, married a Fitzgerald, the register reads that a dispensation was granted. They were second cousins (once-removed), outside the prohibitions of canon law, but a dispensation was obtained nevertheless.

COUSINHOOD OF A SORT

In genealogical research, one always wants to go backward, but sometimes the victim of Acute Genealogia must go forward for a while to relieve the distress, before he can return to his backward path. That is what my data on Dennis Harrigan forced me to do. I traced his son Dennis Jr. to Stillwater, Minnesota, a bustling sawmill town on the St. Croix River, heavy with immigrants from Miramichi, New Brunswick. Dennis and his spouse Catherine Ahearn had seven children between 1867 and 1879, according to the baptismal register of St. Michael's Catholic Church and census records. The third, born in 1873, was named Catherine. Her name meant nothing to me until the newspapers reported the death of Bing Crosby on a golf course in Madrid, Spain, in 1977. One news story mentioned that his mother was born Catherine Harrigan in Minnesota. That was enough for me to take a renewed interest, at my sister Margaret's suggestion, in the 1880-vintage Stillwater photo from our grandfather's collection. Four children had posed for it, two boys and two girls. The oldest, standing, appeared to be about ten. That would have been the age of Catherine Harrigan in the year 1883. The apparent ages of the other three children also corresponded with my records of this family.

I still had to move forward in time, but a stroke of luck soon was to set me again on the backward path so comfortable to genealogists. The luck was a letter from Margaret Harrigan Kendall of Redmond,

Washington. She had been given my address by a Stillwater, Minnesota, librarian, with whom we had both corresponded. She mentioned that she was a first cousin of the late Bing and his brother Bob, the bandleader, and that she too was seeking her Harrigan roots. She wondered who I was. She possessed a letter from a deceased uncle indicating that the Harrigans and Fitzgeralds were "first cousins"; that they had been born on "a small farm in County Cork"; that the "first Harrigan" was John of Skibbereen, who also used the surname O'Brien and was known as Organ O'Brien because he played the organ beautifully in the church at Skibbereen; that the Harrigans and Fitzgeralds settled together in Miramichi, New Brunswick, before moving on to such places as Oshkosh, Wisconsin, and Stillwater, Minnesota. She included in her letter the California address of her cousin Bob Crosby and his wife June.

I mailed Margaret and Bob copies of the Stillwater photo and other data. Bob immediately recognized the older girl in the picture as his mother. He was delighted with it, never before having seen such an early photo of her. I presented him with the original.

VISIT WITH BRIAN MAHONEY

It was now time for a visit to Miramichi, New Brunswick. There in 1978, in the community of Williamstown, now little more than a ghost town ten miles west of Newcastle, I met Brian Mahoney. He was well in his 70s and the descendant of old settlers. He claimed to be related to both Harrigans and Fitzgeralds way back. He had been told so by his long-lived schoolteacher grandmother, Annie Donoghue O'Brien. Without prompting, he remembered from his boyhood a very old man named Mick Sauntry. Mick, he said, had in his old age made a visit back to the village of his birth, "Bally-dee-hall, ten miles west of Skibbereen." By this time, I knew from the records that Michael (Mick) Sauntry was a son of William Sauntry and Ellen Harrigan, and thus blood relatives of my Harrigans. Brian told me that a grandson of Michael had raised a family of twenty-three children, surely a local record, by two consecutive wives. His second wife and some of the children still lived just down the road. I have since met several of these twenty-three children, twenty-two of whom are alive at this writing.

BALLYDEHOB AND SCHULL, WEST CORK

I wasted no time consulting a map of West Cork. There, ten miles west of Skibbereen, was the village of Ballydehob, and a few miles south was the village of Schull. Neither did I delay writing to the priests of the two parishes that served this area on Ireland's southernmost peninsula, at Schull and Goleen. The Schull registers of marriages and baptisms were extant from 1807, but with large gaps during the next two decades. The extant Goleen registers start in 1827. The parish priests kindly searched the barely legible and deteriorating records and came up with a treasury of information.

The records revealed the baptisms of three children of Dennis "Horgan" and Catherine Driscoll between 1811 and 1813, and two more in 1829 and 1830; the marriage of their oldest daughter, Ellen, to William Sauntry in 1828; and the baptisms of six of their children between the years 1829 and 1845. One of the six was Michael Sauntry, baptized in 1830, the man from "Ballydehall" remembered by old Brian Mahoney of New Brunswick. The names of the children from these families corresponded exactly, and the birth years almost always exactly, with New World records.

The records also revealed the baptisms of two children of Timothy Lucey and Ellen Horgan in 1810 and 1813 and of another (John, their youngest) in June 1833, corresponding precisely with the information on John Lucey's Oshkosh, Wisconsin, death certificate.

The *Tithe Applotment Books* were next consulted. Prepared in the 1820s, these records were an attempt to list all occupiers of land (except in the cities) in Ireland by townland and parish, for the purpose of taxing them to support the established Protestant Church of Ireland. In 1827, Daniel "Horragan" and James Fitzgerald, no doubt senior members of their families, were listed as joint occupiers of twenty-two acres in Drinane Mor townland, civil parish of Schull (West Division), and were obligated to pay a tithe of 19 shillings and 7 pence. "Horragan" and "Harrigan," along with Sullivan and Kingston, appeared as the surnames of occupiers in adjacent Drinane Beg and Derryleary townlands, and Luceys were also thereabouts. The townlands of Derryleary and Drinane were on the border of the Catholic parishes of Schull and Goleen. Just off the coast of Derryleary, according to an Ordnance Survey map, were the outcroppings known as Harrigan's Rocks.

Although the names of my direct ancestors, William Fitzgerald and Ann Harrigan, were not found on these records, the names of Ann's sister and brother and of a number of her nieces and nephews on the registers of Goleen and Schull were strong circumstantial evidence of Ann's roots on the Mizen Peninsula. The fact that her relatives were served by priests of both Goleen and Schull, and that a farm shared by a Fitzgerald and a "Horragan" was located on the very borderline of the two Catholic parishes, provided additional circumstantial evidence. (It is possible that William and Ann settled, after their marriage, across the bay between Baltimore and Skibbereen, where, in 1828, according to the tithe applotments for the Parish of Tullagh, a William and a James Fitzgerald were co-occupiers of 41 acres in the townland of Spain, later subsumed by the townland of Ballymacrown.)

The next step on this genealogical odyssey was to determine the present-day occupiers of the old Fitzgerald and Horgan/Harrigan farms. From the Rates Office in Cork City, I learned that the present occupiers of the townland of Drinane were Declan O'Mahony and Michael Donovan; and that nobody had paid taxes on Harrigan's Rocks for one hundred years. The rocks could be mine, I thought. I soon learned through correspondence with a distant cousin-in-law, Mary Margaret Lucey of Ratooragh, Schull, that the Harrigans of long ago had weed-cutting rights to the rocks. The weeds were used for fertilizer.

It was time to write a book: *The Irish Lumberman-Farmer*, published in 1982. It contains extensive family charts, an index of several hundred surnames, and quite a bit of background historical data. Two newspaper editors, in Cork City and in Skibbereen, thought their readers would be interested in just how Corkonians had been getting along in America; so I was hired to write full-page stories for both papers, all about the roots on the Mizen Peninsula of its most famous American son, Bing Crosby. My photo was included, next to Cousin Bing.

THE ROCKS ARE MINE

It was also time to visit West Cork to promote the *Lumberman* book, and to deliver a lecture to the West Cork Archaeological and Historical Society, on the occasion of an autograph session arranged by Jack O'Connell of Schull Books, my distributor. The society wanted to hear about the Corkonians of yore and how their descendants were doing. The Society's witty president, Michael Donovan, assuring me that Harrigan's Rocks were mine for the asking, offered to act as my caretaker. Soon thereafter, he wrote me a comforting letter about how the rocks had "weathered a fine storm and taken on a nice shine." As an honorarium, the Society commissioned a local artist to do an oil painting of Harrigan's Rocks. It is today proudly displayed in the King living room.

THE GENESIS OF MYTHOLOGY

Bear with me briefly for some other items of this visit to the Mizen Peninsula, shortly after the two stories with photos of Bing and me had appeared in the Cork newspapers. On the night that my wife Betty, my sister Margaret, and I arrived in Ballydehob, I was enjoying a pint of Guinness in a local pub when I noticed a young man staring my way guardedly. Finally, he summoned the courage to ask. "You be

2. Harrigan's Rocks, off the coast of Derryleary, Schull, County Cork. Castlepoint and O'Mahony Castle in background. 1983 photo.

3. View from Mount Gabriel, County Cork, author J.A. King in foreground, Schull Harbor and Cape Clear in background. 1983 photo.

4. J.A. King, Declan O'Mahony and son, Con Lucey, by ruins of cottage, Drinane townland, Schull, County Cork. 1983 photo.

5. Ruins of cottage with storage shelf, Drinane townland, Schull, property of Declan O'Mahony. 1983 photo.

the cousin of Bing Crosby?" I responded modestly, "Oh yes, well, sort of."

The following evening found my party in a pub in the sizeable town of Bantry, for a musical evening. The master of ceremonies was married to the head of the local historical society with whom I had corresponded. They maintained a bed and breakfast establishment where we had checked in before going to the festivities in the pub. At one point in the evening, behind his microphone, the master of ceremonies stopped the entertainment to introduce the "cousin of Bing Crosby, come here all the way from California." Nameless, I accepted the applause as modestly as I could. "His wife and his sister are here beside him." More polite applause. "I've been introduced many times," my sister said later, "but never as the sister of the cousin of Bing Crosby."

Just as intriguing was a conversation my wife and sister had with a friendly lady on the little pier at Schull the next day, while I was nervously preparing my lecture to the Society and worrying about my arrogance in daring to lecture to the Irish about the Irish. Not associating them with the "cousin of Bing" but obviously proud of her community, the lady on the pier said, "Do you know that Bing Crosby was born here?"

There is, you see, always some truth in folklore. Well, almost.

So, that is a good part of the story behind the genealogical data in Chapters 4 and 6 ("A Parish in West Cork" and "The Miramichi Irish") in this volume. It is the kind of research, however, that many historians, quite understandably, are reluctant to do. Nevertheless, a growing body of genealogical literature is becoming available, quite a bit of it of high quality, and historians would do well to allow themselves time for the study of some of it.

JAK

_____

Chapter 4

A PARISH IN WEST CORK

Mount Gabriel, on Ireland's southernmost peninsula, rises dramatically 1,339 feet above the rugged Cork coastline. From the top, on a clear day one can view the mountains of Kerry and Cork to the west and north, the coastline east toward the city of Cork, and Clear Island to the south, where Irish is still spoken. Hundreds of thousands of Americans and Canadians have an Irish ancestor sprung perhaps five or six generations ago from the many parishes that can be spied from this mountaintop. For definition of terms used in this chapter, see Note 1: Terminology in Notes and Selected References section, p. 330.

MIZEN PENINSULA ROOTS

An especially large group of emigrants began leaving southwest Cork after the Battle of Waterloo and the Peace of 1815. They followed a migration route, often over the course of two or three generations, that ran from Cork to New Brunswick and Maine, and then westward to Michigan, Wisconsin, Minnesota, and the Pacific Northwest. Little has been written about the Canadian experience of these Irish, and even less about the particular townlands and parishes from which they came in Ireland. But if their descendants have in their family tree a surname like Driscoll, Mahony, Donovan, Regan, Sullivan (preceded with an "O," if you will), McCarthy, O'Brien, Hickey, Coghlan, Kingston, Goggin, Sauntry, Lucey, to name just a few, there is a good chance that the parish of their ancestor's birth can be viewed from Mount Gabriel's peak.

This is the story of one parish, Schull, also spelled "Skull" on the records, at the foot of Mount Gabriel on the Mizen Peninsula. It is not an exceptional story; it could be repeated for hundreds of parishes

33

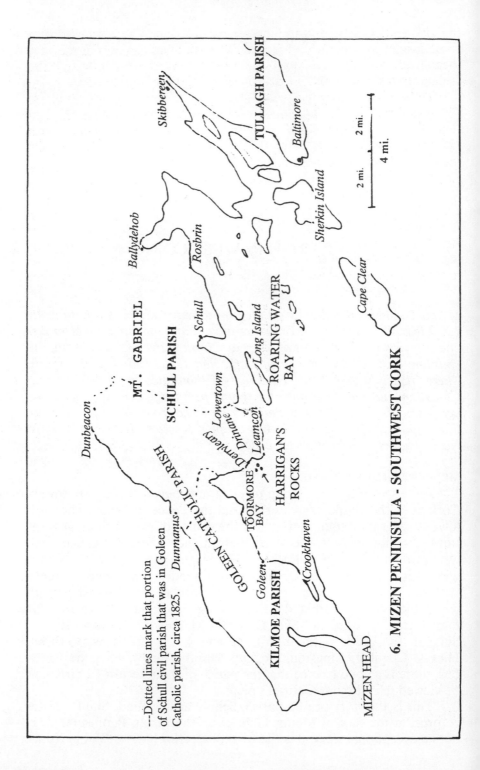

6. MIZEN PENINSULA - SOUTHWEST CORK

---Dotted lines mark that portion of Schull civil parish that was in Goleen Catholic parish, circa 1825.

TULLAGH PARISH

Baltimore

Skibbereen

Sherkin Island

Cape Clear

Ballydehob

Rosbrin

Long Island

ROARING WATER BAY

Schull

MT. GABRIEL

SCHULL PARISH

Lowertown

Dunbeacon

Drinane

Derryleary

Leamcon

HARRIGAN'S ROCKS

GOLEEN CATHOLIC PARISH

Dunmanus.

TOORMORE BAY

Goleen

Crookhaven

KILMOE PARISH

MIZEN HEAD

2 mi.   2 mi.

4 mi.

in Cork and elsewhere in Ireland. It is hoped that the story will offer some insight into just what life was like in the Old Country at the very local level for the pre-Great Famine emigrants who followed the Ireland to Canada to the American Midwest route of migration.

To tell that story we will follow the fortunes of the William Fitzgerald family. He appears on a United States census for the last time, in his old age, in 1870. In that year William and his spouse Ann Harrigan, ages given as 78 for both, although other records indicate they were even older, were living in the household of their daughter Kate McPartlin in Oshkosh, Wisconsin. *(See census data in Chapter 1.)*

William and Ann were married in West Cork, probably in the Catholic parish of Goleen, civil parish of Schull, about 1808. *(See Note 1: Terminology.)* William was a carpenter and small farmer. He and Ann had at least eight children before emigrating to New Brunswick in 1830. There, with many relatives who joined them, they settled in remote Williamstown in North Esk Parish, Northumberland County (known as "Miramichi," for the river), cleared some land, and built log cabins. William and his older sons learned the skills of the logger in the woods and on the rivers. In 1833 and 1835, he and Ann had two more children, Kate and Ann. In 1855 they moved to Oshkosh, where they spent their final years surrounded by children and grandchildren and other families who had followed the same path of emigration from the Mizen Peninsula in Cork.

When William and Ann passed away in Oshkosh in 1873 and 1880, they left no written record of their life journey. No photographs or letters or Bible records have come down, but at least part of the story of their roots in Ireland can be told.

IRELAND

The story begins in a troubled land, in the townlands of Drinane and Derryleary, three miles southwest of the tiny port of Schull. There, among many close relatives, William Fitzgerald worked the marginal and mountainous soil, pursued the carpentry trade with his Harrigan in-laws, and harvested seaweed, used as a fertilizer, from Harrigan's Rocks in Toormore Bay. The weed cutting rights were leased from landlord Richard Edward Hull of Leamcon House, a stone's throw from their cabins. The Hull family owned most of the land in those parts.

The Harrigans and Fitzgeralds spoke Irish, as did about 90 percent of the people of Cork until the mid-19th century. The oldest children of William and Ann received some schooling in English, however, at the little school at Leamcon, close by the Harrigan and Fitzgerald farms. As Catholics living on the borderline of the

Catholic parishes of Goleen and Schull, they were served by priests of both parishes, as noted in Chapter 3.

SOME HISTORY OF SCHULL PARISH

What we know of the earliest history of Schull and West Cork is a blend of folklore, fiction, and fact. (Some of that story is told in Chapter 2, "A Long Inheritance: The Gael and Genealogy"). According to folklore there were three early invasions of southern Ireland from the continent. First were the Firbolgs, a pastoral people. They were conquered by the warlike De Danaans about 1000 B.C., who, in turn were conquered by the Milesian Celts, probably from Spain, about 500 B.C. Some think the Firbolgs and De Danaans, as well as the Milesians, were of Celtic stock.

Archaeological evidence indicates that a hunting and fishing society existed earlier than 6000 B.C. Farmers and herdsmen arrived about 3500 B.C. Bronze workers came about 2000 B.C. The rich copper deposits on Mount Gabriel were worked from perhaps as early as 1200 B.C., according to carbon-dating. The copper was mixed with the tin of Cornwall to make bronze. Ships of many lands anchored in Schull harbor to take on cargoes from the mines at Rosbrin. These mines were abandoned after the arrival of the Milesian Celts, an Iron Age people, but were re-discovered and worked for a time in the 19th century.

The history of Schull and the Mizen Peninsula, anciently known as Ivagha, is tied inextricably to the O'Mahony family from the 5th to the 16th century. The O'Mahonys were among several great families, including the O'Driscolls, O'Sullivans, O'Donovans, McCarthys, who dominated West Cork. A succession of twenty O'Mahony chieftains were undisputed rulers of the Mizen from the 12th to the 16th century. By 1400 they had built twelve castles ringing the Mizen from Dunbeacon to Rosbrin, including one at Leamcon, adjacent to the farms of the Fitzgeralds and Harrigans of this study. They controlled sufficient ships and fighting men to exact a wealth in tolls from fishing vessels from Portugal, Spain, France, Belgium, and England. Roaring Water Bay had become one of the richest fishing grounds in Europe. The cosmopolitanism of the coast, especially the Spanish connection, is evidenced by place names such as Spanish Cove, Spanish Point, Galley Cove, and, on the eastern side of the bay near Baltimore, Spanish Island and Spain Tower.

The O'Mahonys and many other Irish chieftains were only imperfectly Christianized; at least that was an argument advanced by Norman King Henry II of England in 1155, to obtain the Pope's permission and blessing to conquer Ireland, which his knights succeeded in doing for him within the two decades following. In any case, there is little evidence that the O'Mahonys of this era were members of the church hierarchy (none was ever Bishop of Cork or Ross). However, centuries after the Norman invasion there is some record of O'Mahonys among the religious martyrs: in 1594, Blessed John Cornelius O'Mahony, a Jesuit, was hanged; in 1642, Father Francis O'Mahony, a Franciscan, was imprisoned, tortured despite his advanced age, and then hanged with his cincture.

There is plenty of evidence, however, for O'Mahony patronage of Gaelic education. They settled a family of bards, the O'Dalys, near Kilrohane, and the ruins of their bardic school can still be seen. Finin of Rosbrin, an O'Mahony chief, was considered the most learned man of his time in Latin, Irish, and English. Before his death in 1496, Finin had translated into Irish the popular *Travels of Sir John Mandeville*. Finin may have been educated at a local school from which the village of Schull, it is thought, derived its name. The parish church was known in Finin's time as Sancta Maria de Schola and also *Scoil Mhuire*, Irish for School of Mary.

The Irish chiefs regularly fought one another and their Norman and English conquerors, taking various sides. Many of the Gaelic chiefs accepted the "surrender and re-grant" proposals of Henry VIII and his daughter Elizabeth I, by which they abandoned the Gaelic system of communal, tribal ownership and swore loyalty to the English crown in return for personal title to all or part of the tribal lands. English Law was thus imposed on Ireland, eclipsing the Gaelic order of things. But outright confiscation of the lands was extensive in the late 1500s, continuing until the 1690s through the Parliamentary and Williamite wars, when the conquest and confiscations were complete. The lands of the O'Mahonys had been reduced considerably by 1622, when Sir William Hull was occupying the O'Mahony castle at Dunmanus. In that year Hull also obtained a lease on the castle and land at Leamcon from representatives of Conor O'Mahony.

Pirates and smugglers found the many little coves and bays safe haven. As late as the first quarter of the 17th century, twenty-five pirate vessels used the cove at Leamcon (Croagh Bay) as their lair. Sir William Hull was occupier of Leamcon Castle and Vice-President of Munster (Vice-Admiral, appointed in 1609, according to one source). In 1616, he contracted with Sir Richard Boyle, who became first Earl of Cork, to engage in the pilchard fishing business in Cork and Waterford. Hull also made profitable arrangements with the most notorious pirates along the coast. By the time of the Parliamentary War in the 1640s, he had substantially increased his holdings over a wide area of West Cork. The holdings included a lease on the town of Crookhaven, which was attacked in December 1641 by 700 rebels under the Great O Mahowne (O'Mahony), Fionn of Kilmoe, so Hull reported in a claim submitted on October 22, 1642, for damages incurred. O'Mahony forces, he testified, destroyed some of his houses and his fishing cellars at Crookhaven and attacked the pilchard fishhouse at Leamcon Castle, which Hull had built to withstand, he thought, a siege of 4,000 warriors. His family at Leamcon barely escaped with the help of a ship captain he had hired. The captain set fire to the castle, leaving the whole countryside to the rebels.

The rebels carried away about 2,000 barrels of salt from the fish cellars at Leamcon and Dunbeacon, valued at over 600 pounds, and other goods also valued at 600 pounds, including 1,300 sheep worth 173 pounds. Hull further reported that he had an income of 280 pounds a year from rents at Crookhaven town, 280 pounds from lands in Kilmoe and Leamcon, 1,500 to 2,000 pounds from pilchard fishing, and 92 pounds from half the rents at Clonakilty to the east. He counted his yearly losses at 1,150 pounds, in addition to 7,500 pounds in property. At Clonakilty, the rebels destroyed his house, carried away the floorboards, and burned the orchards and gardens.

Hull received 7,679 pounds in claims. The O'Mahony lands he had leased in 1622 were now his and his heirs' in "fee simple," forever. These amounted to more than 1,200 acres in and around Leamcon Castle, including the townlands of Derryleary and Drinane where, two hundred years later, the Fitzgeralds and Harrigans of this study were paying rents to his descendants.

PENAL CODES

The penal laws of the 17th and 18th century were designed to put an end forever to the rebellious behavior of the native Irish. Various codes of marked severity were passed in the two decades following the defeat of the forces under Catholic King James at the Battle of the Boyne in 1690 and the capitulation the following year of Patrick Sarsfield's forces at Limerick. Despite the provisions of the treaty struck with Sarsfield, the English rulers set out to destroy the Catholic Church in Ireland, as the key to the strategy of ending rebellion. All the bishops along with the "regular" clergy, mostly Jesuits, Franciscans, Dominicans, Augustinians, were ordered to leave Ireland by May 1, 1698. They were subject to charges of high treason and punishment by execution if they dared to return. "Secular" clergy, not members of the orders, were required by law to register, post a substantial bond to cover transportation into exile and other costs in the event they violated any of the penal codes, and take an oath of abjuration renouncing the spiritual authority of the Pope and swearing allegiance to a Protestant king forever. There was little room for mental reservations. To the two oaths of supremacy and allegiance was added a declaration against transubstantiation, an essential doctrine of the Catholic faith.

In 1698, 444 priests of an estimated 1,237 (838 of them secular and 399 regular clergy) in Ireland were reported to have been transported, mostly to French ports and Lisbon. By 1703, only two bishops, both in hiding, remained in Ireland. By 1708, the number had increased to three, but one of these was in prison, a second was sickly, and a third was in hiding. By 1710, only 33 priests of a then-reported total of about 1,100 had taken the Oath. Many had even refused to register.

In 1698, 12 priests (9 secular, 3 regular), unnamed, were reported to be residing in the Baltimore Revenue District. One or more of these presumably served the Mizen Peninsula parishes. In 1714, a report of priests who allegedly had visited Cork City contained these items: "Daniel Carthy alias Gehy deceased, East Skull" and "Teige Calleghan, Skull and Kilmoo," after whose name was the notation "refused the oath." In 1731, two Mass-houses existed on the Mizen Peninsula, one in Schull and the other in Goleen. In the same year it was reported that for the parish of Kilmoe and surrounds "fryars frequently landed here from France who disperse themselves through the Country."

At the same time illegal traffic in priests was being conducted with the help of smugglers, especially along the rugged coasts of southwest Cork and Kerry. The smuggling trade was in wine and brandy for the wool that the Irish were forbidden by law to export to any country but England. A Protestant bishop complained at this time that "Popish priests were dayly convey'd thro' said parishes [Kilmoe and Schull] into ye inland Country who are landed at ye harbour of Crookhaven.. .by shipping from France and other countries, which priests, I am credibly informed, are mostly Fryars." On January 9, 1710, William Hull, Justice of the Peace, examined innkeeper Thomas Morgan of Crookhaven. Morgan reported that two years previously one Thomas Grady had spirited two "fryars" ashore at Coosane near Schull, where they were met by Kean Mahon of Meenterory and sheltered by Edmund Hodnett, who provided them with horses and arms before conveying them to Cork City.

In 1719, the Irish House of Commons, with apparent unanimity, approved an elaborate bill against Papists, one clause of which called for branding with a red-hot iron the letter "P" on the cheeks of all unregistered priests. The Irish Privy Council changed the penalty to castration before sending the bill to London. There, the ministers restored the branding provision, perhaps because of diplomatic pressure from Catholic France, and returned the bill to Dublin where the Irish Parliament had the power to reject but not amend. The Irish

House of Lords, objecting to a clause in the bill concerning leases which Catholics had been allowed to make, rejected the whole bill. Regarding these events, historian W.E.H. Lecky of Trinity College, himself a Protestant, wrote: "It is. . .a memorable fact in the moral history of Europe that as late as 1719 this penalty [castration] was seriously proposed by the responsible government of Ireland."

In 1723, the same House passed a fierce new bill against unregistered priests, providing high bounties for Discoverers ("priest-catchers"). But this was more sound and fury than action, as evidenced by the 1731 *Report on the State of Popery in Ireland*. It is a remarkably valuable document. The returns therein, submitted pursuant to an order of the "Lords Committees," were prepared by local Church of Ireland officials, and they covered every diocese and parish in Ireland. They enumerated the number and location of Mass-houses, private chapels, friaries, nunneries, and popish schools, and the number of Catholic clergy. It is clear from the reports by respondents who had no good reason to exaggerate the Catholic presence (they were supposed to enforce the codes) that the Catholic Church was functioning openly in every diocese and in almost every parish, despite the codes. It was evident, even by 1731, that the codes against the practice of the Catholic religion were a failure. The enforcement, if at all, was usually only token and spasmodic. Father William P. Burke in *The Irish Priests in the Penal Times (1660-1760)* remarks that "upon the whole a steady defervescence of bigotry is noticeable after 1720."

The 1731 report indicated that there were 1,445 secular clergy, 254 regular clergy (including friars), "several" bishops, 9 nunneries, 664 Mass-houses, 54 private chapels, and 549 popish schools, in a population of 1,309,769 Catholics in a total population of 2,010,221.

In 1766 there were 480 friars in Ireland, including 231 Franciscans, 147 Dominicans, 68 Augustinians, and 34 Carmelites. Catholics in some areas felt as harassed by itinerant and poorly educated friars demanding fees for their services as they were by tithe collectors for the Protestant Church of Ireland. In mid-century, the practice of the orders of ordaining young, uneducated men to the priesthood before sending them to the continent to study was abandoned on orders from Rome.

The population figures for 1766 also reveal the failure of the codes to win the majority away from the Roman Catholic church. In a total population of 2,158,514, there were 1,407,345 Catholics and 751,169 Protestants. Only Ulster had a Protestant majority. The figures for Catholic and Protestant in Connaught were 246,142 and 23,718; in Leinster, 474,863 and 214,173; in Munster, 491,738 and 134,061; in Ulster, 194,602 and 379,217.

The real success of the codes was in the Protestant acquisition of land. Until the Gavel Act was repealed in 1778, the land of a Catholic, upon his death, had to be divided among all his sons, unless the oldest son apostatized, a recipe that insured the eventual balkanization and impoverishment of Catholic estates. Although quite a few Catholic families managed to evade this requirement (some inheritors formally apostatized but secretly remained Catholics), Catholic ownership of land dropped from about 14 percent at the beginning of the 18th century to about 5 percent by the last quarter of the century.

PRIEST-CATCHERS

Priest-catching does not seem to have been a popular or successful pastime in West Cork, nor elsewhere in Ireland. Professional priest-catchers, seeking bounties, were generally held in low esteem even by the authorities. Two of the most notorious, J. Garcia and Edward Tyrrell, came to grief.

Garcia, said to be a Spanish or Portuguese Jew, arrived in Dublin in 1717, converted to Protestantism, and took up the priest-catching profession. Between 1718 and 1720, he received a total of 125 pounds for his services from Dublin authorities. They tired of him by 1722, after he had made a number of self-pitying and unsuccessful appeals for a pension.

More notorious than Garcia was the fallen-gentleman, Edward Tyrrell, who made several expeditions throughout the countryside in 1712 in search of priests and bounties. In that year he also married. It was soon learned that he had three (or four) other wives. Entrapped, he was tried, confronted with the testimony of his wives, and convicted. Tyrrell was hanged at Newgate on May 23, 1713.

In Limerick, one priest-catcher had these lines cut by his neighbor on the back of his tombstone (as reported by Burke in *Irish Priests in Penal Times*):

> *God is pleased when man doth cease to sin*
> *The devil is pleased when he a soul doth win*
> *Mankind are pleased whene'er a villain dies*
> *Now all are pleased for here Jack Cusack lies.*

Enforcement of the codes against priests and Catholic schoolmasters, especially in the overwhelmingly Catholic countryside, was difficult and even dangerous business. Most magistrates and other Protestant gentry would have none of it and, while lamenting the superstitions of the peasantry, looked the other way. In 1731, for the *Report on Popery,* the mayor of Galway noted that his sheriffs could find no member of the forbidden friars in his town. But the account book of the Augustinian friars has an entry for 1731, reading: "November 9. . . a bottle of wine for ye sheriffs 1s 1d." The same mayor reported that his sheriffs could find no Dominicans in their reputed friary. Yet an entry in the Dominican account book reads: "For claret to treat ye Sherifs in their search, ye 11th [of the month] 2s 2d."

To be sure, there were occasional outbreaks of enthusiastic enforcement, short-lived. In February, 1744, there was a swoop by priest-hunters in Dublin. Father Nicholas English was arrested while saying Mass. Two Dominicans, among others, were caught and arrested. That the chapels were still closed several months later is attested by Viscount Taafe, ambassador to England from Austria. Visiting Dublin, from whence came his own forebears, Taafe found the doors to the St. Stephen's Street Chapel nailed shut by government order. He wrote a letter of complaint to the King of England after being treated badly, he claimed, by Irish government officials.

In 1756, the magistrates of Cork City closed all Catholic chapels and what they called "oratories." They took the keys, after which Catholics armed with fists and clubs tried to open the chapels, attacking armed Protestants who opposed them. There were some injuries to both sides but no fatalities. The chapels were re-opened shortly thereafter, but one priest was held in jail for several months.

Generally, however, the clergy were harassed only to the extent that they were perceived as a threat to property. This was evident during the violence of the 1760s when the Catholic bishops were quick to distance themselves from the secret Whiteboy organization that opposed both tithes and the enclosure of pasture land. Father Nicholas Sheehy of Clogheen, accused of complicity in a murder allegedly perpetrated by the Whiteboys, was executed at Clonmel, County Tipperary, in 1766, a "notorious case of injustice," according to historian W.E.H. Lecky. The head of the hanged, quartered, and disembowelled priest remained spiked over Clonmel Jail for twenty years, and the priest's grave became a place of pilgrimage. During the last of three trials, a witness named Keating testified that Sheehy was in Keating's house at the time of the murder. Poor Keating was immediately arrested on suspicion of being a Whiteboy himself.

Bishops were exercising jurisdiction despite the codes. Quite revealing is the career of Nicholas Sweetman, bishop of Ferns in Wexford from 1745 to 1786. Sweetman was taken under arms and imprisoned briefly in Dublin Castle in 1751, after being charged by a priest whom he had suspended with recruiting soldiers for the Pretender James III. He was released after favorably impressing the Viceroy, Lord Chesterfield, with his urbane good manners, his erudition, and his willingness to cooperate with the authorities. Lord Chesterfield became his lifelong admirer and friend, and Sweetman continued to exercise his ecclesiastical authority, in flagrant violation of the codes. During his long tenure, he had much less trouble from the civil authorities than from priests he considered renegade or incompetent. Sweetman also was distressed by Franciscan friars who disputed his authority in local matters. His battle with the friars raged for twenty years and was carried to the Vatican.

Also revealing is the career of Honora "Nano" Nagle, born in Ballygriffin, County Cork, in 1718 of parents in good circumstances. Her father had managed to hold onto his land while still adhering to the Catholic faith. Between 1755 and 1784, Paris-educated Nano Nagle established a number of schools in Cork City, where her brother Joseph had property and commercial interests. She recruited the French order of Ursulines to establish a community in 1771, and later founded the Sisters of the Presentation of the Blessed Virgin Mary, an order devoted exclusively to the services of the poor.

Some of the more affluent Catholics in Cork City, who had the most to lose, reviled Nano for spending so much money and energy educating "beggars' brats." Some Protestants were alarmed not only by Nano but by "the multiplication of private places of Catholic worship and the swarms of Jesuits." Nano compromised by forbidding her nuns to wear their habits publicly. Fearing repercussions, she even objected strongly when the Ursulines in 1779 decided to flout the codes by donning their habits.

In the final analysis, enforcement of the penal codes turned out to be impossible in a land with a Catholic population of 90 percent outside of Ulster. With few exceptions, priests and their bishops conducted their business in the last half of the 18th century, and even before, with little effective opposition, as long as they did not confront or inconvenience the landlords or magistrates. Hard and brutal incidents of enforcement of the codes appear to be rather isolated and sporadic events, if viewed over the course of the entire 18th century. Certainly, nothing approaching the persecutions of prior centuries prevailed, in degree of barbarity or in numbers.

By mid-18th century, the posting of sentries at "Mass-rocks" was usually a thing of the past. The open-air Masses, romanticized in folklore, continued in many parishes. They were, however, "far more a product of poverty than of persecution of religion itself," believes West Cork historian Father James Coombes of Skibbereen, who has called the author's attention to one Mass Rock in West Cork that could not have been situated in a more vulnerable location.

The open-air Masses were sometimes a consequence of landlords refusing to lease land for a Catholic chapel, or to allow rock-quarrying for its construction, or to permit Mass-houses to remain on land that was being cleared and improved. Even as late as 1781, Lord Doneraile, in a fit of pique, closed every Mass-house on his estate in County Cork. This was after he had been convicted of horsewhipping, kicking, and beating almost to death an 81-year-old parish priest and his housekeeper. Doneraile was furious that he could not get the priest to lift the excommunication of a person living in adultery. The old priest claimed in conscience that he was unable to discuss the matter. The enraged Lord was tried on an assault charge and fined 1,000 pounds.

It is easy to argue that the truly grievous crime of colonial rule during the 18th century was not the enforcement of the codes, ugly as they appeared on paper, but rather the physical and cultural impoverishment of an ancient, proud people. Despite all, the Church survived. It can also be argued that the Church, with its priests, was the chief single force that provided some hope and dignity to the degraded and despairing peasantry. That goes a long way toward explaining the respect that the Irish have given their priests right into modern times.

SET-BACKS

There were some set-backs to the Church in Cork and in Schull. In 1773, Father Jeremiah Harte was appointed Parish Priest of Schull. The following year he took the Oath, renouncing the Popish communion at a ceremony at St. Finbarr's (Church of Ireland), Cork City. This apostasy earned him a living as a Church of Ireland pastor. Even more disappointing to the Catholics of Schull was the apostasy in 1786 of their bishop, John Butler, in the city of Cork. He resigned his bishopric when he was over seventy years of age in order to marry in a Protestant Church and to be eligible to assume his family's inherited title, Lord Dunboyne. He returned to the Catholic faith in 1800, the year of his death, and left 1,000 pounds to establish a Dunboyne Foundation at the seminary in Maynooth.

THE ASCENDANCY

The whole period of what came to be known as the Protestant Ascendancy was also a dark period for the ruling class. Many Ascendancy families fell into decadence over the course of generations. In 1900, one product of the class, the noted writer Standish James O'Grady, wrote with contempt that the Ascendancy Protestants "had once owned all Ireland from the Centre to the Sea, but now. . .they are rotting from the land. . . without having to their credit one brave deed, without one brave word." Dr. Mahaffy of Trinity College, also a member of the Ascendancy, wrote that his class had become "idle, afflicted with boorish ignorance and lacking in public spirit. They neither read books, nor collected libraries and as regards education, they were going backwards - even their women cared for nothing but hunting and racing." But the whole truth over the course of two centuries, as Professor James Donnelly and others have shown, was that many who bore the surnames of these Ascendancy families had themselves fallen into comparative poverty. Some could hardly be distinguished from the native Irish. Even some of the greatest of the landlords were barely clinging to over-mortgaged estates. *(See Note 3: Over-Encumbered Estates.)*

The Protestant Ascendancy was the class of people that were masters of the Mizen Peninsula. Catholics, especially the poor cottiers and laborers, had no practical appeal in the law. Their landlord was often the magistrate. It is not surprising, therefore, that the system of justice merited the cynicism of the masses of Catholics, as expressed in this jingle:

> *The law doth punish man or woman*
> *That stole the goose from the common*
> *But lets the greater felon loose*
> *That stole the common from the goose.*

In Schull parish, circa 1830, as reported in Lewis, *A Topographical Dictionary of Ireland (1837),* a manorial court was held at the Hull castle at Leamcon every third Monday, at which debts under five pounds were recoverable. An ecclesiastical court was held occasionally at "the manor belonging to the Bishop of Ross" (presumably the glebe house occupied by the curate of absentee rector Anthony Trail). Petty sessions were held at Toormore on alternate weeks in matters of grievance.

EDUCATION

Catholic education was proscribed by the penal codes. What education there was for Catholic children, if their parents did not send them to a proselytizing Protestant Charter School (almost none did) was furnished illegally and surreptitiously by the hedge-schools. These flourished from the 1640s, with the death of the Gaelic Bardic schools. The 1731 *Report on the State of Popery* indicates that Catholic hedgemasters were functioning quite openly, if illegally, in many parishes. Little effort, the report indicated, was being made to capture, fine, and imprison them, as the codes demanded. These itinerant scholars were known to give instruction in Greek and Latin as well as in Irish history. There were reports of students illiterate in English who could read Homer in Greek and spout Virgil in Latin.

The codes were relaxed by Acts of 1782 and 1792. Among the *Parliamentary Papers* prepared in the 1820s is a detailed report on the schools. In Schull Parish by 1826, seven of the ten schools were taught by Catholic masters. Historian Father Patrick Hickey gives figures on schoolmasters' stipends and on attendance. They reveal that the poorest Protestant schools were better off than the "best" Catholic schools. The best paid Catholic teacher taught at Schull and received ten pounds a year for a class of forty-two Catholics and two Protestants. The best paid Protestant teachers received 24 pounds at Gubeen for a class of 58 children, including five Catholics, and 25 pounds at Ballydehob for a class of 45 pupils, 4 of them Catholic. The worst paid teacher taught at Leamcon, close by the Fitzgeralds and Harrigans, receiving only two pounds for a class of seventeen Catholics and one Protestant conducted in a structure described as "a miserable little hut." Almost certainly in that squalid structure the Harrigans and Fitzgeralds learned to read and write.

The Catholic schools were supported entirely by subscription of the parents. The religious census taken in 1834 (as reported in the *Parliamentary Gazetteer of Ireland*) revealed that Schull Parish had two Protestant Sunday schools attended by eighty scholars; seven Catholic hedge-schools usually attended in summer by about 243 scholars; and nine other daily schools, two of which (Catholic) "were supported wholly by fees" and attended by 212 boys and 173 girls. Government aid ostensibly came with the advent of a National School System in 1831-32. There was, however, a catch: an application for a National School, even one conducted by Catholics, and a license for the Catholic schoolmaster had to be submitted to the local Church of Ireland rector for his endorsement. In 1836, the Reverend Robert Trail (aka Traill) refused to sign an application submitted by the Catholic school at Ballydehob, even though the school was detached from the chapel as required, with no crucifix, statues, or religious pictures in evidence, as also required.

On September 10, 1844, James McCarthy, middleman of Kilmoe/Goleen, reported to the Devon Commission that the landed proprietors of the area persisted in refusing a site of barren rock for a Catholic schoolhouse, "though a hundred acres of it would not be worth a farthing." A request to quarry slate for the local Catholic chapel, McCarthy reported, had also been turned down. In 1838 the Catholic school at Schull achieved National School status. But as late as 1845, two years before he was to succumb to famine fever, Dr. Trail was still protesting.

MORE UNREST

Despite the relaxation of the codes, unrest continued to be the rule. There were bloody encounters at County Wexford and in parts of Ulster during the Rising of 1798, English cannon and muskets against Irish pikes. General John Moore was ordered to abort any rising in southwest Cork, from Skibbereen to the Mizen Head. He assigned Major Nugent to the peninsula itself, from Ballydehob to Ballydevlin. Moore kept a diary, later published, which explained his strategy: "to forage the whole country [and] to treat the people with as much harshness as possible. . .and to supply [the troops] with whatever provisions were necessary to enable them to live well." The general explained that his "wish was to excite terror and by that means to obtain our end speedily." The plan was successful. "The terror was great. . .the moment a redcoat appeared everybody fled," Moore wrote.

Nugent's five companies, after a three-week campaign, extracted 800 pikes and 3,400 stands of arms "in poor condition." General Moore, who had observed on his way to fight at Wexford that he would be on the side of the rebels if he had been Irish, is well spoken of by some Irish historians. His use of "terror" was designed to eliminate bloodshed. There was no rising, no bloodshed, on the peninsula. Ellen Harrigan, who married Tim Lucey and who lived to be 112, was nineteen years of age at the time of Major Nugent's sweep. Her recollections were reported ninety years later, in the January 19, 1887, *Oshkosh Daily Northwestern.* She told the reporter that her family "was obliged to hide in a cave."

Relations between Catholics and Protestants seem to have improved somewhat in the first quarter of the 19th century. The Catholics maintained a small chapel in Ballinskea townland near Lowertown. It was the closest chapel to the Fitzgeralds and Harrigans. It is quite possible that members of the family were present when the roof collapsed during a celebration of Mass on April 27, 1825. Landlord Richard Edward Hull and Church of Ireland rector Reverend Anthony Trail (father of Robert Trail, referred to earlier) helped Father Michael Prior, Parish Priest of Goleen, to raise subscriptions for a new chapel. Hull donated twenty guineas, a rent-free lease of the site, and permission to quarry rocks and bog-oak for the construction. Trail, "who was always kindly disposed toward his Catholic neighbors," according to one local historian who cited the fact that Trail had forgiven the tithes during the famine of 1822, donated thirty guineas, equivalent of thirty-one pounds ten shillings. He was, however, an absentee rector whose real neighbors were in County Antrim, as we shall see.

7. Ellen Harrigan Lucey (1778-1891), at age 111 in 1890, Oshkosh, Wisconsin. She recalled hiding in a cave during the sweep of the Mizen Peninsula by British troops in 1798.

The religious devotion of the Catholics was reported by a Protestant gentleman in the *Cork Mercantile Chronicle* on December 12, 1825. Describing himself as a "liberal Protestant of Skibbereen," he told how he had ridden in the rain to witness for himself the privations of the Catholics of West Schull and to observe the first Mass said on the Hull-donated site. "I saw from the public road at least 2,000 men and women kneeling on the side of a barren mountain, assisting in silence and in apparent reverence at the ceremony of the Mass, literally no canopy over them but the broad expanse of the heavens, whilst a heavy winter's shower descended on their uncovered heads." Among the 2,000, very likely, were the Harrigans, Fitzgeralds, Luceys, *et al.*

The same Cork newspaper reported on June 21, 1826, that "a commodious and stately temple" for the Catholics of Schull was nearing completion. This particularly soft period in Catholic/Protestant relations was commemorated in a plaque placed in the chapel:

> *To the Glory of*
> *God this chapel was*
> *Erected by Protestants and*
> *Roman Catholics*
> *Founded A.D. 1826*

Almost one hundred years later, in 1919 during the War of Independence, the plaque was smashed into three pieces. Some think that it was a deliberate act of Father T. O'Sullivan, Parish Priest. Others think the stone was broken by accident when the church was being renovated. For a time the pieces were deposited against the back door of the chapel. They were later removed to the parish house at Goleen, with intention to eventually set them in cement for placement in the Lowertown Chapel.

PAYING TITHES

The major grievance of Catholics remained the hated tithe, assessed on Protestant and Catholic alike for the support of the Church of Ireland. Paradoxically, even Catholic priests and dissenting Presbyterian, Methodist and other ministers had to pay the tithe. In Schull Parish, according to the religious census taken in 1834, there were 13,912 Catholics in a total parish population of 15,810. Regular Sunday church attendance was 160 and 130 at the Church of Ireland services at Schull and Ballydehob, with another 240 at three schoolhouses which also served as places of worship. The Wesleyan meeting house had an attendance of 70. The Catholic chapels at Schull and Ballydehob had attendance of 900 and 1700 respectively, with another

950 at the chapel near Lowertown, the one probably attended by the Fitzgeralds and Harrigans.

Until 1823, the tithe each occupier of land had to pay was determined more or less arbitrarily by the authorities. It could amount to as much as ten shillings a year per Irish acre for wheat and potatoes and eight shillings for oats. All pasture land was excluded, thus placing almost the entire burden of the tithe on the Catholic small tillers. By the reform acts of 1823 and 1824, the amount of tithe was fixed at 10 percent of the average price of a barrel of wheat for the seven-year period 1815 through 1821. The price of a barrel was eighteen shillings and six pence a barrel. For Schull and a few other parishes the rate was set at 7 percent, perhaps because of the poor quality and scarcity of tillage land.

The recipient of the substantial tithes for Schull in 1828, the first year under the new system, was the Reverend Anthony Trail, rector. He was the son of Reverend Robert Trail and Jean Dow; was married to the daughter of William Watts-Gayer, Clerk of the Irish House of Lords; and was a nephew of James Trail, bishop of Down and Connor in Ulster. He was also the father of the Reverend Robert Trail who was to succeed him as pastor at Schull. Anthony was an absentee rector, residing in County Antrim where he also held the title of Archdeacon of Connor from 1782 until his death in 1831. He assumed the rectorship of Schull in 1794. That it was a very valuable sinecure is certified by his bishop's testimony, in 1801, that the value of the benefice was 600 pounds per annum. By contract signed on October 25, 1826, by "Richard Edward Hull, Chairman, Special Vestry," and by the two appointed tithe commissioners, Vicar John A. Jagoe (appointed by Trail) and Thomas Evans of Aghadown (appointed by Hull), the absentee rector was guaranteed "850 [pounds] by the year. . .for the space of 21 years from the first day of November [1826] and shall not be liable to any change or variation in consequence of any change or variation in the price of grain during said period." This was a most generous agreement. It was immune from the drastic and continuing fall in grain prices in the decades following the Battle of Waterloo and the Peace of 1815. Irish produce, so vital to England during the Napoleonic Wars, was no longer in as much demand in English markets.

Trail's perquisites also included use of the glebe-house and income from sixty-three acres of land around it, from which an additional 100 pounds income could be derived. Further, in 1829, he received 650 pounds from the Board of First Fruits of the Established Church for construction of the chapel at Ballydehob. Later, he got 208 pounds from the Ecclesiastical Commission for repairs to the Schull church. Trail paid the salaries of two curates. In 1829, they were Reverend John Triphook, who received 80 pounds per annum, and Reverend Alleyn Evenson, who occupied the glebe house and sixty-three acres, from which he derived, according to his own testimony, 100 pounds per annum. The absentee rector also had to pay an undetermined but no doubt substantial sum to his tithe collectors. It has not been determined how much, if any, of the tithes he shared with his superiors (the "living [was] under the alternate patronage of the Crown and the Bishop"), but such sharing was the exception, not the rule. It was said that he contributed to the support of five schools. His son Robert, who succeeded him, was contributing sums of five, ten, and twenty-five pounds to the support of three schools in 1834.

Without any doubt, the Reverend Trail had a magnificent sinecure. So did his curates, especially Reverend Evenson, occupant of the glebe house. This residence was described eloquently and poetically by a contemporary observer, writing for the *Parliamentary Gazetteer of Ireland.* It was "an ancient mansion sheltered down on the shore, in a sunny nook, half-way between the church and the village. . .under the guardianship of a protecting hill, and some old sycamores in solitary magnificence and unpruned luxuriance, their long branches sweeping the lawn [seeming] to say we are here to show that no one should be [as] comfortable as a good minister." Continuing in this spirit, and without a suggestion of irony, the writer spoke of the parish church itself "on a high elevation over the sea" blending into "a tranquil and blessed scene [harmonizing] with that peace which religious worship communicates and which worldliness with all its pretences and promises cannot give, and cannot take away."

Nevertheless, the world was in fact hinting at taking away some of this blessed peace and privilege. The Earl of Mountcashel, fifty miles away, attacked the privileges of his own church in a letter to the *Cork Constitution* (November 24, 1829), citing as a notorious example the "lucrative parish" of Schull which, he said, had not been visited by its rector, Anthony Trail, for many years. Even more disturbed, no doubt, was Father Mahony, Catholic parish priest of Schull, who paid twelve shillings and six pence on eight acres of land. Just as disturbed, surely, were the Harrigans and Fitzgeralds. Daniel Harrigan and James Fitzgerald, listed occupiers of 22 acres in Drinane Mor townland valued (in pounds, shillings, pence) at 14/1/0, were assessed 0/19/7 in tithes. Edward Holland, George Kingston, and Michael Harrigan of Drinane Beg, occupying 24 acres valued at 16/1/0, were assessed 1/2/6. Daniel Sullivan and Tim Harrigan of Derryleary (facing Harrigan's Rocks), occupying 36 acres valued at 37/10/0, were assessed 2/12/5. At 12 pence to the shilling and 20 shillings to the pound, and figuring a laborer's wages at 8 pence per day (if he were fortunate), the tithes on the occupiers of just these three farms represented 141 days of labor per year. These occupiers were paying for the support of a church to which they did not belong, and which they generally abhorred.

It should be noted that the acreages of the listed occupiers are misleading. Most of the farms were jointly owned, the words "and partners" frequently following the names enumerated on the Tithe Applotments for Schull, suggesting that a form of the ancient Irish system of "rundale" was still practiced in southwest Cork, as it was in many other areas of rural Ireland well into the 19th century. *(See Note 4: Joint Ownership - Rundale.)* A more revealing picture of the holdings of the individual occupiers is provided in the responses to the *Poor Inquiry.*

THE POOR INQUIRY

The wretched condition of the masses is underscored in a remarkable document which historians usually refer to as the *Poor Inquiry,* the product of a British Parliamentary Commission. In 1833, the Commission addressed several score of questions to one or more persons, usually clergymen or magistrates, in each parish in Ireland. For Schull Parish, the respondents were Reverend Robert Trail, who had succeeded his father in 1830, and Father James Barry, Catholic Parish Priest of Schull. For neighboring Kilmoe/Goleen, the respondents were magistrates Richard Notter and Lionel Fleming. They all confirmed the appalling poverty. Most of the tenants in Schull were "more properly labourers holding but small lots." Very few occupiers held as many as three gneeves, the amount of land required for grazing about twenty-four cows, reported Father Barry. One-eighth of a gneeve, grazing for one cow, was the usual, with many occupiers being "third or fourth from the head landlord." About two-thirds of the land was held under middlemen, about one-third under head landlords who were "usually absentee." The average annual rental for a gneeve was nine pounds. An acre of first-quality land, which was scarce, rented for 0/18/6, and down to 0/1/6 for the poorest. A cabin and kitchen garden rented for two pounds annually, which amounted to the labor of sixty working days. Part or all of the rental frequently was in the form of labor at the six to ten pence per day prevailing rates.

Unemployment was usual. An adult male could earn four to nine pounds per year. His wife and four children might earn an additional seven or eight pounds as beggars, travelling far into the interior of the country while the father was working his potato patch. Such begging was common, the respondents reported.

An adult working male required seven pounds of potatoes daily (his sole diet, supplemented perhaps with a little milk) to be above the starvation line. Thirty-five pounds of "lumpers" were required for a family of six, two adults and four children. This meant that the six-ton annual production of potatoes on a one-acre plot, a quite usual holding, was consumed totally by this family. Nothing was left over to pay the middleman on Gale Day, the twice-yearly moment of reckoning, except the pig that, perhaps, had been fattened enough with lumpers which the family denied themselves. Hence the stories and the jokes about the pig being part of the Irish family, sharing the interior of the cabin. He was certainly an important family member, a bulwark against eviction.

The usual dwelling in Schull Parish, as elsewhere in Ireland, was a windowless hovel of stone and mud. Very few dwellers had straw for bedding, "heath grass or mountain grass being the substitute." Their clothing was "wretched, perhaps one in six [having] clothing to appear at a house of worship on Sundays," reported Father Barry.

ANTI-TITHE AGITATION IN SCHULL

The troubles had been exacerbated by a severe failure of the potato crop and a cholera epidemic in 1831. Reverend Robert Trail was not nearly as "kindly disposed" to the plight of the Catholics as his father, Anthony, had been. He reported to the Parliamentary Commission conducting the *Poor Inquiry* that, in 1832, "the priests and demagogues excited the most alarming disturbances, which yielded alone to military force." Among the demagogues he had in mind, as we shall see, was surely Father James Barry of Schull. Responding to the same question, Barry reported that "I have never seen or heard of any place more peaceable than this since 1830; in tithe agitation even, there were no outrages worth remark, and none of any other nature that must not be borne with at all times." The events that seemed significant to Trail, but not Barry, are described by Desmond Bowen (*The Protestant Crusade in Ireland, 1800-70*) and others. They were two gigantic anti-tithe meetings. At the first, on June 21, 1832, Father Barry himself was reported as leading his "athletic mountaineers" from Schull Parish, joining a crowd of 20,000 at Bantry. Led by their priests, the people carried banners of green and orange. Tradesmen marched in procession, each trade having its own banner. The banner of the tailors displayed a picture of James Doyle, Bishop of Kildare and Leighlin, with the inscription, "May our hatred of Tithes be as lasting as our love of justice." A picture of Daniel O'Connell, the great leader from Kerry, was on the other side.

At the second meeting, in July 1832, at the foot of Mount Gabriel in Father Barry's own bailiwick, there was an even greater gathering. On a wet day, boats galore from Cape Clear and Carbery's Hundred Isles in Roaring Water Bay arrived in Schull Harbor, with "streamers flapping in the breeze." The surrounding countryside was festooned "with wreaths and garlands." There were fiddlers, bagpipes and drums. Many Protestant dissenters - Methodists and others who also resented the tithes - were in attendance. It is possible that among those present were some of the direct ancestors of President John Fitzgerald Kennedy whose maternal Fitzgeralds, according to the Irish Genealogical Office, farmed near Skibbereen. *(See Chapter 15 in this volume.)*

Another priest-demagogue in prominent attendance at both meetings was Father Thomas Barry, Parish Priest of Bantry, alleged author of some popular satirical verses, quoted here in part:

> *There was a parson who loved 'divershun'*
> *And ne'er was harsh on his flock so few;*
> *'Twas he dressed sleekly, and looked so*
>   *meekly*
> *When preaching weekly to one or two.*
> *They saw him one day and that was Sunday*
> *For early Monday he was off for fun,*
> *To a steeple chase - a hunt or race,*
> *Or else a blaze with a double gun.*
> *The tithe was heavy that he did levy. . .*
> *This reverend Tory, so runs the story,*
> *Lived in his glory 'til twenty-nine*
> *When 'emancipation' impaired his reason*
> *Which he swore 'twas treason*
> *For the King to sign. . .*

The short, relatively peaceful period of Catholic/Protestant relations was definitely over. This was underscored not only by the anti-tithe agitation but by the attitude of Reverend Robert Trail who refused in 1836 to approve the application for National School status of the Catholic school at Ballydehob.

All this was on the eve of the Great Famine when, according to the Relief Committee, 4,476 people died of "fever, dysentery, and destitution" in Schull and Kilmoe/Goleen parishes during one twelve-month period, September 1, 1846, to September 12, 1847. (The population of these two parishes, according to the 1841 census, was 24,548.) Only 352 had the means and the energy to emigrate during the same period.

The Reverend Trail himself died of typhus in 1847. That was the worst year of what English writers called "the distress," when corpses were lying unburied on the streets of Schull and Skibbereen, their neighbors too weak to remove them for burial.

An Englishman who came ashore at Schull in February of 1847 gave this ghastly report:

. . .we proceeded to East Skull on quitting Shirkin. Inland we passed a crowd of 500 people half naked and starving. They were waiting for soup to be distributed amongst them. They were pointed out to us, and as I stood looking with pity and wonder at so miserable a scene, my conductor, a gentleman residing at East Skull, and a medical man, said to me: 'Not a single one of those you now see will be alive in three weeks; it is impossible.' The deaths here average 40 to 50 daily, 20 bodies were buried this morning, and they were fortunate in getting buried at all. The people build [*sic*] themselves up in their cabins, so that they may die together with their children and not be seen by passers-by. Fever, dysentery, and starvation stare you in the face everywhere - children of 10 and 9 years old I have mistaken for decrepit old women, their faces wrinkled, their bodies bent and distorted with pain, the eyes looking like those of a corpse. Babes are found lifeless, lying on their mothers' bosoms. I will tell you one thing which struck me as peculiarly horrible; a dead woman was found lying on the road with a dead infant on her breast, the child having bitten the nipple of the mother's breast right through in trying to derive nourishment from the wretched body. Dogs feed on the half-buried dead, and rats are commonly known to tear people to pieces, who, though still alive, are too weak to cry out. I went into one of the only shops in the place to try and get some bread to give away. I was obliged to leave immediately, for I could not stand the stench. On looking again, I discovered the reason - one body lay stretched on a door. And I saw the outline of a form, although covered with a heap of rags, I perceived was also dead. Instead of following us, beggars throw themselves on their knees before us, holding up their dead infants to our sight. (*The Times,* quoted in *Cork Constitution,* March 11, 1847, and in Donnelly, *The Land and the People of 19th Century Cork, pp. 85-86*)

The mortality rate for the parish of Schull was one hundred a week during the winter of 1846-47. The effect of the famine on the population of the townlands was catastrophic. Between 1841 and 1871, the population of Derryleary dropped from 192 to 62; of Drinane, from 94 to 35; of Leamcon, from 82 to only 5; of Lowertown, from 342 to 132. The total parish population in 98 townlands, 7 inhabited islands, and the towns of Ballydehob and Schull dropped from 17,314 to 8,823.

In all thirty-two counties of Ireland between 1841 and 1871, the emigrants numbered about three million. By 1891, another 1.1 million emigrated. By that year, 39 percent of all Irish-born persons were living outside of Ireland.

In 1848, William Sauntry passed away near Ballydehob, perhaps of famine fever. His widow, Ellen Harrigan, and seven children would join their Harrigan and Fitzgerald relatives in New Brunswick a few years later.

This tragic period in Irish history is called a "hunger," not a "famine," by Cecil Woodham-Smith in her classic study, *The Great Hunger.* During the worst years, 1846-48, exports from Cork of cattle and butter actually increased substantially, and production of grain, increasingly used for cattle feed, also increased dramatically. It has been estimated that Irish food production was more than sufficient to feed the native population.

RELIGIOUS FEUDING AMIDST FAMINE

Strange as it seems, amidst this "distress," the Protestant and Catholic pastors in West Schull and Goleen became embroiled in bitter religious controversy. In West Schull, the secretary of the Relief Committee was the local Protestant rector of Kilmoe, Reverend William A. Fisher. A resident of Altar, a townland between Goleen and Schull, he was also landlord of Toormore, Gorthowen, and Liscaha. In February 1847, he was accused by Father Laurence O'Sullivan and his curate, Father Barrett (Barry?), of using famine relief funds to influence starving Catholics to become Protestant. The two priests refused to hand over to Fisher subscriptions to the Fisher and quit the committee. Father O'Sullivan, afflicted with fever himself, journeyed to Cork City in February to raise funds personally. He explained his reasons in a letter published in the *Cork Examiner* on February 8, 1847, written from St. Vincent's Seminary.

Meanwhile, the Reverend Fisher, an Irish speaker, was successfully recruiting a significant number of Catholics (over six hundred by the end of the famine) to his church, called *Teampall na mBocht* (Church of the Poor) at Altar. Services were in Irish. Historian W.M. Brady, a Protestant who later converted to Catholicism, reported that "the money sent to Mr. Fisher for the relief of the destitute, instead of being distributed in alms gratuitously, was employed in giving labour, and procuring materials to erect this church" *(Clerical and Parochial Records of Cork, Cloyne and Ross,* 1863, vol. 1, p. 176). The converts became known as "soupers," ones who would trade their faith for a bowl of soup. Many of them returned to Father O'Sullivan's church after a mission of six Vincentian priests, who had been successful at winning back soupers at Dingle, arrived in Goleen in the summer of 1848 to help O'Sullivan win back his former parishioners.

Ironically, Father O'Sullivan was later accused by Protestants and some former Catholics of deserting his flock in time of need. They argued that the Catholics turned to Fisher in the absence of their own parish priest. This view has been projected by Peter Somerville-Large in *The Coast of West Cork,* p. 128; by Reverend Desmond Bowen, an ordained Anglican minister, in *The Protestant Crusade in Ireland: 1800-1870,* p. 188; by Eoghan Harris in his play *Souper Sullivan*; and by a BBC television documentary.

The charge has been answered convincingly by historian and priest, Father Patrick Hickey, writing in *The Fold* (April 1986) and elsewhere. He points out that the critics of O'Sullivan base their conclusion on local Protestant folklore and on the absence of records of baptism from February to May. They ignore the fact that the absence of records does not necessarily mean the absence of a priest. At nearby Aughadown Parish, Father Troy noted in the marriage book, "A frightful famine and fever year, alas, a hundred dying weekly, no marriages or baptisms." Also ignored is the fact that the Goleen curate, Father Barrett, is cited in a number of documents for his charitable activities in 1847. Regarding Bowen's claim that, while the Reverend Fisher was ill with fever, the Catholics "quarreled with their priest who fled the community, leaving them without the paternalistic direction he had once given them," Hickey asked Bowen if he could produce any "proper source" for the statement. Bowen, Hickey reports, could not. "He could not," Hickey says, "because it is false."

The facts of record indicate that Father O'Sullivan's absence from the parish was brief. On February 17, the chairman of the Relief Committee, Protestant Richard Notter of Rock Island near Crookhaven, expressed appreciation to O'Sullivan and his curate, Barrett, for bringing food to the starving people. The name of Father O'Sullivan is often cited on subscription lists for February through April, after he had obtained substantial donations from Archbishop Murray of Dublin and others. The Goleen church register indicates that O'Sullivan officiated at two marriages on March 16, and he may have returned even before that.

A DIGRESSION

This chapter and others in this book focus strongly on political and religious tensions, Protestant and Catholic rivalries, the English versus the Irish, the rich against the poor. The peril of this focus is the inevitability of distortion. The class struggle paradigm is useful, but it has its limits. When pushed too far, it turns people into papier-mache characters, lacking the flesh and blood of total human beings. Irish men and women were not solely political and religious creatures. Nor were all Catholics poor, even during the worst years of famine and oppression. Nor were all Protestants, including government officials, without the milk of human kindness and the desire for reform.

Even in the 18th century, Catholic merchants in cities such as Cork and Dublin were amassing considerable fortunes in the provisions business and in other occupations. In rural Ireland, middlemen, strong tenants, and even the hated tithe proctors were frequently Catholic. Some old Catholic families managed to hold onto their estates through the centuries of oppression and confiscation.

There were joy and laughter, amidst the poverty and misery. There was dancing to the fiddle and the pipes at the crossroads on summer evenings, and story-telling by the local *seanachie* at a fireplace on winter evenings. There was feasting at weddings and at wakes. There were local fairs where the small farmer sold his pig, where he enjoyed the musicians and the ballad singers, and where he saw boxing and wrestling matches and other sporting events. The fairs were also famous for the faction fighting among rival bands of young men from different parishes.

Irish poets were still practicing their ancient art and held in high esteem. The blind poet Carolan, who traveled about Connacht most of his life and is said to have been the greatest and last of old Irish bards, died in 1737. But a few great ones followed him. The most famous were Eoghan Rua O'Suilleabhain, born in County Kerry about 1750; Blind Raftery of County Mayo; Piaras MacGeraild (Pierce Fitzgerald) of County Cork, considered the chief poet of Munster before his death in 1791 at the age of 91; and Brian Merriman.

Poet Brian Merriman was born about 1749 at Ennystymon, County Clare, in the west of Ireland. He grew up in the village of Feakle where he was educated by hedge-masters. In *The Midnight Court (Cúirt an Mhean-Oíche)*, a poem written about 1780 and consisting of over a thousand lines of rhyming Gaelic verse, Merriman celebrates the rights of women to sex and marriage and satirizes single men, impotent old suitors, and older women married to young men. One caustic passage attacks the conduct of the administration of justice by the British ruling class.

The Midnight Court is a bawdy, good-humored poem that many an Irishman of Merriman's day could spout by heart in its entirety. One character in the poem, an elderly man tricked by his young bride, has this to say (in a liberal translation by Frank O'Connor, who uses rhyming couplets to suggest the assonantal, stressed-syllable rhyming couplets of the original):

> *And I smiled and I nodded and off I tripped*
> *Til my wedding night when I saw her stripped*
> *And knew too late that this was no libel*
> *Spread in the pub by a jealous rival*
> *By God, 'twas a fact well-supported*
> *I was a father before I started!*

A major achievement of Merriman, who died in Limerick in 1805, was to remind his audience of country people of their Irish identity. They were possessors of a history of poetry and song in their own language, much older than that of their conquerors. The dispossessed and depressed could hold their heads a little higher for the rich and witty verse of their own poet.

Great statesmen in the Irish and British parliaments, such as Edmund Burke and Henry Grattan, both Protestant, eloquently led the fight for justice and reform. Protestant leaders of the United Irishmen, such as Henry Joy McCracken, Robert Emmett, Lord Edward Fitzgerald and Wolfe Tone, gave their lives in the fight for freedom and justice around the turn of the 19th century. McCracken and Emmett were executed; Fitzgerald was fatally wounded and captured in March 1798, and died in his cell; Tone, after being sentenced to hanging, drawing, and quartering, committed suicide in his Dublin cell in 1798.

There were many Protestant landlords and churchmen who were sympathetic and even active in efforts to alleviate the plight of the Irish poor. George Berkeley, Bishop of Cloyne, was among the liberal-minded Established Church leaders preaching toleration of Catholics. As early as 1725, Edward Synge, the son of an archbishop not famous for his sympathy for Catholics, urged repeal of the use of coercive measures against Catholics, in a sermon before the Irish House of Commons. But the liberals, in the last analysis, were too few. Long established vested interests, together with human nature whetted by bribery, even led the landlord class to abandon the Irish Parliament. With the Act of Union of 1801, even the semblance of an "independent Ireland" was traded for rule from London in a United Kingdom.

Nevertheless, the laborers, cottiers, and small farmers of the Mizen Peninsula parishes, among the poorest in Ireland, were not without moments of joy. There were love and marriages, births, music, and a sense of community. When injustice became too great to bear, the Catholic community could organize behind a great national leader such as Daniel O'Connell, or locally around parish priests such as the Barrys of Schull and Bantry, to march by the thousands, pipes playing, as in the great anti-tithe meetings in southwest Cork in 1832.

THE EXODUS

It is unlikely that there was much singing and dancing as the Fitzgeralds and Harrigans prepared for their journey to the New World in 1830-31. In 1831, there was a severe failure of the potato crop, followed by famine and cholera. They were among the very few Catholics with the means to get away, fifteen years before an even greater disaster would occur. Their departure was described indirectly by the respondents to the *Poor Inquiry*. The Reverend Robert Trail reported that ninety families emigrated in 1831, of a parish population of 13,668. Forty left in 1832, and about twelve in 1833. "They were, with few exceptions," he said, "Protestants, and in comfortable circumstances." Father Barry reported similarly: "The emigrants were tradesmen, hardy labourers, and farmers with from 20 to 60 pounds capital [but] few of the last class." Squire Notter of Kilmoe testified that "the emigres are of a better description; in fact, most of the people here, who could afford to emigrate, would do so." As to what country the fortunate emigrants had gone, the answer was "almost universally to the British settlements in North America."

At the ports of Bantry, Crookhaven, and Baltimore were the timber ships from Canada, ready for passengers for the return voyage. Passenger fares had dropped by 1830 to as low as thirty shillings per adult, and half that for children. The Harrigans and Fitzgeralds, by selling their leases in Drinane and Derryleary, must have had ample for the Atlantic voyage, and something to spare. So too the Sullivans, who also farmed in Derryleary. The Sullivans may have been the first to leave.

Michael Sullivan, age thirty, arrived in New Brunswick in 1825, if data on the 1851 census is accurate. His brother Patrick joined him in 1832. William and Ann Fitzgerald and some members of their family arrived in the spring and summer of 1830. Other members of the Fitzgerald family arrived the following year, accompanying the large family of Dennis Harrigan, brother of Ann Fitzgerald. John and Cornelius Harrigan, thought to be brothers of Ann Fitzgerald, arrived in 1830-31. By 1835, they were joined in the Williamstown Settlement by Michael O'Brien and spouse Bridget Jardine, and by John Kingston and spouse Catherine O'Mahoney. About 1840, new arrivals included John Jardine and spouse Susan Goggin, John's brother Richard and spouse Ellen Kingston (sister of John), and John Regan, who soon married Margaret Lucey. Timothy Donovan and spouse Elizabeth Callaghan arrrived in 1842, settling in nearby Strathadam. Timothy Lucey and Ellen Harrigan (sister of Ann Fitzgerald) and their family came in 1847 but soon re-settled in Littleton, Maine. A latecomer was Ellen Harrigan Sauntry, oldest child of Dennis Harrigan, who, as a widow, arrived with her seven children about 1851.

By the time of the Great Famine of 1845-48, no Harrigans, Fitzgeralds, or Kingstons, and few Sullivans and Donovans, were occupiers in Drinane and Derryleary townlands of Schull Parish, but those surnames are found in abundance in North Esk Parish, New Brunswick.

Mary Ann Fitzgerald Blake, when she was 102 years of age in Oshkosh, Wisconsin, recalled her voyage at age seven to New Brunswick. She remembered the "crying among the women" during the six weeks on a sailing ship. Very few passenger lists have been found for arrivals in Miramichi in the 1830s. The entries, however, might have appeared as follows for Mary's Fitzgerald and Harrigan relatives:

SPRING/SUMMER 1830

William Fitzgerald	44
Ann (Harrigan)	44
James	15
Maurice	13
Mary	7
Michacl	5
Daniel	2

1830-31

John Harrigan	30
Cornelius Harrigan	(adult)

MAY 1831

Patrick Fitzgerald	22
John Fitzgerald	12

JULY 1831

Dennis Harrigan	51
Catherine (Driscoll)	49
Ann	20
John William	18
Catherine	15
Michacl	11
Cornelius	8
William	6
Jeremiah	4
Mary	3
Patrick	1
Wm. Fitzgerald, Jr.	21

Miramichi Bay in the spring of 1830 must have been a welcome sight for the seven-year-old and her family. By 1835, Harrigans, Fitzgeralds, Sullivans, and O'Briens were occupying log cabins in the Williamstown Settlement, paying taxes, and finding their main livelihood in the logging industry. The children married and bore children and left their imprint on the marriage and baptismal registers of St. Patrick's in Nelson and St. Thomas in Red Bank, on school rosters and tax returns, in county directories, and on the census of 1851. In that year members of this energetic and achievement-oriented *derbfine* began moving on to Maine, Wisconsin, and Minnesota.

Mary Fitzgerald herself married Limerick-born James Blake in 1844. In 1855, with their five children, they boarded a boat at Newcastle bound for New York City. This was the first leg of a journey to Oshkosh, Wisconsin. In 1926, Mary gave an account of the journey to a student who reported the following in a paper prepared for a class at Oshkosh Normal School:

On the trip from New Brunswick, Matilda Blake, infant daughter, died on the boat. The boat stopped and the child was buried on the shores of Nova Scotia on an island. After arriving at Chicago, they came on to Sheboygan, Wisconsin, reaching port after battling a raging storm on Lake Michigan. At Sheboygan they were met by Mrs. Blake's brother, Maurice, and he conducted them across land on horseback to the southern end of Lake Winnebago. There they boarded a boat owned by John Fitzgerald (no relation), the only one on the lake and river in 1855, and came to Oshkosh.

Thousands of Irish followed this route, from New Brunswick to New York City via a Maine port, by rail or river boat to Albany, then by

8. Headstones, Riverside Cemetery, Oshkosh, Wisconsin, right to left: Ann, wife of William Fitzgerald/died Feb. 25, 1880/aged 99 yrs. 11 mos.; William Fitzgerald/died Aug. 25, 1873/aged 86 years; Joseph M./son of P.&K. McPartlin/died August 15, 1873/age 1 yr. 3 mos.

9. (left) Mary Fitzgerald Blake (1823-1926), daughter of William Fitzgerald and Ann Harrigan, at age 102, Oshkosh, Wisconsin, with great-granddaughter Mary Ellen Kavanagh, 1925 photo; (right) 10. Her sister, Catherine McPartlin (1833-1923), date of photo unknown.

11. Michael Fitzgerald (1825-1927) and Ellen Derby family, Oshkosh, Wisconsin, about 1900. Born in Ireland, Michael learned the lumbering trade in New Brunswick and Maine; in Wisconsin, engaged in provisions business (for lumber camps) with brother Dan; and, when he was well over eighty, went on several timber cruising trips to Maine and to the Pacific Northwest.

12. Historic Mass celebrated in June 1982 at the "Mass Rock" near Schull, County Cork, on property of Bob O'Regan of Cooryorigan. Priests officiating (left to right): An t-Ath Daithi O Foghlu, Denis Kehily, and Patrick Hickey. Bottom: the congregation stands in the rain. *Cork Examiner* photo, June 27, 1982.

rail or canal boat from there to Buffalo, and then by boat and rail to Chicago and Milwaukee. It was a new start for the Blakes, whose children would be surrounded by cousins, aunts, uncles, grandparents. (*See census data in Chapter 1.*) These children are among the "uncounted Irish" in the census enumerations for Wisconsin, 1860 and 1880, which do not reveal the country of parents' birth. They grew up knowing little about the land of their parents, who had good reason to want to forget it. However, some of their descendants have been moved to learn something about that land and the cultural values that have been passed on down to them for three or four generations. Hence this research and this report, which started only with the folklore that these families "had come from County Cork through New Brunswick, Canada." Hence, also, a visit to the Miramichi in New Brunswick and to the Mizen Peninsula of Cork.

RETURN TO ROOTS
What a pleasure it was to locate the small settlement called Williamstown in New Brunswick where these Wisconsin families had lived for a generation, and to become acquainted with distant relatives still living in Miramichi. (*See Chapters 3, 4, and 6.*) What a pleasure it also was to locate the townland and parish in West Cork, and to visit the farms at the foot of Mount Gabriel from which these families had sprung. The land is now sparsely inhabited.

Dairy farmers Declan O'Mahony and Michael Donovan, occupiers of the Drinane land, graciously showed us around, pointing to the ruins of a cluster of stone cabins, almost certainly once the dwellings of our ancestors, and taking us to view Harrigan's Rocks in Toormore Bay, a short walk away. Somehow it seemed good to know that an O'Mahony was once again prospering on land confiscated from the O'Mahonys by the Hulls almost 350 years ago. I was told that the Hulls are not fondly remembered in local folklore. The last local occupier bearing the name appears to have been the Richard Edward Hull who, in 1876, was reported in *Returns of Owners of Land* to be the owner of 2,671 acres in County Cork.

The lead-lined coffin of Hull, who reportedly died in the 1880s, was placed in a vault at the entrance to the old graveyard on the Colla Road. A local historian says that the grave was desecrated during World War II by someone who removed both the remains of Hull and the saleable lead from the coffin. Hull's house at Leamcon has had several owners in more recent years, despite the belief that one of the Hulls haunts the place to this day. A local estate agent, in a letter to the author, writes that "on two separate occasions I showed the place to prospective buyers and they got a most unfavourable reaction from whatever vibes were flying around in it, although they didn't know anything about its reputation for being haunted."

On Declan's property was an old structure long ago used, he said, as a carpenter's shop, perhaps the very spot where William Fitzgerald and his brother-in-law Dennis Harrigan had plied their trade. Distant cousin-in-law Mary Margaret Lucey introduced us to farmer Jack Roycroft, who pointed out the old cemetery on his land near Lowertown where the Luceys, Harrigans, and Fitzgeralds buried their dead long, long ago. The inscriptions on the weathered stones, half-hidden in the weeds, are unreadable today. Jack told us that, when he was a boy, he discovered a *souterrain* (underground chamber and tunnel) containing a skull, beneath the cemetery. May the author be forgiven for imagining that that chamber just might be the very "cave" where Ellen Harrigan remembered hiding with her family during the sweep of the peninsula by General Moore's troops under Major Nugent in 1798.

We hiked to the top of Mount Gabriel where we viewed Schull Harbor, our ancestral farms a few miles to the southwest, Cape Clear far out beyond Roaring Water Bay, and many miles of the grand coastline of southernmost Ireland.

On June 27, 1982, three priests - Fathers Denis Kehily, Daithu O Foghlu, and Patrick Hickey - said Mass on the local Mass-rock in the mountains, at Corrydorrigan, near Schull. Speaking after the Mass, local historian C.G.F. McCarthy recalled the days when it was necessary to hide the priest and place a sentry.

It is fitting, we think, to conclude this chapter with a note of pride in the tough but gentle people of southwest Cork. If an explanation is needed for the achievement in the New World of so many of the sons and daughters of Cork, it will not be found in the suggestion of historian Merle Curti (*see Chapter 19, "Bias: American Historians"*) - that the exposure of the Gael to the Englishman and his language somehow stimulated the poor creature to greater achievement. A better answer, we think, can be found on a mountainside in the remote parish of Schull in rural Ireland on a rainy Sunday in June.

JAK

II
NEW WORLD BRANCHES: CANADA

Chapter 5

THE NEW BRUNSWICK IRISH:
UNCOVERING THEIR ROOTS

Historians of the Irish in New Brunswick have not painted a representative picture of the Irish, especially of the Catholic Irish immigrants who were arriving in the Colony of New Brunswick even before the turn of the 19th century. The historians have tended to focus on the rowdy and the shiftless, the criminals and the drunks, a bias that is readily explainable. Most of the documents on which the historians rely were written by Protestants, the established settlers who had taken with them to the New World and passed on to their children their Old World animosities and suspicions.

The Irish today are becoming a very visible presence in New Brunswick, Canada. One strong sign of the Irish emerging publicly was the formation in 1983 of the Irish Canadian Cultural Association of New Brunswick. The Association annually sponsors the Irish Festival in Miramichi and week-long St. Patrick's Day festivities in Saint John.

The Irish, both Catholic and Protestant, began arriving in New Brunswick before 1800. Many were there before the Loyalists arrived from America in the 1780s. Some came directly from Ireland; others trickled in from older colonies in Newfoundland, Prince Edward Island, and Nova Scotia. Irish immigration stepped up considerably after 1815 and dramatically after 1830. The very large numbers of Irish Protestants, especially Anglicans, Methodists, Baptists, and Presbyterians who emigrated to New Brunswick in the period after 1815 were more acceptable than the Catholics to the Loyalist rulers of the Colony. They were, after all, Protestant. They were almost always literate in English. They could obtain free land, at least until 1829, and immediately start working for themselves.

The grants of free land ended totally in 1829, on the eve of the greatest flood of Irish Catholics. The flood was largely a consequence of reduced fares on the timber ships, a subject discussed in Chapter 1. The many thousands of Irish who arrived in the 1830s joined earlier-arriving Irish, Scots, and English, who had begun settlement in the 1760s and whose families now occupied all the best lots on the river systems.

Without free land, some of the newly-arrived Irish were thrown on the mercy of the port cities such as St. Andrews, Saint John, and Newcastle, and on the vagaries of the timber and shipbuilding industries where unemployment was often the rule. As few as five hundred to one thousand of these Irish, even though a very small percentage of the whole, unemployed and reduced to beggary and hanging around the port cities or committed to alms houses, would have been a sizable and very visible presence to the earlier settlers.

The Catholic Irish that these established settlers tended to see and write about, furnishing the primary sources for future historians, tended to be the relatively few who turned to drunkenness, crime, beggary, public assistance. These were the "rowdies," and historians of the Irish, even today, are quick to focus on them.

New Brunswick historian William Spray, for example, employs the term "rowdy" frequently: "Given the conditions that many of these people lived in and their long tradition of rowdyism, it is no wonder that crime and drunkenness flourished . . .that many of the Irish immigrants were rowdy and difficult to control is evident from many reports from various parts of the province."

The available facts, seasoned with a modicum of imagination and good sense, might lend themselves to a picture of the early Catholic Irish in New Brunswick somewhat different from that painted by Spray and by other historians of a generally Establishment bent. It is possible to make a small try in that direction.

What is "rowdyism"? That might depend on who defines the term and who chooses the illustrations to fit the definition.

THE HANGING OF PATRICK BURGAN

On February 21, 1828, Patrick Burgan, age eighteen, was hanged by the neck from the second-story window of the old jail at Saint John. His crime was "burglary, breaking and entering, and assault." He had stolen twenty-five pennies and, so it was said, a loaf of bread from his employer, John B. Smith, a maker of ginger beer. He had entered Smith's house at the corner of Union Street and Drury Lane during the night. He was arrested the day after by Constable John McArthur.

The jury, all Protestant, recommended mercy, but Judge Ward Chipman Jr. nevertheless pronounced sentence of execution. No doubt the judge intended to teach a lesson concerning such serious breaches of the peace.

On the Sunday night before his execution, young Patrick set fire to his cell in an apparent attempt to burn down the jail. His cell was a dungeon, access to it being through a trap door. He had built a fire near the door hoping to burn a hole in it, or so it was alleged by the jailer who noticed the smoke. Patrick had nearly suffocated by the time the jailer arrived on the scene through the trap door.

The execution took place as scheduled. Patrick was accompanied to the hanging by Fathers McMahon and Carroll. The latter priest had unsuccessfully petitioned Lieutenant Governor Sir Howard Douglas for a reprieve. Patrick's hangman was one Blizard Baine, an Englishman serving a two-year term for robbery. As a reward for his civic service, Baine was released from prison and awarded ten pounds by Sheriff White.

Saint John's Irish Catholics, Patrick Burgan's own class, may well have concluded that the boy was the victim of a rather rowdy system of justice. On the other hand, the *Royal Gazette*, voice of the Old Loyalist ruling class, editorialized piously: "We trust such an example as this will not fail to be a warning, especially to young people, how [*sic*] they tread upon the threshold of iniquity."

Let us look at two more incidents, both used by historian Spray and others to illustrate the stereotypical rowdiness of the Irish.

THE RIOT OF 1822

The 1822 riot on the Miramichi has been reported briefly by several historians. They tell about "unemployed Irish laborers of Miramichi fighting with lumbermen, seasonal workers from the state of Maine. The Miramichi Irishmen "terrorized the inhabitants." Local authorities "lost control and appealed to Fredericton to send troops." A detachment of the 74th Regiment under Lieutenant Davis from Fredericton was dispatched to Miramichi to quell the dispute.

The regimental forces arrested over fifty Irishmen. It was their poor fortune at their trial in Newcastle in July of 1822 to have to face crusty Judge John Saunders, age sixty-eight, an old Loyalist from the state of Virginia, known for his extremely autocratic behavior. Historian James Hanney in *History of New Brunswick* commented on Saunders' charge to a jury in 1821, which had the effect of acquitting George Street, who had killed a man in a duel: "If it is to be taken as a specimen of the legal knowledge of the judges of the day, our bench in the year 1821 could not have stood very high." Saunders was also known for his fierce anti-Irish and anti-Catholic prejudice. Eight years after this trial he went on record opposing the Act of 1830 which removed the remnants of the penal codes and gave Catholics and other dissenters equal citizenship with Anglicans in the Colony of New Brunswick.

The incarcerations and trial were, according to one historian, "without parallel in the judicial annals of the Colony." Judge Saunders made the most of it. For "seditious words, forgery, highway robbery, petty and grand larceny," the Irishmen were convicted and received stiff penalties. Saunders meted out fifty-nine sentences. A number of the convicted received fifty lashes. Twelve stood in the pillory.

Judge Saunders had his day, but the spirit of the convicts outlived him. That spirit is immortalized in the song "Mullins' Boom" ("boom," literally a rigging for snagging logs at the end of a river drive, used as a metaphor for the Newcastle jailhouse with Mullins the jailer). This oldest indigenous song of the Miramichi, as quoted in part below, was composed, it is believed, by prisoner Francis Gleeson. The composer speaks for his fellow convicts:

> *We suffer for that Yankee Brood*
> *Those sharks that bore our wealth away,*
>
> *And punished tho' our cause was good,*
> *To Coward Yankee tricks a Prey...*
>
> *We took no foul unmanly plan*
> *To drive those cunning Spoilers back,*
>
> *But met them fairly man to man,*
> *Fierce rallied on by Musha Whacks...*
>
> *Three Valiant Sons of Erin's Land*
> *Were Singled out by Price's Crew*
>
> *And hotly fought with heart and hand*
> *Stout Darby, Frank and Borris too.*

The meaning of "Musha Whack" (a nickname for a Cuchulain of the Miramichi? a rallying cry?) and the identity of the warriors "Stout Darby, Frank, and Borris too" may never be known. But their activities become at least as heroic as rowdy when told from an Irish point of view. From that perspective the greater rowdiness may well appear to be that of the establishment Protestants against a poor and oppressed people struggling to get their fair share of honest work.

The song itself fell afoul of the law. After evidence was given on March 20, 1823, a bench warrant was issued by Grand Jury Foreman William Abrams, the shipbuilder, to bring the words of the song and its alleged composer, Mr. Gleeson, into court. (The consequences of this bench warrant require further research.)

THE FIGHTING ELECTION OF 1842-43

The Fighting Election involved Chatham on the southside of the Miramichi River and the towns of Newcastle and Douglastown on the northside. The Chathamites were almost all Irish Catholics employed in the yards of shipbuilder Joseph Cunard. The Newcastle and Douglastown citizens were a mixed bag of English, Scots, and Irish, mainly Protestant, employed in the shipyards of Gilmour, Rankin and Company, and Abrams and Company (the same Abrams who twenty years before had sequestered the seditious song and its writer).

The fight was over two Assembly seats. There were three candidates: Alexander Rankin and John Ambrose Street of the northside, and John Williston of the southside. The southside Catholics never had had "one of their own" elected to the Assembly, and though Williston, a lawyer and millowner, was not a Catholic, they felt he would give them fair representation. Certainly, they thought, they would not get it from John Ambrose Street, who a few years before had written that the Irish were "the scum of the population."

In the first election, with balloting from December 27, 1842, to January 5 at various settlements, Rankin and Williston won the seats. The tally was 834 votes for Rankin, 676 for Williston, and 645 for Street. Sheriff John M. Johnson, on request of Provincial Secretary William F. O'Dell, submitted a report on how he had conducted the election. He recounted how, at several polling places, supporters of Williston had blocked supporters of Street from casting their votes, amidst scuffling and fighting. He also referred to a religious aspect of the election:

I much regret that throughout the whole of the Election there has been a strong religious feeling evinced - Mr. Street having been charged by some of the people with having insulted or offended one of the Priests who lately came here, whilst traveling together.

The sheriff estimated destruction of property in Chatham by the Catholic "mobs" at 150 pounds. The election was disputed by Street who had his way with the Protestants controlling the election machinery in Fredericton. A new election, between Street and Williston, was announced by the Sheriff, on instructions from Fredericton, to be conducted from July 17 to July 27, 1843.

The hard feelings were fueled even more by the call for a second election. Bloody fights broke out between the two factions. Clubs and stones and fists were the weapons, and the Irish doubtless were well represented in angry crowds of between five hundred and one thousand. At the polls, thirty to forty people were injured and an elderly publican of Newcastle, James Ryan, died of wounds received. It was reported that two of Williston's leading supporters, Joseph Hea and Michael Dunn of Chatham, rallied the fighters with "orders" in the Irish language, understood by most of the "mob."

That Street's supporters responded in kind is evident in the report of an observer who claimed that a steamer carrying Williston forces arrived at a pier in Chatham with its decks strewn with lumps of coal four inches deep, the lumps having been hurled by the Street men. John Ambrose Street was declared the winner.

The whole incident might be used, although it has not been so used by New Brunswick historians, to illustrate the struggle of the Irish to reach worthy goals, such as fair play in elections and democratic representation, over barriers erected by a Protestant establishment that used whatever levers it could apply, including substantial rowdiness of its own, to deny equal opportunity. The Catholics eventually won this good fight. Shortly after the Fighting Election, the number of seats for Miramichi in the Assembly was increased from two to four. In 1846, Martin Cranney of Chatham became the first Catholic elected to the Assembly. In 1851, James Davidson (of Scots-Catholic roots) became the first Miramichi Catholic to hold a seat in the Legislative Council.

New Brunswick, in the final analysis, became a fine place for Irish Catholics whose ancestors had been among the most destitute people on earth. But it did not happen without a struggle against entrenched Protestants with Old World prejudices, wanting to hold on to their advantages.

CATHOLIC SCHOOLMASTERS

Although the evidence is sketchy, some of it suggests that Catholic schoolmasters were treated severely and unfairly by Protestant school inspectors. The reports of Inspector John Gregory in 1844 are particularly revealing. He found William Broderick, who was teaching in the McKay Settlement of North Esk Parish, Miramichi, to be "suffering from obtuseness of intellect." He drew this conclusion after finding that Broderick could not instruct his thirty-eight pupils, mostly Protestant, in appropriate answers to questions the inspector posed on a passage in the *Book of Revelation*. The inspector was accompanied on his classroom visit by the Reverend W. Henderson, who gratuitously tried to explain the meaning of the passage to the unfortunate schoolmaster.

Inspector Gregory also found the education of Richard Phelan, a thirty year old married man teaching an all-Catholic class at Barnaby River, Miramichi, to be "very defective." The inspector was disturbed by the fact that "there were no Bibles or Testaments" for these children. The religious instruction, alas, "was solely dependent on the Roman Catholic Catechism," which "had been carefully taught to the children who could not read," but "all present could say their Catechism well."

The inspector treated thirty-six year old Presbyterian schoolmaster George Laurence somewhat better, although Laurence gave the wrong answer to a mathematical problem posed by the inspector. Laurence, he concluded, "might acquit himself better on some other occasion," a possibility not considered in the cases of Broderick and Phelan. This same inspector gave a most flattering evaluation of the instruction of James Howe, an Irish Methodist with long experience in Miramichi schools, who had the confidence of both Catholics and Protestants in the community of Williamstown and who no doubt was a teacher of merit.

Howe was succeeded in 1846 by Irish-born James Evers, Williamstown's first Catholic schoolmaster. Shortly thereafter, Evers was falsely accused by a Protestant parent of improper conduct with some of the girls in his class. The teacher's license was revoked by Provincial Secretary John Saunders (son of the judge) on the uncorroborated word of the one Protestant accuser, even though the teacher had been cleared of the charges by the three-man North Esk Parish board of trustees, who conducted a thorough investigation. (The details of this story are given in the next chapter.)

Perhaps the most distinguished teacher in Miramichi was John O'Connor. Of the last generation of Irish hedgemasters, Irish-born O'Connor made his way to New Brunswick where in 1820, at age 50, he opened up School No. 4 at Red Bank-Cassilis. He seems to have been a specialist in starting new schools, reports W. D. Hamilton. By 1842, the last year his name appears on a school return, he had started three more schools: at North West Meadows in 1827; at Holmes's Settlement on the Little South West in 1833; and at Indian Point in 1837.

O'Connor was probably the most senior of many Irish bachelors who plied their teaching craft in Miramichi before 1850. In 1852, when he was eighty-two years of age, he was obliged to do what many other aging former teachers had to do: he threw himself as a pauper on the support of the Overseers of the Poor. As a parish ward he was living at the residence of Alexander Mullin at Sunny Corner in the late 1850s and early 1860s, and at the residence of George Matchett in Sunny Corner in 1864. An unsung hero of education in New Brunswick, he may be buried in an unmarked grave at the cemetery of St. Thomas the Apostle in Red Bank.

THE CATHOLIC CHURCH AND THE IRISH IMMIGRANTS

No account of the reception of the Irish into New Brunswick would be complete without strong focus on the Roman Catholic Church. Yet historians have very much underplayed the importance of the Church. (Spray, in his essay "Reception of the Irish in New Brunswick," does not mention it at all.) There were, to be sure, only four priests in all of New Brunswick in 1818 and only eleven in 1831, but that does not mean that the Church as an institution, whether with resident priests or without, did not provide a sense of community, continuity, and worth to an alien people in an often socially and physically hostile land.

Traveller John Francis Maguire, visiting remote Irish settlements in the 1860s and talking to many old timers who remembered the early days of the century, reported that the Catholics had not made their way easily among the older Protestant population that regarded them with "aversion and distrust" and looked on them as "interlopers and intruders." Maguire found his countrymen to be generally religious, law-abiding, and hard-working. He found no evidence of rowdy behavior distinguishing the Catholics from earlier Protestant settlers.

Maguire was told stories of Father William Dollard of Ossory, Ireland, who was appointed Missionary Priest to the Miramichi in 1825 and who became the first bishop of the new Diocese of New Brunswick (formerly under the jurisdiction of the French Bishop of Quebec). Father Dollard travelled in a canoe with an Indian guide, sleeping on the bare ground under the shelter of the canoe, bringing the Church to the Irish in remote settlements.

Maguire spoke to men who remembered the first tiny congregation at Saint John where in 1818 a tailor, "Andy Sullivan of Bandon," read the prayers because priests were not usually available. Services were conducted in a tiny structure "which the poor congregation were years trying to cover in from the rain and wind and had no means of warming." Maguire was told about an educated man named Flanagan who read "with befitting impressiveness the Epistle and Gospel of the day."

The Catholics of New Brunswick soon overcame their isolation by sheer numbers. By 1871 the Catholic Church was the largest religious denomination, although still outnumbered by the total of all Protestants. Of 285,000 people enumerated on the Census of 1871, there were 96,016 Catholics, 70,595 Baptists, 45,481 Anglicans, 29,000 Methodists, and 28,000 Presbyterians.

Since a majority of the Protestants also had Irish roots, and since there were a goodly number of Catholic Irish settlers in the latter part of the 18th century, it is small wonder that New Brunswick was almost named New Ireland when it was established as a separate colony from

Nova Scotia in the 1780s and the issue of a name was being discussed in British circles. (The neighboring colony of Prince Edward Island was also sometimes referred to as New Ireland.) The British government came down, not too appropriately, in favor of the German name Brunswick in honor of its king and his German relatives.

A PROBLEM WITH STATISTICS

One very questionable notion advanced by scholars such as John Mannion of Memorial University, St. John's, Newfoundland, is that early Catholic immigrants of the 1815-1845 period, at least in Miramichi, tended to be lone, single men, removed forever from their kin in Ireland, who somehow married the daughters of earlier Irish settlers. In *Irish Settlements in Eastern Canada,* Professor Mannion writes: "Only 19 of the 153 nuclear families recorded in the 1851 census [Nelson Parish] had children born in Ireland and genealogical evidence suggests that the majority of household heads had arrived in Miramichi as single adult males, and had married girls who came as child members of nuclear Irish families or the daughters of earlier Irish immigrants born in Miramichi."

My own genealogical and other evidence for a number of families in Miramichi, including many in Nelson Parish studied by Mannion, does not support his conclusion. Although evidence of the surnames gathered from the 1851 Census, tax lists, and school reports for the Williamstown Settlement and Nelson (northside) would seem to indicate that of eighteen Catholic families with Irish-born heads only three were related, genealogical evidence acquired from extensive research in Ireland, New Brunswick, and the United States testifies that all of these families were related by blood or marriage, and that they all came from the Mizen Peninsula in Southwest Cork.

Much more evidence to counter the myth of the Single Rootless Irishman (which fits comfortably with the other myth of the Rowdy Irishman) has been gathered by Peter Murphy, archivist and genealogist for the Diocese of Saint John. Mr. Murphy has painstakingly accumulated hundreds of detailed genealogies of early Irish, mostly in the Saint John area, all neatly catalogued in file after file of three by five cards. He has yet to find an Irishman without kin in New Brunswick.

Professor Mannion's conclusion about single males, even if true for his Miramichi study area, clearly could not apply to New Brunswick as a whole. That has been made evident by the discovery and publication of lists of over 10,000 passengers arriving in the Port of Saint John in the 1830s. A random check of ten of the largest vessels, carrying a total of 1,850 passengers, indicates a 42 percent female component. Typical is the barque *Robert White*, which departed from

Cork on May 30, 1837, and arrived at Saint John on July 24. It carried 137 adult male passengers, 97 females, 54 children under 14, and a crew of 21. Most of the lists give age and occupation of the women ("spinster," "wife," "widow"). Clusters of common surnames, and wives without husbands aboard, point up a pattern of families joining earlier-arriving senior male members.

Perhaps the most compelling evidence that the history of the Irish in Canada has traditionally been written from a highly-biased Protestant point of view has come from Professor Donald Akenson of Queen's University, Ontario. In *Being Had: Historians, Evidence, and the Irish in North America* , Akenson devotes a chapter to the late H. Clare Pentland and his heavy influence on the past generation of Canadian historians. Pentland, Akenson believes, had a sophisticated but enduring bias regarding Irish Catholics. His most influential book, *Labour and Capital in Canada, 1650-1860*, is "not history but social pathology" with a "racist structure." To make his point, Akenson takes some passages from Pentland, removes the words "Irish" or "Irishman," and inserts in their place pejoratives for other ethnic groups:

Some of the [nigger's] misery could have been relieved, it is true, if he had been less inept, indolent, and improvident. . .Thus [the wops] would do anything to get land except save for it. . .It may be wondered whether physical weakness was not an important reason why the [Jewboys] did not seek the heavy work of canal construction, and why employers did not want them.

Professor Akenson's chapter on Pentland in *Being Had* is meticulously researched. His conclusions are worth quoting at some length:

Pentland was a fifth generation Canadian. . .a descendant of an Ulster-Scots weaver from County Down who came to Upper Canada in 1821. The amazing point is that H. Clare Pentland, writing in the 1950s, 60s, and 70s, highly educated, influenced by at least two major schools of European economic history, evidenced the same ethnic cosmology, the same prejudices, that were common amongst the Ulster-Scots of the cottier-weaver class in the three or four decades after the abortive 1798 Rising: an affinity for the lowland Scots, a contempt for the highland Catholics . . .a dislike of the French (who had continually made alliances with the treasonous Irish natives), a mixed admiration-dislike of the 'real' English . . .an equally uneasy feeling about the people of English descent who lived in Ireland (fellow Protestants, but too often anti-Presbyterian), and, most of all, an abiding hatred and contempt for the Irish Catholics, a group seen as scheming, dishonest, feckless, priest-ridden, superstitious, and, in sum, a body of backward pagans. Pentland's book seems to be an important piece of evidence concerning the perdurance of a specific cosmology, running strong just below the surface, for a century and a half in the New World . . . despite Pentland's virulent racism and his fabricating many points of evidence to fit that racism, many Canadian scholars have assimilated Pentland's world view. Only a few have quibbled around the edges concerning that racism, and no one has pointed out directly and in detail the outrageous nature of his racist case.

Akenson believes that Pentland's strong "ethnic cosmology" calls for a study of the mechanisms by which these racial prejudices of the Ulster Scots were preserved in a family for 150 years.

THE "MYTH" OF THE FAMINE

Professor Peter M. Toner of the University of New Brunswick at Saint John has pointed out that "over 90% of the Irish of New Brunswick are descended from immigrants who arrived before the Famine." He says that the Catholic Irish began to arrive before the Loyalists, that they were "the largest [ethnic] group even before the Famine," and that they made their contribution to New Brunswick along with the major [Protestant] groups." Not realizing all this, the Catholics have accepted instead the "myth of the Famine," that they were late-comers, a misconception in large part assimilated from American "Pop" culture. They therefore have been led to believe that "the basis of [New Brunswick] society was laid by others, and that their ancestors merely hitched a ride." Toner believes that "nothing was so damaging as the myth of the Famine [in diminishing] the perceived contribution the Irish made to the province."

Toner's perception of the cause of the problem is troubling. The famine he refers to occurred in the years 1845-48. But there were also failures of the potato crop followed by horrendous famine, starvation, and substantial emigration in the early 1820s and 1830s. In fact there had been twenty-four failures of the potato crop since the year 1728, including fourteen partial or complete failures between 1816 and 1842. The New Brunswick Irish were no strangers to famine, and they no doubt passed on famine stories to their children.

One should be wary, therefore, of blaming the Catholic Irish themselves and American pop culture for ignorance about the early New Brunswick settlements and the vital role played by Catholic Irish. The real cause of ignorance is rooted in New Brunswick history. The pre-1845 Catholic immigrants did not start from scratch with their Protestant "cousins" (Toner's term). Irish, not English, was usually their first language, at least before their arrival in the colony. They left few written records such as diaries or letters. They controlled no newspapers. They wrote no books about themselves. What we do "know" about early New Brunswick has been passed on to us largely by the written record of a ruling Protestant class. The focus of this record has been on the hegemony of the Loyalists, the movers and shakers of Fredericton, and on their significant contribution to the commonweal. When the Catholics manage to thrust themselves into this record, through such events as the hanging of Patrick Burgan, the Riots of 1822, and the Fighting Elections of 1843-44, their story has been told by Protestant sheriffs, politicians, and newspaper editors. Historians have drawn on these sources, and the consequence has been a very biased history of New Brunswick, especially regarding the role of the Catholics. The work of D.H. Akenson - his latest being *Small Differences: Irish Catholics and Irish Protestants, 1815-1922* - has been a refreshing corrective.

The hard facts of history may distress some modern-day New Brunswick Protestants who have been living in harmony with Catholics for a long time. The facts may be even more distressful to academics who have a vested interest in their own lecture notes. They may be upset by a new generation of historians rendering their notes obsolete. But the ire of the myth-perpetuating historians and the salutary desire for harmony should not lead historians to sugar-coat the truth.

At the same time, one should not be led to think that religious tension and prejudice were the most significant aspects of early New Brunswick history, although those aspects happen to be underscored in this chapter. Problems of sheer survival in a wilderness environment kept people busy thinking about more pressing matters than the religion of their neighbors. A body of evidence is available to show that Catholics and Protestants often worked together to solve common community problems. Protestants worked to alleviate the distress of Catholics afflicted with fever and dying on crowded immigrant ships, and some Protestants even gave their lives in the process. The pauperized among the thousands upon thousands of immigrants thrust upon the shores of a sparsely populated colony were not allowed to starve and die at dockside. Tax money that New Brunswickers could ill afford went for the aid of the needy, even as some of these same taxpayers were lamenting the onslaught of the "scum of the earth."

THE SILENCE ABOUT IRISHNESS

Until Cork-born Timothy Warren Anglin began writing as the first editor of *The Weekly Freeman* in Saint John in 1849, there had been no strong voice expressing the viewpoint of the Irish, especially Irish Catholics, nor any medium through which such a voice could counter the prevailing prejudices. *The Weekly Freeman* itself was established as a consequence of the bloody Orange Riot at York Point on July 12, 1849, when the Orangemen, as was their annual disposition, took their parade into the Catholic neighborhood, singing lustily songs dear to their hearts, such as "Kick the Pope" and "Boyne Waters," all deliberately designed to provoke the Catholic citizens of Saint John.

THE FENIAN SCARE

There were several reasons why the Catholics were slow in New Brunswick to organize their own societies and to produce scholars willing and able to write the history of their forebears free of Protestant bias. One reason was the physical and, in a very narrow sense, the cultural handicap of the Irish Catholics who arrived during the first half of the 19th century. English was not their first language. They left no written record of their lives and times, save for church registers and some civil records.

Another reason was the great pressure to prove themselves "good Canadians." This was especially evident in the 1860s when the Fenians in the United States organized an army and proposed to capture Canada, a subject explored in Chapter 7. Some American newspapers, and even elected officials, encouraged the Fenians and said it was only a matter of time before Canada would be annexed to the United States.

The Fenians indeed succeeded in making brief sorties onto Canadian soil from New York and Vermont, and even raised their flag on Campobello Island for a brief spell before the arrival of British and United States warships.

The Fenians were the talk and the fear of the day, and all Irish Catholics in New Brunswick, including the distinguished Timothy W. Anglin, were suspected of being sympathizers or collaborators. Anglin opposed Confederation, the other big issue of that time. As a result, he was accused by Confederationists of being disloyal to the British Empire and even of having plotted against Britain before emigrating to Saint John. Anglin was obliged to publicly condemn the Fenians as a "disgrace." Other Catholics, including the hierarchy of the Church, made equal haste to distance themselves from these wild Irish tribesmen of theirs in America. They rushed to assure their Protestant neighbors that they too were loyal to New Brunswick and, after Confederation in 1867, to the Dominion of Canada.

It is impossible to measure the extent to which the Fenian Scare led the Irish to "go into the closet" rather than publicly proclaim their Irish heritage and insist on fair, accurate history of their pioneer forebears. The effect has been considerable, however, and endures to this day.

THE IRISH EMERGE

In the 1980s, the Irish in New Brunswick began to express pride, increasingly, in their Old World roots, in their New World experience, and in their contribution as New Brunswickers of Irish ancestry. The formation of the Irish Canadian Cultural Association of

13. Celtic Cross erected on Middle Island near Chatham, New Brunswick, in 1984, honoring about 200 Irish immigrants buried in unmarked graves. They arrived in 1847 on two ships carrying famine victims and were quarantined on Middle Island to avoid a typhus epidemic in the community.

14. Farrell McCarthy, Newcastle teacher, founding president of the Irish Canadian Cultural Association of New Brunswick, and wife, Edna Regan. 1988 photo.

New Brunswick was a huge step in "bringing out" the Irish. Under such leaders as teacher Farrell McCarthy of Newcastle and Dr. Danny Britt of Saint John, the Association has encouraged a new breed of historians to discover the real story of the Irish pioneers. Financed by a government grant obtained by the Association, Professor Peter M. Toner has edited a book of essays entitled *New Ireland Remembered: Historical Essays on the Irish in New Brunswick*, published as this chapter was nearing completion. Toner's volume contains a chapter about the first four New Brunswick bishops, including the saintly William Dollard. Two beautifully done volumes of essays, *The Untold Story: The Irish in Canada*, edited by Robert O'Driscoll and Lorna Reynolds, were also published as this chapter was in the process of completion. Turner Huggard of Fredericton has published a most valuable 53-page bibliography, *An Annotated List of Resource Material on the Irish in New Brunswick* (1984). Peter Murphy, the Saint John diocesan archivist, is preparing for publication his extraordinary collection of genealogies. The New Brunswick Genealogical Society, Saint John Branch, has published the extant passenger lists, mentioned earlier in this chapter, for many of the ships arriving in the Port of Saint John in the 1830s. Professor W. D. Hamilton of the University of New Brunswick at Fredericton has done a study of almost 300 families, a majority Irish, in *Old North Esk on the Miramichi*. His *Miramichi Papers* includes an update on the genealogies, as well as an essay on the folk-rhymster Michael Whelan, "Poet of the Miramichi."

The most striking evidence that the days of anti-Irish and anti-Catholic sentiment are long gone came in the results of the October 13, 1987, provincial elections. The Liberal Party headed by Frank McKenna won all fifty-eight seats in the Legislative Assembly, sweeping out of office the Conservatives under Brian Hatfield, who had ruled for seventeen years. "The names of the Liberal Party assemblymen," writes Farrell McCarthy of Newcastle, "read as if one were listening to a role call of the *Dáil* [Irish parliament]: Kenny, Hurley, Maher, King, Duffie, Dalton, O'Donnell, McKee, Murphy, McAdam, Dysart, Mooney, Barry, Lacey . . .the most Irish Legislature in our history."

McKenna was born on a farm near Sussex and attended St. Francis University in Antigonish, Nova Scotia, also the alma mater of Canadian Premier Brian Mulroney. At the nominating convention at Chatham, McKenna received a loud cheer from the three thousand in attendance when he promised funds for the building of an Irish Cultural Center.

McKenna and these Liberal Party members of Irish ancestry are not the descendants of rootless, rowdy men hanging around port cities. More likely, they and their Protestant "cousins" can trace themselves to emigrants who may have been separated from their kinfolk and neighbors in Ireland for a time but who managed in the long run to keep together as families; to build churches, schools, hospitals, and communities; and to pass on their religious and other Old World values to their progeny.

The "emerging Irish" in New Brunswick show no signs of developing the stridency of some strong advocates of Ireland in America. These latter-day grandchildren of Erin in America, however, may be better acquainted than New Brunswickers with Irish history, less influenced by Britain and British culture, and hence more inclined to be critical of the British role in Northern Ireland.

The Irish Canadian Cultural Association, although founded and supported largely (but not nearly exclusively) by Catholics, has provided opportunities at its festivals for Protestants and Catholics to play, sing, and even pray together, finding and enjoying the best values of their Irish heritage. Many who have long ignored their Irish roots for a complexity of reasons have taken a new interest and pride in the Irish contribution to New Brunswick history. They are learning that it is possible to be "Irish" and also "good Canadians."

JAK

———————

Chapter 6

THE MIRAMICHI IRISH

Irish surnames of the Canadian-born abound in the United States censuses for 1850 to 1880 for states such as Michigan, Wisconsin, and Minnesota. But almost nothing has been written about the Canadian experience of these Irish ethnics who avoided the cities and settled on the farms and river systems. A study of the tiny Williamstown Settlement in Northumberland County, New Brunswick, gives us some insight into what life was like for these Irish lumberers and farmers, many of whom lived for a generation and more in New Brunswick and contributed enormously to its economy, as they did later to the economy of the American and Canadian West. The study of Williamstown also reveals how Old World prejudices transported to the New contributed to the destruction of a teacher, a school, and a community.

The story of the Williamstown Settlement in Northumberland County ("Miramichi") is typical of many communities settled by the Irish in New Brunswick and the other Maritime provinces, whose sons and daughters eventually went westward in great numbers.

Williamstown has never been heralded as a tourist attraction, even during the Irish Festivals of recent years sponsored by The Irish Canadian Cultural Association of New Brunswick. But one historian of the Miramichi, Professor W. D. Hamilton of the University of New Brunswick at Fredericton, has called it "the most interesting of the settlements in the Nor'West," because of its colorful, although short, history and because so many of the descendants of its old settlers achieved distinction in a number of fields.

83

REMOTE SETTLEMENT

The settlement is situated inland between the South West and North West Miramichi Rivers, about six miles west of where these great rivers converge at Wilson's Point and flow into Miramichi Bay. Even at its height, if that word is appropriate, in the 1840s, not more than twenty families lived there, on one hundred and two hundred acre lots. There were scattered log cabins. Much land had been cleared for tillage and several farms, despite marginal soil and climate, were considered to be flourishing.

GHOST TOWN

Today the land is mostly scrub. A few occupied houses remain, one being the residence of Gladys Mahoney, widow of Frank Mahoney, a descendant of early settlers. Many dwellings, abandoned long ago, have become playthings of the wind and rain. It is a ghost community, and the ghosts are many. One such ghost is that of old bachelor Cornelius Regan, whose deteriorating hut was still standing in 1982. Old-timers can recall Con's death at age eighty-one in 1924. They say that Father Frederick C. Ryan, pastor of the church at Red Bank, would not allow the coffin of old Con to be carried through the main entrance to the cemetery. Con's mourners had to hoist the box over the fence of St. Thomas Cemetery, where it was buried in a remote corner.

Another unhappy ghost is that of James Evers, Williamstown's first Catholic schoolmaster, who held classes in the 1840s in a private dwelling on what is now Mahoney property. Evers was accused by a Protestant parent of defiling one or more of the girls in his class, of which more later. The crumbled remains of the fireplace of the Fitzgerald log cabin, possibly the one used for the school, now lie hidden in the brush.

"The land was never any good," said old-time resident Brian Mahoney, brother of Frank, in 1979 shortly before his death. That was one of the reasons for the decline of the community. Another was the ups and downs of the lumber industry on which the community depended, the residents being loggers in the winter and farmers in the spring and summer. A third reason was bitter religious factional fighting between Protestants and Catholics.

THE IRISH METHODISTS

The surnames of the first Methodist settlers in Williamstown are familiar ones on the Miramichi today: Tweedie, McLean, Quayle, Hosford, Graham. The Tweedies were weavers and farmers from County Leitrim. The McLeans and Quayles also had Leitrim roots. The Hosfords may have come from Bandon in County Cork. Why

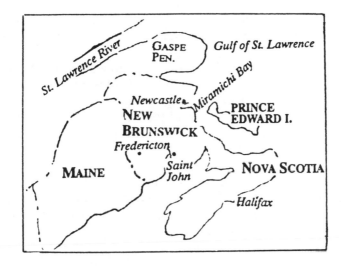

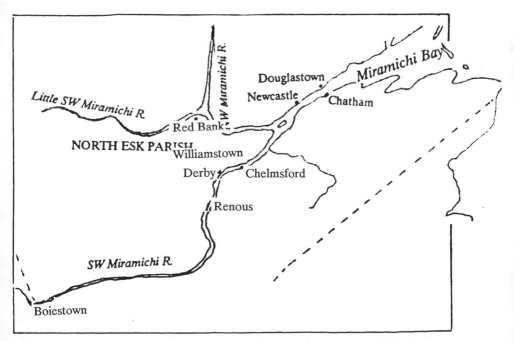

15. (Top) Maritime Region. (Bottom) Miramichi area of New Brunswick, including Williamstown Settlement in North Esk Parish.

they left Ireland is conjecture but one can make educated guesses. These families, way back, had been awarded large tracts of land in Ireland for serving in or financially supporting English armies who waged war against rebellious Irish subjects, especially in the 1640s and 1690s.

As generations passed, there was less and less land to be inherited by individual descendants of the original Protestant adventurers, and some of them could hardly be distinguished in their poverty from their Catholic neighbors. With the end of the Napoleonic Wars in 1815 and the opening up again of European trade ports, there was a steep decline in grain prices in Ireland, which had fed the English military during the wars, and a long general depression was the result. Compounding the problem were the periodic failures of the potato crop. Particularly severe ones occurred in the early 1820s and 1830s. Moreover, the important cottage industry of linen-weaving, the men doing the weaving and the women the spinning, declined radically during the 1820s. These farmers and weavers began emigrating in considerable numbers. They took the six-week passage on the sailing ships plying the timber trade route between British North America and Ireland.

For whatever reasons, some hardy Protestant settlers from County Leitrim began arriving on the Miramichi in 1822. They were not the first by any means. Scots and Irish had been settling since the 1760s and by 1822 occupied most of the desirable lots on the river system.

The first of the Williamstown party was Robert Tweedie, a weaver, accompanied by his large family from Lisduff townland near Carrick-on-Shannon. They arrived in 1822. By 1831, Robert and his brothers Joseph and James and their relative John McLean and his son Joseph had been granted lots of approximately 200 acres each in Williamstown. Another relative, William Quayle, came in 1825, having sailed with his wife and six children on the lumber vessel *Maria of Harrington*. Quayle had served in His Majesty's 10th Regiment of Militia, enduring, according to family folklore, "all the hardships of the Irish Rebellion of 1798." William Graham arrived in June 1824, soon marrying Jane McLean, daughter of John. William and Benjamin Hosford landed in 1831, married Margaret and Mary Tweedie, obtained land grants in Williamstown, and took their places in the Methodist community. Nathaniel Buck arrived from Foxcroft, Maine, marrying Elizabeth Quayle in 1831.

HISTORY OF FRICTION

To understand the friction that later developed between the Methodists and the Catholics of Williamstown, one needs to know something about the background in Ireland of the senior Methodist settler, Robert Tweedie (1785-1855), and his brothers. They were the great-great grandchildren of an army officer from Tweeddale, Scotland, who fought with the forces of Protestant King William III, which defeated those of deposed Catholic King James II at the Battle of the Boyne in 1690. For his services, Robert was rewarded with land in Ireland. In County Leitrim he and his descendants, although masters, at least for a time, of large land holdings, were immersed in a sea of Catholic neighbors and small leaseholders. Their tightly knit Protestant enclave became religiously attuned to the preachings of the Wesley brothers in the mid-18th century.

Many families like the Tweedies understandably developed a siege mentality and a contempt not only for the religion of the dispossessed but also for the "Irish race." There is some evidence that the Tweedies brought this contempt with them to the New World and transplanted it. Robert Tweedie's daughter Isabelle (1830-1915) wrote to a nephew in 1901 expressing her own and her late father's low opinion of Irish Catholics:

When I was a thoughtless girl at home [in Williamstown] our work brought us in contact with rather poor specimens of the Emerald Isle, so I took no interest in the race . . .I have heard my father tell a minister we used to have, a converted Catholic, there was not a drop of Celtish blood in his veins and say he was Anglo-Saxon, pure Scotch on both sides.

Mixed with this contempt, however, was a feeling of nostalgia for the land which had been the family's home for five generations. One of the immigrant members of the Tweedie family recalled the weeping as the family said farewell to friends at the River Shannon. The Tweedies sustained themselves, she said, during fearful storms on their voyage across the Atlantic by singing a favorite Methodist hymn:

> *Away with our sorrow and fear,*
> *We soon shall recover our home.*

The home they found in New Brunswick could hardly be considered desirable. Since the river-front lots upstream were already occupied by earlier settlers, they were obliged to settle inland in a totally unoccupied area of the old Davidson and Cort grant of the 1760s, divided into lots for settlement but accessible only by a narrow trail. Outsiders labelled the place "Irish Settlement," to distinguish it from "English Settlement," a small community of Methodists from Devonshire, on the North West Miramichi River. However, the settlement soon came to be known as Williamstown, perhaps for William IV, who assumed the throne in 1830, but possibly for William III of the

Battle of the Boyne to whom the Tweedie brothers' forebear was indebted for his land in Ireland.

It was tough going for these first settlers. The land had to be cleared, the trees felled and cut and burnt. For many years the planting was done on land covered by tree stumps. Every year a few more acres would be cleared.

METHODIST PREACHER ARRIVES

The Methodists were as fervent in their religion as they were in clearing their land. A circuit-riding Methodist preacher, Reverend John B. Strong of Fredericton, took notes of a visit to the isolated settlement in August 1828. He was greeted by Robert Tweedie and his wife and eight children. They had not seen a Methodist preacher in five years. Mrs. Tweedie wept for joy. "Have I once more fixed my eyes on a Methodist preacher?" she cried. Her children went scurrying to bring the neighbors the good news. Mr. Strong preached a sermon in Tweedie's log cabin and recorded the experience in his notebook:

This good man [Robert Tweedie] was the leader of a little band who had not left their religion behind them in Ireland. For five years he had by means of class-meetings and other simple services, kept the home fires burning as they all prayed for ministers of their own loved church to come and work among them . . .In this log dwelling, these Irish Methodists told the story of their trials in their adopted country. During the settlers' five years in the woods, their faith in God and attachment to the Church of their childhood had been well tested. Persistence in a religious life had encouraged each other to await the arrival of a minister of their own denomination.

Commenting critically on the nearby Baptist Church, which already had its own minister and church structure on the North West Miramichi, the Reverend Strong praised the Irish Methodists for their stout resistance to the heresy of baptism by immersion:

Immersionist theories had in vain been urged upon them with a zeal worthy of a more important cause, while they thus looked for a messenger of the churches.

The truth was that some of the Methodists did affiliate themselves with the Baptists for a short time, full immersion or no. The affiliation was an uncomfortable one for Tweedie's nephew Joseph McLean who married Ann Nutley in a Baptist ceremony in December 1826. Less than two weeks after the ceremony, the following entry appears in the Baptist Church record book:

Ann Nutley, now McLean, for imprudent conduct is under censure of the church, and Brethren James Tozer and John Woodworth are appointed to converse with her and make report.

The nature of Ann's offense is unknown. The censures recorded in the church book are frequent, and for what Christians today would probably consider very minor imperfections.

DISTINGUISHED DESCENDANTS

In any case, Wesleyan Methodism flourished in Williamstown. For some years a log building was used as both a school and church. Three of the thirteen children of Robert Tweedie and Sarah Dowler became Methodist ministers. Among their great-grandchildren was Thomas Mitchell Tweedie (1872-1944), Chief Justice of the Supreme Court of Alberta. A grandson was Lemuel Tweedie (1849-1917), who served as Lieutenant Governor of New Brunswick from 1907 to 1912. Another grandson was William Morley Tweedie, who taught English Literature at Mount Allison University for fifty years. A grandson of original settler James Tweedie (1794-1863) was Hedley Tweedie (1866-1950), assistant in opthalmology at Johns Hopkins University for many years, who later had a private practice in Rockland, Maine. Hedley never forgot his roots in the Williamstown community. For many years he returned to deliver an annual address at the little church.

Perley Quayle, described by Professor W.D. Hamilton as a "teacher and scholar," kept the original Quayle grant under cultivation until his death in 1975, 150 years after the arrival of his pioneer ancestor. His widow was residing in Williamstown in 1983, among a handful of the descendants of the earliest settlers.

The hard-working and God-fearing pioneer Methodists of County Leitrim sank deep roots in Miramichi. These roots were deeper than those of the Irish Catholics from the parishes of Schull and Goleen on the Mizen Peninsula of southernmost Ireland who began arriving in Williamstown in the early 1830s and began departing for the West a generation later. In the United States, the latter produced scores of high achievers in the fields of business, law, government, education, the military, the church, public service, and entertainment. The culture of these Corkonians, in language, religion, attitude toward England, and even in the manner of sharing the land, was not compatible with the cultural soil the evangelizing Methodists wished to fertilize. That is the subject of the next part of the Williamstown story.

THE IRISH CATHOLICS

As mentioned in Chapter 1, the sharp reduction in passenger fares on the timber ships returning to British North America about 1830, from five pounds per person to as low as one pound, made possible the first mass emigration of the Irish and mainly Catholic poor.

Among the arrivals in New Brunswick in 1830 and 1831 were William Fitzgerald, age forty-three, his wife Ann Harrigan, and eight children. By 1835, William and two sons were paying taxes on three 100-acre lots in the Williamstown Settlement, about fifteen miles west of Newcastle. They were joined by more Fitzgeralds and Harrigans and by other close relatives and friends: Regans, Jardines, Kingstons, Sullivans, O'Briens, and Sauntrys. It was a large extended family, a *cineadh* or *derbfine*, which tranplanted itself to the New Brunswick colony over the course of twenty years.

The family seems to have had little trouble acquiring lots in Lower Williamstown, mostly east of Stewart Brook, the Catholic part of the small settlement. John Harrigan (son of Dennis) and William Fitzgerald Jr. were listed, on an 1838 record, as "freeholders . . .by grant of the Crown," but the lots seem to have been shared freely as common property with other members of the *derbfine* in line with the rundale system of rural Ireland. On an August 1835 tax list, the name of Patrick Fitzgerald, oldest son of William, was listed consecutively with two more "Fitzgerald" entries (no first names given), and one "Harrigan" (no first name), and Michael O'Brien. The four lots were each assessed one shilling six pence.

Dennis Harrigan served as Overseer of Highways from 1839 to 1846, according to the minutes of the Court of Quarter Sessions at Newcastle, evidence that the Catholics were becoming part of the total society.

In 1838, the Catholic and Protestant settlers had joined hands in the face of a common threat to their community. Rowland Crocker of nearby Crocker Settlement had diverted the waters of what he called Crocker Lake and what the Williamstown residents called Williamstown Lake, thus severely depleting the water in a brook that flowed through Williamstown. On December 21, 1838, seventeen Williamstown residents addressed a petition to the Lieutenant Governor in Fredericton. They testified that they were all farmers during the summer season and "in the winter cut and haul a few logs off of their farms into the . . .mill stream and drive the logs down into Mr. [Jared] Tozer's mill pond which is and has been a great benefit to the Settlement." The petitioners "have learned that Mr. Rowland Crocker has cut a new out let for the water of [Williamstown] lake and has carried and diverted the [water] to the South West instead of allowing it to flow in its natural and accustomed channel whereby the quantity of water is very much less in the. . .brook and stream and should the [water] be allowed to remain in its diverted state it will not only be injurious to the inhabitants of Williamstown . . .but ruinous to the said Jared Tozer."

The petition was signed by five McLeans (Arthur, Robert, Joseph, Michael, John), three Fitzgeralds (William, Patrick, John), four Harrigans (William, Cornelius, John, Dennis), and by John Regan, Joseph Tweedy, Jonathan Gillis, George McCombs, and Michael O'Brien. What attention Fredericton gave to the petition is unknown.

In 1839, Patrick Fitzgerald attempted unsuccessfully to obtain additional land in the adjoining all-Protestant Crocker Settlement. He was preparing for his marriage to childhood sweetheart Catherine Driscoll, who had arrived from Ireland in that year. On March 25, 1839, Patrick filed a land petition in Chatham, addressed to the Lieutenant Governor. "The land," he petitioned, "is in its natural wilderness state, no improvements having been made thereon." He offered to pay two shillings six pence per acre for the 100-acre parcel "adjoining . . .Roland Crocker's lot." He was surprised to be informed, shortly thereafter, that his bid was rejected. An application had allegedly been filed earlier by William Craig.

Patrick and Catherine married in November. They remained in Williamstown until about 1850, when they joined Patrick's cousin, John Harrigan, and his widowed mother in Chelmsford, on the southside of the South West Miramichi (in 1847, John's father, Cornelius Harrigan, had purchased a lot there from George Flett). John shared the farm with Patrick and his family for a number of years, before Patrick joined his parents, sisters, and brothers in Oshkosh, Wisconsin.

The pattern of sharing lots freely with other members of the extended family as some arrived from Ireland and others moved on to Maine and Wisconsin was in sharp contrast with the practice of the Williamstown Methodists and other Protestant families who quickly obtained legal title to individual lots in the English manner.

Language also set the two groups apart. The Catholic settlers, although bilingual, used Gaelic as their first language. The major divider, however, was religion. The Catholics were as firmly set in their religious faith as the Methodists. They were regularly served by priests of St. Patrick's at Nelson and later mostly by priests of St. Thomas at Red Bank. The marriage and baptismal registers tell the story of the importance of the Church to these early immigrants.

Above all, perhaps, they were interested in education for their children, an education largely denied them and their forebears during the dark days of the penal codes in 18th century Ireland, when Catholic schooling, what there was of it, was administered, more or

16. St. Patrick's Church in Nelson-Miramichi, New Brunswick, site of "Malcolm's Chapel," which was built in 1796 to serve Roman Catholics on the Miramichi. 1985 photo.

less surreptitiously, by the hedgemasters. In Williamstown until 1845 they were hampered by the fact, much as in Ireland, that the official school was, in every sense of the word, a Protestant school. It was taught by Methodists zealous in their desire to win souls for Christ. For them, the Catholics, worshipping as they did in the Popish institution, were among the souls that needed winning.

CATHOLIC VERSUS METHODIST

To the Irish Methodists of Williamstown the sight and sound of Irish-speaking Catholics coming down the narrow trail in the 1830s to take up land in their community could not have been a pleasant one.

Certainly, however, the Irish Catholics had no feelings of inferiority, and they were not about to abandon the religion and other features of their culture which they and their forebears had managed to guard so tenaciously in the Old Country. They had a language and literature and other civilized traditions much older than that of their conquerors.

The first problem that the Catholics faced regarding schooling for their children in their new home in Williamstown was that the local school, opened in 1838, was a *de facto* Methodist institution. The school structure also served as a Methodist chapel. The teachers from 1838 to 1840 were devout Methodists Sidney Fayle and his wife Margaret Howe. The school returns for the two 1839 terms show twenty-two and twenty-three pupils, all Methodists. The teacher for 1841-42 was Catherine Tweedie, believed to be the daughter of Methodist clergyman J. R. McGeary of County Down. Before 1845 only two Catholic children appear on the returns, and then only for a single term. Some Catholic children, especially Harrigans and Fitzgeralds, can be found during those years on returns for Miramichi schools located at inconvenient distances from their homes. It is most likely that the Catholic parents were distrustful of the Methodist instruction.

To understand their fear and their dilemma, one needs to know something about the evangelical zeal of the Methodists of those days. Inspired by the teachings of the Wesley brothers, the Methodists were tireless proselytizers, spreading the Good News of Salvation to all ears they could find. The Reverend D. F. Hoddinott in *From Whence We Came*, a book about Methodist and Presbyterian traditions on the Miramichi, writes that the early Methodist preachers, imbued with the buoyant spirit of the Wesleyan Movement, "felt themselves called of God to win men and women to a personal experience in Jesus Christ and their work was judged not by attendance at services or financial income, but by the number of persons who were led to take a 'stand for Christ.'"

The Methodists must have found their Catholic neighbors to be a stubborn lot, if they attempted any evangelizing. It is likely that they shared the feelings of their leader Robert Tweedie who boasted of his "pure Anglo-Saxon, pure Scotch" heritage." Small wonder that the Williamstown Catholics were not eager to send their offspring to a school administered by Tweedie's band. Their attitude seems to have changed with the arrival of schoolmaster James Howe, brother of Margaret Fayle. Howe was a native of County Tipperary with many years of teaching experience in Miramichi schools. Although a Methodist, Howe had enough of the trust of the Catholics for them to raise the largest portion of the twenty pounds to pay him, and to entrust their children to him, no doubt with the understanding that there would be no proselytizing. It was quite customary in New Brunswick at the time, to the dismay of officials in Fredericton, for the parents to negotiate privately for a schoolmaster and then report his being hired as a *fait accompli* to the local trustees. That Howe did not have the complete trust of the Catholic parents is suggested, however, by the attendance for the six-month term ending January 13, 1845, of Maurice Fitzgerald, age twenty-nine (age shown erroneously as twenty on Howe's return), himself literate, in a class of children ages five to fifteen, quite possibly monitoring Howe's instruction. Twenty-one of Howe's thirty-two pupils were Catholic, as evidenced from his January 2, 1846, return. Curiously, the children of only two Protestant families, the McLeans and the Bucks, appear on Howe's last return. Some Protestants seem to have preferred schools in nearby settlements with mostly Protestant pupils. Some may have decided to continue the education of their children in a private home.

THE CATHOLIC SCHOOLMASTER

Howe's school was conveniently located just across the road from Protestant Joseph McLean's log cabin. McLean's children were in attendance during Howe's tenure, and were enrolled in the class of Howe's successor, Catholic James Evers, whose first six-month term in Williamstown began on April 30, 1846. McLean became upset, however, by Evers' removal of the instruction to a cabin vacated by "the young Fitzgerald" (which could mean Patrick, Maurice, or William, elder sons of William Senior). Shortly after this move, McLean withdrew his five children from the school and raised the dreadful charge that Evers was guilty of conduct of the "grossest nature" and of "defiling" one or more of the girls at the school.

The charge was not unique in New Brunswick, and teachers then, as today, must have been especially vulnerable to it. In 1832, William Beckwith, a schoolmaster in the Parish of Waterborough in Queen's County, was found guilty, after an investigation by three school trustees and the Court of General Sessions (five justices of the peace), of "inconsistent conduct in the school, by indecently touching and interfering with female children under his tuition, and endeavouring to corrupt and deprave their morals, virtue and modesty." The investigators recommended in a report to Lieutenant Governor and Commander-in-Chief of the Province Sir Archibald Campbell, Baronet, that Beckwith be deprived of his license. In 1848, William Ferguson, schoolmaster in the Parish of Delaford, was dismissed by the trustees, pending a hearing on charges of "indecent behavior to his scholars."

In the case of Evers the charge was astonishing in view of his age and long service in the community. An Irish immigrant and bachelor in his sixties, Evers had obtained his teaching license for New Brunswick in 1830. He had taught for fourteen years, most of them at nearby Red Bank, before coming to Williamstown. He had successfully applied for renewal of his license in 1842. His application was accompanied by glowing testimonials to his competence and character by the three members of the Northumberland County Board of Education, all Protestants, including Presbyterian minister James Souter, and by the Catholic priest of Nelson, Father Michael Egan. They testified that Evers "had taught at a parish school in North Esk since the year 1830 . . .he is correct and praiseworthy in conduct, strictly attentive to his duties as a teacher . . .of peaceable and sober habits." The records show that Evers accepted more pupils tuition-free than did any of the other schoolmasters in North Esk Parish. The Catholic church registers at Nelson and Red Bank indicate that he was chosen by some Catholic parents to be godfather to their children. He never received any negative comments, as did at least two other parish teachers, in a column provided for that purpose on forms submitted over the years by the trustees authorizing his government pay bounty (these records are abundant, although not complete). The considerable evidence suggests that Evers was one of the better, more reliable, and competent teachers at a time when many lesser pedagogues were at work in Miramichi schools.

This favorable view of Evers was confirmed by the three North Esk Parish trustees - Anthony Rogers, Robert Forsyth, and John Dunnett - all Protestant but non-Methodist, under whose jurisdiction Evers served both at Red Bank and Williamstown. It was further confirmed by the investigation they conducted immediately after McLean raised his charges in early 1847. They took testimony from pupils and parents under oath, concluding unanimously that McLean's charges were totally without foundation in fact. In June 1847 the trustees once again confirmed their confidence in Evers by reporting to the General Sessions that Evers had taught "to our satisfaction" for the spring term, and they again submitted a favorable report after the end of the following term, Evers' last, all after McLean had raised his charge. Evers' roster for his final term listed the children of the Protestant Buck family. Joseph McLean had been the only parent to withdraw his children from the school.

VENDETTA AGAINST THE TEACHER

But Joseph McLean was not to be denied. Although repudiated by local school trustees and parents for his baseless charges, he decided to take his case independently to a Fredericton bureaucracy with its share of anti-Catholic bias, including a willingness to believe the worst about Papists and Popery and with an equal willingness to play the Orange card against the Green. In November 1847, McLean travelled the ninety miles to Fredericton to raise his personal protest before Provincial Secretary John Simcoe Saunders, signing an affidavit which included among other fabrications a statement that "the Protestant children with the exception of one family have been withdrawn from [Evers' school]."

It is perhaps not surprising that Saunders proceeded to act against the Catholic teacher on the word of one Protestant farmer alone. Saunders happened to be a member of an old Loyalist family from Virginia notorious for its hostile attitude toward Catholics. The secretary's father, Judge John Saunders, was the same judge mentioned in Chapter 5, remembered for his poorly drafted judicial opinions and for the severity of his sentencing of Irish laborers involved in the Riot of 1822. So hostile was the judge to Catholics that, on February 27, 1830, he had entered in the record of the Legislative Assembly a statement opposing the Catholic Emancipation Act for New Brunswick, parallelling an Act passed by the British Parliament (for Ireland) the previous year. The judge's statement, something of a tirade, included the following observation:

It is therefore not only unnecessary but highly impolitic to pass such a law here, which cannot fail to nourish into vigour the influence of that [Roman Catholic] dogma, and thereby introduce a separate organized body, actuated by the same spirit of hostility to our Protestant religion and government, which occasioned the commission of so many atrocities in Ireland.

That Provincial Secretary John Simcoe Saunders, to whom McLean appealed, had inherited his father's prejudices, there can be little doubt. Just four months before McLean appeared with his complaint against Williamstown's first Catholic schoolmaster, Saunders had written his own son, then travelling in Europe, that "the whole country is swarming with Irish Emigrants - not the kind that are likely to be of any uses - either as servants or settlers but will chiefly have to be maintained at the public expense" (July 12, 1847, letter in Harriet

Irving Library, University of New Brunswick at Fredericton, in which Saunders also discusses a bloody fracas that day between the Orange and Green).

McLean had found a receptive ear. On the same day, November 16, 1847, that McLean registered his personal grievance, unsupported by any documentation or by corroborating witnesses, Saunders placed a tiny announcement in *The Royal Gazette* that James Evers' teaching license had been "revoked," no reasons given.

The Williamstown school was closed for the following spring, 1848. The trustees, on orders from Saunders, were obliged to re-open the investigation. Obviously very annoyed with McLean and with Secretary Saunders, they sent a scathing letter to Fredericton, pointing out several bold lies in McLean's affidavit, and declaring:

[we have] carefully perused the deposition of Joseph McLean . . .but consider it unnecessary to go into an investigation . . .again as we investigated the matter before on the same charges preferred by the same individuals under oath in April 1847 . . .all was hearsay and his [McLean's] two sons being required to name the parties with whom Evers was in the habit of behaving indecently towards, and those that were crying on account of his conduct; and they having done so; we gave Evers an opportunity of rebutting the charges, which he did by bringing forward some of the children that attended the school; these we examined on oath . . .and all denied having seen or heard any such transactions as spoken of by McLean's boys in the most positive manner . . .[Evers] also brought forward the fathers and mothers of the children who all stated that they had, after hearing the report, taken much trouble to ascertain the truth and all were convinced [of] its incorrectness . . .we did not remove the School from the Schoolhouse as stated by McLean, neither was it done by our orders, neither do we know when it was Removed, but at the time of the examination spoken of Evers was teaching in an unoccupied private house [belonging to "young Fitzgerald," according to McLean's affidavit] in the middle of the district as appointed by the trustees . . .as to Evers defiling a girl at the school, if McLean knows who it was he had better name her as we know nothing of the matter and cannot investigate it.

The report was signed by all three trustees on February 7, 1848. Three days later, however, trustee John Dunnett had second thoughts. Behind the backs of the other trustees who had charged him with forwarding the report to Fredericton, but who he now claimed were unavailable for consultation, he appended a minority report. In it, he excused himself for not being able to get the support of the other trustees and raised a totally unsubstantiated new accusation against Evers. The schoolmaster, he said, had been charged four years previously with similar misconduct at Red Bank. "There is no doubt," wrote Dunnett, "that Evers has got many of the Irish Roman Catholics on his side, but I am confident in my opinion that he is not fit to have children under his care."

A few days before, on February 4, James Evers had submitted the following petition to the House of Assembly at Fredericton, in a firm and attractive hand:

> The Petition of James Evers of the Parish of North Esk County of Northumberland humbly Sheweth, That your Petitioner is a Schoolmaster and has Taught a School in the Parish of North Esk for the last seventeen years, that in the year one thousand eight hundred and forty two your Petitioner got his Licence renewed, which Licence bears date the twenty seventh day of December one thousand eight hundred and forty-two, That your Petitioner has taught under said Licence ever since and always had his certificate signed by the Trustees until the recent January Session, That your Petitioner applied to the Trustees of the said Sessions to sign his certificate for the last Six Months he had Taught which time ended on the twenty second day of December last and they the Trustees informed him they could not as your Petitioner's Licence had been Discontinued by the Government. This your petitioner found to be true but is up to the present moment entirely ignorant of the cause except by report, your Petitioner having heard causually [sic] that the Government had ordered the Trustees to investigate this matter, called on one of them recently namely John Dennet [the Dunnet name is pronounced *den-net* on the Miramichi] who informed your Petitioner that one Joseph McLean of said Parish had made an Affidavit against him accusing him of improper conduct in his School, your Petitioner requested a Copy of the Affidavit which said Dennet refused, he then requested Mr. Dennet to read the affidavit, this also was denied. Your Petitioner is forced to conclude that his case is singular in the Extreme in many particulars, first in suspending his Licence on the ex parte statements of an individual who to say the least of him does not stand high for Veracity where he is known, secondly in taking away his Licence first and then sometime after ordering an investigation, and thirdly in not sending him a Copy of the charges prepared against or ordering the Trustees to furnish him with one, your Petitioner would court an investigation of any charges that might be brought against him by Joseph McLean or any one else, but as he had no power to move in the matter he is reluctantly compelled to wait their time which may never come, as the Trustees have on a former occasion investigated charges prepared against your Petitioner by the said Joseph McLean and found them entirely without foundation, and your Petitioner is lead to believe that the said McLean has renewed the same charges against him.
>
> Your Petitioner therefore would most Humbly pray that your Honours would take his case into your favourable consideration and grant him the sum of ten pounds as a compensation for teaching a School for the last six Months.
> And as in duty bound will ever pray.
>
> /s/ James Evers

Evers' plight reminds us of the central character in Franz Kafka's haunting novel *The Trial*, about a man who seeks in vain to learn the nature of the crime for which he has been called to court and for which he is about to be punished. There is nothing Kafka-esque, however, about the response of thirteen Williamstown residents who

We the undersigned inhabitants of the Parish of North-Esk residing in the lower Williamstown settlement, do certify that James Evers has Taught a School in our settlement for the last twelve Months ending the twenty second day of December last entirely to our satisfaction, and We consider him a Man of good moral character, and We would wish to have him continue as our Schoolmaster providing he could obtain his Licence again. Dated this fourth day of February one thousand eight hundred and forty eight.

Nathaniel Buck

Dennis Corrigan
Patrick Fitzgerald
John Jordan
John X Megan
    his
    mark

William Nathaniel Buck
William Fitzgerald
Richard Jordan
Michael Harrigan
Bridget X OBryan
    her
    mark
Witness John Kenrogan
Michal Sullivan
Patrick Harrogan

17. Petition of thirteen Williamstown residents, February 4, 1848. *House of Assembly Sessional Records*, Fredericton, New Brunswick.

Return

of the Number of Scholars Taught by James Evers in District N° 10. in the Parish of Northesk in the County of Northumberland for Six Months ending the 22nd day of December in the year of Lord 1847.

N°	Names of Boys	Age	N°	Names of Girls	Age
	Peatrick Herrigan	16		Elizabeth Herrigan	16
	Dennis Herrigan	14		Bridget Kenny	14
	David Cheasgreen	21		Sarah Buck	12
	William Buck	14		Harriet Buck	10
	John Fitzgerald	11		Ruth Buck	8
	William Fitzgerald	6		Elizabeth Buck	6
	James Fitzgerald	4		Mary Regan	6
	Cornelius O'Brien	9		Mary O'Brien	9
	John O'Brien	11		Margaret O'Brien	7
	John Fitzgerald, Less	4			
	Cornelius Regan	1			
	Daniel Fitzgerald	7			
	William Fitzgerald, Less	6			
	Alexander Taylor	10			
	Francis Taylor	8			
16	John Kingston	9	9		

Boys — 16
Girls — 9
The Whole 25

James Evers
Teacher

To Thomas H. Peters Esqr.
Chatham

18. Return of schoolmaster James Evers, for six-months ending December 22, 1847, Parish of North Esk, Northumberland County. *Provincial Archives of New Brunswick*, Fredericton

were quick to sign a petition to accompany Evers' own petition to Fredericton:

We the undersigned inhabitants of this Parish of North Esk residing in the lower Williamstown Settlement, do certify that James Evers has Taught a School in our Settlement for the last twelve Months ending the twenty second day of December last entirely to our satisfaction, and We consider him a Man of good moral character, and We would wish to have him continue as our Schoolmaster providing he could obtain his Licence again. /s/ Nathaniel Buck, Dennis Horagan, Patrick Fitzgerald, John Jordan [spelled *Jardine* on other records], John [his mark] Regan, William Nathaniel Buck, William Fitzgerald, Richard Jordan, Michael Harrigan, Bridget [her mark] O Bryan, William John Horrogan, Michal Sullivan, Patrick Harragan.

The variant spellings of the same surname were typical of the times. The signature of Nathaniel Buck, a Protestant, headed the list, and the petition is in his handwriting. The signers included almost all the parents of Evers' pupils, as well as two senior pupils, Patrick Harrigan and William Nathaniel Buck.

On February 22, the petitions from Evers and his supporters were introduced to the House of Assembly by Martin Cranney of Chatham, Miramichi's first Catholic Assemblyman. But it was not until May that the Provincial Board of Trustees in Fredericton, into whose hands the Assembly had placed the matter, acted. On that day they appointed three Northumberland County justices of the peace (Henry B. Allison, a Newcastle merchant; John T. Williston, millowner of Chatham and a friend of Assemblyman Cranney; and Thomas C. Allan) to get in touch with Evers, furnish him with copies of all documents, and invite him to solicit an investigation of his revoked license, "if he was anxious to proceed with it."

The minutes of the Board do not indicate that Evers at this late date solicited the investigation. By the month of May, the poor teacher must have been in dire straits. Most likely he had "left the country," as later reported, to renew his career. In July 1849, the Court of General Sessions at Newcastle approved the payment of ten pounds to Evers on the recommendation of North Esk trustees James Forsyth, Robert Hutcheson, and George Scott (the latter two having replaced John Dunnett and Anthony Rogers). They testified in a form letter that Evers had been a teacher of "moral and sober habits," that he was "duly licensed," and that he "taught to our satisfaction" during the six-month term ending December 22, 1847.

That is the last factual record of James Evers that has been located. Whether he ever received his final pay is unknown. Where the aging schoolmaster spent his last years and where he found a final resting place is also unknown.

McLean made one more thrust at his Catholic neighbors. On February 16, 1850, he submitted a petition for compensation for an alleged act of arson against his property. The petition was supported by the signatures of eighteen Protestants of Williamstown and Crocker settlements and addressed to the Executive Council in Fredericton. McLean claimed that he had been threatened by Catholics because of his accusations against the schoolmaster. Consequently, his barn and new hay crop were set afire by arsonists. He was "a poor man with a large family" when in 1847 he swore out a complaint against the "flagrant and diabolical" conduct of James Evers. He was only "acting as a parent" with the "welfare of the settlement at heart." The petitioner, in a blatant falsehood, testified that the inquiry by the three trustees conducted three years past "supported [McLean's] charges and required that Evers' license be cancelled."

One can only speculate as to why McLean was able to get eighteen of his Protestant neighbors to lend their signatures to such an obvious falsehood. It is conceivable that they were concerned mainly that their poor neighbor get some recompense for his loss. It is also possible that they did not read the petition carefully and were not very familiar with the events three years in the past. (None of them had children in Evers' class.) In any case, McLean got away with the lie, doubtless because a Fredericton bureaucracy had short memory of events and was unwilling to take the time to check the facts. The petitioners asked that McLean be awarded thirty pounds. The government granted him ten pounds and ordered an investigation of the alleged arson.

Whether the investigation ever took place has not been determined by the records searched so far.

MOVING ON

It may have been only coincidence, but at the time of the alleged arson and consequent call for an investigation, the Fitzgeralds and Harrigans began moving out of Williamstown, mostly for points in Maine and Wisconsin. It was also a time of decline in the lumber industry. Recruiters from the West were generating "Wisconsin Fever"; New Brunswickers with lumbering skills were badly needed in the West.

Maurice Fitzgerald, age about thirty-five, arrived in Oshkosh, Wisconsin, in 1851, and he was soon followed by many other members of the Williamstown extended family. They included his aging parents, three sisters, four brothers, and a number of Harrigan, Lucey, and other cousins and friends. They sought a better life for themselves and their progeny. As we shall see, many of them found what they were looking for, although a few came to tragic ends.

MOST DISTINGUISHED

Three children of William and Ann Fitzgerald - Maurice, Michael, and Daniel, all Irish-born and Miramichi-raised - made notable successes of themselves as lumbermen and farmers in Oshkosh, Wisconsin. Maurice, Dan, and another brother, James, built large brick homes at Fitzgerald Station, south of Oshkosh. Maurice's house burned down in the 1880s (perhaps poetic justice, if indeed he had been involved in the alleged arson on the Miramichi). But the houses built by Dan and James, county landmarks, still stand. Dan's is the "elegant brick structure" described by Harncy in *History of Winnebago County, Wisconsin* (1880).

Of twenty-two granddaughters of William and Ann who lived to maturity, ten became schoolteachers. One of them was Josephine FitzGerald (1858-1931) who spelled her name in the ancient Norman fashion, a leading educator in the Pacific North West in charge of teacher training at Cheney College, now Eastern Washington State University.

The list of achieving descendants is long, and includes: Rose Kavana, great-granddaughter of William and Ann, a graduate of Vassar, principal of Medill High School in Chicago, and author of widely used school textbooks; James Clare Fitzgerald, a school administrator in Oshkosh for many years, who died at age 99 in 1981; George Fitzgerald, now emeritus Professor of Botany at the University of Wisconsin, considered a leading authority on algae; Major Charles M. Fitzgerald (1866-1954) of the United States Army Supply Corps, a grandson of William and Ann; his daughter, Margaret M. King (1899-1984), who, at age nineteen, was appointed Chief Petty Officer in the U.S. Navy, one of the first women and the youngest ever to achieve that rank - and who served twice as national commander of the Yeomen-F organization; Cecil Fitzgerald (1882-1972), youngest brother of Major Charles, who was mayor of Seattle in 1919-20, host to President Wilson, founder of the Washington Motor Coach Company (later sold to Greyhound), chairman of the State Republican Central Committee, and a powerful force in the business and politics of the state of Washington.

Albert Fitzgerald (1868-1938), Maine-born grandson of patriarch William, served as mayor of Tomahawk, Wisconsin. His younger brother, Cornelius, was known as "The Cherry King" of Ferndale, Washington, after his cherries took the grand prize at the Alaska-Yukon Exhibition in Seattle. Lee Hewitt, a great-grandson of William, served for six years as mayor of Alexandria, Minnesota.

Stephen McPartlin (1874-1949), a grandson of William, was founder and president of the Union Insulating Company in Chicago

DROPPED DEAD

Maurice Fitzgerald, a wealthy
farmer near Fitzgerald Statio
dropped dead yesterday morn
while engaged in some work
about the house, cause suppo:
to be heart disease. Decease(
was a brother of Dan and Mil
Fitzgerald, lumbermen of this
city.- *Oshkosh (Wisconsin) Da
Northwestern,* September 30, 1

19. Death notice for Maurice Fitzgerald, son of William Fitzgerald and Ann
Harrigan; photo of his four sons (left to right): Cecil, Charles, Edward, Gerald.
Ashland, Wisconsin, 1894.

20. Cecil Fitzgerald (1880-1971) and niece, Margaret Fitzgerald King (1899-
1984). Seattle, Washington, about 1960. Cecil served as Mayor of Seattle,
1919-20; Margaret was youngest woman, at age 19, to achieve rating of Chief
Petty Officer in U.S. Navy during World War I, and headed her veterans'
organization, the Yeomen-F.

and an original director of the Celotex Corporation. His children include Mary Louise McPartlin (1909-85), long-time administrator in charge of the extension school at Loyola University in Chicago and recipient of many awards for distinguished service; Richard McPartlin, S.J. (1927-82), lieutenant colonel in the Army Chaplain Corps and a theologian at Loyola University, Chicago; John McPartlin, sales manager for NBC radio and later CBS Television in Chicago; and Stephen McPartlin Jr., head of McPartlin Sales Company of Wildwood, Illinois. John Jeffrey McPartlin of Great Falls, Montana, a son of John, is a leading authority on falconry in the United States.

Among the third and fourth generation descendants of William Fitzgerald and Ann Harrigan are James R. Fitzgerald, Professor of Mechanics and Materials Science at Johns Hopkins University, and his nephew Peter Mueller, Professor of Agronomy at North Carolina State University; Irene Mennitt, mother of five, nurse, writer, educator, who has given many years of service to the St. Joseph's School for the Blind in Jersey City, New Jersey; actor and singer Dan Fitzgerald of Miami, who has appeared in scores of films and who at age sixty (in 1988) is the youngest surviving great-grandson of William and Ann Fitzgerald; Michael Fitzgerald, head of Utah's Department of Public Dentistry and president of the National Dental Directors Association; and Richard and Robert Fitzgerald, 3rd great-grandsons of William and Ann, who farm thousands of acres of wheat land near St. John in eastern Washington.

Many cousins and other Irish Catholics from Miramichi, including Harrigans, Sauntrys, Suttons, Mackeys, Walshes, settled in Stillwater, Minnesota, where they played leading roles in the logging, driving, rafting, and sawmill operations of the last quarter of the 19th century. They include Dennis Harrigan Jr. (1832-1915), born and raised in Miramichi, a major building contractor in Minnesota and, later, Washington, and his famous grandsons, Bing and Bob Crosby; Lyman Sutton (1867-1958), great-grandson of Dennis Harrigan Sr., president of the Cosmopolitan State Bank in historic Stillwater, named to the Hall of Fame for his civic service in that historic town; William and John Harrigan, grandsons of Dennis Sr., who founded the Scotch Lumber Company in Fulton, Alabama; their brother Emmet Harrigan, who first moved to Montana where he became general secretary of the Brotherhood of Railway Trainmen and a candidate for the United States Senate, and later headed a 22-member law firm in St. Paul, Minnesota; Gordon Neff, a great-grandson, who introduced the supermarket concept in Los Angeles, where he started a chain of stores; and Colonel Bill Harrigan, a great-grandson, famed in World War I for his rescue of the "Lost Battalion" in Flanders.

Robert Shaw Harrigan of West Hartford, Connecticut, is a talented water colorist. Kate Harrigan of Washington, D.C., has served as a confidential secretary to Senator Mitchell of Maine, and was also largely responsible for organizing two reunions of Harrigans and Fitzgeralds in Seattle in recent years.

Two 3rd-great granddaughters of Dennis Harrigan Sr. are Sister Jean Sauntry, who in 1986 was elected Mother Superior of the Sisters of St. Joseph, East Hartford, Connecticut; and her first cousin, Bernadette Sauntry, who is Sister Jean Michael, a missionary in Papua, New Guinea.

One great achiever was William Sauntry Jr., Irish-born and Miramichi-raised grandson of Dennis Harrigan Sr., and son of his eldest daughter, Ellen. A millionaire and leading figure in the logging industry on the St. Croix River in Minnesota, he ended his own life with a revolver shot on March 10, 1914, in a St. Paul hotel room. The garish house he built in Stillwater, in the Moorish manner and known as "The Alhambra," has become a major tourist attraction.

LEAST DISTINGUISHED

An interesting but uncelebrated member of the *cineadh* was Jack Lucey, the robust, six-foot, two hundred pound grandson of Ellen Harrigan Lucey, shot to death by a drinking companion on July 26, 1888, on the streets of St. Paul. The St. Paul newspaper described him the next day as the former proprietor of a "notorious resort in Hurley, Wisconsin [who] has lately been engaged in operating a floating house of ill fame on the Mississippi River between the city and South St. Paul."

THOSE WHO REMAINED

Several Catholic families remained in Williamstown, chiefly the Kingstons, O'Briens, Sullivans, Jardines, and Regans, although some members of these families also went west. They were joined in Williamstown by Sauntry relatives from County Cork in the early 1850s. These Catholics and their Protestant neighbors soon were able to put the Evers Affair behind them, and some sort of truce occurred. James Howe was brought back to teach. His school roster for July 1, 1851, shows twenty students - eleven Catholics and nine Protestants. Three of the Protestants were McLeans and six of the Catholics were Fitzgeralds, nephews and a niece of Maurice Fitzgerald, most of whom would soon join him in Oshkosh.

The Methodist-Catholic rivalry flared up once again in the 1890s, when Dennis and Michael Sauntry were successive postmasters and named their post office "Ellenstown," after their mother. A political tug-of-war ensued and in 1897 the post office was moved to James

Tweedie's place. But the shrivelled and dying community found it could no longer support a post office. The office was closed permanently in 1912. A grandson of Michael Sauntry, Eugene Sauntry, did his part to keep the community alive. Eugene fathered twenty-three children by two successive wives in Williamstown before his death in 1980 at age eighty-two.

The death of Williamstown would have occurred regardless of James Evers and Joseph McLean and the religious antagonisms. Greater forces were at work. There was the lure of money to be made in the west. There was a severe decline in the New Brunswick lumber industry in the late 1840s after Great Britain had reduced tariffs on timber imported to Britain from the Baltic countries. There was the growing indebtedness typically incurred by lumberman-farmers who were off to distant pine forests and rivers in the winter, neglecting the clearing of land for tillage, and falling more and more in debt to the town merchants. Life in Williamstown and in Miramichi in general was, for the great majority, whether Irish or Scot or English, Catholic or Protestant, very hard at best.

For those who remained, Miramichi proved in time to be a rather good place. Religious suspicions have long since been buried in favor of live-and-let-live. Religion, to be sure, is still quite important to Miramichiers, as evidenced by the many churches, sometimes two or three in tiny villages along the river systems. But at recent Irish Festivals, Protestant clergymen and Catholic priests have prayed side by side at ceremonies honoring the Irish pioneers and those who died on the "fever ships." In Newcastle, a civilized gentlemen's agreement to have alternate Catholic and Protestant mayors, observed at least until the late 1960s, worked for many years to everybody's satisfaction.

Visitors to the annual Irish Festival in July might enjoy a leisurely drive through Williamstown to the old Methodist Church. The cemetery by the church is neatly kept and one will note the names of the earliest pioneers on the headstones. Drive on a few miles to Red Bank and to the Catholic cemetery at St. Thomas the Apostle Church, also neatly kept. There rest the bones of many of Williamstown's earliest Catholic settlers, although some of the graves, including those of Bing Crosby's great-grandparents, Dennis Harrigan and Catherine Driscoll, have no markers. The visitor might want to say a little prayer for old Con Regan whose coffin was denied entrance through the cemetery gate. Eighty-year-old bachelor Con is alone in death as he had been alone in life, but a small stone marks his final resting place, hidden by bushes, in a corner of the cemetery.

And far away in Tacoma, Washington, Vera Fitzgerald Cowan, approaching age one hundred in 1988, a great-granddaughter of William Fitzgerald and Ann Harrigan, might say a prayer in Irish for

Con, and also perhaps for James Evers and Joseph McLean, if she is so inclined.* Vera's father, raised in an Irish-speaking household in Williamstown, was a six-year-old pupil in Evers' fateful class, and no doubt a playmate of Con, also in that class. The Irish tradition remains strong in his daughter Vera. When the author last saw her, she recalled her early childhood in Ashland, Wisconsin, when she sat on the lap of her father, a lumbercamp cook, as he sang to her and taught her the prayers in the ancient Irish tongue. She remembered hopping off his lap to the command: "Bring me my dooth-een!" (Irish, *dúidún*, small clay pipe).

JAK

———————

After completing this chapter, the author learned that Vera Fitzgerald Cowan died in Tacoma, Washington, on August 4, 1988, less than three weeks before her 100th birthday. Vera was truly a child of the Northern Migration Route, from Ireland to the Pacific Northwest. Over the course of several generations, members of her line of the family settled in New Brunswick, Maine, Wisconsin, Minnesota, Washington, and Alaska.

Chapter 7

THE FENIAN ATTEMPT TO ESTABLISH
AN IRISH REPUBLIC

In the year 1866, an army of about 20,000 Irishmen, many of them veterans of the Union and Confederate Armies in the American Civil War, moved from all states and territories toward the Canadian border. Their purpose was to invade Canada, establish an Irish Republic in Exile on a piece of Canadian soil, and gain international recognition as an independent Irish nation. The American Fenian Movement had considerable and lasting effect on the governments of Canada, Great Britain, and the United States.

THE FENIAN MOVEMENT IN NORTH AMERICA

In the 1770s, the colonies in Canada decided not to join the other British North American colonies that declared independence. The Thirteen Colonies that won freedom became a new nation, the United States, which in 1812 engaged England in a second war. England hoped to regain control of her lost colonies, while some United States leaders hoped to annex Canada.

After 1814, a new ethnic dimension was added to the Canadian provinces. To its Acadians, French Quebecois, Old British, American Loyalists, and Old Irish and Scots were added each year thousands of Irish and Scots immigrants. Most of these newcomers or their forebears had fought against England for freedom in their native lands. The Irish, in particular, had a heritage of almost seven hundred years of struggle against English invasion and occupation.

The dilemma faced by the Irish who did not migrate further to the United States was to reconcile loyalty to British Canada with support for anti-English agitation in Ireland. The first generation was too busy struggling to survive in a new land to become active in any struggle in the old. The spread of the Fenian Movement from Ireland in the mid-19th century, however, brought the first large Irish freedom crusade to United States and Canadian soil.

The Fenians were the successors of many organizations that had risen to fight for Irish freedom, had been dispersed or defeated, then had risen again under a new name with leaders for a new generation. Fenianism was born in Ireland in the ashes of the Rising of 1848, an insurrection called for by the Young Irelanders, men like John Mitchel, William Smith O'Brien, Thomas Francis Meagher, and Terence Bellew MacManus. After putting down the rising and transporting to British jails or Australian penal colonies all the leaders who did not escape into exile, England expected some respite from Irish rebellion. It was a surprise to London when, in 1857, the rebellious spirit rose so quickly again in Dublin as the Irish Revolutionary Brotherhood (later Irish Republican Brotherhood) and in famine devastated Skibbereen as the Phoenix Society. It crossed the Atlantic under its more popular Fenian name, which came from the ancient Irish Fianna warrior-heroes.

BACKGROUND OF FENIANISM

In Ireland, James Stephens became Head Center or Chief Organizer of the Irish Republic (C.O.I.R.). Stephens, born in County Kilkenny, was a civil engineer who had escaped to France after the Rising of 1848. He and Thomas Clarke Luby, a Trinity College graduate and son of a Protestant minister and Catholic mother, wrote the original Fenian constitution. This set up a revolutionary military structure with Stephens as supreme commander and with members taking oaths to free Ireland and to be subject to all superior officers.

In Canada, Edward O'Meagher Condon established most of the early Fenian Circles. Condon, born near Mitchelstown, County Cork, emigrated as a child to Newfoundland. His father, a contractor, moved the family to Quebec and then to Toronto, where Edward completed training as an architect and met Sarah Quinn, whom he married in 1866. In 1859, Edward visited New York, joined the Fenian Brotherhood, and returned to Canada to organize Circles. In 1862, he went again to the United States and enlisted in the 164th New York Volunteers for active service in the Civil War. Condon's fame came after the 1867 Fenian trials in Manchester, England, when he ended his speech from the dock with the cry "God save Ireland!" T.D. Sullivan then wrote the ballad "God Save Ireland," the anthem of all nationalists until adoption of "The Soldier's Song."

JOHN O'MAHONY

In the United States, John O'Mahony became Head Center. O'Mahony, born at Clonkilla near Kilkenny, where the counties of Cork, Limerick, and Tipperary meet, belonged to a family long prominent in the area. His great-grandfather and grandfather had opposed tyrannies of the Earls of Kingston, to the extent of horse-whipping one Earl for an insulting remark. His father and uncle had been active in the Rising of 1798. Educated at Cork and at Trinity College, O'Mahony was a recognized scholar in the fields of philosophy and Irish history. He was also a linguist, well-versed in Latin, Greek, English, and Irish. His principal literary work was a translation from the Irish, with many annotations, of Geoffrey Keating's *History of Ireland.*

In his position as The O'Mahony, the title for the head of this ancient family, he believed he "could always count on two thousand men in his quarrel." So, in 1848, he put aside his books and gathered his Gaelic followers, men who simply continued the practice of following the Chief to fight his wars. After O'Mahony's pleas to the leaders to begin the insurrection at Carrick were rejected, he obeyed orders and sent his men home. As the leaders delayed, he recalled some of his forces and attacked police and military barracks in guerilla fashion. When the hopes of a rising were past and a bounty was placed on his head, he turned his property over to his brother-in-law and made an adventuresome escape to France.

In January 1854, O'Mahony arrived in the United States where he tried to restore spirit and unity among his embittered fellow exiles by organizing the Emmet Monument Association. The title suggested the purpose. Before his execution, Robert Emmet had forbidden the writing of his epitaph until "my country takes her place among the nations of the earth."

PROGRESS OF FENIANISM

Personal accounts of Fenianism in Ireland were written by John Devoy, John O'Leary, O'Donovan Rossa, and Joseph Denieffe. Denieffe said that he had returned to Ireland from America because of the anti-Irish Know Nothing Movement. He stressed that organizing had to be secret because the Treason-Felony Act of 1848 allowed the government to transport for fourteen years to life any person who by speech or writing "compassed the intimidation of crown or parliament."

The first mass arrest of Fenians was made at Skibbereen. O'Donovan Rossa and others were held for eight months, tried before a pro-English jury, and then freed on condition that they plead guilty. The publicity generated by the trials was increased by the National

Petition Movement, sponsored by the Sullivan brothers and the evolutionary nationalists of *The Nation*, published in Dublin. The English Prime Minister and the *London Times* had been advocating the right of every people to choose their own rulers. The National Petition Committee collected and presented to Parliament 500,000 signatures requesting a national plebescite. England did not intend to apply to Ireland her own rhetoric about freedom for other European peoples, so the petition gathered dust on the floor of Parliament. The Petition Movement, however, provided a chance for the Fenians, who supported it, to recruit in every county.

The next impetus came from America and the funeral of Terence Bellew MacManus. Sentenced to hang as a Young Irelander in 1848, MacManus received commutation and transportation to Australia. In 1851, he escaped to the United States. In 1861, when he died in San Francisco, the American Fenians decided to return his body to Ireland for burial in Glasnevin Cemetery. The long funeral procession across America and the blessing by Archbishop John Hughes in New York publicized the Fenian and Irish cause. Archbishop Paul Cullen refused to let the body lie in state in the Pro-Cathedral, but intense public feelings resulted in the largest funeral ever seen in Dublin to that time. Father Patrick Lavelle of County Mayo performed the religious rites. (Lavelle was already renowned for his fierce battles against Lord Plunket, the Church of Ireland Bishop of Tuam and a large landholder who was notorious for his eviction of tenants who refused to send their children to the Protestant schools on his estate.)

The funeral provided the opportunity of swearing in as Fenians several thousand country people who returned to their districts to swear in others. Fenianism spread quickly. Men waited for the signal to rise, a signal dependent upon American help that was held up by the Civil War. Fenians in the British Army also awaited the signal. John Devoy reported that there were eight thousand Fenians among twelve thousand regulars in the British Army in Ireland, six thousand among twelve thousand in the unarmed Irish militia, and seven thousand outside of Ireland. Galway-born Thomas J. Kelly, an American Civil War veteran, was sent to Ireland in 1865 to assess the situation and urge Stephens to call an insurrection quickly. Kelly and Devoy said that every British regiment had dedicated Fenians ready to act upon Stephens' repeated promise that 1865 would be the year of action.

In Canada, Fenianism came at a time when advocates of a United Canada were attempting to bring the Maritime Provinces of New Brunswick, Nova Scotia, and Prince Edward Island into a Confederation with Ontario and Quebec. The latter two provinces had been united in 1841 as Canada East and Canada West, but the United

Parliament was not working well. The Confederationists planned to re-separate these provinces and bring in the others for a stronger and more heavily English-speaking Canadian Union. *(See Note 1: Terminology.)*

Edward O'Meagher Condon had established Fenian Circles in several cities, including Montreal, Quebec, Hamilton, and Toronto, all of which had sizeable Irish populations. Assisting Condon were Father John Curley, a Canadian priest; Michael Murphy of the Hibernian Society of Toronto; and William Mackey Lomasney (aka Captain Mackey), who would be killed in 1884 trying to dynamite London Bridge. Despite their efforts, Fenianism never took the strong hold in Canada that it did in the United States, where Fenianism flourished. On a visit in 1858, James Stephens appointed John O'Mahony the head of the I.R.B. in America. In an effort to avoid Catholic Church opposition, Americans used a pledge rather than an oath for membership. To offset the handicap of the Civil War, O'Mahony encouraged formation of whole Fenian regiments, men who would be trained to fight for Ireland. O'Mahony himself organized the First Regiment of the Phoenix Brigade. Michael Corcoran, an exile of 1848, commanded the almost entirely Irish 69th Regiment of the New York State Militia. Captured at Bull Run, imprisoned and released, Corcoran returned to form the 164th New York Volunteers. Thomas Meagher, an 1848-er who had escaped from Australia, had been sympathetic to the South's claim of states' rights. Now Meagher, who had opposed the Union of England and Ireland, spoke in favor of another Union, whose preservation he considered the first duty of every Irish American. He raised a company to join the already over-subscribed 69th and rose to Brigadier General of the Irish Brigade. Meantime, in 1863, he was pledged into the Fenian Brotherhood.

Civilian Fenian Circles were replaced by those in the military, Union and Confederate. In February 1863, Thomas Clarke Luby, sent from Ireland by Stephens, went with Father Edmund O'Flaherty of Indiana to recruit Fenians and collect funds in several states and many Union Army camps. Under the name James Daly, Stephens made a wider tour the following year. With letters from high-ranking officials, he raised money and organized Circles in the Army of the Potomac. Stephens' enthusiasm motivated many officers to head overseas for a rising in Ireland as soon as they were discharged. At the end of the war, thousands of Union and Confederate veterans looked upon their experience as preparation for a war against England. The time seemed opportune: trained Irish veterans had horses and arms; relations between England and the United States were strained; North-erners, heady with victory, were resurrecting the old American dream of annexing Canada.

PROBLEMS IN THE UNITED STATES

As the revolutionary ardor to establish a free republic in Ireland escalated in the United States, there were differences over the plan of attack. Dissension resulted in three Fenian factions by late 1865: the Fenian Brotherhood led by John O'Mahony; the Senate Wing led by William Roberts; and the United Irishmen, who called for an immediate assault on England through Canada.

John Devoy later said that Red Jim McDermott, a spy who infiltrated the movement, "was really more responsible for the Split which took place at the end of 1865 than any of the bigger men. He was constantly fomenting trouble by lying stories which he put in circulation or told 'confidentially' to numbers of people with the intention that they should be spread."

Certainly disinformation fueled the split but, as historians William D'Arcy and W.S. Neidhardt have noted, much can be attributed to internal disputes over power and authority, which came to a head at the Third Fenian Convention in Philadelphia in October 1865. A new constitution changed the organization from authoritarian European style to democratic American style. O'Mahony knew that an army could not function democratically, but he conceded and was elected President. The old central council was replaced by a fifteen member Senate with an elected permanent president, William Roberts. O'Mahony, with the consent of the Senate, appointed Brigadier General Thomas Sweeny to the office of Secretary of War.

WILLIAM RANDALL ROBERTS

William Randall Roberts, born in 1830 in Mitchelstown, County Cork, came to the United States in 1849 and became a very successful businessman and politician in Brooklyn, New York. After he left the Fenians, he was twice elected to Congress from Brooklyn, was a member and president of the New York City Board of Aldermen, and was appointed Minister to Chile by President Cleveland. Contracting paralysis, he returned to New York and was hospitalized for eight years until his death in 1897.

THOMAS WILLIAM SWEENY

Thomas William Sweeny, born in 1820 in County Cork, came to the United States in 1832, worked as a printer, then joined the Army. He served as a Second Lieutenant in the Mexican War (in which he lost his right arm), in the Indian Wars, and in the Civil War. He was married first to Eleanor Clark, second to Eugenia Reagan. Having risen to generalship, he left the Army in 1865 and joined the Fenian Movement. His was the most persistent call for an attack on Canada before one on Ireland, and he tried to convince all factions of the feasibility of his plans. After his Fenian days, Sweeny was reinstated in the United States Army and retired to his home in Astoria, Queens County, New York, where he died in 1892.

All this however was in the future. In 1865, there were several developments that obstructed the Fenian Movement. In Ireland, the British continued the mass arrests begun in the summer. Stephens was captured on November 11. The fascinating story of his rescue from Richmond Bridewell Prison in Dublin on November 24 was told in accounts by John Devoy, outsideman, and John Breslin, insideman, who accomplished the feat under the guidance of Colonel Thomas Kelly.

The Fenians in Ireland seemed immobilized with Stephens again in hiding; with leaders Luby, Kickham, and O'Donovan Rossa in jail; and with American Civil War officers such as John McCafferty and Charles Underwood O'Connell being arrested almost upon landing. The Fenians in America took leadership from the Fenians in Ireland. The question, as Roberts linked up with Sweeny, was which faction would provide leadership.

FENIAN BONDS

Both the O'Mahony and Roberts factions were committed to freeing Ireland by military means. As the year 1865 passed, however, the Senate Wing lost patience with O'Mahony, who was waiting for a "call to action" from Stephens. In December the Senate found an excuse for a clear split with O'Mahony. Patrick Keenan, Fenian agent of the Irish Republic with power to issue bonds in its name, resigned a few days before the Continental Bank Note Company of New York was to issue certain bonds. The bank requested a signature and O'Mahony provided his. O'Mahony insisted that he would have betrayed his trust had he failed to sign in such an emergency, but the Senate deposed him for signing bonds without its consent. Stephens reconfirmed O'Mahony as Fenian head in America and added to the dissension by calling the Senate Wing leaders mad and traitorous.

On January 6, 1866, O'Mahony held a Fenian Congress in New York. The six hundred delegates restored the constitution of the November 1863 First Convention at Chicago and elected O'Mahony Head Center. The only member of the opposing wing who attended was General Sweeny, who made a plea for unity. He was the most experienced military officer present, but he was discounted, probably because he had never officially been pledged to the Brotherhood.

Roberts and Sweeny toured the states to promote a Canadian invasion. Roberts received rousing cheers for his fiery words:

If you will purchase rifles for the arming of one hundred thousand men who are ready to march with General Sweeny, you can annihilate your traditional and actual enemy . . . we can sweep Johnny Bull into the sea. . .if we can get a foothold on which to raise the Irish flag, we shall be recognized. . .let us repeat what is already history, let us show that Irishmen can fight . . .in two months we shall get that foothold of our own, the Irish flag will be raised, and Ireland, free Ireland, will be recognized among the nations of the earth.

On January 20, General Sweeny gave this promise to an audience:

Before the sun of July shall gild the Emerald Isle with its rays, a note of joy will thrill the heart of our native land.

On February 19, the Senate Wing held a Congress in Pittsburgh. O'Mahony was warned by John Mitchel, who was in Paris handling funds, that the American split was having serious repercussions in Ireland. O'Mahony attempted reconciliation by sending two delegates, B. Dorian Killian of New York City and Father John Curley of Toronto. They received no better reception from the Roberts wing than Sweeny had from the O'Mahony wing. Each faction subsequently went ahead with its own plans, and some Fenians participated in activities of both.

PLAN TO ATTACK THE MARITIMES

Fenian leaders began speaking of capturing Nova Scotia for use as a base for their Irish government-in-exile. Killian had met personally with President Andrew Johnson and Secretary Seward and reported that they were privately supportive. Killian reported to the Fenian leadership that the President would recognize "accomplished facts."

In November 1865, Father John Curley bore a letter from Killian to Seward in an unsuccessful effort to get a written agreement. Copies of Fenian correspondence show that the Fenian leaders believed they had verbal commitments and, if they won, would be backed by the American government.

Irish Civil War hero General Philip Sheridan was asked to command the Fenian Army. Sheridan, a Fenian sympathizer, at first agreed, but later declined when he learned that his name as general was wanted to increase numbers. He left things open, however, in case an army could be raised without his name.

The American government sold the Fenians military supplies, ignored Fenian full-uniformed military drills and gatherings, and did nothing to dampen the spirits of the Americans who murmured about "our manifest destiny to annex Canada." The Fenians held large rallies. In March 1866 in Jones Wood in New York City, 100,000 Irish came to hear O'Mahony speak and to cheer American-born Captain John McCafferty, who had just been released from an Irish prison. McCafferty, a veteran of the Confederate Army, had served with Morgan's Raiders.

O'Mahony, previously committed to Stephens' plan for an initial rising in Ireland, began to see the formidable problems of transporting ten thousand or more men across the Atlantic in the face of British control of the seas and Irish harbors. Urged on by Killian, he decided to attack Campobello Island in Passamaquoddy Bay, off the coast of Maine and New Brunswick. Despite the Convention of 1817, Campobello was still claimed by both the United States and Canada. Campobello would be a base for readying forces for invading Canada, for preparing troops for Ireland, for attacking British ships, and for getting recognition of an Irish government-in-exile.

The Roberts faction was working on another plan, so Campobello was not a united project. The newspapers added to the problem by reporting contradictory plans, wild speculations, gross inaccuracies, and information and disinformation on the leadership split. The English government received regular reports on the various plans from Edward Archibald, the British Consul in New York City, who had several spies on his payroll. The Consul selectively passed on these plans to Washington, but the American government had more direct sources of information since it was selling war surplus supplies to the Fenians.

When rumors of planned raids against Canada reached the Maritimes, they aroused Archbishop Thomas Connolly of Halifax. In 1864, Connolly had been upset by a story by Reverend Hutchinson in the *The Burning Bush*, a Protestant journal. Hutchinson, Grand Chaplain of the Orange Order in Nova Scotia, not only accused the Fenians of countless atrocities of imagined or distorted history, but said that they were storing arms in Catholic churches. Connolly publicly denounced Fenianism and denied that churches were being used for arms. In 1866, he again asserted that the Catholic Church was opposed to Fenianism, and he began to speak more kindly of Confederation.

THOMAS D'ARCY McGEE

One reason that the Fenians never gained strength in Canada was the strong opposition of Thomas D'Arcy McGee. McGee, born in 1825 in County Louth and educated in County Wexford, emigrated to the United States in 1842. He returned to Ireland and became active in the Young Ireland Movement. After the Rising of 1848, he escaped to New York, where he founded the *New York Nation*, a paper advocating international revolution and rising of the masses.

According to biographer Isabel Skelton, he assumed that Canada, like Ireland, was oppressed by England and he appealed to the Irish Canadians to seize any chance for independence.

A persuasive speaker and writer, McGee had some initial success, but he had competition from equally gifted Irish exiles. He clashed with Bishop John Hughes and other clergymen. His papers failed in New York, Boston, and Buffalo. His view of the United States changed. Looking toward Canada in 1855, he wrote: "The British provinces of North America are not necessarily miserable and uninhabitable because the British flag flies at Quebec."

In 1857, McGee moved to Montreal, published *The New Era*, disavowed his old republicanism, and began lashing out at Americans and later at Fenians. Starting from a base in Montreal, which had a large Irish population, McGee became a leader in government circles. By 1865 he was Minister of Agriculture and a leading voice for Confederation. Nicholas Davin, historian and journalist, gives McGee credit for turning the heads of so many people that the balance was shifted toward Confederation, especially in the unenthusiastic Maritime Provinces of Nova Scotia and New Brunswick.

The Confederationists believed that an invasion of New Brunswick was likely despite the reported Fenian plan to set up an independent Irish "Acadia" in Nova Scotia. New Brunswick provided a more fertile soil for frightening people into proving their loyalty and patriotism by joining a Confederation against outside enemies. One argument employed successfully by McGee was that the United States would take advantage of the Fenian schemes if they showed signs of succeeding. As already noted, the Fenians believed this too.

McGee was assassinated in 1868, just after Confederation. Patrick Whelan, an Irish Canadian who pleaded innocent and denied being a Fenian, was found guilty on the flimsiest of circumstantial evidence and was executed. Few historians have accepted his guilt. The true story of McGee's assassination is simply not known.

THE BISHOPS TAKE A STAND

In Ireland leading churchmen took opposite sides. Archbishop Cullen of Dublin was pro-English and anti-Fenian. Archbishop John MacHale of Tuam was pro-national and pro-Fenian. The Canadians also had differences. Bishop John Sweeny of Saint John, New Brunswick, and Cork-born Timothy Warren Anglin, editor of the Saint John *Morning Freeman,* both said that the threats of a Fenian invasion might be a hoax to drive New Brunswickers into the Confederation camp.

Pro-Confederation Bishop John Farrell of Hamilton, however, was moved to declare that Fenianism was contrary to Catholicism;

that Fenians were cut off from the Church; and that the Hibernian Society, which had Fenian members, was to be condemned. Bishop John J. Lynch of Toronto refused to condemn the Hibernian Society, but condemned Fenianism for any secret oath-taking. Lynch was soon forced from his middle ground. To avoid riots in 1865 he requested the Hibernian Society to refrain from open parades and celebrations on St. Patrick's Day. The members respected his wishes. They were understandably annoyed on July 12 when the Orangemen held their big annual parade, celebrating the victory at the Battle of the Boyne. They marched through Catholic neighborhoods, singing provocative anti-Pope songs, with never a word from their own clergymen that this activity might be offensive and might generate violence.

The Hibernian Society's grievance might have been confined to oratory at its annual summer excursion to Niagara Falls had not Bishop Farrell, claiming that the Toronto Hibernians might contaminate his people as they passed through Hamilton, forbidden his flock to join the excursion. Things were said in temper. Michael Murphy, as reported in the pro-Confederation *Canadian Freeman*, declared that "such Saxonized threats have no authority, whether uttered by a Catholic bishop or by a renegade and traitor." He then called for three cheers for the Bishop of Toronto. Now Bishop Lynch in Toronto felt that he had to support his insulted colleague by condemning Murphy, the Fenians, and the Hibernians. He still refused to condemn the Irish nationalist ideal (later, he was very solicitous of the welfare of prisoners in the Toronto jail who were accused of participation in the Fenian invasions). Nevertheless, the damage was done to Fenianism in Canada West. Many now believed that Church condemnation of Fenianism and Hibernianism meant Church rejection of the Irish freedom movement. *(See Note 2: Lynch.)*

FENIAN FORCES AT CAMPOBELLO

In early March of 1866, some anti-Confederation leaders in New Brunswick were still ridiculing the Fenian threat as a media myth and pro-Confederation trick. Some newspaper reports had the Fenians heading in other directions, to Mexico or the West Indies. On April 5 the *New York Herald* reported that five thousand men had sailed to capture Bermuda. But on April 9, when O'Mahony's men, accompanied by B. Doran Killian, began to appear at Eastport and Calais in Maine, skepticism disappeared. Whatever the maneuverings of the pro- and anti-Confederationists, there certainly were Fenians near the border.

Ten days before the Fenian forces expected to reach full strength, the British stationed the *HMS Pylades* off Campobello. Seeing the handwriting on the wall and the warship on the ocean, some early-arriving Fenians decided to make one eloquent gesture showing that the Fenians were descendants of the great race of Fionn and the Fianna. The gesture might be romantic, but its symbolism would be understood in the hearts of many Celts. Surely they would be remembered with honor, as the Irish have remembered their martyred heroes since pagan days.

An invasion force of five men proceeded to raid the custom house of Campobello Island, where their only gesture was the taking down and carrying off of the Union Jack. There was no blood sacrifice, no martyrdom, no capture.

On April 17, the 81-gun *HMS Duncan* with over seven hundred troops backed the *Pylades*. The *USS Winooski* almost immediately joined them, a strange alliance. Four more British warships appeared. Too late, the *Ocean Spray*, purchased by the Fenians from war surplus, arrived at Eastport, Maine. There was a stand-off until April 19, when United States General Meade arrived with authority to act. He seized the *Ocean Spray* and the arms on it.

To this barely known and hardly distinguishable border of Maine and New Brunswick, the Fenian threat brought six British warships, two British generals, a British vice-admiral, an American warship, and an American general. About five thousand British regulars and Canadian militia were mobilized to defend Campobello against some six hundred Fenians scattered on the Maine border.

The Fenians produced reactions far out of proportion to their numbers, not only militarily but politically. In New Brunswick Lieutenant Governor Gordon put pressure on anti-Confederation Premier Albert J. Smith to resign on April 10 as Fenians gathered in Maine for the attack on Campobello. Leonard Tilley formed a new pro-Confederation government. The Fenian threat drew New Brunswick into the Confederation camp.

The American press, often suggesting annexation, had urged the Fenians to give up the "impractical" plan of striking first in Ireland. The *New York Citizen* of March 10, 1866, said:

We strike at England, even in Ireland, when we strike at the Canadas. We can there gain a country in which to operate and mature our future plans. . . we have reason to believe that the sympathy of President Johnson and the Secretary of War are with the Fenians; and under this impression we bid Head Centre O'Mahony good speed in his early march on the Canadas.

The *New York Herald* of March 27, 1866, said:

Unquestionably, there is . . .some probability of success to this Roberts-Sweeny plan of operations . . .as for the other scheme of commencing this struggle in Ireland, it appears to us if it ever was the right plan, the time for it has gone by . . .we have only to suggest that if the Fenians are not prepared to strike anywhere, they had better settle up their accounts and stop their warlike assessments on their sympathizing countrymen.

INVASION OF CANADA

Fenian leaders Roberts and Sweeny criticized O'Mahony's project after its failure. They continued with Sweeny's plan for a three-pronged attack on Canada that would set up an Irish government-in-exile, possibly at Sherbrooke or Montreal, where they hoped for local support from Irish Canadians and a neutral stance or support from French Canadians. Fenian forces were to gather in the West at Chicago and Milwaukee, in the center in the Buffalo area, and in the East in northern New York and Vermont. The western and central contingents would divert the Canadian and British forces to Toronto, while the eastern contingents would head for Montreal and Quebec. Sweeny, as he stated in 1865, expected to have ten thousand and possibly twenty five thousand men, three batteries of artillery, adequate arms and ammunition, and a benevolent or neutral attitude of the United States government that waited for "accomplished facts."

In 1865, John A. Macdonald of the coalition government of Canada had called out 2,000 volunteers, but Sir John Mitchel, Commander of the Forces, had said that this was not enough to back his 5,000 regulars in the event of a sizeable Fenian invasion. In the spring of 1866, four regiments of British regulars were sent to Canada, but this did not make Sweeny's plan a fantasy. Sweeny was not an unrealistic dreamer. He had been a successful field officer in the Mexican, Indian, and Civil Wars. He had many historical precedents of relatively small armies conquering great populations.

What was wrong with Sweeny's plan at its time and place in history was not the numerical odds, but that it was a good plan only for a regular army, not for Fenian militias. Sweeny was unable to foresee some handicaps: inability to purchase any artillery or sufficient arms and ammunition; delay and detention of Fenian units coming to the rendezvous points; exaggeration in the number of troops promised by the Fenian Circles; availablity of plans to the press; misunderstanding of the extent of American government backing. The first hitch in Sweeny's plans came when General Charles Carroll Tevis, in command at Chicago, claimed that he could not obtain transport for the men mustered at Milwaukee and Chicago. The next hitch occurred when Brigadier General William Lynch, apparently ill, could not reach his command post at Buffalo.

JOHN O'NEILL

When Lynch failed to arrive, Captain William Hynes, Sweeny's liaison, placed Colonel John O'Neill in charge. O'Neill, born in 1834 in Drumgallan, Parish of Clontibret, County Monaghan, emigrated to the United States in 1848. In 1857, he entered the Army and was stationed for a time at San Francisco. During the Civil War he was wounded at the Battle of Cumberland, was cited for his role in putting Morgan's Raiders out of action, and achieved captain's rank. On November 27, 1864, he married Mary Crowe of San Francisco, at a ceremony performed at St. Mary's Church at Elizabeth, New Jersey, where the O'Neill family resided.

O'Neill's 13th Fenian Infantry Regiment had a base of 115 men, Union and Confederate veterans, whom he had trained in Nashville, Tennessee. As he moved toward Buffalo, he was joined by more troops from Indiana, Kentucky, and Ohio. Others in Buffalo increased his command to about 1,500. The large contingents from New Jersey, Pennsylvania, and lower New York were missing and not expected to arrive until later.

Messages were passed between Hynes and Sweeny about advancing the invasion date. O'Neill thought that the invasion had a chance if it took place before knowledge of the Fenian staging problems reached the intelligence sources, if Civil War raider tactics were used, if the expected additional Fenian forces arrived, and if the Fenians from the East moved at the same time that he did. He preferred waiting for maps and for more officers with experience, but he and Hynes were afraid that delay would allow the whole force of British and Canadian armies to mobilize across the river. After having Hynes put the invasion order in writing, O'Neill found himself with six hundred men, a large number from Buffalo but the majority trained in Tennessee, Kentucky, and Indiana by himself, Colonel Owen Starr, and Captain Haggerty.

THE BATTLE OF RIDGEWAY
In the early hours of June 1, 1866, O'Neill and his troops crossed the Niagara River. Colonel Starr, the advanceman, hoisted both the Irish and Fenian flags. The Fenians went over the back walls of Old Fort Erie, which had a drawbridge and a moat, and captured the small garrison. They took possession of the nearby village of six hundred population. O'Neill assured the citizens that they would suffer no harm or pillaging.

O'Neill then moved to Newbigging's Farm on Frenchman's Creek. Although he had no maps, he had excellent scouts and a gift for piecing together bits of information and outguessing the enemy. Canada West had mobilized about 107 companies and batteries when the Fenian invasion was imminent. Lieutenant Colonel George Peacocke of the 16th Regiment of the regular army was moving from Toronto, via St. Catharines, with 1,400 men and a battery of artillery.

Lieutenant Colonel Alfred Booker was coming from Port Colborne with 1,000 regulars and militia, including Militia Company No. 5, the Queen's Own Rifles, a unit which had many university students from Toronto. Before nightfall, O'Neill received information that the two armies moving toward him had increased to 5,000.

To avoid the pincer movements of Peacocke and Booker, O'Neill moved after dark toward the town of Ridgeway and placed his main body of soldiers within the treeline at Limestone Ridge, three miles north of the town. A second group was placed at a lower fenceline, and a third group of skirmishers stayed further down the slope. Earthworks were thrown up to support the positions. O'Neill hoped to defeat the first column before the other arrived.

Colonel Booker arrived before Colonel Peacocke. Peacocke, late in leaving Toronto, had been going by the army "book," with his men carrying full marching kits, including heavy overcoats. Booker, leaving on time, had correctly concluded that overcoats were not needed in Canada in June and his men need not be hampered with full marching kits. He incorrectly concluded that this was just a military exercise against inexperienced Fenian adventurers who would be routed and chased quickly, like delinquent schoolboys.

When Booker reached O'Neill's position outside Ridgeway, he put his regular troops in front of the militia volunteers. Booker's men carried adjusted Spencer repeating rifles, which got out fourteen shots before reloading was necessary. As a result of the wide publicity, Booker knew that the American government had not sold these advanced arms to the Fenians. What Booker did not know was that he was facing John O'Neill, a military leader of high intelligence and varied experience, who was backed by Owen Starr, another skillful commander.

Booker drove O'Neill's skirmishers back from the lower outpost line, then drove the next group from the upper fenceline. Thinking that this was the main body of Fenians and that any behind them were on the run, Booker brought back his regulars, who had used their fourteen shots, and moved his militia reserves to the front. They moved up the ridge under the illusion that they were pursuing a frightened and retreating rabble army.

Unexpected by Booker, some mounted Fenians in a scouting party came galloping and shouting around the side of the ridge. One of Booker's officers was reported to have exclaimed, "My God, the Fenians have cavalry!" Booker ordered his troops to form a British

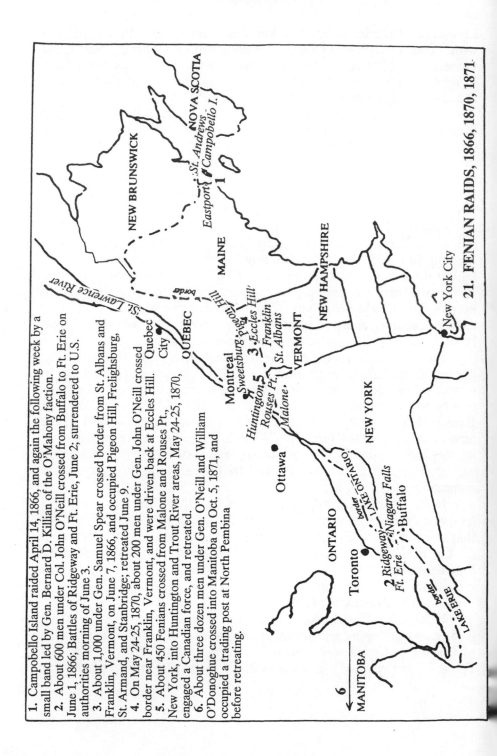

1. Campobello Island raided April 14, 1866, and again the following week by a small band led by Gen. Bernard D. Killian of the O'Mahony faction.

2. About 600 men under Col. John O'Neill crossed from Buffalo to Ft. Erie on June 1, 1866; Battles of Ridgeway and Ft. Erie, June 2; surrendered to U.S. authorities morning of June 3.

3. About 1,000 under Gen. Samuel Spear crossed border from St. Albans and Franklin, Vermont, on June 7, 1866, and occupied Pigeon Hill, Frelighsburg, St. Armand, and Stanbridge; retreated June 9.

4. On May 24-25, 1870, about 200 men under Gen. John O'Neill crossed border near Franklin, Vermont, and were driven back at Eccles Hill.

5. About 450 Fenians crossed from Malone and Rouses Pt., New York, into Huntington and Trout River areas, May 24-25, 1870, engaged a Canadian force, and retreated.

6. About three dozen men under Gen. O'Neill and William O'Donoghue crossed into Manitoba on Oct. 5, 1871, and occupied a trading post at North Pembina before retreating.

21. FENIAN RAIDS, 1866, 1870, 1871.

22. John O'Mahony, headed Fenian Brotherhood in the United States.

23. Thomas W. Sweeny, officer in Union army and Fenian general.

24. William R. Roberts, also headed American Fenians, vied with O'Mahony for leadership.

25. John O'Neill, captain in the Union army, general in the Fenian army.

Military Square. O'Neill immediately recognized his enemy's blunder and took advantage of it. With officers on horseback, he came out of the woods for a counter-attack. He soundly defeated the larger force, sent them into a hasty and disorganized retreat, and chased them back about three miles through Ridgeway.

O'Neill, running out of ammunition, knew that the enemy forces, with Lee Enfields and Spencer repeating rifles and superiority in numbers, might regroup and be joined by Peacocke's column. O'Neill's intelligence sources informed him that nine ships sent by the British to patrol the Great Lakes were cutting off retreat, as well as preventing transport of any reinforcements at the Niagara River and the Welland Canal. *(See Note 3: O'Neill's Forces.)*

Leaving behind six wounded men whom he was able to place in farmhouses, O'Neill returned to Fort Erie. He had to recapture it from a small force under Lieutenant Colonel Dennis of the Welland Battery, who had re-taken the village in his absence. Dennis proceeded to flee from his command, but other Canadian officers put up a fierce fight. The Fenians were again victorious, but had more casualties. The 7th Buffalo Regiment suffered the most. It had already lost Lieutenant Edward Lonergan and Major John Canty, the chief Fenian intelligence officer, and now lost Major Bigelow.

O'Neill received the bad news that the USS *Michigan*, an armed revenue cutter, had stopped the crossing of reinforcements, that Fenians were being imprisoned in Buffalo, and that the American government was seizing all ammunition and supplies cached near the border. Captain Hynes arranged for a retreat. As O'Neill and his men withdrew across the river by means of a large scow attached to a tugboat, they were hailed by the tug *Harrison*, belonging to the *Michigan*, and arrested on orders of General Meade.

O'Neill's official report, in which he noted that his position in an American prison made it impossible to get accurate reports from his officers, had eight Fenians killed and fifteen wounded. A later report confirmed eight killed, but had twenty or twenty-one wounded. Canadian and British reports from various units indicated twelve or eighteen killed (depending on whether deaths from heatstroke and, later, from wounds are counted), and seventy-four to eighty wounded.

Lieutenant Edward Lonergan of the 7th Buffalo was killed on his 21st birthday. He was buried in a mass grave at Ridgeway, but his body was later brought back to be buried in Holy Cross Cemetery at Limestone Hill in what is now Lackawanna. A limestone monument, provided by the Fenians and repaired in 1897 by the Ancient Order of Hibernians, has this inscription:

In Memory of Edward K. Lonergan
Lieut. 7th Regt. I.R.A.
Aged 21 yrs
who fell gallantly fighting
Ireland's enemies on
the famous Field of Ridgeway
June 2, 1866.

The other side of the stone has some lines of verse praising Fenians and condemning tyrants.

On June 6, somewhat belatedly, President Johnson finally called attention to the Neutrality Laws and denounced the invasion.

CANADA EAST

Meanwhile, General Samuel Spear, Commander of the Eastern Wing, the most important division of the Fenian Army in General Sweeny's plans, gave orders to cross the border from Vermont and New York. About three hundred troops under Brigadier General Michael C. Murphy moved into Canada from St. Albans, Vermont. General Sweeny and his chief-of-staff, Colonel John Mechan, were arrested at midnight on June 6, before they could cross and assume command. Murphy's men held a few hill positions and captured some enemy flags before they were forced by troops from Montreal to recross to Vermont, where United States Army troops detained them.

General Spear had escaped from St. Albans after Sweeny's arrest and joined his command at Franklin, Vermont. On the morning of June 7, Spear and about 1,000 men, some without rations and ammunition, entered Canada and raised the Green Flag. They occupied Pigeon Hill and a few other small villages. Spear sent word to Colonel Mechan (no longer in a position to help) that Irish Canadian farmers supported him and that he could hold his own if muskets and ammunition were sent. Spear wanted that foothold for an Irish Republic, but on June 9 he was forced back by about 3,000 Canadian and British troops. *(See Note 4: Spear.)*

In a September 1866 report to Fenian President Roberts at New York City headquarters, Sweeny was highly critical of the behavior of the United States Army:

As to the U.S. Army, it was practically placed at the hands of the British generals, and one detachment under Lieut. Col. Bvt. [Brevet] La Rhett L. Livingston, of the 3rd Artillery, permitted a British force to march into United States territory, in order to cut off the retreat of some stragglers left behind after the final evacuation. After crossing United States ground, by the verbal permission of this American officer, they sabred some of the unarmed men under his very eyes.

According to a Canadian version, the "march" was actually a cavalry charge of the 25th Regiment of the Royal Guides who had arrived from Montreal earlier in the day. One of the cavalrymen, in 1898, gave this recollection of events:

> . . .our captain ordered a charge, telling us to use only the flat side of our swords; and in a minute we were in among them slashing right and left. I saw fellows tumbling head over heels as they were struck . . .we soon reached the boundary line. There a company of United States regulars was stationed, and as fast as a Fenian tumbled over the line he was seized and disarmed. . .We came charging right up to the boundary, but were warned by the American officer in charge not to cross it. Of course we had nothing to do but obey . . .

Sixteen Fenians were gathered up and taken prisoner by the Royal Guards, then transported to jail in Montreal and later to Sweetsburg for trial.

AFTERMATH OF THE INVASIONS: UNITED STATES

Fenian supporters expected only token arrests and releases, but Minister Bruce forced Johnson's hand. Johnson had made a proclamation against the Fenians, but he was accused of delay and complicity. The situation was not improved by the introduction of resolutions in the House of Representatives by Sydenham Ancona of Pennsylvania and Robert Schenck and Reader Clarke of Ohio, in which the Department of State was urged to recognize the Irish nation as a legitimate belligerent and extend aid to the Fenians. Nor was it improved when William R. Roberts, after being released from prison, was introduced and applauded on the floor of the Senate.

Johnson was having domestic disagreements with the Radical Republicans (which would soon lead to his impeachment) and he wanted time to tour the country before the fall congressional elections. There were international matters demanding his attention that were weightier in his eyes than the Fenian problem. The United States and Britain, for example, were engaged in litigation over the "Alabama Claims" (the *Alabama* was a Confederate cruiser-raider supplied and supported by the British). After Campobello, Secretary Seward had informed London that if nothing was done about the claims, the United States would look the other way when the Fenians attacked again. After Ridgeway, the British finally acknowledged the claims, although they were not submitted to arbitration until the Treaty of Washington in 1871.

Johnson made sure that his order for confiscation of arms was implemented. The New York City Fenian militias, arriving in Buffalo too late for O'Neill, were temporarily put in cattle pens with the other troops. Movements of persons of Irish birth and ancestry were forbidden in some parts of the country. Arrests were made of many Irish near the Canadian border. Fenian rallies were broken up and banned. Many Fenians accepted parole conditions and returned to their homes with the help of funds from New York City officials; but many others seem to have accepted the help offered by the American government, which authorized General Meade to provide railroad transportation "to all Fenians now assembled on the Northern Frontier" back to their place of residence.

The American public, remembering the British blockade that prolonged the Civil War, did not want severe punishment for men whose intent was to fight for their native country's freedom. Confederate officers had been treated honorably at the end of the Civil War. Confederate soldiers had been allowed to return to their homes with horse, blanket, and rifle. So too should the Fenians be treated. Roberts and O'Neill were jailed only for a short time. Sweeny and Spear were indicted by a grand jury in Rutland, Vermont, but never brought to trial. In Buffalo in August, the district attorney entered a *nolle prosequi* (unwilling to pursue prosecution) for the remaining officers arrested there.

The *New York Times* of June 13, 1866, denounced England by contrasting the willingness of the United States to enforce the Neutrality Laws against the Fenians with the unwillingness of England to enforce those same laws during the Civil War. The *New York Herald* of June 12, 1866, said that Britain would have been driven out of all North America if the American government had not interfered. Both the *Tribune* and *Herald* claimed that Canada's annexation to the United States was inevitable. By August the *Herald* was encouraging the Fenians to invade Canada again.

Soon thereafter, President Johnson applied for the release of Fenians held in Canada. Concern was shown also for those held in Ireland. On June 18, Representative Ancona of Pennsylvania introduced a resolution, unanimously passed, asking the President what information he had on American citizens imprisoned in Ireland and what steps he was taking to protect them. Johnson replied immediately, and Seward made another request of Minister Bruce in regard to Americans arrested in Ireland after the suspension of habeas corpus in February 1866. Britain said that the handling of the Fenians in Canada was being left to Canada, but promised to release American Fenians in Ireland. This promise was interpreted differently by the parties concerned (citizenship disagreement). On July 23, Representative Clarke of Ohio, a legislator very sensitive to his Irish constituency and a longtime friend of the Fenians, proposed another resolution calling on the President to urge the Canadian and

British governments to release all Fenians held in Canada. This passed 112 to 2, with 67 abstentions. In September, New York State Democratic Party leader Samuel J. Tilden asked Johnson to return to the Fenians all property seized by the United States during and after the invasions. Johnson assented, and the arms and military supplies were returned. The *Ocean Spray*, the Fenian ship confiscated in Maine, had already been returned.

AFTERMATH OF THE INVASIONS: CANADA

The British had little sympathy for those Irish emigrating to the United States. According to Lord Wodehouse, Lord Lieutenant of Ireland, these emigrants were frequently traitors who tried to free Ireland through Canada, or else schemed to return to Ireland "to plot against the Queen and shelter themselves under letters of naturalization." Britain did not want to interfere in Canada lest it upset the Confederation that looked imminent. Minister Bruce did advise the Canadians to try the prisoners by ordinary forms of law and to delay the trials as long as possible to avoid generating sympathy for martyrs.

The British majority in Canada West was not inclined to be lenient. Its country had been attacked and its soldiers killed. The pro-Confederationists among them also were not inclined to follow Bruce's suggestion to "allow the present excitement to abate." The Confederationists could argue for a United Canada by playing up the dangers of invasion by Fenians backed by an expansionist United States. Certainly American press articles showed that annexation sentiments still existed.

The Fenians posed a religious issue for the French in Canada East. The anti-American attitude of their hierarchy dated back to the hostile reaction of the Thirteen Colonies, including those *Bostonnais*, to the Quebec Act of 1774, by which England had granted freedom of religion to Quebec Catholics. In the 1837 Canadian Rebellion, although some of the French junior clergy sympathized with the *Patriotes*, the senior clergy supported the English-speaking *Chateau-Clique*. Quebec leader Papineau had not endeared himself to the French hierarchy when he called for the election of parish priests in his Ninety-Two Resolutions. Neither did the Fenians, when they were being denounced by some Irish Canadian bishops for being influenced by the godless radical ideas of the French Revolution.

The Canadian government could not discount the religious issue because the Orangemen made it an issue. Fenianism was equated with Irish, and Irish was equated with Catholic. (Actually, there were more Protestant than Catholic Irish in Canada West.) Only the *Irish Canadian* had been bold enough to point out in June 1866 "for the benefit of our Orange friends . . .that the leaders of the present invasion, Roberts and Sweeny, are Protestants" and that sixteen of the sixty or more prisoners held in Toronto were Protestants, including a "Scottish-born Episcopal clergyman."

Canadian Attorney-General John A. Macdonald (who would become Prime Minister in 1867) did not want any vigilante justice, although he could do nothing about the rough treatment possibly received by Fenians and others taken prisoner during and immediately after the invasions. In July 1866, Macdonald warned the Mayor of Cornwall against arbitrary acts. Believing rumors that John O'Neill, disguised in a red beard and moustache, had sneaked into Canada for evil purposes, the Cornwall citizens had been mishandling men with red beards. Macdonald sent several rebukes to zealous officials who were arresting Irish Canadians on grounds that they were Fenians. He warned that this would drive Roman Catholics out of the country and swell the ranks of Fenians in the United States.

Contemporary Canadian newspapers reported instances of crop destruction and rough handling of Irish. American newspapers reported instances of Irish who emigrated from Ontario because of fear of the Orange Order. Orangemen justified their actions by claiming that Irish Catholics had sympathized with the vicious plundering of filibustering Fenians. More responsible reports indicated that the Fenian soldiers had treated Canadians with consideration. Major George T. Denison Jr., of Peacocke's cavalry, wrote that he was astonished by the universal testimony borne by the people of Fort Erie to the good conduct of the Fenians: "It seems like a perfect burlesque to see a ragged rabble without a government, country, or flag, affecting chivalrous sentiments and doing acts that put one in mind of the days of knight errantry." *(See Note 5: Prisoners.)*

THE TRIALS IN CANADA

The Fenian trials opened in Toronto in October 1866. Justice John Wilson obviously was not impartial. In his opening address to the entirely Protestant jury of twelve, he blamed the two United States political parties for instigating the invasions to win votes. He said that those who would excuse the prisoners as young and thoughtless should recognize that they came from that depraved class of men found in the major cities of the United States.

A number of prisoners held in the Toronto jail for several months were released for lack of evidence and taken to the border, where they were turned over to American officials. Those held for trial were charged with the capital offense of entering Canada with intent to levy war and being found in arms against Her Majesty. Those who were British subjects, an arguable issue from the American point of view, were also charged with treason. The defense attorneys had little to use against the charges, except technicalities. Witnesses, if summoned from across the border, risked arrest themselves.

By November 17, twenty-six Fenians had been acquitted, but seven were sentenced to hang. Two clergymen were treated inconsistently. Protestant minister David Lumsden was acquitted after an array of character witnesses appeared on his behalf. They included his bishop, his wife, and several fellow ministers. His defense was that he had a drinking problem, and that, in any case, his service as chaplain for Protestant Fenian soldiers was consistent with his religious beliefs.

Catholic chaplain Father John McMahon of Indiana offered in defense that he had administered to soldiers of both sides, but this argument carried no weight with the jury. Nor did the technicality submitted by McMahon's defense attorney, Matthew C. Cameron, that McMahon was being tried as an American citizen under a statute covering aliens. The court presented no proof of McMahon's American citizenship, Cameron argued, and therefore he should be tried as a British subject. What was not brought out at the trial but which was recalled many years later by a Canadian officer on the scene, Major George T. Denison, Jr., is that Denison personally gave Father McMahon the opportunity to return to Buffalo, but the priest chose to remain with the dead and dying. He also could have retreated with O'Neill's forces, but chose to do his duty as a priest. On October 26, an unimpressed jury sentenced Father McMahon to hang on December 13.

Pointing to the outrageousness of the testimony of some witnesses and informants, Bishop Lynch of Toronto and others requested that the prisoners be given new and fair trials, or be released. American Consul Thurston in Toronto also asked for new trials for the condemned men, but was refused, although he was privately assured by high Canadian officials that the death sentences would be commuted. He conveyed these confidences to Secretary Seward who, at the same time, was urging Minister Bruce in Washington to present the matter to the Home Office in London. The executions of those already convicted were then postponed to March 13. Despite continued private assurances that the sentences would never be carried out, concern continued, especially after more death sentences were meted out in January and February of 1867.

The defense counsel for most of the later trials, Kenneth Mackenzie, in a March 11, 1867 report, summarized his work for Consul Thurston, who had hired him. At the termination of the Toronto trials, twenty-one prisoners (including two, Lynch and McMahon, who were tried before Mackenzie had been retained) had been convicted and twenty-two acquitted. Mackenzie, obviously satisfied with his work, noted that the "number of prisoners lodged in the military here was 96 or 97 . . . and only 21 convictions."

At Sweetsburg, the trials of the sixteen prisoners taken during Spear's invasion began on December 13, 1866. The chief counsel for the defense was Bernard Devlin, a prominent barrister from Montreal, who was Thomas D'Arcy McGee's main political opponent in that city. Devlin had been retained by Fenian Headquarters in New York City to act as counsel for all the prisoners held as Fenians in Canada, but on the recommendation of Toronto Consul Thurston he did not participate in the Toronto Trials. In the province of Quebec, however, Devlin received the cooperation of the United States Vice-Consul General for British North American Provinces, C.G.B. Drummond, who on January 3 wrote Secretary Seward that Devlin expected "success in appeal in the cases of those capitally condemned." Three of the accused were sentenced to hang, two received terms of two and three months, and the remaining eleven were acquitted. The Home Office in London criticized the conduct and outcome of these trials, while the *Toronto Globe* criticized the small number of death sentences.

Michael Murphy of Toronto, who enraged the Catholic bishops in 1865, was a special case. He had been arrested in April on a train en route to Montreal, but this was not absolute evidence that he was planning to join the Fenians at Eastport to attack New Brunswick. Murphy made the legal question moot by escaping with a few companions just before the trial date.

On January 3, 1867, the Canadian government officially commuted to twenty years imprisonment at hard labor the death sentences of those convicted during the Fall Assizes. By March 4, Secretary Seward was able to inform the American public that the same commutation had been given to those convicted during January and February.

All of the prisoners convicted at Toronto and Sweetsburg were released by July 1872, excepting Thomas Maxwell, wounded at Ridgeway, who died in prison on September 24, 1869. Father John McMahon was the second Fenian to be released, in the summer of 1869, partly through the intercession of Archbishop Connolly of Halifax, who made a special trip to Ottawa on his behalf. Father McMahon was reinstated in the Diocese of Fort Wayne by his superior, Bishop John H. Luers, and died at Reynolds, Indiana, on April 28, 1872.

It is impossible to account for all of the prisoners taken at Fort Erie and Ridgeway during and immediately after the battles in June 1866. As many as two hundred were arrested, some of them no doubt curious residents of Buffalo who had crossed to observe the action on

the Canadian side, and were held for a time in local jails at Fort Col-
burne and Brantford. Many were released quickly. Others were
transported to jail in Toronto to await trial there, and many of these
were released for lack of sufficient evidence only after spending weeks
and sometimes several months in jail.

It would be remarkable, given the feelings of most Canadians, if
some prisoners and innocent bystanders were not treated roughly.
Canadian Major Denison reported that some of Peacocke's troops
encountered "a few stragglers" and that "four [were] reported shot,
one of whom unfortunately turned out to be a farmer in the
neighborhood, who had foolishly armed himself with a Fenian musket
and bayonet which he was taking home as relics of the raid."

Peter Berresford Ellis, in a piece in *The Irish Sword* (Winter
1986), noted that contemporary reports on casualties varied. Ellis
published what he believed was the first Fenian casualty list with military units and disposition. His research confirmed the names of five
killed in action at Ridgeway, three who died later in Buffalo of
wounds received, and sixteen wounded who were hospitalized in Buffalo or taken prisoner. Ellis noted that his list "seems to confirm the
figures given by O'Neill which coincide with the contemporary newspaper accounts and Major Denison's estimations." O'Neill reported
eight dead and fifteen wounded. Denison reported "six men killed on
the spot and probably one or two may have died since. How many
wounded it is impossible to say." For Ft. Erie, Ellis confirmed two
dead and four wounded (one of whom later died of his wounds). Ellis
could not determine the fate of one Lieutenant Patrick Tyrrell, no
unit given:

A British source reports the capture of this officer, said to be wounded in the thigh.
He was held in Brantford before being transferred to Hamilton. There seems to be
no further reference to him..

Newspapers reported Pvt. Henry Anderson, Queen's Own, as
being buried with military honors in Toronto on June 6, but he soon
turned up alive at Ft. Erie. Rumors that a Fenian had actually been
buried were dispelled when a woman belatedly identified the corpse
as her husband, Pvt. William Smith, Queen's Own.

NATURALIZATION ISSUE

The issue of allegiance and naturalization that arose in the
Canadian trials became especially critical in 1867 when many more
Fenians, among them naturalized American citizens, were arrested on
the other side of the Atlantic. Secretary Seward's concern for the
Fenians was wedded to his general concern for upholding the rights of
all American citizens, born or naturalized. He continued to be confronted, however, with the British policy of Indefeasible Allegiance.

American law recognized the rights of the foreign-born to become naturalized citizens upon swearing allegiance to the United States and giving up all allegiance to their former country and its ruler, but English law did not permit British, including Irish, subjects to renounce their allegiance and become citizens of another country. The British position was explained by Lord Clarendon to the American Minister in London, Charles Adams, during the post-Civil War period of arrests in Ireland of American citizens, some of them veterans of the American Civil War:

No British subject could ever, or in any circumstance, renounce, or be absolved from his allegiance to his sovereign. I have to inform you that her Majesty's Government are advised that it would be impossible that they should recognize any title in any foreign power to interfere on behalf of natural born subjects of Her Majesty whom it may be thought necessary to detain in custody in Ireland.

As a counter to the British claims of allegiance, Adams and his superior, Secretary Seward, made it evident in their diplomacy that United States government efforts to block Fenian military preparations on American soil would be proportional to Britain's willingness to abandon Indefeasible Allegiance and to settle the claims for damages done to Union shipping by British-built Confederate raiders, especially the *Alabama*, during the Civil War. The bargaining position was effective. Britain eventually paid $15,500,000, in settlement of the Alabama Claims, and granted concessions on naturalization. While the diplomacy may have been in the best general interests of the United States, it worked against the specific interests of the Fenians, who were used adroitly by Seward and by his successor in the State Department, Hamilton Fish, as pawns in the game. In 1870, when the Fenians again planned an invasion of Canada, the United States acted to enforce the Neutrality Laws with much more alacrity than it had in 1866.

RISING IN IRELAND AND ERIN'S HOPE

The major thrust of the Fenians after 1866 was in Ireland itself, as James Stephens had always wanted, but continued dissension among American leaders hampered renewal of plans. The O'Mahony wing, which generally supported Stephens, struggled for control. The Roberts wing talked of another Canadian attack. A third wing, which included many veterans of the Canadian expeditions and others who had been released or escaped from jails in England and Ireland, set the Big Rising in Ireland for 1867. This group, headed by Colonel Thomas J. Kelly, managed to depose Stephens of any real authority over the American Fenian Brotherhood.

American Fenians started to leave for Ireland, England, and France. Optimistic reports spurred another effort to unite the factions. The Roberts wing shelved its Canadian plans and went along with the Fenian Military Council, which placed a call in the *New York Herald* (February 17, 1867): "Wanted - 1,000 Cavalry Sabres. Address, with lowest cash price and conditions, box 3074. Wanted - one thousand men devoted to the cause of Ireland, each of whom can defray his own expenses to the amount of $100. Apply in one week at 19 Chatham Street." The results paralleled those of 1866, when men were asked to volunteer at their own expense. The *Herald* reported that "Colonel Downing had more applications than the most rapidly executed calligraphy of his clerks could record."

The Fenians acquired the *Jacmel Packet*, which left New York on April 13 with John F. Kavanagh, a Civil War navy veteran, as captain. The commander was Brigadier-General James E. Kerrigan, former Union officer and Congressman, who had raised four thousand men for the Sweeny-Roberts invasion of Canada. The ship's engineer, S.R. Tresilian, an Orangeman and Mason, had also been active in the 1866 campaign.

Rechristened *Erin's Hope*, the ship was met near Sligo by Ricard O'Sullivan Burke, who informed the Fenians that they had come too late. Scattered risings of men with few or no arms had been quickly suppressed in February and March. After vainly searching the Irish coast for a safe landing place, Captain Kavanagh disembarked thirty-one men at Waterford. Quick arrests were made of twenty-eight, including Colonel William J. Nagle and John Warren, who would provide fuel for the naturalization controversy for the next few years. *Erin's Hope* returned to New York with its arms and supplies.

THE MANCHESTER MARTYRS
The Fenians had both success and failure on September 18, 1867, with the rescue of two American Civil War veterans, Galway-born Colonel Thomas J. Kelly and Cork-born Captain Timothy Deasy, who had been arrested in Manchester, England, the previous week. Kelly had been elected acting Chief Organizer of the Irish Republic at a Manchester Fenian Convention, during which it was claimed that Stephens had abandoned the Home Rising by remaining in America during the early months of 1867.

The rescue was organized by Ricard O'Sullivan Burke, who had been wining and dining in stately homes in England and Ireland under the alias of Edward F. Winslow without exciting suspicion. Burke, born in 1838 near Dunmanway, County Cork, had begun training as an engineer and served in the British Army Cork Militia as a teenager. After worldwide travelling, he joined the Fenian Brotherhood in New York in 1861. He enlisted in the Union Army, organized Fenian Circles in the Army of the Potomac, was given Army training as an engineer, and rose to the rank of colonel.

The plan was such that there should have been no casualties, but fate decreed otherwise. To force open the locked door of the prison van, one of the rescuers fired into the lock. Police Sergeant Brett, peering through the keyhole, received a fatal bullet in his eye. The keys from Brett's pocket were passed outside, and Kelly and Deasy, still in chains and handcuffs, were rushed away. Both returned to the United States.

Sixty men were arrested in a lynch-mob atmosphere fueled by the newspapers. Five were brought to trial on murder charges: William Larkin, William Philip Allen, Thomas Maguire, Michael O'Brien (tried under the name of Gould), and Edward O'Meagher Condon (tried under the name of Shore). There was no reliable evidence at the trial that any of them was the one who fired the shot, but there was much perjured and purchased testimony, a response to the public's "hang-all-the-Irish" mood. All five were found guilty and sentenced to be hanged.

Maguire, obviously innocent and unconnected with any Irish organizations, was pardoned. Condon's sentence was commuted two days before the hanging to life imprisonment, after the reluctant intercession of American Minister Charles Adams (son of former President John Quincy Adams) on behalf of an American citizen. Allen, Larkin, and O'Brien (also an American citizen) were hanged on November 23 in a public extravaganza meant to terrify the Irish of Salford and Manchester. The Irish had already been terrified by crowds beating, kicking, and mauling them since September.

Allen died quickly, but the hangman bungled the job on the others. He had to climb on Larkin's back and kill him. A Catholic chaplain prevented the same thing from happening to O'Brien, and the American Civil War veteran, born in Ballymacoda, County Cork, slowly expired while Father Gadd held the dying man's hands within his own. The injustice of the trials and the grotesque hangings shocked Ireland and America, increased the number of Fenian sympathizers, gave the Irish freedom movement its Manchester Martyrs, increased the opposition to Britain within Irish American organizations, and widened the divide in Anglo-Irish relations.

Peter Rice, who actually fired the shot, later lived in New York. He spoke to John Devoy of his regrets: he had no idea that Brett's eye was at the lock. Fenian leaders told him not to come forward to confess, since this would not have changed the pre-determined verdict and would just have added him to the gallows.

THE 1870 INVASION OF CANADA

Stephens, accused by Kelly and other Fenian leaders of dereliction of duty in the 1867 Rising, blamed the failure of the insurrection on insufficient support given to it by the Americans. Meanwhile, in America, a year's effort had convinced William Roberts that he could not collect enough money for another invasion of Canada. He resigned as President of the Fenian Senate on December 31, 1867. John O'Neill, hero of Ridgeway and now a general, was elected to succeed him. O'Neill and the Senate still looked toward Canada. The Fenian movement, however, seemed more split than ever. O'Neill had opposition from members of his own Senate; from leaders of the O'Mahony wing; and from some Fenians who felt he had criticized or condemned them unjustly in his 1866 report on the Battle of Ridgeway.

In February 1870, O'Neill issued a call for men and arms and gathered pledges. He planned a two-pronged invasion for Queen Victoria's birthday, May 24. One would be launched from Franklin, Vermont, under his own command; the other from Malone, New York, under Colonel Owen Starr. The American and Canadian governments, aware of the plan, thought that talk of the eastern border was a diversion to cover a strike further west with support of Canadian insurgent Louis Riel. Even master spy Henri LeCaron, who had infiltrated O'Neill's headquarters and gained O'Neill's complete confidence, at first believed this.

As the Queen's birthday approached, the British consul in Buffalo reported that 1,100 men had left to join O'Neill and that twice that many had left from Philadelphia. The *New York Times* indicated annoyance that plans had been kept secret from the press and reported that 30,000 had left New York City for the Canadian border. O'Neill well knew that he had no 30,000, but he had pledges of more than 3,000 from various leaders. He expected thousands more, if the expedition led to early successes.

O'Neill planned to capture either St. Jean (aka St. John's) as well as Richmond, where he could control rail and telegraph lines to Montreal. When he reached Vermont, he found only a few hundred troops waiting. The store of arms and ammunition hidden at the border was inadequate, but he hoped it would be sufficient to allow him to win control of a key spot on which to put the Irish flag. On May 25, O'Neill crossed the border with 176 men who had arms but little or no military training and experience.

The Canadians and the British, alerted by LeCaron's reports, had massed their forces with more than 13,000 men in arms. There is a question of how many of the 13,000 were near the border. A local unit of Home Guards claimed to have been the main defenders during the initial moments of the battle. There is no question, however, that Canada wanted to destroy the Myth of Ridgeway. Canadian reports indicate that fewer than 200 were waiting for O'Neill at Eccles Hill, with several thousand at a nearby hill as a backup. O'Neill himself estimated that he faced fewer than 100 Canadians in their front line.

O'Neill had barely crossed the border when he met heavy rifle fire from hidden positions on Eccles Hill. The first volley killed young Private Rowe of Malone, New York, and wounded two others. O'Neill and his officers tried in vain to get their men to move forward, risking fire while gaining a better position. The men later claimed that they could not see targets at which to fire, that their arms were defective, and that they would be facing five thousand enemy troops even if they passed the first strategy point. A disappointed O'Neill later wrote, "for the first time in my life I failed in rallying men or getting them to follow where I was willing to lead." He was forced to order the men who had not already retreated to fall back beyond the range of the rifle fire.

O'Neill then made the following speech, as reported by himself and by John Boyle O'Reilly of Boston:

Men of Ireland I am ashamed of you! You have acted disgracefully today; but you will have another chance of showing whether you are cravens or not. Comrades, we must not, we dare not go back with the stain of cowardice on us. Comrades, I will lead you again, and if you will not follow me, I will go with my officers and die in your front! I now leave you under charge of Boyle O'Reilly, and will go after reinforcements, and bring them up at once.

Having put a third officer, Major Daniel Murphy, in temporary command, O'Neill went with O'Reilly toward camp to try to hasten some arriving troops. O'Neill looked for wounded or missing men, always his concern, according to O'Reilly. When he stopped at a farmhouse, O'Neill was arrested by George Foster, United States Marshal from Vermont, who whisked him away to jail at St. Albans in a carriage that passed through the Fenian camp of about 150 men, who did not fully realize what was happening.

The New York and other contingents, too few in number to have been of much use, arrived too late. The 1870 invasion was over. The Canadians were naturally overjoyed at having avenged themselves for O'Neill's victory at Ridgeway four years previously. The officers praised themselves in their battle reports, and they were joined by the Canadian press and officialdom. *(See Note 6: 1870.)*

The Canadians reported no casualties. O'Neill reported two dead and three wounded, with the number of prisoners unknown.

O'Neill was sentenced to two years in prison at Windsor, Vermont, for violation of the Neutrality Laws.

On May 26, from Malone, New York, about 450 Fenians under Colonel Starr crossed the border as planned. They had delayed because of the shortage of men and the inadequacy of the arms cached for them. Starr's men cut telegraph wires and headed for the city of Huntingdon. They were driven back by 1,000 Canadians. The Fenians reported one casualty, the Canadians none. Both sides reported several Fenians wounded and taken prisoner. Colonel Starr, John Gleeson, and others were arrested by General Quimby, United States Marshal for northern New York. Like O'Neill, these leaders were sentenced to prison terms, but were soon released.

The spy LeCaron (whose real name was Thomas Beach) probably did not exaggerate, as he was often inclined to do, the part he played in the invasions of 1870. When it became evident to O'Neill that an informer had passed plans to Canada, LeCaron turned suspicion from himself by placing it on some of O'Neill's most trusted officers. He thus created tension among the best men, some of whom failed to show up with their expected troops. LeCaron had been in charge of depositing the arms and ammunition near Franklin and Malone and had effectively sabotaged part of the supplies. For his work, LeCaron received a special bonus of $2,000 on the recommendation of Gilbert McMicken, chief of the Canadian frontier detective force.

Basically the reports of LeCaron reaching high Canadian circles were accurate as to the building up of the invasion force at the points in New York and Vermont. In other matters, LeCaron's reports were often complete fabrications. He was paid according to production. He often slandered Fenian leaders with accounts of their personal lives and of their relations with other Fenians. The reports reached Macdonald through McMicken, LeCaron's superior in the intelligence service. The prime minister faithfully recorded all the items he received, both the true and the false, although which was which he had little way of telling. Macdonald's extensive papers and memoirs often report as fact information generated by LeCaron, without his mentioning the ultimate source of the information or disinformation. Unfortunately, some historians who more or less accept Macdonald's voluminous papers in the National Archives of Canada as a reliable source have perpetuated some untruths about Fenianism and Fenian leaders, such as John O'Mahony, William Roberts, Thomas Sweeny, and John O'Neill.

GENERAL PARDON IN THE UNITED STATES

President Grant denounced the Franklin and Malone invasions. (One will never know what his position would have been if they were successful.) O'Neill lost prestige among the Fenians, not just because he had lost but also because he wrote some stinging reports on the lack of cooperation he had had from certain Fenian leaders and their organizations. Yet he still had many devoted supporters.

When Grant was in St. Louis on August 12, he was presented with a petition to free O'Neill that was ten feet long and had two columns of signatures. Grant delayed, but in October proposed that all Fenians imprisoned in Great Britain, Canada, and the United States be freed. Britain was agreeable; Canada was not. Making his own decision on October 13, Grant issued a pardon to O'Neill, Starr, and six other Fenians who had been involved in the May invasions and who were still in American prisons.

American sympathy for Fenianism was evident when the first contingent of Fenians released from British prisons arrived in New York aboard the ship *Cuba* on January 19, 1871. These were John Devoy, Jeremiah O'Donovan Rossa, Henry J. Mulleda, Charles Underwood O'Connell, and John McClure. McClure was born in Dobbs Ferry, New York. O'Connell, born in County Offaly, was a Civil War veteran and naturalized American who had been imprisoned in 1865. The "Cuba Five" were honored enthusiastically by the Irish and by New Yorkers of other backgrounds. In Washington, with both Republicans and Democrats seeking the Irish vote, the House of Representatives passed a resolution 172 to 21 welcoming the Fenians to the capital and to all America. On February 22, the Fenians were given a welcome and reception at the White House by President Grant, as reported the next day in the *New York Times*.

A score of other ex-prisoners arriving during the following months were greeted with the same enthusiasm. These included Thomas C. Luby, John O'Leary, William G. Halpin, William M. Lomasney, Edward Power, Dennis D. Mulcahy, William Roantree, Thomas F. Bourke, John McCafferty, and Ricard O'Sullivan Burke. McCafferty, born in the United States, was receiving his second welcome back from prison, the first having been in 1866. O'Sullivan Burke was not released until 1872 and then spent time with his family in Cork, as he tried to recuperate from the torture and attempted poisonings he had suffered in prison. He came to America in 1874 and was active with Clan na Gael until his death in 1922.

As recognized leaders of the Irish in America, the ex-prisoners formed the Irish Confederation, which brought in many from the old wings but lasted only two years. New organizations formed and old ones revived. Rossa, Devoy, and the British prison alumni became leaders in the most militant of the organizations, Clan na Gael. With John Breslin superintending the project, Clan na Gael later provided County Clare-born John Holland of Paterson, New Jersey, with $60,000 for development of his submarine. The first successful model was named *The Fenian Ram*. The Fenians hoped to use an armed submarine, when fully developed for long-range cruising, to attack British ships and to invade Ireland. It was the United States Navy, however, that was to reap the fruits of the Fenians' submarine project.

O'NEILL'S LAST INVASION

At his trial in 1870, John O'Neill said that prevailing conditions convinced him that there was not the remotest chance of success in invading Canada. He also declared, "My love for Ireland remains the same and my hatred of that flag which to the Irish people is the symbol of tyranny and oppression can never be changed."

After his pardon by Grant, O'Neill thought he found a condition that made a Canadian invasion possible once more: an alliance with the Métis, persons of mixed Indian and white (Scots, Irish, French, American) descent. O'Neill's contact was William O'Donoghue, who had worked for Louis Riel in 1869-70. Riel was a native of the Red River area of the Northwest Territories who had been educated at Montreal. He objected when Ottawa, in 1868, without consultation with settlers, sent land surveyors to prepare for a takeover of the Territories. Their population was about 7,000, of whom 5,000 were Métis. (There is some evidence that Louis Riel's surname came from the Irish "Reilly" and that one of his ancestors was Jean Baptiste Riel of Quebec, who came from Limerick, Ireland, about the year 1700.)

Riel set up a provisional government and threatened full rebellion unless certain rights were granted to the Métis. He executed Thomas Scott, an Orangeman from Ontario who had led the pro-Canadian party. Ontarians saw Riel as a dangerous French Catholic radical. Quebeckers saw opposition to Riel as opposition to French Catholics. The Ottawa government averted the crisis by agreeing to all the rights demanded by Riel as terms for bringing Manitoba into the Confederation of Canada. However, Riel, his aide O'Donoghue, and the Métis were still considered a threat to peace.

In 1871, O'Neill sought backing from the Fenian organizations for a new Canadian invasion. He got support only from a few diehard colleagues. Nevertheless, Canadian and United States authorities were concerned when O'Neill became involved with O'Donoghue, who was talking about an independent nation in the western territories of Canada. Their concern increased in September 1871 when General O'Neill and Colonel Thomas J. Kelly met with Bishop Taché at Fort Garry. It seemed as if O'Neill might have the support of

O'Donoghue, who in turn might have the support of Riel and the Métis.

On October 5, O'Neill and four dozen men crossed from Georgetown, Minnesota, and seized Pembina, Manitoba, where there was a non-garrisoned custom house and a Hudson Bay Company trading post. O'Neill did not receive whatever local support he expected. United States troops crossed the border and captured him and ten of his men. Canada's request for extradition was refused, but the Fenians were tried in Minnesota for violating Neutrality Laws. Acquitted on technicalities, they were released after a few days in jail. (Riel and the Métis rebelled in 1885, after which Riel was hanged.)

O'NEILL'S LAST YEARS

O'Neill finally retired from active military projects. He had been interested in Irish rural colonization projects for many years, even while with the Fenians. He became a land colonizer in Nebraska, toured the East and other parts, and urged Irish audiences to emigrate to the West. His work in colonization has been researched by Sister Mary M. Langan in a master's thesis (1937) for the University of Notre Dame, and by Henry J. Casper, S.J., *History of the Catholic Church in Nebraska*. Langan notes that O'Neill received the support of both Vicar Apostolic James O'Connor of Omaha and the Irish Catholic Immigration Bureau (which contributed $1000 to help settle easterners on cheap and even free land on the barren prairie). By 1877, two colonies in Holt County in northern Nebraska were established with several hundred colonists and were flourishing. One, named O'Neill, received high praise from a reporter for the *Omaha World Herald* (May 25, 1877):

General O'Neill takes great pride in the results of his exertions to build up this part of Nebraska, and well he may, for he has succeeded in establishing his colony with very fine and intelligent people . . .Wheat, barley, and oats are looking well [on the] virgin prairies . . .The colonists are planting quite a quantity of evergreens, and when they grow to make shade, the O'Neill colony will be a grand and magnificent country.

On January 8, 1878, after receiving the Last Rites of his Church, General O'Neill died peacefully from the effects of a stroke. Vicar Apostolic O'Connor officiated at the funeral service at St. Philomena's Cathedral in Omaha. The large crowd attending included O'Neill's wife, Mary; their three young children; and his mother, sister, and brother from Elizabeth, New Jersey.

O'Neill's life spanned less than forty-four years, but in that short time he served honorably as a leader both in war and in peace. The town of O'Neill, Nebraska, with a population of about four thousand today, is a memorial to this man of courage and integrity, an idealist with a vision of freedom, equality, and justice for all people.

A SUCCESSFUL FENIAN RESCUE

The American Fenians and Irish exiles did not forget their brothers in prison. In 1874, Clan na Gael undertook to free Fenian military prisoners with no hope of pardon from penal colonies in Western Australia. In the general amnesty of 1871, the Duke of Cambridge, Commander-in-Chief of the British Army, convinced his cousin, Queen Victoria, to deny amnesty to Fenians in the military. Seventeen Fenian members of the British Army, convicted in 1866, were transported to Australia in 1867 as criminals, along with forty-eight Fenians transported as political prisoners. The escape of John Boyle O'Reilly in 1869 gave the remainder some hope, but their guarded efforts to contact active Fenian organizations had not succeeded. By a strange coincidence, prisoner Martin Hogan saw the address of Peter Curran of New York in an old newspaper article on the reception of the "Cuba Five" by Clan na Gael in 1871. Hogan managed to send a letter to Curran through the help of a priest.

Known as the Freemantle Mission (or Catalpa Rescue), this Fenian effort was most remarkable for keeping complete secrecy from spies, informers, and governments. John Devoy, John Breslin, and Thomas Desmond, veterans of other rescues, did most of the planning. Captain George S. Anthony of New Bedford, with no known Irish blood, manned the Fenian-purchased whaling ship *Catalpa* with a normal crew of mostly Malays, Kanakas, and Portuguese Negroes. The ship left Boston in April 1875. The daring rescue of the six prisoners occurred a year later in April 1876 in international waters off Freemantle, Australia. The other military Fenians had died or escaped or were imprisoned under too close a guard, except for William Foley. Foley, ill and on ticket-of-leave, helped with the rescue plans and then escaped to New York where he died in mid-1876. Rescuers Breslin, Desmond, and Thomas Brennan were assisted by other Irish Republican Brotherhood members who, unknown to the Americans, had previously arrived in Australia to effect a rescue.

Restored to freedom in the United States were Martin Hogan of Limerick, Michael Harrington and Thomas Hassett of Cork; James Wilson (real name McNally) and Robert Cranston of Tyrone; and Thomas Darragh, a Protestant Orangeman from Wicklow. That no royal pardon would have been forthcoming was evidenced in early May, before the success of the rescue was known and confirmed, when Prime Minister Disraeli turned down a petition presented by 138 members of the House of Commons for clemency for the military prisoners.

SOME LASTING EFFECTS OF FENIANISM

The Fenian invasions had important and lasting effects on the governments of Canada, Great Britain, and the United States. One effect, not intended and already mentioned in this chapter, was the settlement of the Alabama Claims.

On the naturalization issue, Fenian activity also bore fruit for the United States. The British Naturalization and Mixed Treaties Act ("Warren Act") of 1870, settled a dispute almost a hundred years old. This act was a direct result of negotiation after the United States tried to intervene in the Fenian arrests and trials in order to uphold the rights of American citizens. The British gave up their claim of Indefeasible Allegiance to the Crown ("Once a Briton, always a Briton") and made it legal, in their eyes, for a British subject to swear loyalty to another country.

From the Canadian viewpoint, according to W.S. Neidhardt:

the most important result of Fenianism was the impetus it gave to Canadian nationalism. The various Fenian raids had a catalyzing effect on confederation and they aroused a new wave of patriotic sentiment among the inhabitants of British North America . . .The Fenian raids convinced many Canadians that safety lay in unity.

Peter Berresford Ellis, in agreement on that point, writes:

Looked at in purely Canadian terms, the attempted Fenian invasion brought about the union of the British North American provinces and welded them together into the modern Dominion of Canada. The initial suspicion and hostility which greeted the proposals of confederation were swept aside in the birth of a new 'Canadian nationalism' . . .it may be rightly argued that without the attempted Irish invasion of 1866 the Dominion of Canada might not have come into existence.

From an Irish and American viewpoint, it can be said that an independent Ireland (albeit minus six counties) might never have come into existence without the Fenians who in death as in life provided an inspiration for those who followed. Fenian graves in the United States are scattered from east to west: Thomas Clarke Luby in Bayview Cemetery, Jersey City, New Jersey; Ricard O'Sullivan Burke in Mt. Olivet, Chicago, Illinois; Thomas Desmond in Holy Cross, Colma, California. Calvary Cemetery in Queens County, New York, has a Fenian Plot and Memorial Monument and is said to be the final resting place of more Fenians than any other American burial ground except for national cemeteries and cemeteries for the Civil War veterans. Some Fenians, such as John O'Mahony and Jeremiah O'Donovan Rossa, were returned to Ireland for burial. It was at O'Donovan Rossa's funeral in Glasnevin Cemetery, Dublin, in

1915 that Padraic Pearse (who would be executed the following year for his part in the Easter Rising) prophesied: "The fools, the fools, the fools! - they have left us our Fenian dead, and while Ireland holds these graves, Ireland unfree shall never be at peace."

Seamus Metress, in *The Hunger Strike and the Final Struggle*, says: "Most important, Fenianism established the cause of nationhood in the minds of many of the Irish working class and peasantry. It was a democratic, socialistic, republican concept of Ireland's quest for independence. The spirit of the Fenians survives today in the prisons and homes of the six counties [British Northern Ireland] from Crossmaglen on the border to Magilligan Camp on the northern shore."

The Fenians of the 19th century inspired a new sense of pride in national identity for the Irish in America, brought new and lower classes into leadership, broadened political horizons, encouraged less reliance on the clergy in politics, paved the way for the Land League in Ireland, served as models for the leaders of the Irish independence movement of the next generation, and showed Ireland that it was not forgotten by its emigrant sons and daughters.

MEF

III
NEW WORLD BRANCHES: THE UNITED STATES

Chapter 8

COLONIAL AMERICA:
SETTLERS ON THE FIRST FRONTIERS

The Irish settled in small numbers in the French, Spanish, and Portuguese colonies of the New World. In much larger numbers they settled in British North America. A foremost historian of Irish settlement during the colonial and Revolutionary period was Michael O'Brien. Many historians, unfortunately, have ignored O'Brien. They have thus given us incomplete or incorrect pictures, and seriously undercounted the Irish in colonial America.

Before the end of the 19th century some historians had created and perpetuated a myth that there had been no significant emigration of Irish to North America before the Great Hunger of the 1840s, and no Irish worth counting before the Revolution. After World War II, various ethnic groups sought recognition for their contributions, not only in two World Wars but in building America. Textbook publishers and vote-seeking politicians conceded to the Irish some Revolutionary War generals and some repainted stereotypes, but the myth largely remained: America was one vast land dominated by the Anglo-Saxon sons and daughters of the American Revolution. When presented with evidence of innumerable Irish names and identifications in the colonies, the Establishment historians claimed that they were "Scotch-Irish" or "Ulster Scots."

MICHAEL O'BRIEN

In the early 1900s one historian set out to discredit the Scotch-Irish myth and to demonstrate the important role of the Irish in early American history. Michael O'Brien (1869/70-1960) was born in Fermoy, County Cork, and educated at the Christian Brothers School and St. Colman's College. After emigrating to the United States in

147

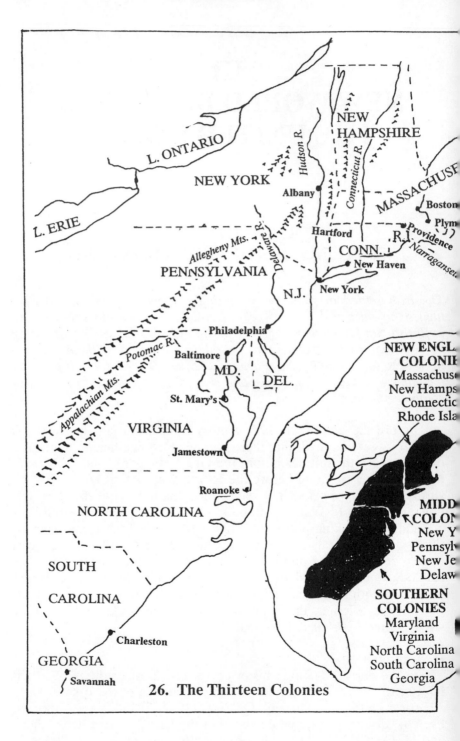

26. The Thirteen Colonies

1889, he began a career of forty-five years with the Western Union Telegraph Company. His job as an accounting supervisor took him to most of the eastern states and allowed him to combine his love of historical research with his non-working time away from home. He wrote more than twenty books and several hundred articles on the contributions of the Irish in America. He was librarian of the Friendly Sons of St. Patrick, historiographer of the American Irish Historical Society, and one of the founders of the Catholic Writers Guild. In 1930 he received an honorary LL.D. from University College, Dublin, for his outstanding professional research and writing on the history of the Irish in America. He died in Yonkers, New York, at the age of ninety. He left behind his extensive publications; voluminous records now at the American Irish Historical Society; and about eight linear feet of papers, notes, and correspondence, now in the library of Iona College, New Rochelle, New York.

Michael O'Brien faced the Scotch-Irish myth after it had reached bed-rock entrenchment. Aiming to inundate its exponents with so much data that the truth could not be ignored, he spent his life researching and publishing information that he found in thousands of documents and archives. His thesis was that the Irish, not the 19th century creations known as Scotch-Irish, had emigrated to every one of the thirteen colonies, that many had become prominent in colonial affairs, and that they had provided officers and soldiers out of proportion to their numbers in the American Revolution.

O'Brien was confronting a line of historians who used a twofold argument running backwards that persists to this day. The first part is that the colonial Irish were hardworking pioneers who brought with them the initiative, industry, agricultural skills, and moral rectitude that had made them superior in Ireland to the "irredeemable natives." The native Irish were indolent, uneducated, agriculturally lagging, incapable of pioneering. Therefore, any Irish colonial immigrants must have been Scotch-Irish. The second part is that the British penal laws and colonial ordinances would have prevented Catholics from emigrating. There could have been very few Catholics since only two of the thirteen colonies (Maryland and Pennsylvania) ever had priests, and even in these two colonies the handful of priests could not serve publicly.

Why have historians persisted in this myth if it is as demonstrably false as O'Brien claimed? One reason is a mind-set by which they copy from each other without checking original sources or without checking colleagues' sources. A second is their assumption that the words *Irish* and *Catholic* were synonymous in the centuries of settlement, an untenable confusion of race and religion. A third is their reluctance to use the research of genealogists and local historians who have painstakingly documented and published mountains of literature on the nativity and ancestry of the pioneers. (*See Note 1: Myth.*)

Michael O'Brien was not the first to challenge the myth, but he was the most single-minded, persistent, and prolific in his documentation of the Irish presence in colonial America. Facing a difficult financial market, he had to work hard personally to publish and sell his books (some were published posthumously). In the introduction to O'Brien's book, *A Hidden Phase of American History*, Joseph Clarke wrote, in the ornate prose of his day:

> To Michael O'Brien, the Irish in America will ever be a debtor. . .he worked in sincerity for the good name of his race on the American continent which has brought him high consideration among historical writers and his countrymen. Besides being an historical work of capital importance, based upon data gathered with prodigious labor from unimpeachable sources, it is such an inspiring record of heroic deeds and sacrifice by the high-souled men of an earlier day, gloriously crowned by the establishment of free government upon this continent, that it will fill with a just pride the heart of every true American and of every Irishman in the liberty-loving little nation beyond the sea.

That colorful tribute was written in 1918 when O'Brien had accumulated and published only half of the evidence he was to gather. The debt to him is great for the carefully constructed data on the Irish in the American Revolution, for his thoroughly researched articles on the Irish in the pre-Revolutionary and the post-Revolutionary eras, and, most of all, for his concentration on the Scotch-Irish myth. His demolition turned up stone after stone so that later researchers had only to follow his steps to confirm his conclusions, to find additional information, and, of course, in some cases, to reinterpret his data in view of later findings.

O'Brien may not have succeeded in destroying the Scotch-Irish myth (the myth is dear to some hearts) but he did force most later historians either to clarify their terms, distinguishing between "Protestant Irish" and "Scotch Irish" and "Ulster Irish," or else to use a Celtic thesis that puts together those from the Gaelic areas of Ireland, Scotland, Wales, and England.

Although O'Brien pointed the way for future researchers, none have followed to the end all the paths he took (except genealogists, perhaps). Full-time historians are aghast at what O'Brien did part-time. Despite the advantage of graduate assistants, doctoral advisees, related archeological finds, microfilms, computers and other modern technology, they usually limit themselves to one area. O'Brien researched and copied data from all thirteen colonies and from parts of these colonies which would be formed into new states. He used town, county, provincial, and state vital statistics of births, marriages, deaths, and burials. Rummaging through records in dusty courthouse basements and attics, he studied land grants, deeds, transfers, wills, probate proceedings, intents to marry, witnesses to documents, guardianships, sureties, claims, contracts, warrants, bond-servant issues, apprenticeships, and criminal matters. In the religious area, he combed church records for baptisms, marriages, burials. He noted cemetery inscriptions, sermons, conversions and expulsions, acceptances to admission, and warnings of non-conformity.

From various government sources, he listed officials, elections, voters' lists, tax rolls, freemen's lists, petitions, militia rosters, and correspondence between leaders. He delved into port records, custom house lists, captains' commissions, mariners' rolls, ships' lists, emigrant lists, arrivals and departures of vessels, sinking and loss of ships, fishery petitions and transactions. He analyzed items in newspapers; the records and advertisements of schoolmasters and merchants; the records of the French-English War, Lord Dunmore's War, the Revolutionary War, and the many colonial Indian wars. He pursued his quest in the private areas of extant personal diaries and records, family histories and genealogies, and genealogists' ancestral tracings. He made use of local historical and genealogical societies and of library collections.

From all of these records he excerpted Irish surnames, Irish references, and Irish identification. His work is so meticulously documented, his lists of names so long, his studies so voluminous, his claims so balanced by explanation, that one essay cannot do justice to his work. What follows is a blend of O'Brien's and the author's own research. Because it would be awkward to distinguish between them, such distinctions will usually not be made.

THE NEW ENGLAND COLONIES

The claim that colonial New England was exclusively English is disproved by the finding that the Irish settled in the 17th century not only in early Massachusetts but as far as Maine and Connecticut. In 1639, when Scotland rose in rebellion, King Charles I and his Deputy in Ireland tried to prevent a similar Irish rising by securing the loyalty of the Irish with a civil and religious Oath of Allegiance. Irish who refused were arrested and transported to the West Indies or American plantations as bondservants. A decade later, Oliver Cromwell transported far greater numbers of Irish Catholics in more degrading conditions as virtual slaves. Genealogical research based on Hotten's *Lists of Persons of Quality, 1600-1700* and Brandow's *Omitted Chapters from Hotten's Original Lists* indicates that some of these transportees from Irish Catholic backgrounds rose from bondage and founded families in New England. Colonial records of the 17th century show children with names such as MacCarthy, O'Kelley, O'Brien, and

O'Sullivan sitting side-by-side with Puritan pupils under schoolmasters with names such as Fitzgerald, Hickey, Murphy, Maloney, and McMahon. Irish names appear in the 17th century on "Deeds and Conveyances Recorded at the Registry of Deeds for Suffolk County, Massachusetts"; on "Residents of Boston Who Signed as Witnesses to Deeds Recorded in Suffolk County"; on various legal instruments, tax lists, and custom house entries; on the vital records and baptisms from towns and churches; and on lists of those who took the Oath that they may have refused to take in Ireland.

O'Brien was asked by his fellow Catholics: "Why mortify us by the continued publication, from the Baptist and Methodist church records, of the names of all those Irish apostates?" He answered that this was the only way to find proof of the Irish presence in New England and other colonies. It was unfortunate, he felt, that they had to abandon their faith to survive; also, some may have been Protestant before coming to New England. These mostly involuntary immigrants had little choice. A powerless minority, they could not even marry except as Protestants. They did not have the support system, as in Ireland, of an underground Church, of hedge schools, and of oneness in faith with the majority of their countrymen.

In 1640, in Maine (then part of Massachusetts), Christopher Lawson purchased from the Indians a large tract on the Kennebec near present-day Bath and named it "Ireland." In 1720, Irish-born Robert Temple chartered five ships and brought over several hundred people from County Cork to settle on the other side of the river in present-day Lincoln County. Trouble with Indians gradually discouraged and drove away the settlers, and the colony passed into history as the "Lost Town of Cork, Maine."

In Scarborough, Maine, marriage and baptismal registers of the First Congregational and the Presbyterian churches testify to the Irish presence with names like Kelley, Mooney, McLoughlin, and O'Brien. Fitzgeralds, Sullivans, and Kellys appear on land transfers, deeds, depositions, and militia rolls. Similar Irish names are on the town and church records of Georgetown, Brunswick, Kittery, Falmouth, Biddeford, Hallowell, Kennebeck, Gorham, Merrill, Livingston, Limerick, Wiscasset, Warren, Canaan, and elsewhere. Georgetown shows twenty-three intentions to marry in which one or both partners had Irish nativity. Brunswick militia company records of 1723 show that fourteen of its thirty-two men were born in Ireland. Georgetown and Warren indicate Irish nativity for many men mustered for the French-English Wars. At the outbreak of the Revolutionary War, nativity alone did not distinguish the Irish, for many were in Maine for the second and third generation.

New Hampshire's provincial records and the collections of the New Hampshire Historical Society for the 17th and 18th centuries mention hundreds of Irish names and Irish places of birth. In 1664, Cornelius Leary, Teague Drisco, Jeremiah O'Connor, and Dany Kelly received grants at Exeter. Timothy Dalton, Philip Carter, Daniel O'Shaw, William Healy, Richard Shannon, and Dennis Brian are some of the Irish identified on 17th century records of juries, petitions, and militia companies.

In the 18th century, Ireland was remembered in the founding of the towns of Antrim, Derry, Londonderry, and Dublin, all in New Hampshire. Portsmouth lists John Fitzgerald and Stephen Pendergass, Irish, as taxpayers. Portsmouth signers of the Revolutionary Pledge included men named Clancy, Dempsey, Driscoll, Furness, and Fitzgerald. Schoolmaster Joshua Tate of Somersworth left a chatty diary that discussed births, marriages, and deaths among the Irish, for whom he had no particular liking. He also described characteristics that he attributed to the Irish, ranging from those of Captain John Garvin, "an admirable ship's master," to Patrick Murphy, an "eminent thief" who stole a child's bag of sugar.

In Vermont (where New Hampshire and New York disputed jurisdiction before and after France relinquished its claim), there are Irish names in council and town records, in local historical society collections, in newspapers, and on muster rolls. The Power brothers, who emigrated from Waterford to Massachusetts in 1680 before settling in Vermont, bred numerous farmers, schoolmasters, and physicians, who settled in Woodstock with an "s" added to their names. Pittsford had its share of Powers, stemming from Jeremiah Power, who came also via Massachusetts.

In Rutland, "John Murray, an Irishman" is identified in 1761 as the first grantee of land, and William Powers of Irish parentage as the first white child born in town. Irish natives Daniel McDuffie and his wife settled in Bradford in 1720, but later moved to Maine where Daniel became a schoolmaster and sent five sons to fight in the French-English Wars. Dublin-born Crean Brush of Westminster was a prominent landower, attorney, and member of the Colonial Assembly. Irish nativity and Irish names like Keenan, McCowen, Ryan, McCarthy, and Murphy testify to the presence of Irish in a dozen other Vermont towns.

The Puritan divines may have been inhospitable to the Irish, whether Catholic, Anglican, or Presbyterian, but the first Governor of the Massachusetts Bay Colony (John Winthrop, who had been educated at Trinity College in Dublin) was not. Irish came in the earliest days of settlement as transportees and redemptioners, immigrants who paid for their voyage by contracting to be bondservants for a definite period. Voluntary immigration was never strong, but from 1633, with the encouragement of Winthrop and of Governor Bradford of Plymouth Colony, Irish families, as well as individual indentured servants, arrived from all provinces. Some of these 17th century Irish were O'Dougherty, O'Brien, Murffie, Maccarty, and Roache in Salem; Murphy, O'Mahoney, and Sullivant in Brookline; Callahan, Moore, Reyley, Healy, and Ireland in Charlestown.

After the disastrous winter of 1630-31, the Massachusetts colonists sent to Ireland for food. Provisions arrived just as they were reduced to subsisting on acorns and mussels. In 1675-76, the colony was again devastated by King Philip's War, in which several hundred settlers were killed and several hundred homes burned. Ireland raised money for relief, sent the ship *Katherine* with supplies, and directed that distribution be made to the poor and needy with no distinction as to religious beliefs.

Two interesting 17th century Massachusetts redemptioners were Cornelius Merry and Matthew Clesson of Northampton. After they had served their bondage and applied for land, they found that their acquired liberty was limited. It did not give them the desirable rights and privileges of citizenship. In 1663, the town granted "Cornelius the Irishman three akers upon condition he build upon it and make improument within one yeer, yet not so as to make him capabele of acting in town affaires no more than he had before it was granted to him." Clesson also was granted three acres. The grants prohibited Merry and Clesson from gaining citizenship, although they had taken the required Oath of Allegiance.

Perhaps the Irish did take the Oath lightly, for Merry was ordered to undergo twenty stripes in 1666 for making seditious speeches against English authority. He survived the stripes and the odds, acquired more land, and founded a family which spread to Long Island and Connecticut, with five generations giving the name Cornelius to the first-born. Matthew Clesson prospered by getting more land in odd parcels. His descendants were prominent as scouts and soldiers in the Indian and border wars. A sixth generation Matthew Clesson served in the Revolution.

The 17th and 18th century records of Massachusetts have hundreds of Irish names. Some have creative spellings that require linguistic detective work, matching with other records, and even a bit of imagination: O'Donnell is hidden under Dwinnell, Cassidy under Capsada, Donahue under Doritha, Fitzgerald under Fitchgerls, McCurdy or McCarthy under Mackerdey, O'Mahoney under Omahoine. Easier to recognize are Molooney, Dayly, Ryon, Barrye, Mackginnis, Obrine, Reila, Malonia, Dorrety, and Meccarty. The founding of the Charitable Irish Society of Boston in 1737 indicates that many of these Irish prospered enough in material goods and felt secure enough in their identity to be able to help others of their race.

In Connecticut, to the hundreds of Irish names on the records can be added the many more poor bondsmen and bondswomen for whom records no longer exist. The lists of original immigrants for the years 1634 and 1635 show that English Dissenters were accompanied to Connecticut by Irish bearing the names of the oldest Irish septs. John Riley and his wife, Grace O'Dea, who came from Ireland in 1634, had many children, as did John's brothers, Garrett and Miles. The Rileys' descendants appear on the Revolutionary rolls under at least five surname spellings. Men named Lynch and Hogan were paying taxes in Hartford in 1659. In New London, in the 1660s, Miles Moore, Michael Rice, Thomas Roach, and John Keenan took the Oath of Allegiance and Supremacy and were admitted as Freemen.

Names such as Mullen, Kelly, Kenny, Rice, Jordan, Sullivan, O'Brien, Carroll, Shay, Driscoll, Connor, Flynn, Murphy, and McGuire appear frequently in 18th century Connecticut at every place where records have been preserved. Joshua Hempstead of New London, Justice of the Peace and dabbler in many occupations, made note in his diary of the Irish sea-captains on the Cork-New London route who disembarked passengers from Ireland on every voyage. In 1741, he officiated at the marriage of "Samuel Wangs, an Indian, unto Barbara Rion, an Irish woman." In his travels to other colonies he suspected almost every "Irish Man" he met of being "Roman," but he did not suspect the Irish of being Scotch.

In Rhode Island, the first Irish were indentured servants or redemptioners. It took time in Roger Williams' colony, so strongly anti-Catholic, for Irish to be above suspicion of being Papists and to be accepted as landowners. Mid-18th century records indicate a number of Irish being admitted as Freemen after taking the required Oath, men with names like Casey, Fitzgerald, Heffernan, Kelly, and Higgins.

ANN "GOODY" GLOVER. The story of one uncounted Irish woman in New England is tragic but worth telling. In 1688, Ann Glover of Massachusetts became a martyr for a faith that she had certainly been unable to practice and a race that she may have tried to hide.

The Puritans, whose claims of being persecuted and of exiling themselves for religious freedom are memorialized in school texts and Plymouth monuments, themselves had few, if any, peers among persecutors of religion, when they had the opportunity. Those of Irish heritage still find it hard to forget the Cromwellian invasions, when the Puritan General killed all before him in the name of religion and the greater glory of God. His soldiers' appetite for killing the Irish was whetted by sermons of Puritan ministers such as the famous Nathaniel Ward who, in 1647 on the eve of the invasion, wrote:

Cursed be he who holdeth back the sword from blood: yea cursed be he that maketh not the sword stark drunk with Irish blood; who doth not recompense them double for their treachery to the English; but maketh them in heaps on heaps, and their country the dwelling place of dragons - an astonishment for nations. Let not that eye look for pity, nor hand be spared, that pities or spares them; and let him be cursed that curseth them not bitterly.

After such exhortations bore deadly fruit at the massacre at Drogheda, Cromwell himself was pleased to report to the English Parliament that "the enemy were about 3,000 strong in the town. I believe we put to the sword the whole number .. in this very place [St. Peter's Church] a thousand of them were put to the sword, fleeing thither for safety." This was followed in October 1649 by the massacre of 2,000 men, women, and children at Wexford, after which Cromwell reported to his Puritan constituents that he thought "it not good or just to restrain the soldiers from their right of pillage, nor from doing of execution on the enemy."

The 17th century New England theocracy produced little Cromwells, all prodigious writers, all self-justifiers, all thundering against abominations, which would be anything that did not adhere to the narrow beliefs of the Puritan divines. The Irish in Massachusetts may have tried to keep a low profile, but they obviously were ready victims for pastors looking for "abominations."

Increase Mather, born in Cambridge, Massachusetts and educated at Harvard, took another degree in Dublin in 1658. As pastor of Old North Church and later president of Harvard, he became a religious and political decision maker in the colony. He was asked to give an opinion on water trials for witches. Suspected witches were bound and cast into wells or deep water. If they kept their heads afloat, it was assumed that they were indeed witches and confederates of the devil, and thus guilty; so they were killed. If they sank, they were innocent and acquitted, but, of course, quite dead. In 1684, Increase wrote the opinion that this was a fallacious and non-scriptural way of trying witches, and set the stage for more dramatic types of trials with witnesses, testimony, and role-playing.

Although the Salem witchcraft trials of 1692 were not greatly different from contemporary ones in Europe, they became a shame to the community. Twenty years later, the convictions of the deceased witches were annulled. Somehow, lost in history and never annulled, was the conviction of Ann "Goody" Glover, whose death had preceded the famous trials by four years. From the writings of Increase Mather and his son Cotton, we can get clues that Goody's real crime and abomination was not just being a witch, but being Irish and, worse, Catholic. The last would have been grounds for banishment, since Catholics were forbidden to enter all the Massachusetts colonies.

Banishment was not enough for Cotton Mather, who did much writing about his own mystical visions, soul-searching, and body-punishing. The innocent souls of children had been blackened and ensnared by an agent of the devil in Rome. In his *Magnalia*, Mather describes Goody Glover as "one of the wild Irish," a secret Papist, who "profest herself a Roman Catholick and could recite the Pater Noster in Latin very readily." Goody was imperiling what Mather considered the holy purpose of the Puritan settlements in New England "to raise up a bulwarke against the Kingdome of Anti-christ which the Jesuits labour to build up in all parts of the world." His fierce and frequent cries that the French Jesuits and the Quebec Catholics must be destroyed show clearly from where he expected the anti-Christ to descend if New England did not continue to attack and burn settlements in Maine and northward.

To Increase and Cotton Mather, Ann Glover was a symbol of all that they abhorred. With magistrates, physicians, and other ministers, they examined the children of her master, John Goodwin. The children claimed that Goody had bewitched them and sent them into fits. As the interrogations continued, the children responded with bigger and better tales. Some historians today assert that Cotton Mather was the most brilliant man of his era (his father being the second); that he was pious and possessed an encyclopedic mind; and that he was a master of sciences and several languages. They also point out that he meticulously investigated the stories told of Goody, and of Goody's daughter Mary; and that after investigating, he sincerely believed the children's stories.

Cotton Mather wrote that the "vile hag" Goody caused the children "to fly like geese, and be carried with an incredible swiftness through the air." He accepted and encouraged the witness who had seen Goody fly through the air and "had seen Glover sometimes come down her chimney." Mather reported that the devil spoke through her in devil's tongues at the trial. The terrified woman had reverted to speaking her native Irish.

Goody was jailed for several months, during which time more children advanced to the spotlight and added their stories of dark terror and enchantment. Mather reported that when he visited her and asked her to say the Lord's Prayer, she did so in Latin, Irish, and English, but could not end it. Since it was common belief that the prayer could not be completed by a Catholic or a witch, this confirmed her guilt. On November 16, 1688, Ann Glover was hanged in Boston. *(See Note 2: Ann "Goody" Glover.)*

By November, the main excitement had diminished. Goody, after all, was just a menial, not an important person in the community. She rated only a casual entry in the diary of Samuel Sewall, who was preparing his cabin on the *America* for a trip to Europe. On November 16, he wrote, "The Upholsterer tells me that the Ship is loaden too much by the head and sails badly. About 11 A.M. the Widow Glover is drawn by to be hang'd. Mr. Larkin seems to be Marshal. The Constables attend, and Justice Bullivant there."

Sewall was to be the presiding judge at the witch trials in 1692, about which much has been written. Nineteen witches were convicted and hanged, one of them being a woman who had tried to befriend Goody Glover and her daughter. The community hysteria did not begin to abate until the witch hunters accused the colonial leaders and the new governor's wife of involvement in witchcraft. In 1697, Judge Sewall publicly accepted his "blame and shame" for his part in the trials, and afterwards spent a day in each year in fast and reparations for his guilt.

But no one repented the 1688 execution of Ann Glover, who was quickly forgotten along with her daughter who had been spared from the hangman. There was no let-up for anti-Catholicism in New England. In 1700, Massachusetts passed an anti-priest law, similar to that of New York and broader and more severe than the 1647 act. "Roman Catholics," said John Adams in 1765, "are as scarce [in New England] as a comet or earthquake." What Irish there were in New England were intermarrying with Yankees, joining Protestant churches, and diluting their Irish identity. Perhaps a few stood by quietly and sadly each year while the pope was hanged in effigy at Boston Common, until George Washington's prohibition, in 1775, of this annual ritual.

If any did try to pass their Irish heritage to their children, they may have told them of Ann Glover, convicted as a witch in 1688 for speaking Irish and praying in Latin.

THE MIDDLE COLONIES

Records of colonial New York provide a wealth of information on Irish pioneers. The earliest reference is to John Colman, one of Henry Hudson's crew, who was killed in an encounter with Indians. In 1641, Cork-born William Hayes came from Curacao to act as physician to the Dutch. The Minutes of the Burgomasters and Schepens note James Farrel, an Irishman, in 1656; James Brady (aka Jeems Braddy) in 1660; Thomas Higgins in 1661; Thomas Lewis in 1662. John Anderon who dwelt and traded in Catskill is recorded as "Jan

Andriessen de Iersman van Dublin." At least Jan was identified as Irish. Dennis McCarthy, Hugh O'Neil, William Walsh, and John Fitzgerald are listed as Dutch.

During the English rule in New York, Governor Dongan recommended that natives of Ireland be sent to the colony. Soon Irish settled in Albany, Orange, Columbia, Westchester, Ulster, Queens, and Suffolk counties. They gave Irish names to their homes and farms, but most of the names have died out.

The Huguenot, Presbyterian, and Reformed Dutch churches of New York have several hundred Irish names with peculiar spellings on their registers. The Reformed Dutch church at Kingston has fascinating records which note the Irish birth or parentage of people with the following names: Jerri Karrol, William Bel, Moses Cavener, Hanna Cotain, Huyg Flanengen, Hue Tachety, Andries Kermer, and Molly Kammel. Also interesting are Fort Orange (Albany) Dutch Reformed records noting as Irish Cornelius Kalleheyn, Hendrick Hogan, Cathalynjje McManus, Pieter Maccarty, and Johannie Fine.

Unless one looked carefully at the historical studies of Newtown and Hempstead by James Riker Jr. and Henry Onderdonk, one might not consider searching Long Island records for any but Dutch and English. Some Irish had settled in all New York's Long Island counties in the 17th and early 18th centuries. Several married into the noted Riker family, as, at a later date, did William James MacNeven, a leader of the United Irishmen of 1798. MacNeven, who had received his medical degree in Vienna, was appointed to one of the ten professorial chairs when Columbia College and the New York College of Physicians and Surgeons merged in 1813. He was a frequent contributor to medical journals and, according to author Thomas Gallagher, "one of the first and finest teachers of those discoveries and doctrines which raised chemistry into a science." MacNeven is buried with his wife in the Riker Family Cemetery in Queens, New York, but has a monument at St. Paul's in Manhattan.

Two other United Irish exiles who lived and were eventually buried in New York were Samuel Neilson, Presbyterian minister from County Down, and Thomas Addis Emmet, brother of the famous Robert who was hanged, drawn, and quartered publicly in Dublin.

Staten Island's Irish association dates back to Thomas Dongan of County Kildare, Governor of the Province of New York from 1683 to 1688. Always fond of the island, Dongan acquired 25,000 acres there, on part of which the present community of Dongan Hills commemorates his name. He successfully fought New Jersey's rather reasonable geographical claims and kept Staten Island for New York, although the boundary dispute was not settled officially for another one hundred and fifty years.

Staten Island was put on the Irish transportation map when Daniel O'Brien added a stop there to his stage-coach and stage-wagon service from Manhattan to Philadelphia via Amboy. He had an Irish competitor, Darby Doyle (aka Darbe Dyall), who with his wife and brother provided all aspects of service: stage boats, coaches, building, repairs.

One can do a scholarly research project and find Irish names on all New York records from Suffolk County to the Adirondacks to the Mohawk Valley. It is more exciting, however, to wander among old cemeteries in places like Manhattan, Albany, and New Paltz and find tombstones bearing Irish names among the graves of Dutch, Huguenot, and Anglican pioneers. *(See Note 3: Methodists.)*

In New Jersey, many names beginning with Mac and O in colonial probate records are clearly Irish: James O'Bryan in 1739, Philip O'Brien in 1742, Edmond O'Brien in 1757, William O'Brien in 1759 - all in different areas. Many testamentary documents have names like O'Neill, O'Hanlon, O'Hara, and Kelly. The records of the Reformed Protestant Dutch churches at Hackensack and Schraalenburgh have the marriage of Irish-born Dennis Sweeney; the birth of William, son of Mykel Kelly; the birth of Nelly, daughter of Dennis McGahagan and Catarina Nagel; the birth of Jacob, son of Patrick Sullivan. The records of the First Presbyterian Church at Morristown show the marriage of Peggy O'Brien; the baptism of Mary McMahon; the deaths of Francis McCarty, James O'Hara, and John O'Neil; the acceptance of Sarah O'Connor. Under the spelling of "ffeitzgered" (the double initial consonant being an ancient form of capitalization), Edward Fitzgerald bought 100 acres in Salem County in 1703. Another Fitzgerald appears as Gerrit Fitzgarril. Fitzgeralds are on official records of eight counties of New Jersey in the 18th century.

The vast immigration of Irish to colonial Pennsylvania has been called all "Scotch-Irish", but history, as well as names and birthplaces of settlers, belies this. When William Penn founded Pennsylvania in 1682 with the idea of religious freedom for all, he brought with him a number of Irish, mainly from Cork and Wexford, whom he described as having "substance" and "property." That many were Catholic is shown in the records of the Franciscan missionaries who visited them during the reigns of Kings Charles II and James II.

After Penn's proprietorship was suspended upon the accession of William and Mary, he was able to regain his rights to the colony only by accepting certain conditions. He had to accept the English penal laws against Catholics and a Test Act barring Catholics from public office. Nevertheless, Irish immigration continued, since the Quakers conceded an irregular kind of religious liberty by avoiding application of English laws.

Early immigration from Ireland to Pennsylvania was mixed: Quaker, Protestant, Catholic. Quakers had suffered imprisonment for not conforming to the Church of Ireland. Presbyterians had been deprived of statutory rights and privileges by the Test Act. Catholics had been persecuted the most severely by the penal laws which aimed to wipe out religion, race, and culture. Even Church of Ireland members had found that economic and political measures made them second-class citizens, losing in Ireland their rights as Englishmen.

The most significant immigration of Irish Quakers to America occurred between 1680 and 1750, with Pennsylvania becoming the major receiver after its founding. Quaker converts in Ireland were English and Scots settlers who had replaced their swords with plows. Only one Quaker family with a distinctly Irish name, O'Mooney, emigrated to Pennsylvania, and, in the colony, the increase of Quakers from Celtic stock was negligible. Yet the Irish Quakers, though mostly not Celtic, must be counted as Irish. They identified themselves as Irish, and were identified by others as "Irish Friends."

Colonial Pennsylvania Protestants with old Irish names had no doubts about their Irish pre-Norman roots. Those whose ancestors had been Norman, English, or Scots had a heritage of becoming Irish during their generations in Ireland. Most Protestant Irish brought to Pennsylvania that same burning desire for freedom and passion for justice that led such Protestant nationalists as Henry Joy McCracken and Lord Edward Fitzgerald to rebellion and death in Ireland before the end of the 18th century.

A great number of Irish immigrants were Catholic. Mass was said in homes by priests who preached in the Irish language. St. Joseph's Church, founded in Philadelphia before 1729, was opened or closed depending on how strictly the penal laws were being enforced. Before 1745, Catholics had settled in Carlisle, where, with only rare visits from priests, they kept their faith alive and planted the seeds for an Irish Catholic community still identifiable in the 20th century.

Philadelphia was the starting place for the Irish in Pennsylvania, but they spread quickly to farming communities and to the wilderness that would become farms. Catholics, in particular, saw the advantage of maintaining a low profile in areas remote from officialdom. Runaway servants, whose masters sold them to undesirable new masters or who refused to release them at the end of their terms of bondage, disappeared into the outlands.

In all colonies, a master had authority to add to an original term of servitude on various grounds, some improbable technicalities and some very minor infractions. Indentured servants and redemptioners hotly resented abuses that kept them in bondage for additional years and frequently appealed in court, sometimes successfully, for their rights. Penal transportees, feeling it was less likely that they would get justice from a court that considered them fortunate to have gotten a term of servitude instead of the gallows, were most likely to try to escape to a new place and a new identity.

The Quakers, despite their professed toleration, had some members who were concerned that they might be outnumbered by the Irish, especially Papists. Quaker committees, Anglican ministers, and Assembly members combined to procure passage of bills levying duties on Irish immigrants and taxing those who brought over Irish indentured servants. Ships' captains avoided payment by landing in New Jersey or Delaware, and Irish immigration continued to flow to and through Philadelphia. In 1717, Irish settled in Lancaster County, in 1720 in Bucks County, in 1723 in Cumberland and Dauphin counties, and in 1724 in York County.

The land on which the present city of Pittsburgh sits was sold in 1783 by its Penn family proprietors to two Irish immigrants, James Craig and Stephen Bayard. The land passed to another Irish immigrant, James O'Hara of County Mayo, who willed it to his daughter, Mary Croghan, who had married an Irishman. But Pittsburgh had an even earlier Irish history as the site of English Fort Pitt and French Fort Duquesne. Indian trader George Croghan of County Sligo is credited with having been the first "English" white man active in the area. In 1760, Fort Pitt's army and civilian listings had names such as John Sinnott, Margaret Doyle, Patrick McCarthy, and Richard McMahon. Back in 1756, Fort Duquesne's French chaplain registered the baptism of Ellen, daughter of Irish Catholics John and Sarah Condon, who had reached the fort after being captured by the Shawnees. Many of the French entries identify Irish Catholic children, parents, godparents, and bridal couples who had been Indian captives.

In the American Revolution, Irish enlisted enthusiastically to fight against England. When the Continental Congress called for recruits in 1775, Pennsylvania led the way by providing six of the first ten companies of the Continental Army. What started as Thompson's Rifle Battalion in the Carlisle area increased from six to nine companies, two predominantly German, seven predominantly Irish. Names such as these abounded: Matthew Dougherty, William O'Hara, Patrick Sullivan, Michael Fitzpatrick, Daniel Mangan. After Meath-born General William Thompson was captured, Colonel Edward Hand, born in County Offaly (then Kings County), took command.

Morgan's Rifle Corps, recruited from western Pennsylvania and the Shenandoah Valley, was described in English correspondence as a band of wild, lawless, and disaffected Irishmen. English observers came closer to the mark than historians who, perhaps not having looked at the muster rolls, call Morgan's Corps "Scotch-Irish." The rolls are composed largely of men with names like Daniel Callahan, John Hickey, Patrick Lynch, Patrick Donahue, and Maurice Sullivan.

The regiments of Colonels Hand, Magaw, Shaw, and Haslett, all four Irish natives, covered the Continental Army's retreat from Long Island. Major John Kelly destroyed the bridge at Stony Brook as the Army left Trenton. Captain William O'Neill kept the British army at a standstill at Brandywine. Frontier rifleman Timothy Murphy shot British General Fraser out of his saddle at Saratoga.

The number of Irish in the Pennsylvania Line was far out of proportion to their numbers in the colony. General Lee wrote that the Line of Pennsylvania could properly be called the Line of Ireland. The British agreed, one of their officers writing in 1776 that the rebels in the Pennsylvania Line "consist chiefly of Irish redemptioners and convicts, the most audacious rascals existing." By 1781, the British realized that the audacious rascals, whose ancestors had been ground into relentless servitude and poverty in Ireland, had ground the British Army to a halt.

DELAWARE AND MARYLAND

In Delaware, the Swedish and Dutch settlers arrived first, but the Irish appeared in the province before the end of the 17th century. In 1689, Bryan MacDonnell and his wife Mary Doyle, from Wicklow, settled on 100 acres in Newcastle County. Bryan had served for three years in an Irish Volunteer Regiment loyal to King James II. He signed his will MacDonnell, but some of his descendants changed the spelling to McDonald, McDonalc, McDaniel, and even McDowd. The land and will books show that Bryan settled among Irish neighbors: Murphy, Dowling, Delaney, McGinnis, McCarthy, McMahon, and others. Several hundred Irish names are found on the marriage and baptismal records of the Swedish Church in Wilmington, including Francis O'Nayle, James Macgraw, Robert McCarthy, Patrick Fitch Patrick, Jeremiah Sulivane, Dennis Sullovain, John Goggin, and Timothy Mahoney. Marriages far outnumbered baptisms, suggesting that legal reasons, not intermarriages, sent the Irish to a Swedish-speaking pastor. Lay Catholics probably administered the Sacrament of Baptism under the condition of necessity, then hoped for a priest to arrive to perform the solemn ceremonies and to record the baptism.

The attempts of George and Cecil Calvert, the first and second Barons of Baltimore, to establish a proprietary colony in Maryland with religious freedom for all seemed successful when the General Assembly passed the Edict of Toleration in 1649. The Edict, however, had a short life of five years. During the English Civil Wars, Virginia invaded Maryland, deported any priests who had not fled or hid, and excluded Catholics from toleration. When Lord Baltimore regained control in 1658, he had to accept some limiting conditions, but the climate was still at least as favorable to Irish Catholics and Dissenters as in their homeland.

The official but incomplete lists of original settlers who set sail in 1633 in the *Ark* and the *Dove* indicate English whenever nationality is shown. The ships put in at Barbadoes for supplies and repairs. According to tradition, some Irish joined the passengers. When Leonard Calvert applied for five thousand acres on the basis of having paid for transport of twenty-five able-bodied men to the colony, he included "Daniel an Irishman." However or from wherever the Irish came, they were in Maryland from its foundation.

The first confirmed Irish settler appearing on extant records was Brian Kelly, in 1634, the first year of the colony. In 1635, Kelly appears on land records in St. Mary's County. He appears a few years later in a court case with fellow Irishmen Baltasar Codd and Cornelius O'Sullivant.

Identified Irish on 17th century land grants, wills, and judicial papers were John Kelly, Richard Darcy, Hugh O'Neile, William Ryley, Philip Conner, and David O'Doughorty. Less identifiable by name, but Irish by their own claim, were Peter Bathe, Hugh Conn, Nicholas Keyn, Nicholas Keating, Samuel Lane, Robert Lee, Stephen Marty, John Minnhane, Marke Pheype, Michael Rochford, Joseph Walker, and George Yeedon. In 1678, the *Encrease* brought a shipload of Irish servants from Youghal, County Cork. All assigned to William Sharpe of Talbot County, this group included Margaret Gerrard, Morgan Connell, John Coughlan, Daniel Dalley, Cornelius Driscole, Morish Dulin, John Feakins, Patrick Freeman, Thomas Smith, and Thomas Shehawne.

In 1683, a six thousand acre tract in present-day Cecil County was granted to Edmund O'Dwyre and fifteen other Irishmen who had come as indentured servants several years before. It was called New Munster and O'Dwyre named his first home plantation Fethard. New Munster was adjacent to Roscommon-born George Talbot's 100,000 acre tract known as New Connaught and Wicklow-born Brian O'Daly's similar tract of New Leinster. Other Irish called their grants after their native places: Darby Nolan at Bandon, John Lane at Charleville, Pierce Nowland at Fethard, Alexander Mullany at Sligo, Robert Lynch at Dublin, William Russell at Carlow.

In the 1680s, Colonel William Stevens of Rehobeth asked that a Presbyterian minister be sent from Ireland. Reverend Francis Makemie, born in Donegal and licensed at Lagan, answered the request. In 1683, he founded what is credited with being the oldest continuously active Presbyterian church in America. The "Father of

Presbyterianism" worked in other colonies and founded other presbyteries, but Makemie was first called to and associated with Maryland.

In 1714, a historic controversy broke out among three Irishmen struggling for supremacy. Governor John Hart of Cavan represented the Protestant side; Charles Carroll and his kinsman, Thomas MacNamara, the Roman Catholic. The current Lord Baltimore was an absentee proprietor who had apostatized in 1713 from the Roman Catholic Church. The Assembly was Protestant. That toleration was greater in Maryland than in England is indicated by the fact that this struggle went on for several years with victories and defeats on both sides.

In 1716 the ongoing controversy was fueled by the trial of William Fitz-Redmond and Edward Coyle, charged with "drinking the Pretender's health and preaching contemptibly of the King." The Irish Catholics in Maryland, who had sympathized with James II in 1688, sympathized with his son, James III, the Old Pretender, when he tried to regain the throne. Fitz-Redmond (a nephew of Carroll) and Coyle had expressed their favor by loading four of the great cannons on Courthouse Hill and firing them in honor of the Pretender. Thomas MacNamara, the attorney for the defense, challenged Governor Hart with "Let me see who dares to try Fitz-Redmond and Coyle by this Commission." Carroll, as agent for the Proprietor, produced a writ giving him the right to decide on the fines for the defendants. The Governor had Carroll summoned before the Assembly for exercising powers without taking the anti-Papist oath. When Carroll denied that the oath was in force, Hart said it was, and recorded his opposition to employing any Papists in public affairs.

While Carroll, a strong and clever man, was fencing with Hart, MacNamara added to the action. The Governor objected to his dramatic behavior in court. Lord Baltimore, from across the sea, advised MacNamara to submit. When he refused, the Assembly barred him from practice. MacNamara now proved himself as adroit as Carroll. He made his official appeal so complicated that his lordship had to hire three top lawyers in England. The lawyers advised the Proprietor to veto the Assembly's action and MacNamara was restored to the Bar. He spent the next three years until his death contesting with the Governor.

Hart was probably relieved when he was appointed Governor of the Leeward Islands and bade farewell to Maryland. Unfortunately for him, Irishman Hart found there another belligerent Irish lawyer who engaged him in litigation and appeals. Even worse, he had an uncontrollable Assembly.

Unless sentenced to permanent exile, bondservants could apply to return home when they had worked out their freedom. Joshua and

Robert Doyne, brothers who had been transported to Maryland about 1670, returned to County Wexford. The journey turned out to be the first leg of a round trip, since both men then emigrated as freemen in 1680. Joshua brought his wife with him to the promising new land.

A family that turned down an offer to return to Ireland was that of the Courseys from Cork. In 1658, newly arrived siblings Henry, John, William, and Catherine Coursey were granted eight hundred acres on the Wye River on Maryland's eastern shore. This estate, and those of several other Coursey kinsmen arriving before and after them, increased to thousands of acres. Most spelled the name Coursey, but one Captain Henry spelled it Courcy. In his will, he asked his sons to resume De Courcy (or de Courcy) as his family had spelled it in Ireland. He said "from the respectable and public manner in which my ancestors emigrated from Ireland, it cannot be believed that any necessity of concealment induced them to alter the original spelling." He blamed the spelling change on avoidance of a frenchified name because of poor relations between France and England. The de Courcys were descendants of the Anglo-Norman knight, John de Courcy, who conquered northeast Ulster in 1177, was made Earl of Ulster in 1181, and soon acquired through marriage a large tract of land around Kinsale in southwest Cork.

In 1763, William de Courcy of Wye River, Maryland, declined an invitation from cousins to return to Ireland to press a claim to be recognized as the 25th Baron Kingsale (Kinsale), an invitation that had recently been eagerly accepted by distant cousin and sailor John de Courcy of Rhode Island, who was already seated in the Irish House of Lords. William of Maryland chose not to dispute the matter. Abjuring all titles, he remained in Maryland. His descendants would not be Irish peers but United States citizens.

All 17th and 18th century records indicate increasing numbers of Irish in Maryland. Before the Revolution, Irish had settled in every county. During the Revolution, Irish served in the militia and regular regiments in great numbers. The muster rolls were rich with names of Irish-born, such as Thomas Bryan of Waterford, Thomas Forbes of Kildare, Martin Burke of Galway, and Farrel Hester of Roscommon. Names like Lynch, Kelly, and Murphy appear again and again.

Most famous among Revolutionary era leaders of Irish descent were the Carrolls. Charles Carroll of Carollton, grandson of "Charles the Emigrant," who arrived from Kings County in 1688, was a signer of the Declaration of Independence. Although his Catholic religion banned him from public office, he was an observer at the First Continental Congress. In 1776, when the religious restriction was removed, he became a delegate to the Continental Congress. Daniel Carroll, son of an Irish emigrant who became wealthy in Maryland and second cousin to Charles on the maternal side, was a leading constitutionalist. As a delegate to the Constitutional Convention, he wrote the Tenth Amendment, protecting states' rights. Daniel's younger brother, John, was the first Roman Catholic bishop of the United States. Starting with only twenty-four priests who had to minister to thirteen states and wide undeveloped territories, he charted the course for the Catholic Church in a country that would grow far beyond the dreams of the founding fathers.

VIRGINIA

The founding of Jamestown in 1607 began the continuous English colonization of America. The Virginia Charter of 1609 required the Oaths of Allegiance and Supremacy, abjuring Romanism and the Pope. Irish coming to Virginia were expected to be loyal to the current English sovereign and to conform to the Established Church. The 1641 proclamation of Governor Berkeley and an Act of the Assembly indicated fear of the presence of Catholics, English or Irish. In 1640, enforcement of laws against Catholics had become critical in England and in the part of Ireland actually controlled by the English. Priests had fled or hidden, but eleven known priests in England and ten in Ireland were found and executed in 1641-42. The situation was reflected in Virginia, which made attacks on Maryland on the grounds that the colony tolerated the practice of their religion by Catholics, that priests might cross into Virginia to exercise their ministry, and that Maryland was providing a refuge for Puritan emigrants from Virginia. The penal laws of England were confirmed by the March 1642 Act of the Virginia Assembly, part of which stated:

. . .according to a statute made in the third year of the reigne of our sovereign Lord King James of blessed memory, that no popish recusants should at any time hereafter exercize the place or places of secret councellors, register, comiss: surveyor or sheriffe, or any other publique place, but be utterly disabled for the same. . .none should be admitted into any of the aforesaid offices or places before he or they had taken the oath of allegiance and supremacy. . .and it is further enacted that the Statute in force [of James I] against popish recusants be duely executed in this government, and that it should not be lawfull under the penalties aforesaid for any popish priest that shall hereafter arrive to remaine above five days after warning given for his departure.

Nevertheless, one Irish-born Catholic priest risked the penalties. Alexander Plunkett was ordained in France in the Capuchin order and took the religious name of Christopher. He arrived in Virginia in 1680, probably to serve as a missionary on the estate of a relative, John Plunkett. He was arrested in the winter of 1689-90 and transported to "an island." (*See Note 4: Christopher Plunkett.*) One of his chroniclers, an Irish Capuchin writing in 1741, reported that

Christopher Plunkett suffered many brutalities before dying on this island in 1697, in his forty-eighth year.

In 1705, toleration was granted in Virginia to Protestant dissenters, but Catholics were deprived of the right to vote, declared incompetent as witnesses, and made liable for strict enforcement of the penal laws. In 1745, an order was issued for the arrest of priests suspected of crossing from Maryland. In 1756, fearful of the Jesuits and the influx of Irish immigrants, the Assembly ordered that the Oaths be taken anew in the colony.

The Irish in colonial Virginia will not be found, therefore, on Catholic church records, which, of course, are non-existent. Despite the limited information on other documents, the Irish can be found in the earliest settlements through inspection of Anglican (later Episcopalian) Church entries, ships' lists, delivery receipts for prisoners and bound transportees, musters of settlements, land grants, and deed transfers. In 1621, the ship *Flying Harte* landed Irish colonists at Newport News. In 1622, eight hundred Irish were transported for service on the plantations, with the warning that Irish Tories and convicts must be purged of their dangerous religious and political views.

Some Irish came as free adventurers and merchants, but most came as penal set-term or long-term bondsmen, or as indentured servants. The servant class included artisans, builders, traders, and schoolmasters, who were able to work out their redemption. The convict class, usually indicated by ship captains as sold for periods of seven to twenty years with their masters having ownership rights to resell them, had an advantage over their black counterparts. Their color could assist in escape.

Hotten's *Original Lists* have 17th century Virginia immigrants with names such as Murfie, MacBrian, Riley, Cassedy, Carroll, and O'Mullin. On these lists and other records immigrants Desmond O'Bryan, Teague Naughton, Patrick Conly, Brian Kelly, Dennis Hogan, and Donough Garvie testify by name to their Irishness. Richmond land office records indicate at least three hundred old Irish names on a list of 1623-1666 immigrants. Denis MacCartie (whose descendants were cousins of George Washington) received a land grant in 1691, and many other McCarthys received land grants thereafter. In the 17th and 18th century, grants to men with names like Burke, Brady, Brennan, Dermott, Fitzgerald, Hogan, Leary, Rourke, and Sullivan prove that the Irish continued to take up land.

The records at Christ Church (Episcopalian) in Middlesex show hundreds of Celtic and Norman-Irish names, including these christenings: Bryan Harkins, February 20, 1663; Cornelius Mullins, August 25, 1666; Katherine Farrell, April 12, 1685; Charles Mullins, November 14, 1686; Phebias Macguire, March 29, 1687; Elizabeth Hickey,

April 1, 1705. The Protestant Episcopal church of Overwharton Parish, Stafford County, for 1720-1758, records births for children with surnames Callahan, McCarthy, Heffernan, Carney, Kenney, Higgins, Murphy, and Kelly. Revolutionary War records of men serving in Virginia regiments have numerous Murphys and Kellys with many spelling variants.

Many Irish names appear on passenger lists from Barbadoes, Nevis, Antigua, Jamaica, and other West Indies islands, one 1678 list having at least ninety Irish names. These lists give significant under-counts for several reasons: (1) the Irish were registered English on the basis of their last port of embarkation; (2) the English were trying to destroy Irish nationality, and so Irish were frequently classified as English or British (Oliver Cromwell's son Richard wrote that transportation to the West Indies might make Englishmen and Christians of the heretic Irish); (3) Irish found it possible to lighten restrictions and oppression by accepting the English designation; (4) prudent Irish whose ancestors or themselves had been slaves or convict transportees anglicized their names before coming to Virginia or other colonies to avoid the danger of being returned to servitude; (5) many of the children and youths gathered up or kidnapped in the Cromwellian terror of the 1650s and shipped as slaves had no memory of their Irish surnames.

One of the important colonizers was Colonel James Patton, born at Newtown-Limavady, County Londonderry, Ireland, in 1692. In 1736, he received a grant of 120,000 acres west of the Blue Ridge Mountains. As owner and master of a ship, he made at least twenty-five trips to Ireland to bring over more than seven thousand people, mostly redemptioners, who served a set time to pay the cost of transportation, and then were free. Many followed Patton to his grant west of the Alleghenies and settled Draper's Meadows (now Blacksburg) in 1748, and Burke's Garden in 1754, the former named after Irish pioneer Eleanor Draper, the latter after Irishman James Burke, who had been one of Patton's redemptioners and frontier scouts.

Because of Patton's birthplace, these frontier families are often called Scotch-Irish, even by local historians. Patton, however, recruited not only Ulstermen of Scots ancestry but also Ulstermen of old Irish ancestry and Irish from the other three provinces. This is evidenced not only by his ship's ports and by the several Drapers and Burkes, but by surnames of other settlers: Boyle, Coffey, Doherty, Donaghue, Dillon, Ingles (aka English, a completely hibernicized name then), Laverty, Lawless, McGaughey, McCarthy, McCreary, Moore, Mooney, Tracy, and Fitzgerl (aka Fitzgerald).

Some of the first families of Virginia have descendants who barely recognize their Irish roots. The immigrant ancestor of the Meades was Andrew Meade, an Irish Catholic, born in Ballintober, Barony of Kerrycurrihy, County Cork, who emigrated near the end of the 17th century. The Sullivants (who added the *t*) trace back to Daniel Sullivan, who also emigrated from Munster in the late 1600s. Dennis Callaghan, who emigrated as a servant and became a businessman, gave his name to the town of Callaghan on the westward trail. Most of the Fitzgeralds came as bondsmen, but quickly became masters themselves of other servants. Some of the variant spellings in the records include: Fitzjarrell, Fitzgarrall, Fitzgerrall, Fisjarrel, Fitzgarl, Fitz-Garald, Fitzgirl, Fitchgerrald, and Fegarrell.

GEORGIA AND THE CAROLINAS
    Although the English charters of the Carolinas (1663) and Georgia (1732) expressly excluded Catholics, treatment was not as severe as in the colonies to the north. Hotten's *Original Lists*, Brandow's *Omitted Chapters*, and other records show many Irish coming from Barbadoes and elsewhere in the West Indies with names such as Cornelius Dunnohoe, John Fitzjarrall, and Ann O'Neal. As far back as the initial settlements of the colonies, there are records of Protestants and Catholics from all four provinces of Ireland.
    In North Carolina, Council journals and land records have frequent references to unquestionably Irish settlers with names such as MacCarthy, McGuire, Regan, Fitzgerald, O'Quinn, Leary, Sullivan, Kelly, Burke, and Shea. Almost every colonial parish register that has been preserved has variants of Murphy: Murf, Murfree, Murfry, Murphee, Morphew, Murfey.
    In South Carolina the first large contingent of Irish came in 1670. Three ships that left England in 1669 with intended settlers stopped at Kinsale, Ireland, to take on Irish emigrants. Another stop and boarding was at Barbadoes, where Cromwell had transported so many Irish in the early 1650s. The colonizing expedition was described as "English, Irish, Bermudian, Barbadian." Another shipload of English and Irish came in 1671 on *The Blessing*.
    The master of the *Carolina*, part of the original fleet of three ships (two were wrecked), was Captain Florence O'Sullivan. The only three of his ninety-three passengers named in full were Joseph Dalton, Priscilla Burke, and Teigue Shugeron. O'Sullivan himself became one of the leaders of the new colony. He received a lot at Old Town and a large grant across the river from Charles Town (now spelled Charleston). Michael Moran, emigrating as a servant, rose in a year to be elected to Parliament. Teague Canty, who came from Barbadoes, received a large land grant on which he brought up a family producing many descendants. Richard Kyrle (aka Kirle), described as "an Irish gentleman," was chosen governor in 1684. James Moore,

who was the son or grandson of Irish chieftain Rory O'Moore (hero of the Rising of 1641), was a member of the Council and chosen governor in 1700. In 1709, a 3,500-acre share of an older patent was named Lymerick Plantation by its purchaser, Michael Mahon, from Limerick via Barbadoes. In 1734, Irish immigrants founded a settlement called Williamsburgh Township, which was also known as "Irish Township."

The register of St. Philip's Parish in Charleston has marriages, births, and burials with names like Cusack, Lynch, Roche, Fitzgerald, Fogarty, Sullivan, O'Hare, Reilly, Casey, Delaney, Dougherty, Obryan, and Murphy. In 1809, David Ramsay, State Historian, said: "But of all countries, none has furnished the Province with so many inhabitants as Ireland. Scarcely a ship sailed from any of its ports for Charleston that was not crowded with [Irish] men, women and children."

Georgia records indicate that the first jury impaneled by Governor Oglethorpe had unmistakable Irish names. Although Georgia had many redemptioners, indentured servants, and people released from jails, there must have been some free Irishmen of enough civil substance to serve as jurors. The Irish were encouraged to emigrate by the General Assembly, which promised to give favorable consideration to their petitions for land grants. Old maps of Georgia have 18th century settlements called Limerick, Ennis, Clare, Killarney, Cork, Blarney, Tyrone, Belfast, Newry, Donegal, and Dublin. About forty-five rural places were called by Irish family names. The cities of Atlanta, Augusta, and Dublin were founded by Irishmen named Mitchell, O'Brien, and McCormick. Other towns were named after Revolutionary heroes like Fitzgerald, McDonough, and Jasper.

SCHOOLMASTERS

In the last decade of the 17th century, penal laws in Ireland became even more oppressive than before. A reward was placed on the head of any Irish Catholic schoolmaster. Penalty could be death, but usually was transportation with a term of servitude in the West Indies or the American colonies. Some stayed in Ireland as on-the-run hedge schoolmasters, some were transported, some escaped by emigrating on their own. Therefore, it is not surprising to find so many Catholic Irishmen engaged as tutors, bond or free, for the children of the early colonists.

In addition to the Catholic masters, there were younger sons of Protestant farmers, merchants, and the well-to-do, who had older brothers waiting for the inheritance. They usually had to choose between buying a commission in the British Army or buying their way into medicine or law. Desiring none of these, they had emigrated. Those who came without money and those who felt unfitted or unprepared for arduous work used teaching as a stepping stone to opportunities in land or trade. So many Irish found teaching congenial and satisfying that they monopolized the profession.

The first Swedish and Dutch of Delaware were poor people who had no educators until the coming of the Irish Catholic and Presbyterian schoolmasters. Of Georgia, historian E. Smith said: "There was no one to teach the children of the colonists save now and then a wandering Irish schoolmaster who taught a subscription school for a few months of the year." In Maryland, indentured Daniel Dulaney served as a schoolmaster until he qualified as a barrister; other Marylanders took the same route. Virginia and the Carolinas have many records of Irish who started as teachers but then moved onward and upward. Critics have claimed that some of these schoolmasters, like the Irish natives, were ill-educated. Yet one advertisement for a runaway bondservant, Thomas Ryan, said that he could easily be identified if caught because he did not speak English, only Irish, but could be tricked into speaking French, Latin, and Greek.

In Pennsylvania, many of the first schools in Philadelphia and in frontier settlements were taught by Irish immigrants. A famous example is the "Log College" at Neshaminy, Bucks County, founded in 1728 by Antrim-born Dr. William Tennent. Lacking in fancy construction, but abounding in good instruction by Tennent and his sons, this frontier school provided early training for some of the most prominent men in Colonial and Revolutionary America.

In New York, the Dutch had set the pattern of having common schools, something unknown at the time in England. When Irish Governor Dongan came to the colony, he found that the Dutch had established schools thirty years before the English takeover and had continued to educate in the thirty years since. Meantime, the children of English settlers were educated only if their parents found and could pay a private tutor, or if they were sent back to England. The previous royal governors had been arguing with the Colonial Legislature over schools, but Dongan ignored the red tape. In 1685 in Manhattan, he established the first free school under the English regime. Jesuit priest Henry Harrison was placed in charge. The school was suppressed by Dongan's successor in the days of the Glorious Revolution with its deep bigotry. The idea of the free public common school did not arise again until after the American Revolution.

For a hundred years, much of the void in New York was filled by the Irish schoolmasters. In 1704, Thomas Flynn was teaching in Wind Mill Lane in Manhattan, while Edward Fitzgerald was teaching in New Rochelle. Reverend Thomas Colgan taught at Trinity Church (Anglican) in Manhattan from 1725 to 1731, then at Grace Church in Jamaica from 1732 to 1755. Reverend Richard Charlton replaced him at Trinity. Some other pre-Revolutionary War Irish schoolmasters were Myles Reilly, James Magrath, Cornelius Lynch, James Farrell, and James and William Gilliland. Dr. Samuel Clohissey (aka Clossy), surgeon and graduate of Trinity College in Dublin, was appointed to teach at Kings College (Columbia) in 1764. He joined Robert Harper, who had moved up from ordinary schoolmaster. Robert, born in Ireland in 1733, brought over many Irish families to settle in Broome and Chemung counties.

It is in New England, however, that the Irish schoolmaster became a legend. Contrary to some popular beliefs, the Puritans did not establish schools for children of the ordinary people. Neither Plymouth Colony nor Boston had common schools for forty years. In 1672, Martin O'Shane, an Irish scholar from Galway, taught children of the first families of Boston. In 1680, Margaret, "wife of Willyam Heally, Iershman," was teaching in Cambridge.

In the 18th century, Irish schoolmasters became the rule throughout New England, especially in New Hampshire. A writer in *The New England Historic-Genealogical Register* (vol. 64, 1850) said:

Many aged people of the present day in New Hampshire will remember the stories told by their fathers of the old Irish schoolmasters. Those schoolmasters were almost always of good families at home and were well-educated and men of enterprise. Of this class was John Sullivan, of whom it was said that he could speak Latin and French with ease and fluency when he was one hundred years old.

John, the son of Major Philip O'Sullivan who had fought with Sarsfield at Limerick in 1690, emigrated from Cork to New England in the 1730s as an indentured servant and schoolmaster. His descendants include General John Sullivan of Revolutionary War fame, as well as some governors and federal and state senators and judges.

SEA CAPTAINS AND MARINERS

Early New England was a base for merchant and fishing ships. There are records of Irish captains, fishermen, and shipwrecked or abandoned mariners who became settlers. A colony of fishermen led by Kelley, Haley, and McKenna was formed on the coast of New Hampshire in 1653. About the same time, Daniel Sullivane of Hartford had his own vessel trading with Virginia and the West Indies. In the last decade of the 17th century, Captain Thaddeus McCarty made many trips in and out of Boston Harbor. In the records of trade with Ireland, there were frequent reports of confrontations when an Irish ship refused to salute the English flag. Sea captains of all nations were quite independent, and varied back and forth from merchant to privateer to pirate. The maritime history of 18th century New England is one of Irish captains, shipbuilders, and seamen, with Irish the common language on some ships.

By 1775, the majority of captains of American vessels, in New England and other colonies, were Irish-born or descended from Irishmen. British warships in the Revolution delighted in capturing Yankee Irish captains and crews. Among the New England captains who were captured and later escaped were Timothy Connor, John Murphy, and Francis Mulligan. Other Revolutionary commanders sailing out of Boston were William Burke from Marblehead; William Malone and James Burke from Newport; Jeremiah Hegarty, Richard McCarthy, Thomas Fitzgerald, and John McGraw from Salem; Thomas Quigley, Michael Melally, and Dennis Farrell from New London.

The first command of Michael Melally, born in Ireland in 1745, was the *Oliver Cromwell*, the largest ship in the Connecticut Navy. Despite the thundering name of his ship, Melally had no notable engagements with it. After he was transferred to the captaincy of the brigantine *Nancy*, he forced the British *Le Despencer* to strike her flag. When this prize was refitted as an American privateer still bearing the name *Le Despencer*, Melally commanded it in many successful engagements, especially on Long Island Sound. As for the *Oliver Cromwell*, it was captured under another command, and its crew of entirely Irish and Welsh were taken to England.

Jeremiah O'Brien and his five brothers, sons of Morris O'Brien of Machias, Maine, were the first to haul down the British flag on a regular warship of the British Royal Navy. After many other successful engagements, Jeremiah was caught off New York and imprisoned in the *Jersey*, the prison ship that attained long-lasting notoriety and became a symbol of man's inhumanity to man. O'Brien managed to survive, unlike thousands of other wretches (whose suffering is commemorated by a large monument at Fort Greene Park, Brooklyn, New York), but was brought as a prisoner to England, from where he succeeded in escaping after eighteen months.

THE IRISH CONTRIBUTION

The basis of Michael O'Brien's thesis was that the Irish settlers in colonial America were truly Irish. To prove this, he extracted old Irish names, Norse-Irish names, and Norman-Irish names from thousands of records. He also extracted names of Irish immigrants who could have had Scotch or English ancestors with names common to the three countries. He went beyond the names to match them with other records that would identify their nativity or that of their parents. If all the documents of the time called them Irish, if their names were Irish, if they saw themselves as Irish, if the English saw them as Irish, if they gave their settlements Irish names, if they joined Irish societies, well then, they were Irish.

O'Brien used many examples to show that his surname listing actually minimized his Irish count. Others with non-Irish names could also be Irish. A Whitcomb who emigrated from Galway in 1720 turned out to be the son of a Roman Catholic named MacKirwan, whose family had been in Meath before Galway. Two Gaelic words *cior bhan*, pronounced "keer-waun," literally meaning "white comb" or "white tuft of hair," explained the change. Some others that O'Brien traced were King, an anglicization by pseudo-translation of MacConry (-ry from *righ*, meaning king); Clark from O'Clery (O'Clery meaning grandson of a clerk); Ford, a mistranslation of *Macgiollarnath* (*ath* meaning "ford"), which is a corruption of *Mac Giolla na Naomh.*

"No one denies a good percentage of the people of the North of Ireland who emigrated to America were descended from Scotchmen brought over in the Ulster plantation," O'Brien wrote. "Their families had been in Ireland for many generations; in numerous instances they intermarried with the Old Irish families; they were natives of Ireland; their children grew up Irish, while yet, of course, retaining the religious beliefs brought by their ancestors from Scotland. But religion by no means makes nationality."

The question, then and now, was not whether the Irish immigrants were Catholic, but whether they were Irish. That Catholics could not practice their religion in the colonies did not make them less Irish. Nor were they made less Irish by having had ancestors who conformed to the Established Church in Ireland, or by having joined a Protestant church themselves. That many Irish in frontier America gave up all religious practice did not cause them to cease being Irish. Religion and nationality are not indissolubly linked.

Nor did any of these circumstances mean that the Irish, whether Catholic or Protestant, did not bring with them into their Protestant communities values prized by their Gaelic culture, and thereby enrich those communities with the Irish love of language and schooling; with acceptance of what today is called "assertiveness" in women; with rebelliousness in the face of rank injustice; and with the wit and charm, sometimes seasoned with a modicum of the blarney, so useful in the political arena where the Irish in America have been eminently successful.

O'Brien determined from his research into names, ancestral birthplaces, and colonial records that (1) the Irish came from all provinces of Ireland, not just Ulster; (2) they came from a wide range of class and education; (3) a strong majority belonged to the old Gaelic stock or the Norse and Norman-Irish who had "become more Irish than the Irish;" (4) Scotch and English-descended natives of Ireland who considered themselves Irish were just as Irish as the German and Irish-descended natives of the United States were American.

O'BRIEN AND OTHER HISTORIANS

During and after O'Brien's years of research and publication, there have been historians who seem to have enjoyed demeaning O'Brien, and others who have tried to ignore him. But his massive compilation of facts and records cannot be ignored by impartial historians, although they may disagree with some of his interpretations. Critics who have not done the equivalent of the quantity and quality of O'Brien's research tend to become mean-minded as they go off on tangents, or overstate his case.

Wayland Dunaway, attempting to refute O'Brien and ignoring evidence, tried to claim as Scotch-Irish those who identified themselves as Irish by joining the Friendly Sons or Friendly Brothers of St. Patrick, rather than the Scots' Thistle or St. Andrew's Societies.

David Noel Doyle, who said he had no partisanship, nevertheless said that O'Brien erred in not recognizing that the Ulster Scotch-Irish and the native Irish immigrants had a separate existence in America and lived in two separate worlds, a carry-over from their two distinct worlds in Ireland.

Forrest and Ellen McDonald and Grady McWhiney have proposed a "Celtic thesis" based on hereditary cultural traits. They placed the law-abiding, work-ethic English in the northern colonies and the laissez-faire, unmaterialistic Celts, whether Irish, Scotch, or Welsh, south of Philadelphia, a thesis that not only seems to stereotype but also is contrary to the evidence of researched genealogies and ethnic records in all colonies.

Maldwyn Jones, not accepting the Irishness of Ulster at any time, said that religion and nationality were synomymous and were so transferred to the colonies.

Leroy Eid, who sometimes praised and sometimes criticized O'Brien, has claimed that the Celtic thesis "explains a great deal about the history of that ill-known group of 'wild Irish' that loomed so large on the frontier in colonial America and in the antebellum South." Eid seemed to give some credence to Giraldus of Wales and his descriptions of the late medieval Irish by stating that the boisterous and undisciplined characteristics Giraldus outlined could be seen in Appalachia in the 1980s.

Perhaps, if Leroy Eid had been with Burgoyne's Redcoats in the Revolution as they were attacked by Morgan's Rifle Corps, he might have thought that these "wild Irish" guerilla fighters and sharpshooters were descended from Giraldus' tailed Celts or natives with bodies half-man, half-ox. Some of Burgoyne's officers wrote imaginative and fantastic descriptions of these "savages." One of the more subdued descriptions reads:

> Morgan's men were armed, each with a rifle, tomahawk and a long knife. They were dressed with flannel shirts, cloth or buckskin breeches, buckskin leggings and moccasins. Over these clothes they wore hunting shirts, made, for most part, of brown linen, some of buckskin and a few of linsey woolsey. These shirts were confined to the waist by belts in which they carried their knives and tomahawks. They wore caps on which appeared the words 'Liberty or Death.'

No tails except as decorations.

Harry Dunkak has not joined the historians who have enjoyed attacking O'Brien for his daring to do more research than those with higher academic credentials. Dunkak wrote:

> Admittedly he [O'Brien] was not a trained historian with an earned doctorate in history. There should be no question, however, about his intentions, devotion, research, and number of publications. . .He researched diligently and meticulously. . .in spite of many obstacles and difficulties, for the most part he succeeded in his chosen task. Michael J. O'Brien demonstrated the Irish race's success in the development of early America.

Dunkak placed in perspective a man whom he called "an unheralded Irish American historian."

Michael O'Brien may sometimes have become emotional and nationalistic in his phrasing, but he was answering equally emotional and nationalistic opponents (whose fathers had perhaps enjoyed the 19th century comic caricatures, printed by major newspapers and periodicals, routinely depicting the Irishman with a tail and with ape-like features under a stove-pipe hat), and he was writing in a period of wordy prose style. By saturating his readers with evidence, by piling up fact after fact and list after list, by confronting historians with their own words, by referencing all his sources, O'Brien showed beyond question that the Irish, and not only the "Scotch-Irish," were in America in significant numbers in the 17th and 18th centuries.

SUMMARY

Michael O'Brien refuted the "No Irish Before the Revolution" and the "No Irish Before the 1840s Famine" myths created and perpetuated by major historians and left unchallenged by their colleagues. He and the authors of this book do not claim that the Irish were the only builders of the Thirteen Colonies. What they do claim is that the Irish played an important, overlooked, and uncounted part in early American history: in founding colonies; in clearing the land and establishing settlements; in expanding the frontier; and, later, in winning independence of the colonies from England.

MEF

———————

Chapter 9

WISCONSIN: LUMBERMEN AND FARMERS

In rural America the Irish were quieter than their big city kinsmen, but the fact of their pervasive presence is evident in the churches, the hospitals, the schools and universities, the communities with distinctively Irish aspects, all over the rural West. The Irish came early to Wisconsin, lured by fur-trapping and lead-mining and, in mid-19th century, lumbering and railroading.

At Erin Prairie in St. Croix County in western Wisconsin the landscape is dominated by St. Patrick's Catholic Church. The cemetery contains a magnificent group of statuary, depicting four angel trumpeters heralding the glorious victory of the Resurrection. The headstones are lettered with Irish birthplaces and surnames: Donahue, Kennedy, Padden, Ross, Gherty [*sic*], Garrity, Maloney, Wells, Stephens, Murta, Riley, Moore, Dean, Mead, Meath, Gill, LaVelle.

The Irish pioneer presence in very rural Erin Prairie is no aberration. The Irish had been coming into what is now St. Croix County to farm before 1850, and by 1870 there were two hundred Irish-born farmers in the township of Erin (Prairie) alone. This presence preceded that of the Germans, Scandinavians, and Poles, and was felt in all three great movements into Wisconsin in the 19th century. First, there were the fur trappers, then the lead miners, and after them, the lumberers, farmers, and railroadmen.

The 1860 United States census recorded Irish-born Patrick and Michael Golden, and the families of Irish-born Joseph Shanahan and Thomas Riley, all of them occupied as fur traders and farmers across the St. Croix River from Osceola, Wisconsin, in Chisago County, Minnesota. Shanahan and his wife, Nancy Doyle, were natives of

179

County Wexford, and the first of several Wexford families, including Tyrrells, Sinnotts, and O'Learys, to establish a community in rural Franconia Township. The bones of many of them are interred in the neatly kept little cemetery behind St. Francis Chapel. Many of their descendants, some with the surname Rochel (the Catholic Irish Tyrrells married the Catholic German Rochels), can still be found on the Wisconsin and Minnesota sides of the great St. Croix River.

In the township of Monches (which was called O'Connellville until 1848 in honor of the Irish statesman) in Waukesha County, the three-steepled church erected by the Carmelites stands high atop Holy Hill. This church is shown in a striking photograph included by Fred L. Holmes in his book *Old World Wisconsin,* published in 1944. Holmes' chapter on the Irish was, at that time, one of the very few accounts of the Irish presence in rural America. He cites a number of Wisconsin rural communities that were founded by the Irish. They include the communities of Erin in Washington County and Merton in Waukesha County (where Malloy, Murphy, and McConville Lakes perpetuate the memory of the first settlers, almost all from Killarney, County Kerry, in 1842); the townships of Emmett, Shields, and Elba in Dodge County (Irish settlers from Canada and Maine in the 1840s); Bear Creek, Winfield, and Dellona in Sauk County (Irish farmers as early as 1845); Fond du Lac, Eden, and Byron in Fond du Lac County; Westport in Dane County; Evansville in Rock County; Lebanon in Waupaca County; Poygan in Winnebago County; and several townships in Brown County, including Wrightstown and Askeaton, the last named after a parish in County Limerick. Old Fort Winnebago, now Portage in Columbia County, contained five hundred Irish-born in 1850, one-third of its total population.

In rural Meeme township in Manitowoc County, according to Holmes, the community center was St. Isidore's Catholic Church. The country public school, attended by all the Catholic children, produced a number of notables, including Thomas J. Walsh of Montana, a Democratic United States Senator from Montana from 1913 to 1933, and John Barnes, a justice of the Wisconsin Supreme Court.

The 1846 *Wisconsin Territorial Census* for rural Erin Town[ship] in Washington County lists 454 residents, 259 males and 195 females, at least 90 percent of whom had Irish surnames. On the same census for Emmett Town[ship] in Dodge County, population 775, about 71 of 160 household heads had Irish surnames. In Muskego Town[ship], Waukesha County, population 867, about 55 of 153 household heads had Irish surnames.

From an Irish community at Greenfield, Milwaukee County, came Jeremiah Curtin, one of America's greatest linguists. Curtin was fluent in seventy languages, including Irish. He often travelled to Ireland to gather folktales which he translated into English and published under such titles as *Tales of the Fairies*, *The Ghost World*, and *Myths and Folk-lore of Ireland* .

"Even those Wisconsin pioneer Irish who did not read English," reports Holmes, "could repeat with feeling many of the old ballads and songs. The accuracy of their memories as to the dates of local events would stultify the written record." Holmes mentions Tom Croal, living in 1944 near Hill Point in Sauk County. Croal was possibly the last of the Irish *seanachies* (bards, story-tellers) in Wisconsin.

EDUCATION

In the field of education the Irish were long dominant. "No other foreign nationality, comparable in numbers," wrote Holmes, "has had so many of its sons and daughters enter education. It would be quite an exception to discover an Irish home with girls where one or more were not teachers." John Callahan, who spent his life in the teaching profession and served as State Superintendent of Schools for over twenty years, had three daughters, all teachers. Of the twenty-two granddaughters of William Fitzgerald and Ann Harrigan of Oshkosh who lived to maturity, ten were schoolteachers (*see Chapter 6*).

POLITICAL LIFE

In politics the Wisconsin Irish, like their kinsmen in the eastern cities, produced political leaders in abundance. They have ranged from former Governor Patrick Lucey and Wisconsin-bred Senator Thomas Walsh of Montana, to the late Senator for whose political style the term McCarthyism was invented. This political tradition goes back even before statehood came to the Territory of Wisconsin. At the first constitutional convention in 1846, of 112 elected delegates, Edward G. Ryan of Racine was one of twelve with distinctively Irish surnames (O'Connor, Madden, Manahan, etc.). He "was among the leading advocates of the adoption of the Constitution," reported delegate Moses M. Strong, "towering above all others in the magnetism of his zeal and the power of his eloquence." At the 1848 convention, of the seven foreign-born delegates among the sixty-nine in attendance, five were Irish-born. They were Patrick Pentony of Mequon, John Doran of Milwaukee, James Fagan of Grafton, Garrett Fitzgerald of Milwaukee, and William Fox of Fitchburg. A number of the native-born also had distinctively Irish surnames. At the last session of the Territorial Legislature in 1848, Timothy Burns of Iowa County was elected Speaker of the House, and Thomas McHugh, Secretary of the Council.

BUILDING THE CHURCH

In building the Catholic Church, the Irish had no peers save for the Germans who were also coming into Wisconsin in great numbers in the 1840s. Of 382 churches founded in Wisconsin as of 1896 (see Heming's *The Catholic Church in Wisconsin),* 113 were of Irish origin, while 172 were German and 41 French, with many of the latter, established as mission stations for the Indians, having been subsumed by Irish clergy and parishioners.

THE SINSINAWA DOMINICANS

Founded in 1847 by the Italian-born Father Samuel Mazzuchelli (known as "Father Matthew Kelly" to the lead miners), the Sinsinawa Dominicans increased in numbers to over 1,800 members in mid-20th century. The first four who entered were daughters of Irish lead miners and farmers. Under the leadership of Sister Emily (Ellen Power, born in County Waterford and the daughter of a local farmer), the order established St. Clara's Academy and College at Sinsinawa; Edgewood and Rosary Colleges in Madison, Wisconsin, and River Forest, Illinois, respectively; scores of elementary and high schools in thirty-five states; two collegiate institutions in South America; and colleges in Switzerland and Italy. "She insisted that her sisters be well trained," writes archivist Sister Marie Laurence Kortendick, O.P., "and sent them to colleges and universities whenever possible, even the artists to Europe for study in Rome and Florence. She also invited eminent scholars such as Orestes Brownson to lecture at Sinsinawa." Of 1,699 sisters in 1950, 49.7 percent were of Irish descent. The congregation in 1987 numbered 1,230.

LEAD MINES

The mines near Galena in Illinois on the Wisconsin border produced 55,000,000 pounds of ore in the mid-1850s, during a boom that had its origins forty years before. One of those attracted by the lure of lead was John Furlong. He was one of many members of his family who fought in 1798 at the Battle of Vinegar Hill, overlooking Enniscorthy in County Wexford. At that battle, it was Irish pikes against British muskets and cannon. The Irish, in a futile last stand on the high ground, were slaughtered. John Furlong was one of the few pikemen to survive the battle. Captured, he was impressed into the British Army and sent to Canada. There, through French connections, he and other Irish heard of Julien Dubuque and the lead mines in the West. He and some compatriots deserted the Army and made their way to the east bank of the Mississippi River. Near Galena, they began mining for lead ore.

27. Mother Emily Power (1844-1909), born Ellen Power at Barrettstown, Tramore, County Waterford, daughter of David Power and Bridget Kelly; served as Mother Superior of the Sinsinawa Dominicans from 1867 to 1889 and as Mother General from 1889 to 1909.

27a. Mother Mary Samuel (1868-1959), born Ellen Coughlin at Faribault, Minnesota, the daughter of Cork-born Daniel Coughlin and Ellen O'Mahoney; took the religious name of Samuel, after Father Samuel Mazzuchelli, missionary to the Irish lead miners and farmers in southwestern Wisconsin; served as Mother General of the Sinsinawa Dominicans from 1909 to 1949.

When Illinois became a state in 1818, Furlong purchased land just south of what would one day be the site of St. Clara's Academy. In 1824, he and some of his friends, including Michael Burns and Thomas Carroll, struck a rich vein of ore at Cave Brach and called the site Vinegar Hill. In 1829, John Furlong's wife gave birth to a son, William, the first non-Indian child born in the township. The descendants of Furlong worked the mines until about 1934. In 1967, a great-great grandson, Earl, re-opened them for tourists.

Many descendants of the pioneer Irish miners live today in the communities of Shullsburg, Darlington, Seymour, and Willow Springs, in Lafayette County, as well as in the adjoining counties of Grant in Wisconsin and Jo Daviess [sic] in Illinois.

FIRST ST. PATRICK'S DAY PARADE

In 1837, Father Patrick O'Kelley was appointed by Bishop Résé of Detroit the first permanent pastor of a Catholic parish, St. Peter's, in the city of Milwaukee. He immediately began building the first Catholic Church, St. Peter's. He departed in 1842, the year before the first St. Patrick's Day Parade in that city. On March 17, 1843, over three thousand Catholics assembled for a great parade and religious ceremonies. The number was astonishing in view of the population of the city, which would have been considerably less than the 9,400 and 11,000 reported in 1846 and 1847, the Irish and Germans constituting half of that population. Eighteen parishes, many from outside of the city, were in the line of march, with flags, banners, and martial music. St. Peter's Church, at the end of the line, was too small to contain one-tenth of the spectators, according to a report by Father David O'Hearn in the May 19, 1843, *Milwaukee Sentinel.*

The organizers of the parade, it should be noted, had a political motive, to convince church authorities, by their sheer numbers, that Milwaukee, not Green Bay, deserved to be chosen as the permanent See for the Wisconsin diocese. It was one St. Patrick's Day when many of the members of the considerable German Catholic community marched with the Irish. The relations between the German and Catholic communities were not always harmonious.

LUMBERING

Following the lead miners, the next great influx of Irish into Wisconsin came with the emerging lumber boom in the 1840s. Boards and laths were needed to build the cities of Chicago and Milwaukee and the growing communities on the Mississippi and other river systems. Ties were needed for the railroad lines a-building. Wisconsin had the timber, and the river systems on which to drive the logs to the booms in the sawmill towns. Maine and New Brunswick, especially, had the woodsmen whose skills were needed so desperately. The woodsmen, most of whom were Irish and Scots and Welsh, or Yankees from the Maritimes and New England, came flocking to Wisconsin. Humphrey Desmond's study of Irish settlers who had arrived in Wisconsin from 1835 to 1849 led him to the conclusion that most of them had resided in the East before arriving in Milwaukee. The large number from Maine and New Brunswick were spurred by a depression in the lumber industry there, and by the lure of work, money, and, always, land in the west.

HOW DID THEY GET TO WISCONSIN?

Until the railroad line from Chicago to St. Louis was completed in 1853, the settlers in the lead region of southwest Wisconsin came mostly by way of the Ohio River from Cincinnati, or through New Orleans and up the Mississippi to St. Louis, then by a smaller boat farther up the Mississippi and Fever rivers to the docks at Galena, a bustling frontier town in the 1830s. The New Orleans-Mississippi River route was the one taken by David Power and his family, one of whose members was Ellen, the future Sister Emily of the Sinsinawa Dominicans. (David, dispossessed from land in County Waterford occupied by his family for centuries, had sailed out of Southampton with stops at Waterford and Queenstown on the ship *Asia.*) David was preceded to the lead region by his oldest son Louis, who was soon recruited to the priesthood by Father Mazzuchelli.)

By 1850, other routes to Wisconsin, especially from Maine and New Brunswick, were also well travelled. Isaac Stephenson, a lumberman whose career took him from New Brunswick to Maine to Michigan and Minnesota, and finally to the United States Senate, told of leaving Bangor, Maine, for Wisconsin in 1845. Stephenson embarked from Bangor for Boston in October 1845 on the steamboat *Penobscot.* At Boston, he took the Boston and Albany Railroad ("one of the important transportation lines in the country," he observed). The passenger trains he described were no more comfortable than a modern freight car:

There were only two windows, about sixteen by twenty inches in size, on each side of the cars to afford light and air and such glimpses of the passing landscape as we were able to take. The floors were carpeted and in place of modern upholstered seats were three-legged stools which would be moved about at will. In the middle of each side of the cars was a sliding door similar to those now in use in box cars.

The train ran on "strap rails," the modern, standardized track and rail system being still a thing of the future. Trainmen led a precarious life, moving from car to car via handrails attached to the sides.

At Albany, given the choice of boat or train, Stephenson took the cheaper route. He boarded the *Northern Light* of the Clinton line for the five-day trip on the Erie Canal. The boat was towed by horses at walking pace. (There were express boats towed by horses at trotting pace that could make it faster.) Sleeping berths were set up along the sides of the hull for the full length. Thirty or forty passengers were crowded together in cramped quarters, so much so that Stephenson had thoughts of getting off and taking the train. He had no privacy day or night. He was so uncomfortable that he welcomed the chance to help the Irish boys on the tow horses. Their lot struck Stephenson as being very hard:

They worked practically day and night with only short intervals of rest taken on deck or wherever they could find a place to lie, seldom, if ever, took off their clothes and bore the brunt of hardship of this mode of travel. They were always ready to yield their responsibilities to me and clamber aboard the boat to rest, and I found it diverting to ride the horses which controlled the progress of the *Northern Light*. Whenever the stern of the vessel was veered to the bank of the canal to permit passengers to alight I was usually among those who took advangage of the opportunity, and out of a total journey of three hundred and sixty miles rode the horses, I think, for at least a hundred. During the last leg of the journey some of the impatient passengers bribed one of the boys to urge his mount to greater speed, a cardinal offense, and the lad was discharged upon our arrival at Buffalo.

Stephenson saw a telegraph line for the first time, paralleling the canal along the New York Central Railroad right of way. At Buffalo, Stephenson took the steamer *Empire* to Monroe, Michigan. Monroe had recently been connected by rail to Chicago. The weather on Lake Erie was bad; a strong gale forced the ship into harbor at Cleveland, where Stephenson saw two vessels run aground on the beach and another with a hole in its side above the water line. After a stop at Monroe, the *Empire* continued north to Lake Huron and around the Michigan Peninsula to Lake Michigan and down to Milwaukee, but not without more troubles. It ran into a gale on Lake Huron and sought refuge for three days in Presque Isle, Michigan. High seas greeted it again on Lake Michigan, a gale having blown in from the northeast. "The vessel rolled and pitched to such an extent that I was more or less bewildered and many of the passengers, keeping close to the heaving staterooms, were awaiting in fear and trembling the end of what appeared to be their disastrous journey." Again the boat pulled into harbor for safety, this time at Grand Haven, for two days until the storm abated and the lake calmed.

Stephenson arrived in Milwaukee at the north pier at the foot of Huron Street on Wednesday morning, November 15, 1845. During his stay in that city he saw "as many as seven or eight hundred people land . . .on steamers from Buffalo, packing their belongings with them; and I have seen them by the hundreds in a vacant lot bargaining for cattle and wagons with which to begin life and establish a farm on the unbroken prairie."

The English traveller James Johnston wrote of his journey in 1850 to the American West. When Johnston got to New York City he had two choices of routing westward. One was by Philadelphia and Pittsburgh. The other, a cheaper one and taken by most immigrants landing in New York City, was through Albany and Buffalo.

At Albany, Johnston, like Stephenson, had the choice of a train or the cheaper Erie Canal boat. The gentleman Johnston took the train and so, he reports, did many of the immigrants. Near Rochester, he observed the following:

. . .one of the emigrant trains which every day proceed from Albany and Troy to Buffalo, on their way to the Far West. There were women and children of all ages, and the ragged and lively, though often squalid-looking Irish, were mixed up with the more decently clad and graver-looking English, Scotch, and Germans. The fare from New York to Albany by water, and thence to Buffalo by railway, is five dollars a head, though the poor strangers are liable to much imposition in New York on the part of a set of men called runners who waylay them on landing and profess to give them information, with the view only of cheating them of their money.

The fare from New York to Chicago, said Johnston, "is fifteen dollars a head, which is about 10 pounds for a man and his wife and two children." Although he noted that the English, Scotch, and Germans seemed to be better provided for than the Irish, he suspected that "Pat's ragged coat, as the captains of the steamers know well, often conceals more gold than the decenter garments of the emigrants from other countries."

At Buffalo, steamers were in waiting for the immigrants to take them to Detroit or other Michigan ports (especially Monroe) and thence to Chicago by rail. Johnston estimated that about five hundred a day were making their way from Albany to Buffalo by rail, and then by boat to the Michigan port, a voyage that took seventeen hours. Rail from Detroit across southern Michigan to New Buffalo took eleven hours more. Steamboat from New Buffalo to Chicago took another four. At Chicago, Mr. Johnston boarded a boat for Milwaukee, which took six hours. The journey to Chicago had covered 518 miles and taken thirty-two hours.

A Welsh immigrant, Reverend Benjamin W. Chidlaw, arrived in New York City on November 2, 1835, after a 41-day voyage. He left Albany by steamer: "160 miles for half a dollar," he wrote a friend in Wales. "From [Albany] we went by canal to Buffalo, 306 miles for four dollars, from here on a steamship to Cleveland, 250 miles for two and a half dollars. From here on the canal to Portsmouth along the Ohio River for four and a half dollars. From here on the Ohio by steamship for Cincinnati, twenty miles for one dollar."

To go west from an east coast port was unavoidably a complicated business of getting on and off a number of boats and sometimes trains.

THE IRISH AND HISTORIANS

It was thus that the Irish diaspora reached Wisconsin. To just where within the state they dispersed has been documented by Sister Grace McDonald in *History of the Irish in Wisconsin,* originally a doctoral dissertation for the Catholic Univerity of America in 1954. Sister McDonald reported the Irish presence in every corner of the state, describing the Irish role in politics from 1836-1900, and in business, religious and social life. Unfortunately, she grievously under-estimated the actual *number* of the Irish in Wisconsin, depending as she did on the summary statistics for the United States censuses for 1850-70, which reported only the Irish-*born* (second largest of the foreign-born groups in the state, but only 5 percent of the total population). The enormous number of those of Irish parentage, whose families had settled for a time in Canada or the eastern cities, are not treated as Irish in the statistics. Historian Merle Curti also ignored surname and genealogical data, relying solely on the 1850 to 1880 census data, in his classic study of Trempeauleau County, Wisconsin (*The Making of an American Community: A Case Study of Democracy in a Frontier County,* 1959), in which he drew conclusions about the performance of the Irish compared to other groups.

Sister McDonald's and Merle Curti's conclusions based on misleading data bases have served to perpetuate the distortion in American history books, especially the myth about most Irish immigrants settling in the eastern seaboard cities. They also tend indirectly to lend credibility to studies such as Kerby A. Miller's *Emigrants and Exiles,* in which the author advances the thesis that the Irish Catholics were peculiarly unsuited for adaptation to life in America. *(For further critique of some historians of the Irish, see Chapters 5, 8 and 19 in this volume.)*

FURTHER WESTWARD

The Irish diaspora on the "Northern Migration Route" continued westward in the last quarter of the 19th century. Many of the sons of the lumbermen and farmers took up railroad work and followed the railroads to the ore ports of Ashland, Superior, and Duluth, where one finds heavy concentrations of Irish on the United States censuses of 1880 and 1900. Many Irish were to be found in Virginia, Minnesota, during the development of the great iron ore mines of the

Mesabi Range in the last quarter of the 19th century. The Irish continued westward into the Dakotas, Montana, Idaho, Washington, and California (*see Chapters 12 and 13*).

The most important part of the story of the Irish in America is not told by the Irishman-as-exile or Irishman-as-misfit theorists. It is told by an angel trumpeter among the statuary in the rural cemetery at Erin Prairie in western Wisconsin, with his note of belief that a person's life has meaning and that one could nourish that meaning in the lands of the western American frontier.

JAK

Chapter 10

IOWA: PIONEERS AND SODBUSTERS

Before the American Civil War, there were substantial clusters of Irish settlers in all the midwestern states and territories. They settled in lake and river towns. They settled in mining, lumber and railway communities. They took up undeveloped potential farmland as it was opened to claims. They migrated not only as individuals and families, but also as part of planned colonies. One can look at Iowa for some examples of rural prairie colonies founded and formed to be Irish Catholic.

THE PRAIRIE LAND

There were Irish pioneers, explorers, and trappers in Iowa in small numbers in pre-Revolutionary times. They had migrated before it was United States territory and they continued to migrate after the United States acquired it in 1803 as part of the Louisiana Purchase. The records of these early Irish are sparse, but we find some of them in the reports of the French and Spanish Catholic missionaries.

The expanse of wilderness in Iowa and the whole Louisiana Territory, along with the French background of its trappers and explorers, gave the Irish of "the itchy foot" a feeling of freedom and equality. They knew that they might seldom, if ever, see a priest, but that was also true in the British North American colonies and in the homeland from which they had come.

There are few Irish-born in Iowa now, but the immigration that swelled from the 1840s to the turn of the century made those of Irish descent a significant proportion of a state usually identified as German. On the 1980 census, 24.9 percent of Iowa residents responded "Irish" for the first or second specific ancestry. That made the Irish, although several generations removed from the Old Country, the third largest ethnic group in Iowa (Germans and English were first and second). More significant was that the figure placed Iowa eleventh of the fifty states in the *percentage* of residents of Irish origin.

After 1803, Iowa was settled gradually by pioneers from the seaboard states who wanted more land, and by arriving immigrants who found that only in the West could they obtain the acres for which they hungered. Throughout Indiana, Illinois, and Iowa, there were settlements of Irish who had landed initially in Philadelphia, New York, Boston, Quebec, or New Orleans, then made their way north or west with a possible stopover in Chicago. In the 1840s, Iowa was more appealing than Indiana or Illinois, not only because of its fertile soil, many rivers, and good drainage, but because little of the Iowa Territory had been assigned under the land acts. The only advantage the few settlers already farming in Iowa had over newcomers was that they were already there. A man could settle on any unoccupied land, and, as head of a family, claim a quarter section of 160 acres on payment of $1.25 an acre.

A powerful incentive for taking up land in the West was the opportunity to escape the Nativists ("Know Nothings") in the East where, before mid-century, the inflammatory polemics of such well-known native Americans as Samuel F.B. Morse helped to generate arson and other violence against Catholics, their clergy, and their church and convent structures. This situation provided the motivation for countless numbers of Catholics to move to the western frontier where the Know Nothing movement was not nearly so virulent.

On the Mississippi, three or four trips were made during the high water every spring, and a steamboat could be taken as far as Prairie du Chien and St. Peter's. Keel boats, however, still carried "much of the business," according to an 1827 report, and such voyages were "long, tedious, and expensive."

1836 WISCONSIN TERRITORIAL CENSUS

The Wisconsin Territory was organized in 1836, and a census of the areas of "considerable settlement" was immediately ordered by Governor Dodge. This census record, searched by J.A. King, tells of the presence of the Irish in the Upper Mississippi River Basin. It covers the area of the present states of Wisconsin and Iowa, and as far west as the Missouri River and Bismarck, North Dakota. The most populous counties were Des Moines (6,257); Iowa, now Lafayette, Grant, and Iowa counties in southwest Wisconsin (5,234); Dubuque (4,274); Milwaukee (2,893); and Brown, including Green Bay (2,706). The record shows heads of household by full name, the number of males and females, 21 and over, and the number under 21. King's search revealed negligible Irish in Des Moines and Milwaukee counties (where large numbers of Irish arrived in the next few years) but sizable numbers in Iowa and Dubuque counties.

In Iowa County in 1836, at least 765 residents, or 14.6 percent of the population of 5,234, were in households headed by a person with a distinctly Gaelic or Norman-Irish name, for example, Brady, Burke, Carlin, Doling [*sic*], O'Hara, O'Neil, Roach. In Dubuque County, 843 (19.7 percent of the population of 4,274) were Irish. These were lead miners and farmers. The figures do not include Jo Daviess County in Illinois, where there was a heavy concentration of Irish in or near the frontier town of Galena.

The estimates of the Irish are conservative. Names such as Norton, Harper, Shepherd, Meade, and Smith, have not been counted as Irish, unless listed in a sequence indicating an Irish "colony," such as this one in Dubuque County, where the the census record shows the following names in sequence: Norton, Regan, Duggan, Torn, Corkery, Cunningham, Killer [Kelleher], Garner, Fanning, Drake, Shepherd, Halligan, Finn, Mott, Grenbeck, Currin, Harper, Quigley. The residents of these households numbered 201, including 97 males and 31 females over 21, but 11 of the 20 households included at least one female over 21. This clearly was not a "wild Irish" frontier community of rootless, alienated males, but was distinguished instead by family builders. The household of Daniel Duggan had 6 males and 4 females over 21, and 9 children; that of James Fanning, 8 adult males, 5 adult females, 6 children; that of Patrick Corkery, 2 adult males, 2 adult females, 6 children; that of P. Quigley, 1 adult male, 3 adult females, 8 children; while the James Cunningham household, no doubt a boarding house, had 15 adult males, without women or children.

GARRYOWEN

An early settlement of farmers and lead miners was at Sinsinawa, now in southwestern Wisconsin (*see Chapter 9 in this volume*), with Irish from County Wexford arriving about 1820. Another was at Garryowen, now in Iowa, twenty miles from Dubuque. Garryowen was settled in 1838 by Irish mostly from Cork and Limerick. The settlement was first known as Makokiti. After some heated debate between the men of Cork and Limerick the name was changed to Garryowen in the 1850s. The first church was erected in 1840; the first Mass was said that summer, perhaps by Bishop Jean Mathias Loras or Father Samuel Mazzuchelli, both legends in those parts.

In 1840, the congregation numbered about 100; in 1841, 250; in 1843, 600. The resident pastor was Father Perrodine. Visiting the parish at that time, Father Mazzuchelli wrote that there was not a single Protestant proprietor in the township. At about this time, according to the *Miner's Express*, some "respectable looking" Irish from

New York State arrived and settled in homes already provided for them. Fifty families came directly from Ireland in 1841-42. A school, the first operated by the church in the Diocese of Dubuque (established in 1837), was functioning in 1842. One instructor was Dennis A. Mahoney of Limerick, later editor of the first *Dubuque Herald* and a state senator. In 1855, the Sisters of Charity arrived at the invitation of pastor Jeremiah Trecy.

The community prospered, and by 1939 St. Patrick's, Garryowen, had seven "daughter" parishes and modern grade and high schools.

WEXFORD

One particularly interesting settlement was founded by an Irish priest, Father Thomas Hore, at Wexford in Iowa. Father Hore was born in 1796 in the parish of Our Lady's Island (Ladyisland), Barony of Forth, County Wexford. He completed his theological studies at St. Kieran's College at Birchfield in Kilkenny in 1820. The timing was auspicious. In that year Dr. Patrick Kelly, head at Birchfield, was appointed bishop of the newly-established diocese of Richmond, Virginia. Dr. Kelly asked Thomas to go with him to America. Thomas did go, and was ordained by Bishop Kelly when they arrived in Virginia.

Bishop Kelly returned to Ireland before two years had passed, but young Father Hore remained in Richmond. For six years he attempted to continue the mission of serving Catholics throughout the state. When he began to suffer serious health problems he returned to his native diocese of Ferns in Wexford. After his health improved, he became a successful parish priest and church builder in Annacurra and Killaveney. After the new church of St. Kevin was dedicated in April 1844, no one would have predicted that Father Hore would again be involved in an American mission. But then no one saw the shadow of the Great Hunger hovering over the parish.

In the fall of 1845, Ireland experienced a severe failure, through blight, of the potato crop. County Wexford did not depend on the potato for its economy and continued to send profitable exports of dairy products and produce to England and continental Europe. By 1846, however, with continued famine and, ironically, continued and unreduced export of grains, pork and dairy products, the small cottagers, leaseholders, and laborers in Wexford began to feel the famine. Cholera, typhus, hunger, and death from starvation were all around.

Some left Wexford to look for work elsewhere in Ireland, but found that all the poor of Ireland were on the roads trying to save themselves the same way. Some found the money to emigrate. It was a decision to leave land and loved ones for an unknown future, but also a chance for the family to survive. Some started with their families for the ports, saw death on the roadside, and then learned at the ports that they did not have enough advance money for the passage, not to mention government dues for embarkation, head tax, and various fees demanded by opportunistic agents for arranging passage.

Father Hore at first looked to the British for help, but British authorities, committed as they were to an economic *laissez faire* (no interference by government) policy, would not enact even temporary regulations that would permit the Wexfordians to keep enough of the great quantities of food that were going for export. With conditions desperate, Father Hore decided that the only way to save the remainder of his people was to organize an emigration while passage and first-support money could still be obtained. He met with his parishioners and spoke to them of his early experiences in America. He began preparations by contacting emigrants who had already opted for an America that would have changed considerably since Father Hore left it.

The first plan was to go to Arkansas where Father Hore had an Irish contact: Bishop Andrew Byrne. After becoming the first bishop of Little Rock, Arkansas, Meath-born Dr. Byrne had returned to Ireland several times looking for nuns and priests for his diocese and encouraging people to emigrate. By October 1850, Father Hore had his group of emigrants ready and they made the first step from Dublin to Liverpool. In Liverpool they met Bishop Byrne, who gave Father Hore full authority to function as a priest for the Diocese of Little Rock.

In November 1850, more than 450 sailed on the *Ticonderoga* from Liverpool to New Orleans. After a difficult winter ocean crossing of five weeks, they traveled another difficult 400 miles up the Mississippi by riverboat. When Father Hore and his hopeful but weary Irish immigrants reached their Promised Land of Little Rock, they met their first great disappointment. What Bishop Byrne had not realized was that most of the Arkansas land suitable for farming was already occupied. There was no place large enough for the 450 Wexfordians to settle as a group. They searched for a month in Arkansas, then most of the disheartened families went upriver to St. Louis to await Father Hore's investigation of a location in Iowa, which had been their second choice before they left Ireland.

The bishop of Dubuque, Iowa, was Reverend Jean Mathias Loras, a French missionary who had been appointed First Ordinary in 1837. During a trip to Ireland he had shown concern for the sufferings of the people and had supported a colonization project that never materialized, although individual Irish families emigrated to his diocese. He had succeeded, however, with the founding of the monastery of New

Mellaray in Iowa by the abbot of Mount Mellaray in Waterford. Conditions looked promising in a diocese that already had a monastery, so Father Hore looked into the land situation and found that also promising.

During his search, the situation back in St. Louis had deteriorated. Some of the waiting Irish had run out of funds and had no means of support. No longer could they afford to buy the farmland of their dreams even at $1.25 an acre. They had therefore taken what employment they could get in St. Louis and elsewhere. Some were lured to the Far West by visions of gold.

Father Hore finally found a site in the diocese, in Allamakee County, that seemed to have all the natural advantages for the kind of colony his people wanted. The Winnebago Indians in the area had been evangelized by French missionaries in the 17th century. Father Samuel Mazzuchelli had worked among the Indians in the 1830s, but little was done by the United States Church Mission after that since there were few Catholic settlers in the county. When the Indian land claims were voided and the lands were put on sale in 1851, Father Hore was able to purchase over three thousand acres between February and April. However, only eighteen families of the original Wexford *Ticonderoga* emigrants joined him. They, along with a few other Irish families who had joined the group in America, officially founded the colony in March of 1851 and named it Wexford.

Some of the names of these first settlers were Murphy, Bulger, Esmond, Nolan, Finn, Fennel, Brickley, Heatley, Heyfron, Sullivan, Kavanaugh, Stafford, and McKeogh. They stayed first with nearby helpful and friendly French settlers. Within a month, they had completed construction of most of their homes. Atop an earlier French-Irish mission "station," they also built a church, a high-priority item linking them to the Ireland they would never see again and serving as their foundation on which to build new lives amid alien corn.

The church was dedicated on April 23, 1851. The day is significant. Wexford, Iowa, was one of the few Irish American settlements that did not dedicate its first church to the Virgin, St. Bridget, or St. Patrick. Following a Wexford custom, the settlers named their church for the saint whose feast day was celebrated on the day of the church's dedication or completion. April 23 happened to be the feast of St. George. Thus the little church in Iowa took on a very English name, that of England's patron saint.

Father Hore and his settlement flourished. By 1857, Wexford had reached a nice country-farm settlement size of about four hundred. Allamakee County numbered about six thousand Catholics. A second monastery for the New Mellaray Trappists had been built at Wexford (the first was near Dubuque). Father Hore had founded seven other parishes in the county. He may have been disappointed that he was not able to keep the whole Wexford group together, but he had the satisfaction of knowing that he had established an Irish Catholic colony in Iowa.

In 1857, Father Hore was granted his lifetime wish to go on a pilgrimage to Rome and the Holy Land. Before he left Iowa, he divested himself of property held in his name. He would never see Iowa again. After his pilgrimage, he returned to Wexford, Ireland, where he died in 1864. The memorial tablet in his last parish church at Cloughbawn may not honor his memory as the founder of an Irish American colony, but the small town of Wexford, Iowa, and the many Catholic churches in Allamakee and surrounding counties are memorials to this pioneer, circuit-riding pastor.

LIZARD CREEK

Much farther to the west in Iowa is another Irish colony founded about the same time as Wexford. On the banks of the Lizard Creek, about twenty miles from Fort Dodge, a group of Irish settlers, mostly from County Clare, took advantage of the good soil and abundant river waters of Iowa. The names of some of the first families were Broderick, Calligan, Collins, Condon, Connors, Donohue, Donovan, Ellis, Farey, Fenton, Ford, Griffin, Hickey, Kelley, Morrissey, McCabe, Quinn, Russell, and Walsh. They had to have been strong farmers or merchants in Ireland, for the very poorest cottiers and day-laborers could not afford the cost of the passage or the cost of American land, cheap as it was at $1.25 per acre.

When these colonists settled on Lizard Creek, they were expecting a rail line to come through their town. It never came, and so they were left totally to their own resources. One problem was the presence of the Sioux Indians. The Irish colonists got little help from the military in dealing with the Sioux. Another problem was that of the hard-to-cut prairie grass, five feet high. Breaking the soil, which was good, took oxen and at least two men. The many streams and rivers, fine for the colonists' water needs, were an almost insurmountable obstacle to transportation. Food was scarce in the first years of settlement. The families learned to eat maize, wild animals, and other kinds of Indian food.

Gradually, a village was built on the plains. An inn for hunters and other travellers was constructed. The settlers naturally wanted a church but they had not come with a priest and could count only on itinerant missionaries. A log building for use both as a school and as a Mass-house was erected by original settler James Fenton. Even before Fenton's double-house was completed, the people were being served occasionally by a priest from Iowa City who said the first Mass at Lizard Creek in 1855 at the home of Sylvester Griffin.

In 1856, the first Catholic Church opened at Fort Dodge and the settlement on the Lizard was counted only as an out-station of that parish; and so the Lizard colony followed the frontier pattern of "stations" with Mass once a month in different farmhouses. In 1871, the settlers finally built their own church and named it St. Patrick's on the Lizard. They were given a resident pastor the next year. By then they were looking forward to a flourishing colony.

The railroad that the government had planned and abandoned years ago at last came into being, but it did not come through the Lizard settlement. The people were separated by some six miles from the railway station, and thus isolated from the transportation necessary for profitable farming. No one on the Lizard had been involved in the kind of politics that decreed where railroads would go, increasing by their location the value of the land holdings of speculators.

Undaunted, the tradespeople of the Lizard, if not the farmers, moved to the railway and a new town was born around the stationhouse. It was called Clare, after the county from which a majority of the settlers had sprung. The Lizard settlement deteriorated slowly but never really died, even when St. Patrick's, giving way to a new church at Clare, reverted to a mission outpost.

St. Patrick's Church burned to the ground in 1930, but even in that Great Depression time the descendants of the old settlers built a new church within the year. St. Patrick's on the Lizard exists as a testimonial to courageous Irish pioneers from Clare and as an inspiration to visitors to the mission outpost.

PIONEER LEGACY

The Irish in plains states like Iowa faced many dangers and endured many hardships, but they persevered in their plan to conquer the wilderness. The reminiscences of the old timers were usually pleasant because they tended to remember the good and forget the bad. The settlers at Wexford were thoroughly religious people who spread their faith throughout the county. The settlers at Garryowen brought Catholic schooling to the frontier. The settlers on the Lizard had the satisfaction of knowing that after the first few years they were never without the services of a priest.

The Irish in Iowa got along well with the French, who were there before them, and whose population did not increase. They also got along with the Germans, who settled at the same time as they, and whose population did indeed increase. The pastors of the Iowa Irish colonies searched for isolated settlements on the edge of the frontier where there were no missions or priests. They continued the mission to the Indians, many of whom had been converted before their arrival and who outnumbered the Irish as Catholics when the settlements were founded.

The Garryowen, Wexford, and Lizard pioneers encouraged other settlers to take up nearby lands in Iowa and they helped promote Irish Catholic colonization in the West. Iowa was only a temporary frontier of an expanding America. In 1856, Father Jeremiah Trecy, pastor of Garryowen, led a group of settlers from Iowa to the Nebraska Territory, where they founded another St. Patrick's Colony. In 1879, the Irish Catholic Colonization Association was organized in Chicago to foster movement from the East of immigrants and their offspring to planned colonies, large and small, on the comparatively inexpensive lands of the western United States.

St. George's Church in Wexford, St. Patrick's in Garryowen, St. Matthew's in Clare, and St. Patrick's on the Lizard, stand as monuments to the spirit of Irish pioneers, not only of Iowa, but of all the rural Irish settlements of the United States.

MEF

Chapter 11

TEXAS: SOLDIERS, PRIESTS, EMPRESARIOS

*Present-day Texas has thriving Irish American communities so numerous
that it ranked fourth among the fifty states, according to the 1980 United
States census, in the number of residents identifying themselves as of Irish
ancestry. Irish pride has been evident on St. Patrick's Day when the river
has been dyed green in San Antonio. Nevertheless, the contribution of
the Irish to early Texas is often overlooked. Some writers ignore the presence of the Irish under Spain and Mexico, perhaps because they tend to
ignore the history of Texas before its independence. Others have classified the Irish as British or Anglo-Saxon. "British" may have been techni-
cally correct after January 1, 1801, when the kingdom of Ireland was
declared defunct and Ireland was made part of the United Kingdom, but
"Anglo-Saxon" was never correct. In hearts and aspirations the Irish
remained a people apart, holding to their traditions as they fought for
freedom. Those who emigrated to Texas rejected English rule and kept
their Irish heritage as they pledged loyalty to Spain, Mexico, Texas, and
eventually the United States.*

SPANISH TEXAS

The Irish reached Texas as permanent land settlers in the 1820s,
decades before Texas became part of the United States, but they were
not the first Irish residents on Lone Star soil. They had been preceded for two centuries by Irish soldiers, priests, administrators,
explorers, and pioneers under the flag of Spain. These were *na
Géanna Fiáine*, "the Wild Geese" (emigrés from Gaelic armies who
fought on Irish soil in the 17th century) and their descendants. They

199

had fled to Spain and elsewhere in Europe. Many of them adventured, in time, to New Spain. Eventually they found their way to Texas and the southwest United States.

Spain had claimed Texas in the 16th century on the basis of the remarkable expeditionary feats of such leaders as Cabeza de Vaca, De Soto, and Coronado. Settlements were made in New Mexico and Arizona, but unfavorable conditions, especially the hostility of the Indians, handicapped early mission attempts in Texas. However, after La Salle led an expedition down the Mississippi to claim for France all lands drained by the river, and in so doing crossed part of Texas, the Spanish knew that they had to confirm their claim. They did so by establishing missions backed by fortified settlements called presidios.

For a hundred years there were scattered Spanish settlements and missions in Texas. Some lasted, some decayed. The name Texas came from a mission founded in 1690 near Neches, called Francisco de la Téjas, which name had come from the Spanish pronunciation of a Caddo Indian word, *téjas*, meaning *friends*. When the Texas tribes turned out to be unfriendly, the missionaries withdrew from that area, but the name remained to describe the vast province.

HUGO O CONOR

When Spain seriously established presidios and appointed good administrators, Texas flourished. One of the greatest administrators was Hugh O' Connor, born in Dublin in 1734. He served in Spain, Cuba, and Mexico. He became known to the Indians as Capitan Colorado because of his red hair, and to the Spanish as Hugo O Conor. He served as Governor of Texas from 1767 to 1770, presiding over the dedication of the cornerstone of the great San Jose Mission in San Antonio in 1768. In 1772, he was appointed Inspector General and Comandante General of the northern province of New Spain, and was charged with bringing order to the far-flung colonies and providing security from the Indians on the entire northern frontier. Within a few years, O Conor accomplished this by establishing a line of presidios stretching 1,500 miles from Texas to California.

O Conor was not the only Irishman to adopt a Spanish name. The records of the troops show obviously Irish names and often Irish identification. In Spain and its colonies, O'Donoghue became O Donoju, Murphy became Morfi, O'Brien became Obregon, Berrigan became Barragan. Even if the Irish surname remained unchanged, the first name would become Spanish, and thus we have Ricardo Nolan, Juan Moran, Florencio O'Leary, Bernardo O'Higgins, Arturo O'Neill, Pedro O'Daly, Marcos Keating, and Patricio Macarty.

JUAN AGUSTIN MORFI

One Irish Franciscan with a Hispanicized name, Juan Agustin Morfi, is an important primary source for United States historians. Father Morfi, a priest-historian, wrote a several-volume history of the early Southwest, *Viaje de Indios*. When he traveled to the Mexican provinces with Comandante General de Croix, he kept a journal that provided for his first-hand history. When he visited Texas, he made notes for an objective and detailed account of life in the 1770s on the frontier of New Spain.

Late 18th century censuses and land records indicate the presence of Irish-born settlers under the Spanish crown. In Nacogdoches in eastern Texas, among those easily identifiable as Irish are Philip Nolan of Belfast, James McNulty of Munster, John Oconor of Connaught, James Maconilt, Richard Sims, William Barr, Thomas Blain, and Francisco Cornegay. All were Spanish subjects holding land under allegiance to Spain. In the first decade of the 19th century, more Irish families were recorded nearby, including Patricio Fitzgerald, Miguel Quinn, and Timoteo Barrett.

GENERAL JUAN O'DONOJU

These were not all submissive Irishmen, accepting what Spain decreed without protest. As part of Mexico, Texas was also part of the movement for independence from Spain. Almost all of the Irish in Texas seem to have supported Mexican independence, which was affirmed in 1821 in the treaty *Plan de Iguala* by General Juan O'Donoju, the last viceroy of New Spain. Ignacio Obregon and Miguel Barragan were Wild Geese descendants whose own descendants became closely identified with Mexico for generations.

It is sometimes forgotten that the Spanish colonies had settlers other than Spanish, just as the British colonies had settlers other than English. The descendants of the Irish in Mexico became Spanish-speaking Mexicans or English-speaking Americans, depending upon which side of the Rio Grande they inhabited at the end of the United States war against Mexico (1846-1848).

FATHER MIGUEL MULDOON

General O'Donoju's chaplain, Father Miguel Muldoon (son of an Irish father and Spanish mother), is part of Texas history, but he died before Texas became part of the United States. Lina Trigg's *Father Miguel Muldoon: The Story of an Early Pioneer Priest* is an especially good source of information. Muldoon appeared on the scene at a time when Mexico was struggling to free itself from Spain and some adventurers were trying to slice off Texas for themselves. One of the leading adventurers was an Irish American named Juan Augustus

Magee who invited Irish mercenaries, mostly men without a country, to join him. Father Muldoon, concerned more about people than politics, felt that the tactics of Magee in 1812-13, James Long in 1819, and other freebooters were more likely to bring chaos and tyranny than order and liberty. He asked to be assigned as a missionary to the new American colonists who, in contrast to the adventurers, were applying legally to Spain or Mexico for land.

An American, Moses Austin, had secured a colonization grant from the Spanish government. Before the claim could be fulfilled, two things happened: Austin died, and all of Mexico, including Texas, became independent of Spain. In 1821, without waiting for authorization from the insecure Mexican Congress, Austin's son Stephen started bringing his settlers to Texas from the United States. In early 1823, after Emperor Iturbide's coup dissolved the Congress, a substitute junta confirmed Austin's grant. In April 1823, after Iturbide was forced to abdicate, a reassembled Congress reconfirmed the grant.

Among Austin's "Old Three Hundred," as the first settlers were called, were some Irish-born and many with far-back Irish roots. Some identified as Irish had surnames Allen, Callaghan, Clark, Cummins, Fitzgerald, Hughes, Jackson, Kennedy, Kelly, Lynch, McCormick, and Moore. When the group arrived at their Texas site, they found two Irish-born families, homesteaders like themselves, already living in the area. They also found Father Muldoon, whose life would become intertwined with the lives of the Austin colonists.

Father Muldoon is not remembered in church or Texas history as a preacher who brought back to the Catholic faith the lax or fallen-away Irish on the frontier. Nor is he remembered as a padre on horseback who braved the elements and covered thousands of miles to found and visit Indian missions. Yet his record of "converts" is remarkable, or unremarkable, if one understands that one hundred percent conversion was expected. Mexico, even in its Spanish days, recognized the wisdom of having permanent, self-interested settlers who cleared the land, tried to make a profit, helped each other, and did not look for constant aid from the government way down south. Mexico was aware, however, of the danger of immigrants who would be so independent that they would ignore the government, its laws, and its religious unity.

In order to enter Texas and to acquire land grants under Mexico as well as under Spain, settlers were required to give up past citizenship and swear allegiance to their new government - and they did. No doubt many lightly gave up United States citizenship to secure rich acreage in Texas. They expected few demands from the many turbulent governments that rose and fell in distant Mexico City. Settlers had to profess allegiance to the Catholic Church, and no doubt many also did this lightly. Spain had considered the Church to be an integral part of government with some mutual overlapping powers, but the Church had struggled constantly to separate itself from politics and warfare. Independent Mexico, influenced by freemasonry, was anti-clerical and anti-Church. It persecuted the Church by expelling friars and hierarchy, by making its own appointments of the unfit to clerical offices, and by closing schools, hospitals, and missions. Yet, since it wanted a surface religious unity by which being a good Catholic meant being a good subject, it provided that the national religion be Roman Catholic.

Father Muldoon, who had an easy-going disposition, was always happy to accept the conversions of the United States emigrants, or to certify as Catholics those who claimed to be such. He may not have challenged questionable claims, but he followed up on his certified and his baptized Catholics with baptisms and marriages of their children.

The term "Muldoon Catholic" has survived in Texas to describe someone who is Catholic only on the surface. Nevertheless, Father Muldoon was respected by the Texans of his era, whether genuine Catholics or land-converted Catholics. The monument erected to him at La Grange says that he is a "forgotten man" of Texas history; that as resident priest and friend of Austin, he contributed much to the success of the colonial venture. The records of Mexico, Texas, and the Catholic Church show that Father Muldoon acted an an intermediary between the Austin colony and the distant Mexican government; that he helped in difficulties with nearby Mexican comandantes and garrisons; that he intervened successfully in conflicts between the settlers and the Indians, including those involving hostage-taking by the Indians and the similar drafting of Indians for work by the settlers; that he worked for the independence of Texas from Mexico; and that he was appreciated in his own time by President Sam Houston of the new Republic of Texas.

In addition to the Roman Catholic Church, there was another condition that became a problem for Stephen Austin and later for Sam Houston. This problem was slavery. Moses Austin's original permit from the Spanish government had allotted a minimal grant to each married man of 640 acres; to his wife 320 acres; to each child 120 acres; to each slave 80 acres. The Mexican government abolished slavery in Texas, as in the rest of Mexico, but old settlers were exempted and were allowed to keep their slaves. (Although the children of these slaves were born free and slave-trading within Texas was legally forbidden, the settlers used occasional decrees from short-lived governments in Mexico City, legal loopholes, and evasions to import more black slaves.)

EMPRESARIOS

Americans in the southern states and tenant farmers in Europe might have looked in vain at the vast fertile and vacant acres of Texas if Spain and Mexico had not encouraged immigration with a system of empresario grants. Prior to the 1820s, homesteaders in the United States had gone into default because of the high cost of public land and bureaucratic tangles over it. Peasants and farmers in the British Isles and Europe had been devastated by the Napoleonic Wars. Spain beckoned with grants for about $100 at most, for those, preferably Spanish and Mexican, who would improve and settle lands in Texas or elsewhere in northern Mexico. Even when United States land prices dropped in 1821, there was the offer of better and cheaper land in newly independent Mexico's Texas province. Families wanted land; Mexico wanted families to settle and secure Texas.

Mexico offered grants of land to empresarios who would contract to find and settle colonists. The empresario was given a contract to provide a specified number of colonists within a specified time for an area defined and surveyed by the Mexican government. Each head of family engaging in agriculture would receive what was called a "League and Labor" of 4,605 acres (4,428 acres of grazing land and 177 acres of farming land). A single man, seventeen years or older, would receive one-third of a league, or 1,476 acres.

After the land was settled as agreed, the empresario was rewarded with fifteen leagues (or *sitios*) and two *labors* - almost 67,000 acres. The conditions included allegiance to the Mexican government, obedience to its laws, and profession of Catholicism.

The Irish seemed to be good candidates for settlers under these conditions, and, in the 1820s, the Mexican empresario Martin de Leon sought Irish for his Texas colony. Long under British colonial rule, they had no problem abandoning an allegiance to Britain that they did not feel. Ireland at this time was going through an especially bad period of depression and famine after the long Napoleonic Wars, for which it had been heavily taxed. Catholics had not yet been emancipated and even Presbyterians were not extended the same rights as Anglicans. For these reasons and no doubt others, De Leon's colony near Victoria, Texas, attracted John Linn, an Irishman who had been a successful trader in licit and illicit goods and who was looking for new fields to conquer. Linn's father was a college professor who had supported the Rebellion of 1798 and escaped from Ireland with a price on his head. John, who inherited his father's idealism and possessed as well an adventuresome and entreprenurial spirit, recruited many Irish for De Leon's colony.

The Irish immigrating to the southern American states after the Napoleonic Wars found conditions difficult. The available land was too expensive to buy. Second and third generation settlers, who now saw themselves as pure native Americans, resented new settlers, especially Irish and Catholic ones, taking away what they perceived as their own deserved opportunities. Often lacking any specific skills, the Irish had difficulty finding paid work in a slave-oriented community. So, along with many poor southerners and families from the Mississippi and Ohio Valleys, they looked to the desirable and unpopulated plains of Mexican Texas.

PROTESTANT IRISH

Another group, Protestant Irish, had emigrated from Ireland to Charleston, South Carolina, then tried Alabama, and finally moved to Texas in 1830 despite the requirement for homesteaders to profess the Roman Catholic faith. Mary K. Galloway in "The Irish of Staggers Point" describes how they put down their roots in present-day Robertson County. At Staggers Point, they erected a fort to repel Indians, fought against both Indians and the elements, rebuilt Staggers Point after destruction, and managed to hold on to their settlement. They built the Presbyterian Old Irish Church of Red Top Prairie and invited other Presbyterians to join them.

The Mexican government was far away and seeds of discord were being sown in the Presbyterian community at Staggers Point. Some there were already imbued with the idea of making Texas independent of Mexico and then annexing it to the United States. For this colony of Irish Protestants, one of the very few settlements of non-Catholic Irish in Texas, the desire to be free of Catholic Mexico was not an unlikely one.

SAN PATRICIO AND REFUGIO

John Flannery in *The Irish Texans* records many details of two settlements with an understandably different attitude from that of the Staggers Point settlers toward the Mexican and Catholic connection: San Patricio and Refugio, founded by two pairs of Irish empresarios. Even before these empresarios had received their contracts, there had been Irish settlers on the lands, as well as some Mexicans, Germans, Danes, and others. These settlers, in the view of Mexican authorities, were too few to secure the land. Fuller colonization was needed. Thus the contracts were given to the Irish empresarios, who undertook the recruiting of immigrants for San Patricio and Refugio and at the same time tried to assimilate peacefully the families already on their land grant.

John McMullen and his son-in-law James McGloin from County Sligo were given the contract for San Patricio de Hibernia in 1828, to be completed by 1836. McMullen had previously tried business and colonization in Mexico, where he had become aware that many Mexican empresarios had failed because they could not get the required number of colonists during the period of their contracts. He felt that the place to look for colonists was among those who had already committed themselves to emigrating from Ireland but had not found a satisfactory place to settle. McMullen and McGloin went to New York and Philadelphia, where they recruited newly-arrived Irish looking for an opportunity to leave the port cities, and they made arrangements for the trip to Texas.

The first two shiploads, with a resident priest, arrived in Texas in October, 1829. They endured many hardships before they were able to move from Copano Bay to the Nueces River crossing, where they were assigned their promised land. Mexico, with its government in turmoil, was slow in confirming the land titles. Not until 1831 did the founding empresarios and some of their colonists have their grants legally confirmed. After that, things went more quickly. By 1836, the population of the town of San Patricio numbered six hundred, quite a crowd in the days when Dallas, with a population of two families, both Irish, was known as a "town."

Two other Irish empresarios, James Power of Wexford and James Hewetson of Kilkenny, founded the Refugio colony. Their grant in 1828 included the abandoned Refugio Mission which the Mexicans were anxious to reactivate. Coming close to the six-year deadline for completion of the contract, Power and Hewetson decided to recruit directly from Ireland (an 1830 Mexican law banned North American immigrants). Power returned to his native Wexford, gave impassioned speeches from his sister's house and in the area surrounding Ballygarrett, and found 250 families, mostly from Wexford, willing to emigrate and become landowners in the almost unbelievable land of Texas. Hewetson, a medical doctor who had come to Texas with Stephen Austin's original group, used emissaries to recruit in other parts of Leinster and found several hundred would-be emigrants in this southeast province of Ireland.

JOURNEY FROM IRELAND

As was customary, the journey from Ireland had to be made in stages. From an Irish port such as New Ross or Wexford City, the emigrants had to go to Liverpool, then to New Orleans, then to Texas. Troubles beset each shipload: stormy seas; shortage of water and provisions; cramped shipboard conditions leading to cholera and typhus ("ship fever") epidemics; necessity to abandon supplies as ships were endangered by seas and disease. Some died on the Atlantic crossing or in pest-ridden New Orleans or in the final port of Copano. Others, ill or bereft of head of family, dropped out at New Orleans with a promise to join the colonists later. Probably no more than one-half to two-thirds of the healthy and enthusiastic families who had left Ireland finally reached Refugio.

Those who survived and arrived received 4,428 acres of grazing land, a labor of 177 acres of farmland, and land for a house in town. This must have seemed like a minor kingdom to tenant farmers and landless laborers coming from County Wexford, where only about a dozen estates of the landed property owners exceeded 4,000 acres. The Mexican government moved more quickly at Refugio than at San Patricio and confirmed two hundred grants before the end of 1834. Some of the earliest grantees were Irish natives Nicholas Fagan, Robert Hearne, Isabella O'Brien, and John Sinnott.

The empresarios could not limit their colonies to Irish immigrants, because they were required to honor the property rights of Mexican-Texans already on the land, and because they were supposed to encourage, despite little success in such attempts over the years, more Mexican settlers. The San Patricio and Refugio colonists, nevertheless, were in the overwhelming majority Irish and Catholic and anti-slavery. This prevented an immediate clash with the Mexican government, the kind of clash already arising elsewhere from the different political attitudes and religious beliefs of the settlers from Kentucky, Tennessee, and other states of the South.

INDEPENDENCE MOVEMENT

Mexico did not succeed in her goal of populating Texas with naturalized Mexican citizens who would be loyal to the hand that fed them with large land grants. Most Irish would move with the winds of change. They would support the independence of Texas. They would, in turn, also support the annexation to the United States. But there were some who would do neither. The two positions are reflected in the actions taken by Power and Hewetson.

James Power favored Texas independence, took an active part in the Texas Revolution, favored annexation to the United States, and signed the State Constitution when Texas became the 28th state in the Union. He did not live to see the advent of the Civil War when Texas tried to take advantage of its perceived right, written in its annexation agreement, to withdraw from the United States.

James Hewetson, Power's partner in the Refugio colony, opposed annexation. Hewetson, who like Power had married into a wealthy Mexican family, returned to Mexico before the winds of war arrived and left the administration of the colony to his partner. He continued to accept Mexico as his adopted country, and died there in 1870. Thus we do not find monuments in Texas today in honor of this man, who was one of its pioneering Irish empresarios.

Some empresarios had failed to fulfill their contracts and had their claims rejected. There were, however, on the land of their rejected grants settlers who had been brought by the failed empresarios and some who had drifted easily into Texas from the Louisiana Territory. By the 1830s, many of the Irish were affected by the ideas of the Americans settling beside them. These Americans, Catholic on the Mexican records only, spoke of Texas as if it were their country, not part of Mexico. They voiced their preference for slaves, black or Indian, to work their huge land holdings and to facilitate turning their ladies into gentlewomen without household chores. As Mexico talked of stricter enforcement of its regulations, to which the settlers had agreed in order to get their land, the Texans talked of independence, and so did most of the Irish among them.

In 1836, Texas had three major groups of colonists: the Irish-born and Irish-descended; the Mexican and Spanish-descended; and the Americans, some of whom for fifteen years had put up only a weak pretense of being Roman Catholics and of being loyal to Mexico. (There were minor groups of Germans and other Europeans.) During the first skirmishes in 1835, most of the Irish had thrown in their lot with the Americans. Colonies such as Refugio and San Patricio could not postpone any decision, since they were at the crossroads of battle. According to John Flannery, the Irish who had hesitated at first because they felt unity with the values of their Mexican neighbors moved quickly to the Texas side, especially when confronted with the tyranny of Mexico's General Santa Anna.

In the battles that ensued, three of the largest Irish colonies - Refugio, San Patricio, and Victoria - had the greatest losses of the War for Independence, in lives, property, livestock, and crops. A dozen Irish-born died at the Battle of the Alamo. More than fifty Irish-born died at Goliad and Coleto Creek. More than thirty gave their lives at the Battle of the Nueces.

Although Mexican troops were ordered back south across the Rio Grande after the Battle of San Jacinto, the War for Texas Independence did not end then and there. The Mexican government, not recognizing or accepting the loss of Texas, sent several generals north over the next ten years to try to win back the territory. The Lone Star Republic had a white population of barely fifty thousand as opposed to Mexico's six or seven million. The Irish and other settlers had to defend themselves from the invading Mexican troops who saw them as ungrateful foreign rebels; from their own Texas troops, mostly hired latecomers without any property interest in Texas, who held up farmers and seized their produce and who imprisoned traders and divided their goods; from continual raids of the freebooters and bandits who roamed the plains driving off livestock, robbing traders, stealing from homesteads, and murdering without cause; from the Indians, especially the Comanche, who took advantage of wartime conditions to attack and massacre the colonists, whom they looked upon as trespassers on Indian territory.

ANTI-CATHOLIC FEELING

In the early 19th century there was no overt antagonism between Catholics and Protestants. According to Spanish and Mexican terms for land acquisition, all settlers were nominally Catholic. After the War of Independence, the Mexican-Spanish priests, with the exception of Father Muldoon and a few others, withdrew to Mexico. During Texas' nine years as a republic, only two priests were active in saying Mass in the vast territory. With no ecclesiastical jurisdiction, the standing of these priests was questionable. Their ties to Mexico and Spain were cut, and Rome did not grant them renewed authority to function as priests.

John Odin, C.M., appointed Vicar-Apostolic in 1841 and later first bishop of Galveston, reported that thousands of Catholics had not seen a priest or had services of one since they had come to Texas. Some Irish said that their opportunity to hear Mass was even less than that of their grandparents in penal days. Understandably, Protestants resented having to conform for land ownership purposes, just as Catholics had resented similar laws in Ireland and England. Yet, with the Mexican government gone and with Catholics in low profile, it is hard to understand the rise of anti-Catholic hysteria. Arise it did, notably when Father Odin founded a convent in Galveston and announced that he was going to Europe to recruit missionary priests and nuns.

With the excuse that the Irish had wavered before taking sides at the beginning of the hostilities, some American-born settlers brought into the open anti-Irish and anti-Catholic feelings. They chose to overlook the fact that the Irish had fought and died for the Texas cause from Goliad in 1835 to Nueces in 1842. They raided the Irish ranches and stole from the homes left empty while the men were out fighting Mexicans, Indians, or other raiders.

It developed, therefore, that a number of Irish Texans looked with fear on Americans who tended to put the Irish into a single category, when actually the Irish could easily fit into at least three categories. The first Irish, such as those in the Refugio colony, had come directly from one province in Ireland, had much in common with one another, and had good rapport with the Mexican Catholics who helped them settle. The second were the Irish such as those in the San Patricio colony, who had come via Philadelphia or New York from many parts of Ireland, and who had learned to adjust to the non-Irish by first learning to adjust to different kinds of Irish. The third group were second, third, and later generation Irish who had spent time in the United States and who felt that the persecuting Anglos in Texas were a minority who would settle down as Texas settled down. They had a lot in common with these Anglos, who like themselves had come from the United States in search of better opportunities.

It is true that the Irish in all three groups had a difficult time deciding where their allegiance was at the very beginning of the War for Independence, a war initiated by the Texans. The first and second groups did not understand why they or the Mexican Texans would want to be free from Mexico and a government seat so far away that enforcement of law was negligible. The third group, closer to the Anglos, realized that Texas independence was just a stepping stone to admission to the United States. When the Mexican troops marched on Texas, nevertheless, the Irish in all three groups tended to stand and fight solidly for the Republic of Texas. Without consciously knowing it, they had become Texans first. This made it easier for them to fight for the United States against Mexico, after Texas voted to be annexed to the United States and the war began. The Irish stood firmly for Texas *and* the United States, and thus became Americans.

THE ST. PATRICK'S BATTALION OR LEGIÓN DE EXTRANJEROS

According to government statistics cited by Francis B. Heitman, the United States Regular Army had a total of 637 officers and 5,925 enlisted men on May 13, 1846, when the United States declared war on Mexico. The Army expanded quickly. The government figures show that the total serving at some time during the war, both regulars and volunteers, was 115,847, of whom 111,063 were enlisted men. Enlistment records show that about one-third were of Irish birth. It is thought that about one-half of the total forces were Catholics, mostly foreign-born.

The desertion rate was one of the highest of any war in which America engaged, although enlistment terms and practices made the designation "deserter" controversial. Heitman reported 9,207 deserters, with about 4,000 deserting in Mexico. Some of the deserters ended up fighting for Mexico. One unit called *Las Compañías de San Patricio* or *Legión de Extranjeros* was led by Galway-born John Riley (aka Juan O'Reilly and Juan Riley). Mayo-born Lieutenant Patrick Dalton was second in command.

The San Patricios consisted of two companies, first formed as an artillery unit, then as infantry. As the name indicated, the unit was largely Irish but also included some Germans, other Europeans, and Irish Mexicans. The unit's banner had a coat-of-arms of Mexico on one side. On the other, it had, as described proudly by John Riley in an October 28, 1847, letter from prison to his former employer, Charles O'Malley in Mackinac, Michigan:

I forgot to tell you under what banner we fought so bravely. It was that glorious emblem of native rights, that banner which should have floated over our native soil many years ago. It was St. Patrick, the harp of Erin, the Shamrock upon a green field.

The San Patricios distinguished themselves in several battles and developed a reputation for fighting bravely and fiercely. The last battle in which they participated took place against General Winfield Scott's troops on August 20, 1847, at Churubusco, four miles south of old Mexico City. After a do-or-die battle and defeat, thirty-five San Patricios were killed and eighty-five captured, including John Riley (now an Acting Major) and Lieutenant Dalton. United States Army casualties included 16 officers and 139 of their men killed, 876 wounded, and 40 missing, including losses at the Battle of Contreras (aka Padierna), fought on August 19-20. Scott, estimating casualties for the two days at both battles, reported that 4,000 Mexicans were killed or wounded. He gave a more exact count of prisoners, 2,637 of them, including two ex-Presidents of Mexico.

The San Patricios, manning artillery at the San Mateo convent and at the bridge to Churubusco, were blamed (or credited) with inflicting most of the American casualties. This explains the rage of Scott's men against *Los Patricios*, many of whom had used skills acquired in the American Army against their former comrades.

Seventy-two San Patricios were charged with desertion from the United States Army. At the first court martial at San Angel, from August 26 to September 3, twenty-nine men were sentenced to hang. Scott pardoned two and revised the sentences of seven to fifty lashes on the back with a rawhide whip and the branding with a letter "D" for deserter on the cheek. Among the latter was John Riley, whose death sentence was commuted to imprisonment for the war's duration on the grounds that he had deserted before war was declared. In his defense Riley also claimed British citizenship.

On September 10, 1847, sixteen of the hangings took place at San Angel. Four more were hanged at Mixcoac, about two miles north of San Angel, on September 11. The remaining forty-three prisoners from St. Patrick's Battalion were tried at Tacubaya, from August 23 to September 7. Three were sentenced to lashes, branding, and imprisonment; one to forfeit all pay and allowances; three to be shot to death; and thirty-six to be hanged. General Scott granted a number of commutations, leaving thirty to face death by hanging. These thirty were obliged by Colonel William S. Harney, who was assigned to conduct the hanging, to wait below Chapultepec Castle until the American flag flew from it. The castle, a former residential palace that had been converted to a military college, was protected by its position on the heights and by some recently improvised fortifications. Its defenders, in the castle and on the perimeter defenses, included about 800 Mexican regulars and 47 cadets, ranging in age from about eleven to nineteen.

On the morning of September 13, the doomed San Patricios watched as Scott's infantry, after a heavy artillery bombardment, assaulted the perimeter defenses and the heights of Chapultepec. According to Mexican tradition, one of the cadets, refusing to surrender to the invaders, wrapped himself in a Mexican flag and committed suicide by leaping from a window high on the heights and shouting "Viva Mexico!" As soon as the American flag flew over the Castle, the hangman sprang the traps on the thirty San Patricios who had been obliged to wait and watch the battle from below.

The San Patricios do not appear as heroes in American history books, but the Mexicans honor them, just as they honor the cadets. In recent years commemorative ceremonies that have been held at monuments dedicated to the *Niños Heróes* (Boy Heroes) at Chapultepec and to the San Patricios at Villa Obregon (San Angel). In 1960, a fine commemorative medal was struck with the inscription AL HEROICO BATALLÓN DE SAN PATRICIO, 1847, encircling an eagle and a Celtic cross. The accompanying brochure describing the medal states in the words of the Villa Obregon monument that it was in memory of the SOLDADOS IRLANDESES DEL HEROICO BATALLÓN DE SAN PATRICIO MÁRTIRES, QUE DIERON SU VIDA POR LA CAUSA DE MÉXICO DURANTE LA INJUSTA INVASIÓN NORTEAMERICANA DE 1847. (In memory of the Irish soldiers of the heroic San Patricio Battalion, martyrs who gave their lives for the cause of Mexico during the unjust North American invasion of 1847.) *(See Note 1: Irish.)*

MEF

Chapter 12

CALIFORNIA: LURE OF GOLD AND SOIL

*No major studies have been published of the rural Irish of California.
Yet, according to the 1870 United States Census, thirty-eight of the fifty
California counties had an Irish majority among the foreign-born population in a predominantly rural state. More than a century later, in 1980,
the United States Census Bureau reported that California, first in population, was also first among the fifty states in the number of residents who
reported "one specific ancestor" as Irish.*

DUBLIN, ALAMEDA COUNTY

The city of Dublin, forty miles east of San Francisco, has a rich
and very Irish history. In the spring of 1853, when the bandit Joaquin
Murrieta was hotly pursued by a posse of California Rangers, he
would sometimes pause in the laurel trees a short distance from the
home of Irish-born farmer Jeremiah Fallon in what is now Dublin,
California. Murrieta signalled his presence with a whistle. If the
coast was clear Jeremiah responded with a quail call. Murrieta and
his band would then receive the hospitality of the Fallon household.
The Fallons were also entrusted with delivering messages to Don Jose
Maria Amador, the largest landowner in the valley, whose residence
was more closely watched.

On one occasion, late at night, Murrieta knocked on the door of
the residence of Michael Murray, another Irish immigrant and the
brother-in-law of Jeremiah Fallon. Mrs. Murray answered. A soft-
spoken man told her in Spanish: "Don't be afraid, no harm will come
to you. My men are hungry. Do you have some bread?" After the

men were fed, Murrieta insisted on paying for the food with a five dollar gold piece.

Who were these Irish who befriended the notorious outlaw? The story of Jeremiah Fallon, his spouse Ellen Murray, and their Irish neighbors is worth the telling, reflecting as it does the extraordinary mobility and adaptability of thousands of Irish who crossed an ocean and a continent to reach California, sought gold in the mines for a short time, but ended up tilling the soil in the rich valleys of the state.

Jeremiah Fallon was baptized James Fallon, son of Thomas Fallon and Ellen McGovern of Lurgan, Elphin Parish, County Roscommon, Ireland, according to an August 8, 1815, entry in the Elphin Parish register. In 1834 at age eighteen, Fallon boarded a sailing ship for New York City. Among the passengers were Michael Murray and his younger sister, Ellen (aka Eleanor), also of Elphin Parish. Jeremiah and Eleanor fell in love during the long voyage, but their marriage plans had to wait almost five years. She and brother Michael remained in New York for a time.

Jeremiah sought his fortune in New Orleans. A shipbuilder by trade, he constructed two ships and became known as Captain Darby Fallon. By 1838, he had become successful enough hauling timber down the Mississippi to New Orleans to send to New York for Eleanor. The marriage register of St. Patrick's Catholic Church in New Orleans indicates that "Darby Fallon" married "Ellen Murray" on May 22, 1838. Four of the children of Jeremiah and Ellen were born in New Orleans. These included twin daughters who died in infancy.

Meanwhile, Jeremiah's brother-in-law, Michael Murray, unmarried, had left New York City to take up farming near St. Joseph, Missouri. Michael soon turned his eyes further westward. During a visit by Jeremiah and Ellen, Michael convinced them to join him on a wagon train to California. Jeremiah returned to New Orleans and sold his boats and business.

In the early spring of 1846, Jeremiah, Ellen, their two children (John and Ellen), and Michael Murray yoked up their oxen and joined a wagon train. Every wagon, according to a story passed on to a great-granddaughter, had a cat in it to keep the mice and other pests out of the grain the emigrants carried. At one point during the long and dangerous journey across the rivers, plains, and mountains, the wagons were approached by a band of Indians. The Indians had never tasted white bread. Ellen Fallon laid out a red and white linen table cloth. The chief appreciated the style, as well as the warm bread. He later sent a hunting party with fresh meat to the wagon train.

According to family folklore, the Fallon and Murray wagon left Missouri in a group headed by George F. Donner and James F. Reed. They separated from the Donner Party, so the story goes, at Fort

Bridger, Wyoming, after deciding to push on with little rest. The Donners chose to rest for a few days, a decision of fateful consequences. Thirty-nine of 87 members of the party perished, most of them after being entrapped by an early snowfall in the High Sierras, and most of the survivors had been driven to cannibalism. *(See Note 1: Donner Party.)*

The Fallon family and Michael Murray arrived in Mission San Jose on October 18, 1846, with Fallon's wagon pulled by a big white ox called "Whitey." Whitey the ox had been badly crippled in Nevada by arrows from an unfriendly band of Indians and left behind to die. Nevertheless, the faithful ox followed the train and was found the next morning among the other oxen. Whitey was hitched up again and hobbled across the Sierras into Mission San Jose. He later helped pull the wagons into Dublin. "He was a beloved member of the Fallon family, much a part of the household," Jeremiah's great-granddaughter, Veronica Keifer, was told.

At Mission San Jose, Spanish quickly became the language of the Fallon family. A daughter, Mary Catherine, was born on May 17, 1847. According to folklore, she was the first child of other than Spanish or Indian parentage baptized at the Mission (she would one day marry her first cousin, Luke Murray). Ann and Daniel were born in 1850 and 1851, Rodger and William soon following. Michael Murray found a bride at the Mission, Irish-born Amelia (Emily) Nash. The old Mission register records the baptism of their son, Daniel Murray, on November 4, 1852, his godparents being Robert Livermore and his spouse, Josefa Higuera. But tragedy struck when John, oldest son of the Fallons, picked some green plums in the Mission garden, sickened, and died.

In the spring of 1849, a very handsome young man with a lovely wife, age sixteen, arrived at the Mission after a long and difficult journey with a group of about eighteen people from the District of Hermosillo, Sonora, Mexico. The couple were Joaquin Murrieta and his spouse, Rosita Feliz. Rosita had scurvy from lack of vegetables. She was nursed back to health by Ellen Fallon and Mary Jane Norris, wife of Leo Norris. (The Norrises were Irish Catholic settlers from Kentucky's Nelson County, a center of Catholicism which included Bardstown, site of a Catholic seminary.) Joaquin worked in the vegetable gardens, returning the kindnesses of the Irish settlers with many favors of his own.

Gold fever arrived at Mission San Jose in 1848. Jeremiah Fallon and Michael Murray headed for the Mother Lode. Joaquin Murrieta, Rosita, and Joaquin's brother, Jesus, also headed for the gold fields east of Stockton. Anti-Mexican sentiment was running high. According to a mixture of fact and folklore, the Murrieta brothers tried mining on the Stanislaus River but were constantly harassed and driven up river by Anglo miners. As was the practice with many enterprising Spanish and Mexicans, in the evenings Joaquin dealt a gambling game called monte in his blue tent. Both on the river and in the tent he was sometimes robbed, cheated, and beaten, as were other non-Anglos, especially the Chinese. At Murphys New Diggins, now known as Murphys, near Angels Camp in Calaveras County, Rosita was reportedly assaulted by some Kentuckians, Joaquin was tied to a tree and whipped, and Jesus was hanged.

Joaquin gave up any further attempts at good citizenship. He swore revenge. After taking Rosita to their adobe residence in what is now Niles Canyon, between Dublin and San Jose, Joaquin became head of the most notorious outlaw band in the nation. His gang's escapades were heralded in newspapers across the land. Hundreds of crimes were credited to him, even when they occurred simultaneously in Sacramento and San Diego.

Murrieta, who was both Catholic and Mexican, became a fearful symbol for the Know Nothing Nativists, people suspicious of anybody except Anglo-Protestants. The Know Nothing Movement in the Far West was directed mainly against the Mexicans and Chinese and to a lesser extent against the Irish. Some of the Irish, in fact, embraced the prejudices of the Anglos against the Mexicans and Chinese. For the Spanish, "El Famoso" Joaquin became the personification of the struggle of Spanish and Mexican "Californios" to retain their lands, laws, and culture against the tide of the Anglos.

It is small wonder that the Irish Catholic settlers in Dublin, some of whom had experienced Know Nothingism in the East and who had keen memories of persecution for their race and religion in Ireland, identified sympathetically with Murrieta, giving him refuge as he was pursued by what they considered to be self-righteous Anglos. It is equally unsurprising that Murrieta was befriended by Don Amador, whose cattle herds and horses were being devastated by poachers on their way to the gold fields, by Indians with whom he dealt very brutally (*see Note 2: Amador*), and by Captain Fremont, commanding the California Battalion, who "requisitioned" many of Amador's horses, for which he was never reimbursed.

Authoritative historians of Murrieta, such as Charles Callison and the late Frank Latta, are convinced that the posse under Sheriff Harry Love did not kill the real Joaquin Murrieta at the shootout at Cantua in the San Joaquin Valley. Only one man in Love's twenty-man posse claimed to be able to identify the bandit. There were at least five "Joaquin" gangs in the state whose crimes, some of them heinous, were credited to Joaquin Murrieta. Nevertheless, Sheriff Love and his deputies presented to authorities the severed head of the man they claimed was Joaquin Murietta and collected the bounty authorized by the Legislature.

When Jeremiah Fallon viewed the severed head on display in San Francisco, he supposedly remarked very quietly, not wanting to endanger his old friend who he believed might still be alive: "That head isn't Joaquin's. Murrieta was a blonde. This one belongs to some poor damned Indian." So the story was told many years later by a daughter who heard her father's words and was entrusted with the secret.

Jeremiah Fallon and Michael Murray fared better than their friend Murrieta in the gold country. They obtained sufficient capital to purchase land from Amador in the Amador Valley. He was fighting a losing battle against poachers. In a document dated October 28, 1850, Jose Maria Amador and his wife, Soledad Alviso Amador, deeded 1,500 varras (about 246 acres) to Jeremiah Fallon for $1,500. The land was just south of what is now Interstate-580. Shortly thereafter, Michael Murray acquired from Amador a parcel just north of 580.

On the 1852 census for Contra Costa County, the Jeremiah Fallon and Michael Murray families were listed consecutively with families headed by the following ranchers and farmers: Christopher Stamerman (Germany); Jose M. Amador (California); James Brien (Ireland, with wife, Mary, and six children, the three oldest of whom appeared to be living in the household of neighbor Carrel W. Ish); Michael Murray (Ireland); Carrel W. Ish (Tennessee); Jeremiah Fallon (Ireland); Augustine Bernal (California); Jose Siguria (vaquero, birthplace not given); John W. Cottinger (a lawyer, birthplace not given); Robert Livermore (England). Several laborers were listed, including John Galvin (age 24, Maine) and Edward [Kenner?] (age 64, Ireland). Eleven Indians, occupation "domestic" or "vaquero," were also enumerated, first name only. In October 1852, the pioneering community in the area at the foot of Mount Diablo, stretching today from San Ramon through Dublin to Pleasanton, consisted of 49 males and 34 females.

Shortly thereafter, Tennessee-born James Witt Dougherty and Thomas D. Wells arrived in Dublin, along with William Glaskins. The hard-pressed Don Amador soon deeded ten thousand acres at $2.20 per acre to Dougherty and his partner Glaskins (Doughterty later purchased Glaskins' interest). He also deeded three square miles north of Dublin, in the vicinity of what is now San Ramon, to Leo Norris.

Fallon and Murray soon had acquired over one thousand acres. Amador eventually sold off all of his vast holdings and died in relative poverty at Watsonville. He was buried in Gilroy.

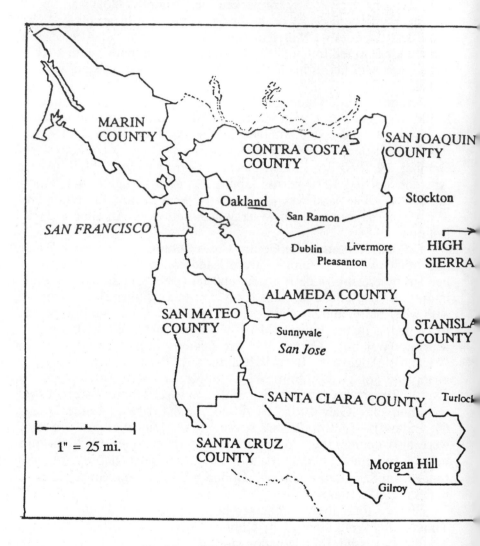

28. Map of San Francisco Bay Area.

TOM DONLON

1834-1859   A NATIVE OF LONGFORD, IRELAND.
HE PLEDGED $50 TO HELP BUILD OLD SAINT
RAYMOND'S CHURCH IN 1856. WHILE WORKING
ON THE CHURCH, HE FELL FROM THE ROOF AND
WAS KILLED AT AGE 25. A SCHOOL IN DUBLIN
WAS NAMED FOR HIM BY VOTE OF THE
STUDENT BODY.

29 and 29a. Old St. Raymond's Church, Dublin, California, and Donlon plaque, 1988 photos.

30 and 31. Eleanor Fallon (1815-96), wife of Jeremiah and sister of Michael Murray;
headstone in St. Raymond's Cemetery for Jeremiah Fallon (1815-64) of County
Roscommon, who emigrated with Michael Murray.

32. Michael Murray, born in County Roscommon in 1809; settled in Dublin,
California, in 1852; three schools, a school district, and a town were named for him.

San Ramon Church

	Sub	Pd
Jeremiah Fallon	$ 30 .	30 .
Edwd Storan	50 .	50 .
Walter Walsh	40 .	40 .
Bernard McLonghli	25 .	8 .
Mc Devany	25 .	25 .
Lawrence Leicester	25 .	25 .
Jn Garrity	25 .	25 .
Mc McCollier	30 .	30 .
Wm Murray	25 .	25 .
Peter Murray	20 .	20 .
Jn Nash	20 .	20 .
Lawrence Nash	30 .	20 .
Mc G. Stiggins	20 .	10 .
Dm Rattigan	10 .	10 .
Geo Johnston	5 .	5 .
Ed Caran	25 .	25 .
Jn Leicester	20 .	10 .
Ja Donlan	10 .	10 .
Thos Donlan	50 .	
John Murray	10 .	10 .
Dominic McGrath	10 .	10 .
Leo Norris	30 .	30 .
Mary Burke	10 .	10 .
James Whelan	10 .	
Tc cary	$ 535	

Subscr   Paid

Brought over	3 535	
Francis Alviso	20 .	
Marks [BERNAL]	2 .	
Francisco Bernal	20 .	
Guadalupe Bernal	20 .	
Teresa Bernal	10 .	
Sean Livermore [LIVERMORE]	50 .	40 .
Casimer Livermore	10 .	
Teresa Livermore	10 .	
Mc Cleary	10 .	
Jn Murphy	15 .	15 .
Peter Arhold	20 .	20 .
Thos Hart	5 .	5 .
Thos Murphy	10 .	
J. Hallaghan	5 .	
Paul Buckler	5 .	
Mr FitzGerald	10 .	
Wm Norton	3.50	2.50
Jes. Engelmeyer	5 .	5 .
Wm Tehan	10 .	10 .
James David	2.50	2.50
Wm Lynch	10 .	10 .

Micheal Cleary $5

33. Donors' List, for the construction of the San Ramon Church Old St. Raymond's , 1859. A second page of the list cites the following additional subscriptions: W.N. Norris pd. $10; Leo Norris pd. $10; Michael Farr pd. $10; Walter Walsh pd. $10; John Meyer pd. $10; and John Green pd. $10.

The first families were soon joined by several score of others, the largest part of them bearing Irish surnames, such as the following: Martin and Horan (from Kings County, now Offaly), Lynch (from New York), Tehan (from County Kilkenny), McMee (from County Donegal), McDermid (from Missouri), Layton (from Virginia, with an Irish-born spouse), Donlon, McGrath, Green, and Flanagan (from County Longford), Murphy (from County Monaghan, via Saint John, New Brunswick), Lyster (from County Roscommon, via Sydney, Australia), and others with Irish surnames whose places of origin have not been determined: Redman (aka Redmond), Devaney, Walsh, Fitzgerald, McLaughlin, McCann, Nash, Farr, Lavan, Garrity, Rattigan, Higgins, Burke, Hart, O'Callaghan, Cleary, Whelan, Collier, Norton.

William and Patrick Murray, brothers of Michael, arrived from County Roscommon with their families in the 1850s. So did Dominick McGrath and several Donlons, believed to be related to McGrath, from nearby County Longford - Tom, his sister Elizabeth, Peter, and John Donlon. John and his wife, Mary (aka Margaret) McGovern, had spent several years in New York City, where their first child, James A., was born. Jeremiah Fallon's sister, Alice Kelly, came from Nova Scotia with her family. Two Nash heads of household, shown on the 1860 census, were most likely close relatives of Michael Murray's wife, Emily Nash.

The odyssey of Lawrence Lyster and Sarah (Moran) of County Roscommon covers three continents.   On September 20, 1839, Lawrence and Sarah and three children sailed on the ship *Crusader* from Kingstown, Ireland, for Australia. In Sydney, where Lawrence worked as a stone mason, they had at least three more children before emigrating to San Francisco in 1852, and in that year their youngest child of record, Elizabeth, was born. Shortly thereafter, the family moved to Dublin, where Lawrence died in 1861. *(See Note 3: Pioneer Families.)*

Cited with the Donlons, Lysters, Fallons, and others on the Donors' List, year 1859, for St. Raymond's Church in Dublin, was William Lynch (1828-1910). Lynch was born in Flushing, Long Island, New York, in July 1827 or 1828, the son of Michael Lynch and Elizabeth Smith. Orphaned young, he went to work as an apprentice carpenter at age fifteen, and after five years became a journeyman carpenter. In late 1848 or early 1849, he boarded the pilot boat *W.G. Hackstaff* for San Francisco, and, according to a plaque in Dublin's old cemetery, the boat passed through the Straits of Magellan and arrived in San Francisco on June 25, 1849 "after 6 months of buffeting strong winds and waves."

A long letter dated September 18, 1849, that he wrote to a relative, Samuel Smith, gives a vivid picture of his experiences during his first three months in California. (*See Note 4: Lynch Family.*) Lynch wrote that he purchased and took with him to the "gold digans" the following tools:

... .shovels, pickes, crowbars pans gold washer and all thay empliments of ware that was neady . . .thay [the] next thing i ingage my pashage up to a small town cald Stockton, this a bought [about] a hundred & fifty miles from San fran cisco i [stayed] thare a fue dayes and heard all cindes of storeys   while thare i saw meney how [who] were destute of menes [means] to get to the mindes   thay wod sel every thing thay had at a very low price   meny things i bot myself and put them with my bageag untill i got ready to start for [there] myself. . .

The letter described how Lynch was delayed five days because of the high prices charged by the teamsters, eighteen to twenty cents a pound, for carting supplies on mules over the mountains to the mines.

But i evenchaly reach thare and it was a hard lucking sight i tell you   i cud not see nothing but a soled bed of rockes   thinkes i to my self this is a purty place to luk for gold after cumming the distenes of 18 thousand miles   but how somever i lucked over all this truble and cept a stif uper lip, and tuck my pick in one hand and shovel in the other and pan on handle of my pick and went [off] like any other gold diger and presed to the rocky hill and in a fue minets i found a lump of gold that wade 2 ownses i dug in with good curage all day digin a bout with little sucksess   i past three weaks in the digins and my ganes was but little . . .

Lynch further reported that the most a miner could make per day was from eight to ten dollars:

... .i give you my word all those poor devils in the mindes have to work for every cent thay can get for thay have to dig in a soled bed of stones and this is a small discripshon of the gold digans . . .

That was enough for Lynch to abandon the gold fields and take up his carpentry trade in San Francisco. He wrote that many people with whom he was acquainted in that city had died without a friend to console them, and that as he himself was writing this letter he was sitting at the bedside of a sick man who had been "a good frind to mee when i was sick." He complained of the shortage and expense of housing and of his not being able to get

a shanty not hafe as your oald cowshed without painge a hunderd dolars a month But thay are building up from those hills very fast so it makes my buisness very brisk Carpenters are getting from 12 to 14 dolars per day   Bording is from 14 to 25 per week and washing from 6 to 8 dolars a dusen and you can gow and by surts [shirts] for a doler a pice   clothing is as cheap hear as it is home   Sow if you now aney of your frindes cumming to Calaforney you can tell them thay nedint over burding them selfs with clothing   But cosce [coax] them to stay away if you can . . .the gold is here but the trubel and mersey [misery] you will have to undergoe in gitting here and your life is worth all the gold that aney fre[e] men can earn to pay one fore his trubel.

Although William Lynch expressed his intention to return to the gold fields in a few weeks, other records indicate he spent most of the next year engaged in the carpentry trade in San Francisco and Santa Clara counties. In the spring of 1850 he took a $2,000 contract to repair the adobe for the Vallejo family at Mission San Jose. While there, he pre-empted a one-quarter section (160 acres) and planted potatoes. Unfortunately, a plague of grasshoppers made this venture unsuccessful. At Mission San Jose he met Leo Norris and, most importantly, Leo's daughter Mary. Soon thereafter, Norris and Lynch became partners in the purchase from Don Jose Maria Amador of the land heretofore mentioned in what is now San Ramon, just north of Dublin. The first crop they planted was barley and they began to prosper. Lynch built houses for himself and his father-in-law. The community known today as San Ramon was, for a while, called Lynchville and, sometimes, Limerick.

The Mission San Jose register records that William Lynch, age 25 and a native of New York, accepted the Catholic faith on March 25, 1853, William Norris serving as godfather. This was doubtless a requirement for his marriage the following month to Leo's daughter, Mary. Seven children were born to William and Mary Lynch. William did not practice the Catholic religion, however. He was a charter member of the local Masonic organization, but he always saw to it that his wife got to Mass on Sunday, so recalls his only surviving granddaughter, Viola Lynch Jones, 92, of Walnut Creek, California.

SQUATTERS

Many of those who arrived in the Dublin-San Ramon area in the 1850s set up tents and squatted on lands with cloudy titles but claimed by James Witt Dougherty and others. The acquisitive and aggressive Dougherty, Protestant and American-born, held to his land tenaciously, acquiring more and more. He would lease but rarely sell. As a consequence, he was sometimes at odds over land boundaries with other, mostly Catholic, owners and squatters. Dougherty's rugged individualism sharply contrasted with the attitudes of the Catholic, Irish-born settlers who seem to have brought with them from Ireland a modicum of the ancient tradition of extended families and the feeling that land should be shared. (*See Note 4a: Dougherty.*)

John Green, an Oakland druggist born in County Longford, arrived in Dublin in 1857 and set up a tent on land claimed by both Dougherty and Michael Murray. Murray invited Green to move closer to his home. In 1862, Green purchased a piece of Murray's property for $6,000, but he still had to deal with Dougherty, who also claimed the parcel, and he settled with him out of court for $900. Green constructed the first general store and post office in Dublin. When he died in 1895, his beneficiaries, according to his last will and testament, included three sisters in County Longford. His son Joseph (1864-1921), a graduate of Santa Clara College, became nationally known as a leader in the field of energy and supervised the construction of hydroelectric systems in northern California. He married Annie McCann in 1887, had four sons and three daughters, was active in Catholic Church work, and died in Palo Alto.

In 1853, Alameda County was formed from portions of old Santa Clara and Contra Costa counties. Dougherty, Fallon, Murray, and Green served on the board of supervisors during the early years. Murray Township was named after Michael Murray. So was the Murray School, established in 1856 on land donated by Murray and Fallon, or so they thought until Dougherty also claimed part of the land, after which he donated what he thought was his share for the school. Murray and Fallon sold off parcels on reasonable terms to squatters and others. Leo Norris sold off a large parcel to Protestant Joel Harlan, whose house "El Nido" (The Nest) is today a tourist attraction.

The 1961 Ordnance Survey Map bears witness to the early Irish presence, with names like Devany Canyon, Dougherty Hills, Donlan Canyon, Tehan Canyon, Collier Canyon, Norris Canyon.

Construction of St. Raymond's Church began in the late 1850s and the Donors' List survives. It contains forty-eight names, at least thirty-six of them Irish. The Spanish donors included the widow and two adult daughters of Robert Livermore. The widow pledged fifty dollars. Also on the Donors' List is the name of Dominic McGrath, a ten dollar contributor. He later married one of the Murrays, and they were to establish a fiefdom in Ventura County, of which more later. Tom Donlon, age twenty-five, pledged fifty dollars. That sum was exceeded by no one, but young Tom did not live to make good his generous pledge. In 1859, while working on the construction of the church, he fell from the roof and was killed. A street and a school in today's Dublin are named after him. In 1860, the church was consecrated by Archbishop Alemany of San Francisco and Father Federa of Mission San Jose. Michael Murray provided two sets of vestments and a solid silver crucifix. Once a month Father Kelly of St. Mary's in Oakland arrived on horseback to say Mass. In 1866, Father John Cassidy officiated at the marriage in the church of William Tehan and Ellen Fallon.

Dublin's post office was known for many years as Dougherty or Dougherty's Station, vying with the unofficial name Dublin, which appeared in print for the first time on an 1878 county map. The community was conveniently situated at the crossroads of two main trails. One proceeded from Monterey through Dublin to Martinez, thence across the Carquinez Straits to Benicia and on to Sacramento; the other from Oakland to Stockton, and thence to the gold fields. The Alamilla Springs, now just off the intersection of Interstate 580 and Interstate 680, provided a convenient rest stop for travellers and horses. The small community prospered by growing grain and raising pigs, cattle, and sheep, and by providing bed and board for weary travellers.

By 1870, Dublin had two hotels, a blacksmith's shop, a shoe-maker, a church, a schoolhouse, and Green's general merchandise store. In 1879, the largest landowners in Alameda County were Charles McLaughlin and James Witt Dougherty. McLaughlin owned most of the hilltops west of Dublin. Dougherty, the second largest owner with 17,000 acres, possessed much of the rich flatlands. Although Dougherty died on September 30, 1879, he was listed on the 1880 census, age 66, in a household with five children, two servants, two Chinese cooks, and nineteen farmhands. Dougherty's only son, Charles, tried unsuccessfully for many years to incorporate as the "City of Dougherty" a plot of land he had inherited in the then-unincorpo-rated town of Dublin. He was consistently rebuffed by Irish-domi-nated Boards of Supervisors. Charles enjoyed the things of this world, including expensive cars and European and Asian junkets in the soci-ety of the rich. He left the superintending of the Dougherty Ranch to Rodger Fallon, son of Jeremiah. The plaque beside the grave of Rodger, who died a bachelor in his seventies in 1932, reads: ". . .renowned for his honesty and integrity and proficiency with the *ri-ata* [rawhide rope] which sometimes was up to 70 feet in length."

Hill owner Charles McLaughlin was unrelated to the brothers Owen and Bernard McLaughlin of the Dublin Catholic community. Charles was a Pennsylvania-born capitalist and railroad builder, who resided in San Francisco. He was shot to death in that city on December 13, 1883, by a disappointed sub-contractor who had fought McLaughlin in the courts for many years to obtain payment for work completed on a railroad right-of-way from San Jose to Stockton via Niles Canyon.

Beginning about 1870, a number of Danes, Germans, Portuguese (from the Azores), and Chinese, arrived in Murray Township. By 1900, Dublin and vicinity had truly become a melting pot. Today, the valley is the scene of suburban sprawl, high tech industry, numerous shopping malls, and considerable affluence. Camp Parks (now an Army Reserve training base) and the Santa Rita Prison are nearby. In a now-isolated corner of the growing city is Heritage Park. It is the site of a neatly kept old cemetery where lie the bones of Tom Donlon and other early settlers. Many plaques describe the odysseys of the pioneers. The Protestant plots are mostly to the left of a paved lane, the Catholic plots to the right, closer to Old St. Raymond's Church, which still stands. The most impressive monument, about eighteen feet high, is over the bones of James Witt Dougherty (1813-1879) and the dog that was doubtless his most loyal admirer. A plaque beside the stone reads: "Carlo, his faithful dog, outlived him by 3 years. As Dougherty wished, his dog was buried at his feet."

Also in Dublin's Heritage Park is the Murray School, now a museum maintained by the Dublin Historical Preservation Association, of which Dan Downey, a native of County Down, was serving as president in 1988. Active with Downey in the Association was Peter Hegarty, a Dublin city councilman, with ancestral roots in County Mayo. A short walk east of the Heritage Park and southeast of the Hibernia Bank, on the southern tip of land once owned by James Witt Dougherty, is the Lord Dublin Howard Johnson Hotel. There, proprietor Louise Clark maintains a heritage room, where a large photograph of Old St. Raymond's Church hangs on one wall. Many descendants of the early settlers still live in the area. Some of them are active in three associations devoted to preserving the old landmarks. Virginia Bennett, retired Dublin librarian, has written a valuable history of the community, *Dublin Reflections.*

LIVERMORE, ALAMEDA COUNTY

In 1851, Thomas McLaughlin settled on the banks of a stream known as the Old San Joaquin in eastern Santa Clara (now Alameda) County, and engaged in farming. The year before, Edward B. Carrell took up government land at Corral Hollow, about eight miles east of Livermore. He and three partners built a tavern, The Zink House, on the old Spanish trail, where they served wayfarers for a number of years. In 1856, Captain Jack O'Brien, a sheepherder, discovered coal at Corral Hollow. Subsequently, he and Carrell organized a flourishing coal business. Carrell kept a diary which reveals the daily life of an enterprising Irish entrepreneur of the period. Here is a sequence of entries for 1857, from "Edw'd B. Carrell, his Book": *(See Note 5: Carrell's Diaries.)*

Thursday, January 1, 1857. . .At home in Corral Hollow. 2 P.M. went to look for old Sorrel but could not find him. . .Wright [Horatio E. Wright, a partner of Carrell] says H.T. Johnson lives at Tobaga or Panama, in case I should pass that way.

Friday, Jan 2. . .Went to look for old Sorrel & found him near Charley. 4 P.M. stoped at Murrys, Supper & Bed $1.00. At Hayward whiskey $1.25. Light rains during the day. ["Murrys" was house of Michael Murray at Dougherty's Station/Dublin, between Livermore and San Jose.]

Saturday, Jan 3. . .Got breakfast from old Doc 10 A.M. [met] Markey from Hayward, gave him some coal. 1 P.M. left old Sorrel at livery at San Antonio at $1.00 per day. At Henry's Dinner & Whiskey 62-1/2 cents. Going to San Francisco [on the ferry] 50 cents. [Old Doc's place was on the old road just north of present Decoto.]
    Sunday, January 4, 1857. . .found Wright at Globe Hotel. . .took dinner there. . . went to see the San Francisco Minstrels. . .50 cents.
    Monday, January 5. . .9 A.M. went to see the Wild Yankee at Mountain Museum. Received from him 7 dollars on account. Went with Wright to see him pay his passage to New Orleans. Left $60 with D. McKay [a barkeeper]. . .Seen Wright off on the John L. Stevens at 5 P.M. [The Wild Yankee is a reference to the famed James Capen Adams, known as Grizzly Adams, an actor who performed with two bears and a dog at Adams Mountaineer Museum in San Francisco, and who sometimes visited Carrell's Zink House.]
    Tuesday, January 6. . .2 P.M., went to see the old Bear Man & received ballance of account $24.00. The old man gave me a free ticket to see the Snake Charmer.

Five years later, the diary records this entry after a devastating flood, highly destructive to Carrell's mining operations:

Saturday, March 1, 1862. . .Started home this morning & Mr. Murphy came home with me. We got home at 7 P.M., the road between Murrys and Harts is very bad, clear & fine all day wind is N.W. ["Murphys" was the ranch of Edward Murphy, a native of County Monaghan, born in 1820, the son of Dennis Murphy, a surgeon who served with the British Army in the War of 1812. "Harts" was the saloon and half-way road house of Thomas Hart, situated on the banks of Las Positas Creek near Livermore.]

On the 1860 census for Alameda County, John C. O'Brien, 38, and Edward Carroll (*sic*), 37, sharing the same dwelling, were listed as miners born in Ireland. Their real estate was valued at $10,000 apiece, with no personal property of value. Their coal and sheep-herding ventures attracted many Irishmen and others to the Livermore area, and many of them became prominent in the valley. One such was Michael Mulqueeney, born in County Clare about 1844. He emigrated to Canada at age 20, and four years later departed for California, arriving in San Francisco on the *Panama* in April 1868. He soon purchased some land, and by 1883 up to eight thousand of his sheep were grazing on eight thousand acres of his property. Michael Mulqueeney had become the indisputable king of the sheep industry in his section of California.

After the death of Edward Carrell in the 1880s, the new owners of the coal-mining operation named it the Tesla Mine, and the community at Tesla flourished until the floods of 1911 doomed the mines.

Many Irish came to the Livermore-Pleasanton area with the rail-roads. Some, like James Aylward, were attracted by business oppor-tunities. Aylward developed the Livermore Spring Water Company in the 1870s. In 1870, the Irish-born in Alameda County numbered

34. James Concannon (1847-1911) and Mary Ellen Rowe family, at Tesla, near Livermore, California, about 1900. James, born in the Aran Islands, established the vineyards and winery which still bear his name.

NATIVE AND FOREIGN POPULATION OF CALIFORNIA, 1870

COUNTIES	NATIVE TOTAL	BORN IN STATE	FOREIGN BORN TOTAL	BRIT. AMERICA	ENG. & WALES	IRELAND	SCOTLAND	GERMANY	FRANCE	SWEDEN & NORWAY
Alameda	14,382	7,332	9,855	733	665	2,657	315	1,292	283	43
Alpine	485	150	200	36	38	25	18	19	7	34
Amador	5,449	2,561	4,133	120	409	490	41	326	152	16
Butte	7,428	2760	3,975	154	366	492	98	430	129	35
Calaveras	4,677	2,699	4,218	70	286	466	51	409	356	43
Colusa	5,088	1,938	1,077	106	98	246	33	215	20	14
Contra Costa	5,791	3,146	2,670	208	549	723	214	302	79	42
Del Norte	1,580	1,058	442	11	40	71	9	53	7	12
El Dorado	6,287	2,909	4,022	126	407	418	128	584	151	63
Fresno	4,974	3,787	1,362	23	149	78	10	52	33	10
Humboldt	4,646	1,974	1,494	548	180	383	51	138	24	41
Inyo	1,164	251	792	71	76	122	20	122	40	8
Kern	2,157	683	768	31	34	96	13	74	26	9
Klamath	793	368	893	33	51	137	17	56	6	21
Lake	2,483	1,060	486	42	55	171	13	45	3	6
Lassen	1,178	365	149	15	41	35	6	25	3	1
Los Angeles	10,984	6,921	4,325	65	248	471	65	635	317	28
Marin	3,761	1,931	3,142	183	181	948	64	273	134	58
Mariposa	2,192	1,155	2,380	32	219	222	37	148	113	14
Mendocino	6,147	2,946	1,398	319	108	260	65	160	9	120
Merced	2,196	894	611	42	46	119	11	56	18	6
Monroe	805	64	125	16	13	22	4	22	1	3
Monterey	7,670	4,519	2,206	192	230	441	80	186	121	29
Napa	5,394	2,438	1,769	114	169	512	55	272	48	49
Nevada	10,479	5,070	8,655	392	2,324	1,806	158	582	237	99
Placer	6,167	2,579	5,190	201	549	816	104	571	73	76
Plumas	2,414	887	2,075	122	248	237	46	159	99	55
Sacramento	16,228	7,106	10,602	542	905	2,429	187	1,634	179	109
San Bernardino	3,328	1,661	660	32	170	78	34	85	18	3
San Diego	3,743	1,629	1,208	122	98	172	36	140	29	11
San Francisco	75,754	38,491	73,719	2,367	5,419	25,864	1,687	13,602	3,548	1,170
San Joaquin	14,824	6,578	6,226	305	535	1,581	123	1,084	189	55
San Luis Obispo	3,833	2,320	939	56	70	101	34	94	33	5
San Mateo	3,497	1,935	3,188	192	197	984	66	258	87	60
Santa Barbara	6,538	4,362	1,246	66	134	189	34	118	92	13
Santa Clara	17,241	9,267	9,005	690	796	2,865	153	1,007	481	96
Santa Cruz	6,758	3,619	1,985	187	196	596	66	285	49	35
Shasta	2,937	1,147	1,236	38	85	167	29	209	51	11
Sierra	2,816	1,305	2,803	221	494	496	69	344	106	32
Siskiyou	4,321	1,763	2,527	62	128	246	35	241	87	24
Solano	11,263	4,532	5,608	488	471	2,443	176	643	82	53
Sonoma	15,656	6,923	4,163	565	383	1,281	137	642	84	92
Stanislaus	5,147	1,881	1,352	94	149	317	35	179	44	71
Sutter	3,949	1,492	1,081	61	114	276	50	240	34	33
Tehama	2,834	1,009	753	41	51	125	19	135	11	10
Trinity	1,397	712	1,816	45	93	201	20	171	37	20
Tulare	3,977	1,727	556	39	50	71	18	78	5	5
Tuolumne	4,182	2,468	3,968	82	386	559	80	389	141	40
Yolo	7,778	2,809	2,121	193	224	489	62	483	30	38
Yuba	6,144	2,760	4,707	167	283	927	73	434	162	23
	350,416	169,904	186,749	10,690	19,216	54,421	5,150	29,701	8,068	2,967

35. 1870 U.S. Census data, from *Official and Historical Atlas Map of Alameda County* (Oakland, 1878). "Other Foreign Born" are not included.

2,657, or 27 percent of a foreign-born population of 9,855, and 11 percent of a total county population of 24,237. A sampling of area census sheets for 1870, Livermore Township households (outside the city but with a Livermore Post Office address) reveals that 30 of 127 households had Irish-born heads and many more were headed by Irish-surnamed individuals born in Canada and eastern states. The settlers were listed as farmers, usually with real estate valued in the $2,000 range. If John O'Brien, listed as sixty years of age and living with his wife, Mary, fifty-eight, was the Captain Jack who was once the partner of Edward Carrell, he was less affluent in 1870 than were some of his former sheepherders and miners. According to the census, he had no real estate and only $500 in personal property.

The Concannon Vineyards. A later arrival in Alameda County's Livermore area east of Dublin was James Concannon (1847-1911), who settled in Tesla in 1883. He was the founder of the winery which received prominence during President Reagan's visit to Ireland during his first term of office. The President was met at the airport by the Irish head of government, Garrett FitzGerald, to whom he presented a six-litre bottle of 1979 vintage Concannon Petite Sirah.

James Concannon was an Irish-speaker and native of Inishmaan, the middle island of the Aran Islands in Galway Bay off the west coast of Ireland. James descended from the O'Concannons of County Roscommon who fled to Galway during the Cromwellian expulsions of the 17th century. At Spiddal in County Galway, James' grandfather's grandfather, objecting to paying tithes to the Protestant Church of Ireland, removed himself to Kilronan in Inishmore, largest of the Aran Islands. A generation later, his son brought the family to Inishmaan, where "the English flag had never flown." So goes the family folklore passed on to the present generation. Irish memories are indeed very long.

James arrived in Boston in 1865 and worked for the Singer Sewing Machine Company for a while before joining his Uncle Peadar in Augusta, Maine. There James worked as a hotel bellboy, was promoted to hotel manager, and after a return visit to his home in the Arans, married Ellen Rowe in Augusta in 1875. Soon after, he and Ellen, with their first child, journeyed west, where James took up sheep ranching in Oregon for a short time before settling in the Mission District in San Francisco. He sold books door to door before obtaining an agency for rubber stamps, a novelty then sweeping the country.

James worked the stores in San Francisco and travelled up and down the Pacific Coast from the Canadian border to Mexico by coach, stage, horseback, and foot. In 1883, he purchased forty-seven acres of land for $1,200 in the Livermore Valley, Alameda County, and there installed his wife and four children. He studied viticulture and wine-making in the archives of the University of California at Berkeley, imported fine cuttings from France, and started the vineyard at Tesla which was to become famous. Meanwhile, his brother Martin, who had arrived from the Aran Islands, was put in charge of the vineyard while James toured Mexico under the banner of his rubber stamp business.

In Mexico City, James got an idea for cleaning up the streets of the city and sold the idea to city officials, who gave him the cleaning concession. His work came to the attention of Mexican dictator Porfirio Diaz. James, who had become fluent in both spoken and lit-erary Spanish, approached Diaz with the opinion that Mexico had ideal soil and climate for a wine industry. In 1890, Diaz granted him a concession to supply proper grape cuttings to the Mexican haciendas. Diaz sometimes accompanied the Aran man with a military escort from hacienda to hacienda, where Concannon distributed the grape cuttings, as well as pamphlets on viticulture which he himself had writ-ten in Spanish.

His brother Martin came down to Mexico to superintend the model vineyard of Senator Raigusa, the dictator's son-in-law, at Celaya. Since the wine business was now occupying James fulltime, he also sent for Thomas, a half-brother in the Arans, to take over the Mexican rubber stamp business. (Later, Thomas gave up the lucrative business to return to Ireland where, according to the writer Seumas MacManus, he became the first Gaelic League organizer, founding branches all over Ireland.)

Back in Livermore, James saw his wine business grow. One of his best friends was Archbishop Joseph Alemany of San Francisco, who had first advised him to take up land in Alameda County. James was often a dinner guest at the Archbishop's residence, where the conver-sation was in Spanish. The archdiocese became the first and best cus-tomer for the fine altar wines produced by Concannon Vineyards.

James attended a lecture given by Seumas MacManus in San Francisco in 1907, a year after the great earthquake. MacManus later wrote that he was much impressed by this "short, sturdily-built, bearded man. . .[of] quiet, forceful personality. . .keen-eyed, keen of mind, with intense interest in his native land." MacManus visited Concannon in Livermore, where he reported receiving the hospitality of the large Concannon family and where he met many Irish "exiles," as he called them, and their offspring, who had been colonizing Alameda County since the 1850s.

James re-visited Ireland four times, the last in 1909 after he had experienced a stroke and knew that his death was near. He was surely a fine example of an Irishman who had done well in the Land of Opportunity across the great ocean, and must indeed have been an impressive figure to his countrymen. During his last trip, after a visit to the Arans, he went to Dublin, where he addressed a Republican group in the Irish language and conversed with leading Republicans Hyde, MacNeil, Pearse, Griffith, Alice Milligan, and others he had long admired from afar.

James Concannon died in 1911. He and Ellen had raised five sons and five daughters, all of whom were active in the family's business and in church and civic circles. Son Joseph Concannon took over the operation of the business. Upon his death in 1965, Joseph Jr., a graduate of the University of Notre Dame, headed operations. The family business was sold in 1980, but a grandson of the founder, also named James, was employed in sales in 1988. The story of his grandfather is a far from unique one of the mobility and adaptability of a poor emigrant from the most remote outreaches of western Ireland who sank deep roots in American soil.

CENSUS DATA

It would be wrong to think that the Fallons, Murrays, O'Briens, Concannons and their neighbors were isolated examples of the rural Irish in California. The census of 1870 tells another story. In a state population of 537,000, the Irish-born numbered 54,000. Of 187,000 foreign-born, 29 percent were Irish, by far the largest foreign-born presence in the state. Perhaps twice that number were first generation sons and daughters of Irish immigrants, born in "British America," or in Maine, Massachusetts, California, or other states. A cursory check of surnames reveals that the Irish were represented significantly in the 10,690 enumerations of California residents born in "Canada East" and "New Brunswick," and in the 350,416 native-born, including 119,904 California-born. By 1870, the typical Irish immigrant was married with family, the children California-born; families were usually large, one child born every two years, as was the custom.

In 1870, the only truly urban county of the fifty counties was San Francisco. There the native-born population was 75,754 and the foreign-born 73,719, of which 25,864 or 35 percent were Irish-born.

The Irish were the predominant foreign-born group in thirty-eight of fifty California counties. Even in partly urbanized Los Angeles County, 19 percent of the Irish-born were listed on the 1870 census as farmers by occupation, and in partly urbanized Sacramento County, 9 percent.

While it is evident that the Irish were the largest urban group in California, it is equally evident that they were the largest rural group among the foreign-born.

THE GREAT VALLEY

In 1870, the population of the rich San Joaquin and Sacramento Valleys from Redding to Bakersfield was 150,096. This figure includes the following 16 counties: Butte, Colusa, Fresno, Kern, Merced, Napa, Sacramento, San Joaquin, Solano, Stanislaus, Sutter, Tehama, Tulare, Tuolumne, Yolo, and Yuba. The Irish-born numbered 10,760, or 23 percent of a foreign-born population of 46,536. They were by far the dominant foreign-born presence in thirteen of these sixteen counties (exceptions Fresno, Tehama, Tulare).

If those with Irish surnames born in "British America" are fed into the stew (at least half had Irish surnames) the figure jumps to 11,997 Irish, or 26 percent of the foreign-born population.

If we consider the fact that the typical Irish head of household in 1870 was a family man with children born in the New World, the 11,997 figure easily triples (as the author's cursory analysis has indicated) to about 35,000, conservatively estimated. That is 23 percent of the total population of 150,096 in the sixteen valley counties.

The figures for Sacramento, the most populated county in the valley, and partly urbanized, reflect the valley as a whole. The Irish-born numbered 2,429, or 23 percent of the 10,602 foreign-born and 9 percent of the 26,830 total population.

Who were these Irish who sank roots in the San Joaquin Valley? What was the route of migration? What baggage of Irish cultural values did they bring with them? What obstacles did they face? An attempt has been made to answer these questions in this chapter, and previously by Patrick Blessing in an unpublished doctoral dissertation for the University of California at Los Angeles, *West Among Strangers: Irish Migration to California, 1850-1880.* His study was limited to only two California counties, Los Angeles and Sacramento, both partly urbanized. His zealously accumulated genealogies for two thousand Irish-born male heads of household need to be repeated for the Irish in the truly rural areas of the state. The total task is awesome, but will be eased by work that has already been done by busy genealogists and memoir-writers throughout the state, if historians are willing to seek out and take advantage of their work. Some of it is work of high quality, but needing collation. Some examples:

The McCabes of Stanislaus County. One such genealogical study and memoir was prepared by Alice McCabe Geiger before she died in Walnut Creek, California, in 1972 at the age of ninety-eight. Alice was the daughter of San Joaquin Valley pioneer Edward McCabe (1827-1894). She tells her family's story elegantly and movingly in a posthumously and privately printed book, *County Cavan to California:*

Edward McCabe (1827-1894) and the 'Irish Colony' in the San Joaquin Valley. Like the story of the Fallons, Murrays, and Concannons of Alameda County, it is a saga of mobility and adaptability.

Edward McCabe and his future spouse, Catherine Greenan, were born in Cran townland, Parish of Drumgoon, County Cavan. They arrived in Boston in 1843 with their parents when Edward was sixteen and Catherine about ten. Edward learned the shoemaking trade in Boston from his future uncle-in-law. In 1846, Edward sailed around the Horn to Monterey, California, a five-month journey by clipper ship. He carried aboard some boots and shoes, which he exchanged for hides at Monterey to send back to Boston. In the fall of 1846, he arrived on the same ship in Yerba Buena, soon to be re-named San Francisco. Edward and friend James Dunlap, a surveyor, went to work for Jasper O'Farrell, plotting the street system.

Edward was in San Francisco in 1848 when news arrived of the gold strike on the American River near Sacramento. He, Dunlap, and four others joined the gold seekers. Their prospecting was so successful that Edward was able to send a few bags of gold dust, $2,000 worth in each bag, via clipper ship to his mother, then living in Quebec, Canada, and his uncle in Boston. The arrival of the gold dust was sensational news. It was possibly the first gold from California to reach either Boston or Quebec.

The prospecting netted Edward about $150 to $200 per day, enough of a stake to buy ranching property and quit prospecting. In 1853, he returned to Boston via the Isthmus of Panama, contracted yellow fever and was nursed back to health at Aspenwall on the eastern side of the Isthmus by a Good Samaritan, a kindly Irish-born stranger to him named James Boyle.

Edward married Catherine at Abington, Massachusetts, in December 1854. After a visit with relatives in Philadelphia, the couple journeyed to Quebec to join Edward's mother and other members of the McCabe family. From 1855 to 1857, Edward engaged in fur-trapping at *Trois Rivieres*. About 1857, he boarded the *City of Panama* in New York, bound for the Isthmus of Panama. He was a cabin passenger. The cargo included the McCabe household furniture and a load of shoes. Catherine and two children, one born in Quebec, the other in Boston, joined Edward in California the following year.

The gold rush was still on. The McCabe family took up residence at Gold Springs, near Columbia in Tuolumne County. Edward owned a share of a mine. Other Irish miners often stashed their gold at the McCabe house until it could be shipped to San Francisco on the Wells Fargo stage. The gold mines peaked by 1860. Edward sold his share of the holdings and moved to Copperopolis in adjacent Calaveras County, where copper had become king. Edward and other Irish families unhappy with mining decided to establish themselves in the San Joaquin Valley.

In 1866, Edward visited a wilderness area of the valley and purchased a section of land a few miles from the present city of Turlock for six to eight dollars per acre. He dismantled his house at Copperopolis and transported it almost one hundred miles by wagon to his new property.

Mrs. Geiger's memoirs include the names of several Irish families she remembers from her childhood. The 1870 census reveals the names she mentions and many others. In Empire Township, Paradise City post office, Stanislaus County, the census recorded the following mostly Irish-born household heads and their families on farms valued, in most cases, in the four to six thousand dollar range: John McGovern, Michael McGovern (Louisiana-born), Hugh Quinn, William King, William McGinn, Peter Kelly, Michael Kehoe, James Kilkenny, Edward McCabe, Michael Kerrigan, Daniel Gallagher, Patrick Heeney, Michael Hershiam, Thomas O'Donnell, Lawrence Fitzgerald (a tinsmith), Thomas Corkery (a butcher), Edward Kelley, and James McCabe.

A grain crop was sown, fruit trees and vineyards planted. The land soon bloomed with oranges, apples, pears, olives, peaches, plums, mulberries, figs, and grapes of the vine. The families of the settlers also grew prolifically, but native-born children are not counted as Irish on the 1870 United States census. The Irish-born in Stanislaus County by 1870 numbered 317, or 23 percent of the foreign-born population of 1,352 in a total population of 6,499. Irish surnames were also in the majority among the 94 heads of household born in British North America, and were at least 25 percent of the native-born population of 5,147.   Irishmen from Maine, Massachusetts, and elsewhere abounded.

Edward McCabe purchased the 800-acre "Wright Ranch" and another parcel of 160 acres. In the early 1880s, he acquired three and one half-sections (640 acres per section) on the west side of the valley in Merced County.

SOLANO COUNTY

In 1870, the population of Solano County included 11,263 native-born and 5,608 foreign-born, of which 2,443 were Irish-born. It was a very rural county with a strong Irish presence. There is much about the Irish pioneers of the Suisun-Fairfield community, between Sacramento and Vallejo, in the *History of the Catholic Community in Suisun-Fairfield, 1861-1986*, published in 1987 by The Centenary Book Committee of Fairfield, California. The first entry in the register for the new mission church at Suisun was dated November 1862, for the

36 and 37. Edward McCabe (1827-1894) and Catherine Greenan (1832-1901) both born in County Cavan. They settled on a farm near Turlock, California, after spending several years in the mining country.

38. Dominick McGrath (1827-1908), born in County Longford; emigrated to New York at age 18, then to Alameda County, California, in the 1850s, where he raised sheep and where he married Bridget Murray; then to Ventura County, in the 1870s, where he and his family farmed over 5,000 acres.

baptism of Albert, son of Albert Knorp and Margaret Cronan. The pioneer families, mostly Irish, many of them having purchased land for farming and cattle raising after a stint in the gold fields, bore these surnames: Trainor (County Armagh), Casey, Devlin, Bradley, Allen, McDermott, Fitzpatrick, Lang, Higgins, McCarron, Griffin, Burke, Connelly, Foley, Deane, Hurley, Edmonds, Russell, Sullivan, Riordan, Horan (County Wexford), Hennessey, Lynch, McGary, McGinty, Corcoran, O'Neil, Murphy, Goodwin, Knorp, Vest (County Cork), Lenehan, Reed. The Trainors came from County Armagh, the Vests from County Cork, the Horans from County Wexford. The remarkable Kate Kennedy *(see Chapter 16)* obtained her first teaching job in Suisun in 1856.

VENTURA COUNTY

In 1870, the future Ventura County was still part of Santa Barbara County. The population included 6,538 native-born and 1,246 foreign-born, of whom 189 were Irish-born, exceeding any other foreign-born group. Arriving in Hueneme Township in the 1870s was the Dominick McGrath family. Dominick, born at Derryshannage, Cashel Parish on the River Shannon, County Longford, Ireland, about 1827, was the fifth of six children of Peter McGrath and Mary Davis. It is said that at age 18, six-foot tall and broad shouldered, he arrived in New York City with his older brother Peter and his future brother-in-law, "Uncle" John Donlan. According to his daughter, the late Nellie Leonard, Dominick first obtained work with an English couple in Connecticut at four dollars per month. Later, with John Donlan, he cleared forest land in Joliet, Illinois, then returned east to work in the foundries of Manhattan and Brooklyn for six years. Father Brady, a priest and reported relative, helped him with funds for passage to California via the Isthmus of Panama. Patrick McGrath arrived in San Francisco in the early 1850s, settled in Alameda County, worked for wages on a sheep ranch in the Livermore area for four years, and soon had one thousand head of sheep of his own.

John Donlan and his family also settled in Alameda County, close to the Fallons and Murrays. In 1867, Dominick married Bridget Donlon, 22, half-sister of John Donlon. *(See Note 6: McGrath Family.)* In 1876, Dominick and Bridget moved to the Oxnard plains in southern California, where the family was listed on the 1880 census for Hueneme Township, Ventura County. Bridget bore fourteen children, ten of whom lived to adulthood. She died in 1888, while giving birth to her last child (stillborn). Dominick and his sons acquired over five thousand acres of farm and grazing land, and at one time the family owned four miles of beachfront land. One could walk from Montalvo to Hueneme without leaving McGrath land. In the early years, Dominick raised barley, corn and lima beans, and later the family engaged in large dairy operations.

Dominick died of cancer on December 23, 1908. A little book, *The McGrath Story*, privately printed in 1972 by Elizabeth Leonard and Yvonne Bodle of Oxnard, has extensive genealogies. The authors traced almost four hundred McGrath descendants. In 1948, the grandchildren of Dominick and Bridget had a problem with the distribution of the 5,020-acre estate, but they solved that problem quickly and neatly, their unique manner of doing it attracting international attention:

Four [McGrath] men drew cards. . .The first drawing was made for the order in selecting the parcels. Dominick McGrath [son of Hugo McGrath] turned the high card to draw for the Hugo McGrath estate. Robert McGrath was second, Frank McGrath third, and Joe McGrath fourth. Tension became almost unbearable, not only for those present but for the many family members at home awaiting the outcome. The brothers were calm, although the attorneys in the room reported the scene was tense and dramatic in the extreme. All was conducted with the utmost of good will. Then in the order thus decided, they drew from four cards, each representing the parcels of land. And that was how the Dominick McGrath Estate of 5,020 acres was divided in just a few fleeting moments.

Among the descendants of Dominick and Bridget McGrath were several priests and nuns, including a grandson, the late Reverend Robert E. McGrath of the Augustinians, who taught at Villanova University; the late Monsignor Harold V. Laubacher, onetime pastor of St. Paul's Church in Los Angeles; Maureen Aggeler, Order of the Sacred Heart; and Gladys E. Wines Leonard, Order of the Immaculate Heart of Mary.

A number of other members of the Dublin, Alameda County, community also settled in Ventura County near the McGraths. They included Irish-born John Scarlett and his wife, Anna Lyster; James A. Donlon, oldest child of John and Mary [McGovern]; and Peter Donlon, perhaps James' uncle and brother to the Thomas Donlon who was killed during the construction of St. Raymond's Church.

SANTA CLARA VALLEY

No account of the rural Irish in California would be nearly complete without mention of the fabulous Murphy family. The head of this family was Martin Murphy Sr., born in County Wexford, Ireland, on November 23, 1785. He married Mary Foley in Ireland. In 1820, with a large family that included a number of adult children, Martin and Mary emigrated to Frampton in the Province of Quebec, Canada, where they settled for twenty years. About 1840, they moved to St. Joseph, Missouri. There they purchased land and farmed, but were met by considerable misfortune. A malaria epidemic took the lives of Martin's wife, Mary, and three of their grandchildren, offspring of Martin Jr. Martin, now nearing sixty years of age, was advised by missionary priest Father Christian Hoeken to move to California where he believed the climate and soil were more favorable and where the Catholic Church was well established. In 1844, Martin and his sons, with the help of Captain Elisha Stevens, organized a train of about a dozen wagons. They hired trapper and mountaineer Caleb Greenwood and his two sons as guides. Among the non-Murphys in the caravan were Dr. John Townsend and his wife. (Dr. Townsend is thought to have been the first American physician to settle in California. Townsend Street in San Francisco is named after him). This historic party of about fifty-three men, women, and children included twenty-six of the Murphy clan: five sons and four daughters of Martin Sr., nine grandchildren, and a number of Miller and Martin in-laws. The party crossed the plains and mountains under intolerable conditions, reaching Sutter's Fort on the Sacramento River on December 15, 1844. They were the first to bring wagons across the High Sierras into the Sacramento Valley.

Daughter Mary and husband James Miller moved on to San Rafael the following spring, where they acquired land from Timothy Murphy, also from County Wexford, of whom more later.

John and Daniel Murphy, sons of Martin Sr., took up gold mining near Angels Camp in Calaveras County and were immediately successful.

Martin Murphy Jr. purchased land in the Cosumnes River Valley, southeast of Sacramento, as his base of operations, planting wheat. He proceeded to do a flourishing business with John Sutter of the fort in Sacramento, serving the 49-ers, who were as hungry for food as for gold. Martin Sr. applied for Mexican citizenship on January 28, 1846, and purchased the Mexican grant of Ernest Rufus on the river. Later that year, Martin Sr. and two of his sons acquired Rancho Ojo de Agua de la Coche near the present town of Morgan Hill, in Santa Clara County. They erected an adobe house below what came to be known as Murphy's Peak, west of Morgan Hill. Soon all members of the Murphy clan, including Martin Jr., were gathered in Santa Clara County. Martin Jr. sold off his large holdings on the Cosumnes River for $50,000. Martin J.C. Murphy, son of Martin Jr., continued the family tradition of land acquisition. Acquiring large tracts in the Santa Clara Valley, the members of the family soon came to own almost contiguous ranchos in a thirty mile stretch, seven miles wide, from Sunnyvale to Gilroy. The Murphy domain was a match for that of the strongest of the Gaelic chieftains of Old Ireland, and beyond their dreams in wealth.

The head of the clan, Martin Sr., preferred that his children hold title to the American fiefdoms. With his daughters Ellen and Johanna acting as hostesses, the widower kept open house in the adobe, on the road leading from San Jose to Monterey. There were no inns in the valley for weary travellers. So, in the Irish tradition, old Martin became famous for his hospitality in this frontier land where pilgrims often were desperate for food and lodging for the night.

Son Bernard built a chapel on the land and named it after his father's patron saint; that name is commemorated today in the town of San Martin, between Gilroy and Morgan Hill. In 1850, Ellen married Charles M. Weber, a founding father of the city of Stockton, at a ceremony performed by a Jesuit priest. Charles, a Protestant, accepted the faith of his wife, a requirement for joining the closely-knit and very Catholic Murphy clan. The story of the Murphy and Weber connection and the involvement of these families in the histories of the Sacramento and Santa Clara Valleys has been told by George P. Hammond in *The Weber Era in Stockton History*, and I have drawn heavily from this source. Daughter Margaret married Thomas Kell.

Morgan Hill, near Gilroy in the Santa Clara Valley, was not named for a hill but for the man, Morgan Hill, who acquired a large ranch there when he married Diana Murphy, daughter of Daniel Murphy of San Jose and a granddaughter of Martin Sr. Sunnyvale in Santa Clara County was known as Murphy's Station in the early days, named for Martin Murphy Jr., who owned Rancho Pastoria de Borregas on which the present city of Sunnyvale is located. Mary Murphy of Yuba County, a Donner Party survivor (no relation to the Martin Murphy family), married Charles Covillaud, a large landowner. In 1850 at a public meeting the town of Marysville was named for her. She became famed for her hospitality to miners who were ill or in trouble.

Denis Martin, a member of the Murphy-Stevens wagon train of 1844 (whose sister was married to one of the sons of Martin Murphy Sr.) settled at Woodside in Santa Clara County. He became one of the first and, for a time the most successful, lumberman in the valley. In 1856, he built the first Catholic church in the county. It was dedicated by Bishop Alemany, who named it St. Denis Church, for the patron saint of its donor. Denis' good fortune declined, and he died in poverty in San Francisco, according to an account of his life published on June 20, 1903, several years after his death, in the diocesan newspaper, the *San Francisco Monitor*.

His brother John Martin settled in Dublin, California, in the 1850s, and died there at the age of 87 in 1883. A headstone inscription in the old cemetery indicates that he was born in Kings County,

Ireland. A plaque beside the stone claims that he had been a member of one of the rescue parties that came to the aid of the ill-fated Donner Party in 1846, but the records do not support this. The records do show, however, that his brother Denis, a member of the Murphy-Stevens Party, came alone and on snowshoes to the rescue of young Moses Schallenberger of the same party. Moses had been left behind at what came to be known as Donner Lake, but which could more appropriately be called Murphy Lake after the senior member of the group that first brought wagons over the pass two years before the Donner Party.

In 1850, Virginia Reed, a survivor of the Donner Party of 1846, married John M. Murphy (son of Martin Sr.) of the Murphy-Stevens Party of 1844. John became a man of prominence in San Jose, as mayor, sheriff, dry goods merchant, and dealer in real estate and insurance, before his death in 1892.

Two Irish pioneers in Santa Clara County who were not kin of the Murphys were Dennis J. Oliver and D.C. McGlynn, brothers-in-law from Menlough, Lough Corrib, County Galway. They gave the name of their place of birth, but not the Irish spelling of it, to today's Menlo Park.

MARIN COUNTY

Another Murphy, unrelated as far as is known to the Martin Murphy clan, was Timothy, the legendary Don Timoteo Murphy, a 300-pound pioneer of San Rafael, California. He was born in 1800 at Coolaneck in County Wexford, according to Jack Mason in *Early Marin*. *(See Note 7: Timothy Murphy.)*

Timothy worked for the London meat packing house of Hartnell and Company, which sent him to Peru in 1826, and two years later to Monterey, Upper California, to help operate the Monterey branch, which soon failed. Turning misfortune into fortune, in a few years he acquired a considerable fortune trapping coastal sea otters, and, at the same time, acquiring the friendship of many influential people at the Presidio, including Mariano Vallejo. In 1837, Governor Alvarado appointed Murphy administrator of the mission at San Rafael, recently secularized, and he served in that capacity from 1837-49. He also became the agent for 1,400 Indians in the Marin area (serving until 1851), and alcalde and justice of the peace at San Rafael.

The jovial Don Timoteo was well-liked by the Indians, whom he addressed in their own tongue and whom he encouraged to practice the agricultural and other skills taught to them by the missionaries. Much of the mission land and livestock had legally become the property of the Indians following the secularization decrees of 1833. The Indians, however, had only recently been a Stone Age people, and the several decades of experience at the missions had not prepared them sufficiently for dealing in business with the Europeans. Once they were removed from the protection of the Franciscan Fathers, they were easy prey to entrepreneuring Yankees and Spanish, hungry for land. Murphy and Vallejo felt that the Indians would be better off under their own protection, rather than being victimized by land seekers less sympathetic to the Indians. Vallejo and Murphy boasted of treating the Indians kindly, even as Vallejo moved cattle and grapevines from Indian lands to his own Sonoma Ranch, and even as Murphy preempted mission cattle and sold the hides, beef and tallow in Sausalito. The Indians accepted employment on what should have been their own ranches.

Don Timoteo Murphy acquired 21,678 acres by grant from Governor Micheltorena in 1844. He sponsored rodeos and threw lavish parties at his two-story adobe house in San Rafael, welcoming Mexican officials, Yankee settlers, and Indians alike. He died a bachelor in 1853, leaving a considerable estate, although much of it had been lost after he fell victim to a Yankee swindler. On his deathbed, he deeded 217 acres to Archbishop Joseph Alemany of San Francisco for the foundation of a school. The bulk of his estate was passed to his brother Matthew and nephew John Lucas. Murphy's adobe was later purchased by Timothy Mahon. The Marin County Civic Center is today located on Timothy Murphy's grant.

James Miller, also a native of County Wexford and who has already been mentioned in connection with the Murphy-Stevens Party, built his home on what had been Murphy's land. He had come to Canada in 1828, migrated with his wife, Mary Murphy, to Missouri in 1841, and then, in 1844, joined the wagon train to California that Mary's father, Martin Murphy Sr., had helped organize. Moving from Sutter's Fort in Sacramento to San Rafael, James Miller acquired land from Timothy Murphy. James and his son William soon prospered, driving cattle to Marysville to barter beef for gold dust. William, educated by the Jesuits at the college at Santa Clara, built the Marin Hotel in San Rafael with convict labor. He was mayor for six years and owned as much as 8,000 acres, which made him, according to one account, the county's largest taxpayer. He died in March 1916.

MINING

The Silver Kings. Surely the most hugely successful of the Irish in mining were the four partners known worldwide as the "Silver Kings." They were John W. Mackey, James G. Fair, William S. O'Brien, and James C. Flood. The first three were born in Ireland; Flood was born in New York, of Irish immigrant parents. All four spent the early 1850s prospecting and mining in California. O'Brien and Flood opened businesses in San Francisco in the 1850s and dabbled in mining stock. After the Comstock Lode in Virginia City, Nevada, was discovered in 1859 by Irish prospectors Peter O'Riley and Patrick McLaughlin, O'Brien and Flood amassed a fortune through their San Francisco brokerage firm.

Mackey and Fair had been prospecting in California and Nevada. After hearing of the McLaughlin-O'Riley strike, Mackey and partner Jack O'Brien crossed the Sierras, took pick and shovel, and went to work as laborers in the mines. Mackey took the stock certificates in which he was paid and invested them in a supposedly exhausted and worthless mine, The Kentuck. With a loan from James Phelan (whose son would later become mayor of San Francisco), he sank a new shaft and hit a rich deposit.

Fair arrived in Virginia City in 1865. He joined forces with Mackey, Flood and O'Brien. The partnership challenged the "Ralston Ring," the deputy for which was William Sharon. Sharon was the most hated man in the Comstock, delighting in lending money to miners against the security of their properties and then foreclosing when payment was past due. He detested Mackey, Fair, O'Brien, and Flood. He reported gleefully to William Ralston in 1872 that he had sold "those four Irishmen" for $100,000 a controlling interest in a mine thought to be worthless, after over a million dollars had been spent in unsuccessful exploration.

The rest is history. The story is told well by Roger McGrath in "The Silver Kings" (*American Irish Newsletter*, September 1987). The vein was found at the 1,500 foot level, ore so rich that waste rock had to be added to it for processing through the stamp mill. It was the Big Bonanza, the very heart of the Comstock Lode. From 1873 to 1882, the mine yielded sixty-five million dollars worth of gold and silver. The Silver Kings were indescribably wealthy.

Bodie, Mono County. The bad men of Bodie, California, on the Nevada border deserve mention. Bodie is a ghost town today, but in 1880 was a thriving community of 5,300 souls. It was known far and wide as the very toughest town in the Old West.

When Professor Roger McGrath of the University of California at Los Angeles began his research on Bodie (*Gunfighters, Highwaymen, and Vigilantes: Violence on the Frontier*), he did not know that he would be telling a story mostly about the *Irish* in the Old West. Soon, however, he found that "the Irish were irrepressible, they leaped out of the original source material with every bit of research I did."

The United States census for the year 1880 revealed the dominant Irish presence. In the Bodie population of about 5,300, the Irish-born numbered 850, the Canadian-born 750, and a goodly portion of the latter had Irish surnames. Additionally, a sizable number of the American-born had Irish surnames.

The Irish were on both sides of the law, among the hanged and the hangmen. Some were murderous thugs, like the members of John Daly's Gang, and others, like Patrick Reddy, rose to prominence in the legal profession.

Almost everybody carried a gun in Bodie, and shootouts were a common occurrence. On Thursday morning, June 1, 1879, one of the most famous of these occurred in Patrick Gallagher's Shamrock Bar when big Alex Nixon, County Tyrone-born, was knocked to the floor by one Tom MacDonald. Both drew guns. Nixon got hit in the side. "My God, I'm shot," he gasped, just before he collapsed. He died within two hours.

That was just one of many violent altercations that occurred in Gallagher's and the other forty saloons which, by 1880, graced the community.

When the Indian wars broke out in the Owens Valley (after Indians surrounded the cabin of Mary Maguire and killed her son, age six), many Irishmen were on the good side of the law, although the Indians may have quarreled with that judgment. Captain Moses McLaughlin and officers with names such as O'Neill, O'Malley, and Kelly, were able to turn the tide against the Indians. McLaughlin, a very aggressive and ruthless commander, is remembered for his slaughter of the Indians at Whiskey Flat.

The sheriff's department at Bodie had a tradition of Irish lawmen, with names like McQuade, O'Malley, Kerrigan, and Brodigan, but sometimes it was hard to tell the lawmen from the badmen. Members of the Daly Gang were deputized for a time by the sheriff's office. The gang was probably the most vicious band of cutthroats the Old West had ever seen, making the James Boys and the Clantons appear saintly.
ts

The Daly Gang all sported Irish names, like William Buckley, James Masterson and Three-Fingered John McDowell. They were finally hanged after a brutal murder of a settler to even a grudge. They had been pursued by a vigilante committee who, having captured them, promptly tried them and set them all on the scaffold. The local newspaper reported Bill Buckley's last words: "I want you [addressing a friend] to see about getting a coffin for me. . .Adieu, boys. . . all of you must go to my wake in John Daly's cabin tonight." He also dictated a letter to a brother in the city of San Francisco: "Give my first and my last love to my mother in Ireland. Don't let her know that my death was by the ignominy of the gallows. . . God bless you all. I have hope yet in a merciful God and savior."

Besides the nightlife in George Callaghan's Can Can Restaurant, Dick McAlpin's Parlor, Gallagher's Shamrock, and the other pubs, Bodie went in big for horse-racing. The fastest horse in the country was reported to be a mare named "Nellie," property of Charlie O'Malley.

C.J. Murphy opened up and operated the major toll road into the mountain town, and over this road came such goods as the "Whiskies from Cork City, Ireland," popular in the saloons and dance halls.

One of the town toughs was 240-pound, six-foot two-inch Eugene Markey, a sometime fire warden, sergeant in the National Guard, and police officer who, on occasion, would go on a drunken spree and shoot up a saloon or two. He was also known far and wide for his prowess at arm wrestling. In 1880 at the miners' union hall he fought Rod McInnis for the "collar and elbow heavyweight title of Bodie." Thousands of dollars were bet on Markey by his friends, but McInnis defeated him.

The National Guard unit at Bodie included non-commissioned officers with such names as Fahey, Kearney, Markey, and O'Brien, and privates with names such as Boyle, Carroll, Costello, Finnegan, Lyons, McGrath, Mullin, O'Donnell, O'Keefe, Phelan, Shea, Thornton, Tobin, and Whelan.

The Irishmen of Bodie, although almost all carried guns, were not without political solutions to problems. They were quick to rise to the assistance of the Land Leaguers in Ireland when asked for help. Within months after Charles Stewart Parnell, head of the Land League, visited the United States, the Bodie chapter of the Land League was established. Judge John Ryan gave a stirring speech at the first meeting in the miners' hall on December 22, 1880: "For seven centuries, Ireland has been fighting for liberty. . .Those who have gathered here tonight should not respond as Irishmen, merely, but as citizens of the leading republic of the earth and aid in liberating the oppressed people from English rule." Music and songs accompanied the meetings, where featured speakers included chapter presidents Thomas Ryan and John F. McDonald and such leading citizens as Judge John McQuaid, J.C. McTarnahan, Father John B. Cassin, and Patrick Reddy.

Patrick Reddy. Reddy began his legal career in Bodie, where he frequently defended with great skill some of the worst toughs and murderers. He became the most renowned trial lawyer west of the Mississippi. Conceived in County Carlow, Ireland, he was born in 1839 in Woonsocket, Rhode Island. He came to California in 1861, worked as a laborer in Contra Costa County, and as a miner in Placer

County and (after crossing the Sierras) in Virginia City, Aurora, Darwin, and Montgomery.

Reddy earned a reputation for recklessness in the mining camps. In 1864, he was shot in the arm by an unknown assailant in Virginia City and lost the arm. Thirty-three years later this loss did not stop him from lunging after a man in a Sacramento post office who was standing over a woman and brandishing a gun. In the scuffle, Reddy managed to jam a finger between the hammer and the cylinder of the revolver as the assailant, Peter Hulsman, cocked it. When Hulsman pulled the trigger, the hammer fell on Reddy's only thumb. Reddy, with the help of a bystander, wrestled Hulsman to the floor. Reddy had his bleeding thumb bandaged after the police arrived and was reported by the *San Francisco Call* as "continuing on down the street as if nothing unusual had happened."

But that is getting ahead of the story. Shortly after the loss of his arm, he married and began the study of law. In 1867, after getting his license, he practiced in Independence in the Owens Valley. In 1879, he moved to the booming town of Bodie where he set up shop in what the *Bodie Standard* described as "the most imposing law office outside of San Francisco." He still occasionally went on a spree, saloon to saloon, challenging all comers to arm-wrestling.

He was known in the courts of Bridgeport and Bodie for his commanding voice, his carefully prepared briefs, his almost total recall, his beautiful diction, and (despite his American birth) a lilting Irish brogue which captivated judge and jury. He developed a reputation for supporting the underdog, often without fee, and was known to slip twenty dollar gold pieces into the hands of destitute miners. He founded the Bodie chapter of the Land League of Ireland, was a delegate to the state constitutional conventions of 1878-79, and was a state senator from 1883 to 1887.

While still maintaining a law office in Bodie, he opened another in San Francisco in 1881. With the addition of junior partners William H. Metson (whom Reddy trained in Bodie) and J. C. Campbell, the law firm prospered and, as in Bodie, Reddy often represented the underdog. He was quick to the scene of a miners' strike in Coeur d'Alene, Idaho, in the 1890s, when the mine owners, with the help of federal and state troops, attempted to destroy the miners' union by hiring strikebreakers, shooting the union leaders, and incarcerating hundreds of miners in fenced enclosures. The *San Francisco Bulletin* reported that "he distinguished himself against the best legal talent in the Northwest in the numerous cases which grew out of those labor troubles."

In San Francisco, in the twilight of Reddy's career, law students crowded into the courtroom to watch him perform. Patrick Reddy died of Bright's Disease at his home in San Francisco in 1900. At his bedside were his wife of thirty-six years, Emma, and his younger brother, Ned Reddy, with whom Patrick had come to California in 1861. He is reported to have died with a smile on his face. Later that morning, when word of Reddy's death reached the United States Circuit Court in San Francisco, the judge ordered the court adjourned for the day in honor of Patrick Reddy.

His estate was valued at $250,000, a considerable fortune at the time; but he had earned over three million dollars in his law practice by charging substantial fees to rich clients who wanted the best. Most of this three million had been given away. He had made many trips back to the mining regions of his youth and seldom returned without one or two of the old boys who were crippled by accident, disease, or old age. If they were still alive after hospitalization, for which Reddy always paid, he would grub-stake them and send them back to wherever they wanted to go.

The wild western town of Bodie, generating the starkest of contrasts, brought out the worst and the best in its sons from the Land of Saints and Scholars. Patrick Reddy was surely among the very best, a remarkable Irishman who can take his place on a list of the greatest defenders of the underdog in the American West.

TUOLUMNE AND CALAVERAS COUNTIES

The town of Murphys in Calaveras County was named for the brothers Daniel and John Murphy, sons of Martin Murphy Sr. They arrived in July 1848 with two associates, Henry Angel and James Carson. They set up camp and soon found a rich ore deposit at a creek site which became known as "Murphys Diggins," later Murphy's Camp or just plain Murphys. The traveller William Redmond Ryan *(Personal Adventures in Upper and Lower California,* London, 1852) reported that an "Irish ranchero named Murphy" at the upper crossing of the Stanislaus River kept a trading post, was married to a sister of the local Indian chief, and furnished the Indians with clothing and other goods in exchange for their services in digging for gold. Ryan's report of the marriage of one of the Murphy boys to the Indian girl was vigorously denied by members of the Murphy clan of Santa Clara County *(see note under Prendergast, Thomas F.),* where the Murphy brothers soon settled with their father and other members of the family.

It is unfortunate that most of the literature on the Irish in the mining counties tends to focus on the devil-may-care attitudes and lawlessness of the miners; a story of rootless, single men who abandoned civilized and Christian values as they zealously pursued their personal pleasure, wasting away their earnings on booze, gambling, and women. A refreshing respite from this point of view comes from Professor Louis Bisceglia of California State University of San Jose. He studied the minutes of meetings during the years 1857-71 of The Hibernian Benevolence Society (HBS) of Columbia, Tuolumne County, in the heart of the Mother Lode The minutes reveal 241 members and 40 unsuccessful applicants. Occupations are listed for 126 miners, 16 laborer-miners, 14 owners or professionals, 6 hotel keepers, and 2 skilled artisans, with an average age of 32.9 years.

The minutes indicate that the major concerns of the HBS were preparation for the annual March 17th and July 4th celebrations; welfare payments for destitute miners; dignified burial for the dead; and fund-raising for the Catholic Church and school. Bisceglia's study of the naturalization and other records for Tuolumne and Calaveras counties indicated that the Irish were by far the quickest among foreign-born groups to file papers for citizenship. In 1877, the Irish were the largest registered-to-vote group among the foreign born. They were one-fifth of all the voters. Between 1854 and 1872 in Calaveras County, over 26 percent of all "first intent" papers were filed by the Irish-born.

Bisceglia concluded that the minutes of the HBS and the other records he analyzed "allow a different glance of miner society - one apart from the usual view of a lawless, raw and hard-driving group." The Irish of Columbia organized themselves with civility, sacrificed individuality for community, and provided superb training for citizenship.

Bisceglia's study of the assessment rolls and census data indicated that the Irish were, in 1869, poorer than other groups. The property of thirty-four percent of the Irish, but only 12 percent of the non-Irish, was valued at less than $100. One needs to look critically at such figures before concluding that the Irish were less successful at mining than were other groups. By 1869, the great days of the Mother Lode were over and the mountains were dotted with sleepy hamlets and ghost towns. The most fortunate, energetic, and enterprising of the Irish had come and gone, countless numbers of them having made their poke and headed for the fertile valleys to purchase farm and grazing land, as the evidence elsewhere in this chapter has suggested.

HISTORIANS

A new generation of American historians is re-writing the history of the Irish in California and in the American nation. Dennis Clark in *Hibernia America: The Irish and Regional Culture* has pointed up the variety of the Irish presence in the West. Irish names abound of traders, explorers, cattlebarons, silver kings, politicians, priests. General Alejandro O'Reilly was in charge of the Spanish armies during

Spain's mid-18th century entry into the Far West. "Honest Joe" O'Cain was trading otter skins with Aleuts and Russians from California to Alaska as early as 1800. Sailor John Milligan (who jumped ship with John Cameron, aka Gilroy) was teaching Indians weaving at Salinas in 1814. Jose O'Donaju arrived with Spanish troops at the Los Angeles mission in 1834. Irish-born John G. Downey was elected Governor of California in 1860. He and his Spanish wife, age twenty-one in that year, have been the youngest couple to the present time to reside in the governor's mansion. Irish-born William Mulholland engineered the vast hydraulic system to pump water from the Owens Valley to the city of Los Angeles. In the 1890s, the fabled "Klondike Mike" Mahoney pioneered trails in Alaska and the Yukon.

Patrick Blessing, in his already-mentioned doctoral dissertation, noted that Governor Downey, who gave his name to a city in Los Angeles County, contributed land worth over a million dollars to the Protestant University of Southern California. When his bishop questioned the gift and sent for Downey to ask him if he had left the Church, Downey told the bishop, to his astonishment, that "the work these men were doing was just as acceptable in the sight of God as the work of our church." Blessing dug deep into the shared values of the "peasant element" in Irish society, a necessary ingredient for understanding the adaptation of the Irish in the New World. These values included emphasis on group equality, disdain for attempts to move up the occupational scale at the expense of the kin group, a view of real estate as a fixed element in a kinship whole, and adherence to family-based cooperative work patterns. Blessing and other scholars have noted that these values were markedly at variance with the rugged individualism of the prevailing Anglo-Protestant culture. Unlike historian Kerby Miller, however, Blessing did not find these values, in the balance, to be crippling. Instead, he was struck by the "relatively smooth adjustment of individuals from a peasant background whose values were most at variance with the beliefs of a native white society."

All studies of the rural Irish in California, including this one, will inevitably suffer from serious methodological flaws. Blessing's two thousand genealogies covered only males, only the Irish-born, and only two counties, both considerably urbanized. Bisceglia, focusing on two sparsely populated mountain counties, was handicapped by the paucity of records of the Irish who came and went between 1850 and 1870, never meeting the census enumerator or any other record-keeper. This chapter, focusing largely on Irish settlements in the great valleys, is impressionistic, although the United States census figures that have been cited speak quite strongly for the pervasive Irish presence in the grazing and farming lands of California, even before 1870. Many counties, however, still remain to be studied. It is hoped that this chapter will generate both criticism and further research. The importance of seeking out the genealogical literature cannot be overemphasized.

SAN FRANCISCO: THE URBAN IRISH

James P. Walsh and R.A. Burchell have done excellent studies of the San Francisco urban scene. Burchell, in *The San Francisco Irish: 1848-1880*, notes the uniqueness of the Irish experience in San Francisco. He maintains that San Francisco in 1850, unlike the cities of the eastern seaboard, had no entrenched Anglo-Protestant class, holding tenaciously to its property, power, and privileges against the tide of newly-arrived foreigners. In San Francisco, Anglo-Protestant and Irishman began the race on the same starting line. By 1860, the Irish had established the Hibernia Bank, and a significant number had become part of the city's political, business, and professional elite. John Sullivan, a founder of the Hibernia Bank, was a member of the Murphy-Stevens Party of 1844. Burchell says very little, however, about the considerable number of Irish in the city's poor underclass.

Professor Walsh of San Jose State University has noted that the "reforming" faction in San Francisco in the 1850s was motivated less by a desire to clean up corruption in politics than by a desire to destroy the political support of State Senator David G. Broderick, a Catholic Irishman. The merchant-dominated San Francisco Vigilance Committee raised a private army and, for a short time, took over the reins of the city government without the consent of the electorate.

"Among those who cried the loudest for law and order," says Walsh, "were men of property who evaded their taxes and others who felt secure enough to negotiate with the city compromise settlements of unpaid taxes and their penalty fines." They had found that Broderick, soon to become a United States Senator, possessed little sympathy for the greedy merchant class, and identified instead with his working-class constituency, a large part of which was Irish and Catholic. He also belonged to the anti-slavery wing of the Democratic Party. Since Broderick's integrity could not be questioned, the Know Nothings aimed their attack at the worst element of the lower party levels, lynched four Irish rascals, and deported a score of others.

Know-Nothingism in San Francisco was short-lived and largely ineffective. By 1881, four Irish Catholics, including Broderick, had been elected to the United States Senate, and Irish Catholic John Downey had served as Governor of the state.

BIAS

Stuart Miller, in *The Unwelcome Immigrant: The American Image of the Chinese Immigrant, 1785-1882*, claimed that the Irish in California were the Western Know-Nothings, the Nativists who led the battle to expel Chinese immigrants and who bonded with the Anglos to claim white privileges over non-whites. Although there is some truth to this - the Irish were by far the dominant foreign-born group in California and many had adopted the racist viewpoint of the Anglo-Protestants - the Irish role has been exaggerated. Blessing points out, for example, that the rioters in 1871 came from all levels of society, even as self-righteous Anglo community leaders were blaming the occurrence on "American hoodlums, Mexican greasers, Irish tramps, and French communists." In fact, says Blessing, there is no evidence at all that the Irish were involved in any significant numbers in the Chinese lynchings. The overwhelming majority of the Irish community and their churchmen were as appalled by the rioters as they were by the Anglo business leaders whose real concerns were a desire for cheap labor and the suppression of Irish-led union agitation for higher wages and better working conditions.

Regarding the "Massacre of 1871," the bloodiest riot in Los Angeles history, in which a number of Chinese were killed by mobs, the great Anglo-Protestant historian Hubert Bancroft, with a fine eye for racial physiognomy, wrote that it was easy to recognize many whites who attacked the Chinese as "men of Hibernian extraction in whose countenance you could easily distinguish the brute nature that controlled all their actions."

THE IRISH LEGACY IN CALIFORNIA

It may be true, as Blessing's data indicates, that by 1900 the Irish-born had ceased to be an important contributing factor in California. By then, however, they had laid an enormous foundation in churches, schools, universities, local and state governance, labor union organizations, and business enterprises. Awareness of Irishness is kept alive by scores of Irish clubs and organizations (for which one can find listings in Cull and Concannon, *The Irish Directory*). San Francisco has two Irish monthly newspapers, *The Irishman* and the *Irish Herald*, the latter published by John Whooley, a native of Skibbereen.

The most enduring and valuable legacy that the Irish emigrants to California brought with them from Ireland in the 19th century may well have been the religion they passed on to their children. In the San Joaquin Valley where this author lived during the 1950s and 60s, there was hardly a parish without a pastor or curate who spoke with the softly accented English of his birthplace in the Emerald Isle.

The Irish of California today, although dispersed in heterogeneous communities and quiet about their Irishness (except perhaps on March 17), are still very much a cultural presence in the state. In March 1988, in the Dublin settled by the Fallons and Murrays and other Children of Erin over 130 years ago, four men named Michael Halloran gathered at Jimmy O'Gil's Irish Bar, in the building that was once John Green's general store. They were there to celebrate St. Patrick's Day to the rhythmic clacking of the spoons of Michael O'Dea, manager of the bar and a former champion Irish spoon player. Although they lived in nearby communities, three of these Hallorans were meeting each other for the first time. Michael James Halloran of Orinda, a San Francisco corporate attorney and chairman of the Orinda Planning Commission, descends from Great Famine immigrants from County Clare who first settled in Hamilton, Ontario, then moved to Montana for work in the copper mines, before the Dust Bowl conditions of the 1930s produced another famine, driving them to Long Beach, California. Michael Joseph Halloran of Concord is assistant superintendent of the San Ramon Valley school district (adjacent to the district that included the old Murray School), and his son Michael Paul is a recent graduate of Cornell University who intends to become a science writer. Their Hallorans landed in New Jersey, then worked their way West to Bismarck, North Dakota, where they established the Grand Hotel. Michael Joseph's grandfather, it is reported, once took his six-month old son to shake hands with Sioux Chief Sitting Bull. The fourth Halloran at the gathering at Jimmy O'Gil's pub was Michael Benedict of San Ramon, owner of a tire company and, in 1988, president-elect of the San Ramon Chamber of Commerce. His great-grandfather settled in Port Arthur, Texas, later moving to California to become superintendent of the Texaco refinery in Long Beach.

The ancestors of the four Michael Hallorans, who turned their eyes to the West, shunning the eastern seaboard cities, were among the uncounted Irish that are the subject of this book.

JAK

For the Tormey family of County Westmeath and Contra Costa County, see Note 8 in "Notes and Selected References" for this chapter, p. 345.

Patrick J. Dowling's interesting CALIFORNIA: THE IRISH DREAM *(San Francisco, 1988) came to the writer's attention too late for comment in this chapter. Dowling's sketches of Irish pioneers in Marin, Santa Clara and other counties confirm the early Irish presence in rural California.*

Chapter 13

PLACE NAMES FROM OCEAN TO OCEAN

*Few of us have the opportunity to name a river, town, or county, but ear-
lier generations did. Most people are familiar with Dutch names in New
York, Spanish names in California, French names in the Old Northwest,
and Indian names in all states. Travelers aware of these and of Irish
names in Europe, such as the famous Schottengasse "ring" in Vienna, are
often unaware of Irish place names in the United States. The Irish in
America, like other immigrants, used names that kept alive the memories
of their homeland and of national heroes.*

Since the Irish settled in great numbers in all the colonies in pre-
Revolutionary America, we have many Irish place names in the original thirteen colonies. The Irish continued to emigrate after the Revolution, and left their marks on local, county, and state maps from
coast to coast.

Some of the earliest and largest colonies were the great plantations of New Leinster, New Munster, and New Connaught in Maryland, names which survive only in local usage and folklore. But the
towns of Mayo and Tyrone are on the Maryland map today. The city
of Baltimore was named for the Irish title of the Maryland proprietor,
Cecil Calvert (Lord Baltimore), and comes from an Irish phrase
meaning "townland of the big house."

Here is a very small sampling of Irish place names in the United
States, with the names of the states in which they are found:

Antrim - Michigan and elsewhere.
Armagh - Pennsylvania.
Cork - New York (Fulton County), Georgia, Ohio, Virginia.
Derry - New Hampshire, Pennsylvania, elsewhere.
Donegal - Pennsylvania.
Dublin - Georgia, California, elsewhere.
Erin - New York, Tennessee.
Erin Prairie - Wisconsin.
Fermanagh - Pennsylvania.
Galway - New York (Saratoga County)
Hibernia - New York, New Jersey, Florida, elsewhere.
Kildare - Wisconsin.
Kilkenny -Minnesota.
Limerick and New Limerick - Connecticut, Maine.
Londonderry - New Hampshire, Vermont, elsewhere.
Monaghan - Pennsylvania.
Newry - Georgia, Maine, Minnesota, Wisconsin, Pennsylvania.
Roscommon - Michigan.
San Patricio de Hibernia - Texas.
Shannon - Georgia, Illinois, Mississippi, Missouri (Shannon County), North Carolina,
    South Dakota, Washington (Lake Shannon), and Iowa (Shannon City).
Sligo - Pennsylvania.
Ulster - New York.
Vinegar Hill - Illinois (a township).
Waterford - New York (Saratoga County), Iowa, Vermont, Virginia, Mississippi.
Wexford - Iowa, Michigan (Wexford County).

Some places named in the 19th century and earlier came from family names. Here is a very small list of such places:

Barry - Missouri (Commodore John Barry, of Revolutionary War fame, "father of the
    United States Navy").
Burke - North Carolina (Thomas Burke, governor 1781-82); Georgia, New York,
    Vermont (Edmund Burke, British parliamentarian of Irish birth and blood, strong
    spokesman for Irish and American colonial rights).
Callaghan - Virginia (Dennis Callaghan, pioneer in Allegheny Mountains).
Carroll - Maryland and elsewhere (Charles Carroll of Maryland, Revolutionary
    patriot and signer of Declaration of Independence).
Fitzgerald Station, now Old Fitzgerald Station Campground - Winnebago County,
    Wisconsin (three Fitzgerald brothers of County Cork and Miramichi, New
    Brunswick).
Greeley - Colorado (founded by Horace Greeley, newspaper publisher, anti-slavery
    leader, loser to Grant for Presidency in 1872, famous for phrase "Go West, Young
    Man, Go West."
Kearney - Missouri (General Stephen Kearney, who commanded the western armies
    of the United States in the Mexican War); also Kearny, New Jersey (Major
    General Philip Kearny, killed in the American Civil War.
McDonough - Delaware (Commodore Thomas McDonough, War of 1812).
McMullen - Texas (John McMullen, Irish empresario).

Meagher County - Montana (General Thomas Meagher, leader of the Irish Brigade in the Civil War, later governor of Montana).

Murphy - California (miner who discovered gold there); North Dakota (a superior court judge).

O'Brien - Iowa (William Smith O'Brien, Irish patriot and Young Irelander).

O'Neill - Nebraska (Fenian General John O'Neill).

O'Neals - California (early settler Charles O'Neal).

Sheridan - Illinois, Kansas, Wyoming, Montana, Nebraska (General Philip Sheridan of American Civil War fame).

Sullivan County - New York, Pennsylvania, New Hampshire, Tennessee (John Sullivan, a general under George Washington).

St. Patrick's, Missouri, could be included on this list. Like Santa Claus and the North Pole, also place names in America, St. Patrick's is known to all those who collect postmarks. The postmaster is deluged annually with letters to be postmarked March 17. He also provides special St. Patrick's Day envelopes. The community was settled in 1833 by Irish Catholics who built a church the following year. They first called their community North Santa Fe, because it was near a branch of the famous trail. The name was changed to St. Patrick in 1858, and a shrine to Ireland's patron saint was built a century later, in 1957.

Hundreds of Irish place names in Michigan and Wisconsin and further westward reveal the marks of Irish settlers in the 19th century, as they established settlements from ocean to ocean. Many of the sons of the lumbermen and farmers took up railroad work and followed the railroads to the ore ports of Ashland, Superior, and Duluth on Lake Superior, where one finds heavy concentrations of Irish names on the United States censuses from 1850 to 1900. The Irish are heavy in number among the men who developed the great iron ore mines of the Mesabi Range, in the last quarter of the 19th century.

For Minnesota, the United States Post Office *Zip Code Directory* lists such places as Avoca, Clontarf, Corcoran, Dalton, Donnelly, Fergus, Foley, Gibbon, Iona, Kelliher, Kennedy, Kilkenny, Kinney, Scanlon, Tracy. By 1870, the log boom town of Stillwater, though its name is not Irish, was more than 75 percent Irish in population, a great number of them having arrived from Miramichi, New Brunswick. In St. Paul and Minneapolis, the Irish presence was also substantial.

For Nebraska, the same directory lists Avoca, Brady, Brandon, Carroll, Cody, Dalton, Emmet, Kearney, Kennedy, Kilgore, Lynch, McCool, McGrew, Merriman, Milligan, Mitchell, Murray, O'Neill, Sutton, Gibbon, Ragan.

For South Dakota: Brandon, Burke, Butler, Creighton, Doland, Harrington, Hayes, Hurley, Iona, Marty, McLaughlin, Mitchell, Quinn.

For North Dakota: Bantry, Colgan, Driscoll, Elliott, Emmet, Fingal, Finley, Keene, Kenmare, Martin, McCanna, McCluskey, Regan, Sutton; also counties Burke, Dunn, Walsh.

For Montana: Brady, Clancy, Condon, Conner, Dillon, Ennis, Garryowen, Geraldine, Hays, Kevin, McCabe, Moore, Norris, Ronan, Seeley.

For Idaho: Burke, Carey, Coolin, Deary, Dingle, Donnelly, Downey, Emmett, Gibbonville, Iona, Kingston, Mackay, McCall, Moore, Moyle, Mullan, Murphy, Rathdrum. There are counties bearing the names of Fallon, Meagher, and Toole.

For Washington: Boyds, Brinnon, Buckley, Burley, Burton, Carrolls, Cheney, Colton, Connell, Conway, Cunningham, Cusick, Finley, Galvin, Harrington, Ione, Joyce, Kingston, La Conner (after J.J. Connor, an early settler), Malone, McCleary, McKenna, McMillin, Reardan, Redmond, Roche Harbor.

Americans veterans of World War II who served overseas will recall the ubiquitous slogan "Kilroy was here," scribbled in toilets and elsewhere, wherever there were American troops, sometimes even before the troops arrived. Backpackers in the highest of California's Sierras will unfailingly learn that Irishmen preceded them. The hiker will find on the Ordnance Map for Silver Lake such places as Mahon Camp, Cody Meadows, Martin Meadow, and Jim Quinn Spring. In or near Yosemite National Park, the stout mountaineer on Donahue Pass will note Donahue Peak at 12,023 feet. Not far away are Rafferty Pass (10,000 feet) and Rafferty Creek, Delany Creek, Sullivan Lake, Ireland Lake, Ireland Creek, Maclure Creek, and McGee Lake. Elsewhere in the park are McGurn Meadow, Norris Camp, Hogan Mountain, and Keyes Peak, to cite just a few names that remind us that the kin of Kilroy have been there before us in the High Country.

Some places ought to have been named for an Irishman, but were not. In the southern Sierras, at the 8,000-foot level, is the Mineral King Valley, discovered by Harry Parole and an Indian helper in 1862. Harry, a roamer, was born in Ireland as Harry O'Farrell. At San Gregorio on the California coast, he was known as a champion fighter and was jailed more than once for brawling. After a judge in Redwood City defeated him in a fight, Harry, feeling disgraced, changed his surname to Parole and wandered the southern Sierras, hunting, trapping, and prospecting for gold. In 1862, Harry and his Indian friend followed the canyon of the Little Kern River upstream. Their horses became skittish near the top of the pass, and so the two explorers had to walk through a narrow gap. They beheld what was surely one of the most beautiful and inaccessible valleys on the continent. It was shaped like a bowl. No white man and few, if any, Indians had ever set foot in it before. Deer grazed innocently and bear cubs wrestled while their mother watched, unfrightened by their first experience of the human presence. Today, the valley is part of Sequoia National Park, and has been kept in a near-wilderness state, accessible only by a narrow and tortuous road, by a park service zealous to retain the beauty that Harry O'Farrell aka Parole and his Indian friend saw for the first time over one hundred years ago.

CANADA

Let us not forget Canada. The early Irish presence in Newfoundland (17th century) is suggested by O'Donnells, Patrick's Cove, Port Kirwan, Saint Brendan's, and an island named "Ireland's Eye."

In Nova Scotia, one finds Conway, Kingston, Lyons Brook. Mahone Bay, Meaghers Grant, and New Waterford; and on Prince Edward Island are Irishtown and O'Leary.

In New Brunswick, the settlements with Irish names are far too numerous to mention in their entirety here. An attractive map prepared in the early 1980s by Father Leo J. Hynes and Peter Rafferty and published by the Irish Canadian Cultural Association of New Brunswick lists about two hundred localities where Irish settled - and the earliest year of their arrival, mainly during the first half of the 19th century. To name just a few: McCluskey (1847); Gillespie Settlement (1845); Wicklow (1833); Dungarvon River (1842); Quigley Island (1826); Nowlanville (1827); Irish Settlement (1819); O'Donnell Settlement (1834); Shannon Brook (1821); New Ireland (1818); Donegal (1841); Irishtown (1821); New Bandon (1820); Cork (1842); Kerr Lake (1817); St. Patrick's Lake (1786); Hibernia (1830); Irish River (1819); Erin Go Bragh, now Barnesville (1820); McNallys (1822); New Ireland (1833); Doyles Passage (1784).

In Quebec, the French, who were there first, understandably supervised the naming of places, yet St. Patrick's Church in Quebec City, completed in 1833, says something of the Irish presence. In *Saint Patrick's, Quebec*, Sister Marianna O'Gallagher notes that the Irish population of Quebec City around 1830 was about 7,000 of a total of about 32,000 in this old French city. Father McMahon, the pastor in 1835, reported that he had six thousand souls in his congregation. Elsewhere in Quebec, one finds Cowansville, Sully, Sutton, and Tracy, in a sea of French place names.

In Ontario are Barry's Bay, Burk's Falls, Collins Bay, Creighton, Dunnville, Eganville, Erin, Holland Landing, Keena, Killarney, Mitchell, Naughton, Sutton, Tara, and Waterford. There is an

Erindale Campus of the University of Toronto, which has a faculty
that includes such fine scholars as Cecil J. Houston, Professor of History and an authority on Canada's Orangemen (*The Sash Canada
Wore*). Professor Houston has pointed out that in 1871 the ethnically
Irish Protestants and Catholics were 34 percent of the population of
the province of Ontario, the largest of eighteen ethnic groups officially
recognized by the census.

In Manitoba: Carberry, Cowan, Killarney, McCreary, and suspi-
ciously Irish-sounding Rorketon.

In Saskatchewan: Beatty, Broderick, Dollard, Hanley, Hoey,
Kelliher, Kennedy, Killaly, Lang, Lanigan, Macklin, Shamrock.

In Alberta: Boyle, Donnelly, Innisfree, Innisfail, Magrath, Ryley,
Shaughnessy.

In British Columbia: Courtenay, Flood, Golden, Haney, Kelly
Lake, McBride, McConnell Creek.

In Yukon and the Northwest Territories: Hayes River, Kennedy
Channel, Meighen Island, Mayo and Mayo Lake, McCabe Creek.

Place names do not always reveal the early Irish presence in frontier communities. Charles M. O'Malley of County Mayo settled in
Mackinac County in northern Michigan in 1836, and was joined by a
large number of other Irish families. By 1840, O'Malley operated a
general store and his business was flourishing. He represented the
county in the state legislature in 1846-49, and was later a justice of the
peace in Mackinac. As a member of the legislature he raised the ire
of Henry R. Schoolcroft, an American ethnologist and former
Superintendent of Indian Affairs for Michigan, by his successful effort
to change the Indian names of various counties in Michigan to Irish
names, such as Roscommon, Clare, Emmet, Antrim, and Wexford.
O'Malley was a close friend of John Riley, who achieved fame during
the Mexican War as the officer in charge of the San Patricio Battalion,
which fought for Mexico (*see Chapter 11*).

Sometimes a place name is Irish, but a bit disguised, such as
Flinton, Pennsylvania. It was named for John Flynn, born in 1801 in
Tulsk, Ogulla Parish, County Roscommon, Ireland. According to
W.D. Hamilton in *Old North Esk Revised* (1988), Flynn emigrated to
New Brunswick, and settled in North Esk Parish, Miramichi, where he
petitioned for land in 1824, and declared that he was a native of
Ireland, age 22, and a resident of New Brunswick for two years. In
1827, he married a neighbor, Avisia Kingston, and settled on the
Portage River. By the 1830s, he was one of the principal taxpapers in
the county and his lumber business was thriving. In 1844, however,
amid a general collapse of the lumber industry, Flynn declared
bankruptcy.

In the mid-1850s, John and Avisia and six of their married sons re-settled at Janesville, Cambria County, Pennsylvania. They were attracted by the virgin white pines along the Susquehanna, much like the forests of New Brunswick. Soon the family members had acquired the local hotel, the livery stable, the grist and sawmills, a general store, and a private family cemetery. Their major business, however, was lumbering. "Their part in what became one of the 19th century's greatest lumbering operations," writes Professor Hamilton, "was a significant one, and their woods headquarters on Clearfield Creek became known as Flynn Town, later Flinton, Pennsylvania."

John's oldest son, Edward, almost lost his life in a river drive in New Brunswick in 1851 (his partner, John Allison, was drowned). He was, however, to die in a logging accident in Cameron County, Pennsylvania.

John Flynn's son Anthony, who was a partner with his brother Patrick in the A. & P. Flynn Lumber Company, was famed during his lifetime for his ability to organize the drives on the rivers and the operations in the woods. On his deathbed in 1900, with his caulk-shoes beside him, he instructed a nephew on how to clear a massive pine log jam on Clearfield Creek, a task requiring a hundred men and eighty logging teams.

Shieldsville, Minnesota, memorializes Irish-born James Shields, the only person to serve as United States Senator from three different states: Illinois, Minnesota, Missouri. Shields was a practicing lawyer; supreme court judge in Illinois; governor of the Oregon Territory; California railroad commissioner; land commissioner in Washington, D.C.; and brigadier general in the Mexican and Civil Wars. As a rural land colonizer in Minnesota, he organized several townships, including Erin, Kilkenny, and Shieldsville, where his first official act was the building of a Catholic church overlooking Lake Mazaska. James Shields, whose statue represents Illinois in the National Statuary Hall in the nation's capital, left a legacy from ocean to ocean.

It would need a book in itself to list all the Irish-born and Irish second generation settlers who gave their surnames or Irish place names to what became their settlements in the United States, or to list all the people of Irish descent whose achievements motivated admiring citizens to name places after them. One has only to consider the number of schools, roads, airports, public buildings, cultural centers, and parks that have been named for President John F. Kennedy.

MEF and JAK

Chapter 14

ST. PATRICK'S DAY CELEBRATIONS

The most famous St. Patrick's Day parade is held in New York City, but other gala parades celebrate March 17 in cities and towns everywhere in the United States. In the metropolitan New York area, permanent parade committees sponsor smaller editions of the annual Irish march up Fifth Avenue. Thus, in March, one can cheer the grand marshal, bands, pipers, county associations, and Irish American organizations in the Big Parade, and then repeat the enjoyment another day by watching resplendent parades on main streets an hour from Manhattan: Brooklyn, Staten Island, and Rockaway Beach within New York City; Nutley, Newark, and Jersey City in New Jersey; Brentwood, East Islip, and Garden City on Long Island.

EARLY CELEBRATIONS IN AMERICA

In British North America, the Protestant Irish were the first to surface with pride in their Irishness. In colonial days, they were the only ones who could initiate a public Irish celebration. Catholics were officially banned in all of the colonies, although they were tolerated in Maryland and Pennsylvania as long as they kept a low profile.

The earliest celebrations were not parades, but banquets, meetings, or fund-raising efforts. The first March 17th celebration of which there is a record of its being "public" was in Boston. This was the 1737 celebration of Boston's Charitable Irish Society, which was Irish Protestant.

In Charleston, South Carolina, the newspapers in 1771 reported a dinner of Irish gentlemen on the occasion of St. Patrick's Day. In 1772, the dinner was accompanied by the ringing of bells in town. In

1773, a much larger public dinner was held by the St. Patrick's Club, also known as the Friendly Brothers of St. Patrick. Two noted members were Edward Rutledge, a signer of the Declaration of Independence, and his brother John, a governor of South Carolina. Both were sons of an Irish Protestant immigrant from County Longford. After a Revolutionary hiatus, the Charleston organization re-organized itself in 1786 with a charter and the name "Friendly Brothers of Ireland," with Pierce Butler, a United States Senator, as president.

In Philadelphia in the 1770s the Society of the Friendly Sons of St. Patrick celebrated March 17 with banquets. The membership rolls included Generals Wayne, Butler, Hand, Irvine, and Moylan, as well as other officers of the Continental Army. George Washington was adopted as an honorary member. Another member, Protestant like most, was Thomas McKeon, who was president of the Continental Congress, a signer of the Declaration of Independence, and a governor of Pennsylvania. McKeon, who was also president of the Hibernian Society for the Relief of Emigrants from Ireland, always identified himself as Irish.

The Friendly Sons of St. Patrick of New York was officially organized in 1784, a year before the organization of the first Catholic Church in New York. The New York Friendly Sons, like their counterparts in other cities, became more tolerant of their Irish Catholic brethren as time went on. The support of the Protestant Friendly Sons was important in a state like New York which had discriminatory laws against Catholics for many years after the Revolution. Until 1821, under the Jay Alien Clause, the State of New York required immigrants seeking naturalization to renounce allegiance to and jurisdiction of any foreign authority, including the Pope," in matters ecclesiastical as well as civil." This was a serious matter for Catholics. American-born fared better than Irish-born and some were elected to the state legislature.

In 1902, John Crimmins of New York's Friendly Sons of St. Patrick published his research on Irish American celebrations before the year 1845. He had found the records of thirty-eight different Irish organizations in Connecticut, Georgia, Maryland, Massachusetts, New York, Pennsylvania, Rhode Island, Virginia, and South Carolina. Crimmins limited himself to what he called "prominent, notable and curious instances," but he realized that there might have been unrecorded celebrations in small villages and on the frontier.

ST. PATRICK'S DAY PARADES

The idea of celebrating St. Patrick's Day with a parade belongs to the Revolutionary Period and to the mid-19th century. Recent historians, perhaps over-reacting in their pride, have taken an earlier date for the first St. Patrick's Day Parade in New York. In 1762, some Irish-born militiamen marched to a St. Patrick's Day breakfast in lower Manhattan with band playing and flags flying. The practice continued each year as leading citizens of Irish heritage were honored on March 17 with a Fife and Drum corps reveille. Parading from house to house was incidental. A civil parade with religious connotations was anathema to staunchly Protestant New York and smacked of Romanist processions and invocation of the saints.

Colonial America did have celebrations in honor of St. Patrick's Day, but the public military parade is associated with Revolutionary War times. St. Patrick's Day was enthusiastically observed in the American Army during the Revolution by celebrations, military drills and parades, and "time off."

On March 17, 1776, the day that the British evacuated Boston and the Americans took possession, George Washington authorized "Boston" as the parole (password) for the day and "Saint Patrick" as the countersign. He made General John Sullivan the Brigadier of the Day.

In 1778, while Washington's Army lay at Valley Forge, the Irish were insulted by the display of a "Paddy" effigy by the Pennsylvania Germans and the New England troops. To avoid a serious confrontation, Washington settled the affair by ordering an extra drink for every man under his command in honor of March 17, thus making all of his troops celebrate the day.

In 1780, Washington's General Orders for March 17 congratulated the Irish Parliament for its fight to remove the heavy and tyrannical oppressors, and for its operations in support of America's similar cause. He also directed that all fatigue and working parties cease for the day and that celebrations be permitted in the camp.

On the same day, Colonel Francis Johnson of the Pennsylvania Line, certainly as heavy an Irish as "Scotch-Irish" group, issued an order for a little rum to the corps to celebrate St. Patrick and the Kingdom of Ireland. The camp parole was "Saint," and the countersigns were "Patrick" and "Shelah." The day began with music and hoisting of the colors exhibiting the United States' thirteen stripes, the harp, and an inscription, "The Independence of Ireland."

Records indicate the Continental Regiments at West Point had a great parade on March 17, 1781. In March 1782, officers in the Pennsylvania and South Carolina regiments held all day and night dinners in honor of St. Patrick.

NEW YORK CITY'S FIRST OFFICIAL PARADE

In New York City, the first government-sponsored St. Patrick's Day Parade took place in 1779. With New York City occupied by the

British and the fortunes of the redcoats declining elsewhere, it was important for the British to make a show of British and Irish amity. Such a show might influence the Irish among the rebels, who enlisted in the Continental Army only for short periods, to stay on their farms instead of showing up for a new muster.

Thus the British organized the first real St. Patrick's Day parade on record in New York City with a large Loyalist corps. The parade was staged by five hundred members of Lord Rawdon's Volunteers of Ireland, a unit that had fought valiantly for several years. This was a true parade, with marching maneuvers, banners, uniforms, bands, full military display. It was a parade of Irish, a St. Patrick's Day Parade in pro-Tory New York City. Such an event could not have been predicted two years before, in 1777, when a Catholic priest had been arrested for saying Mass. Lord Rawdon's forces, to be sure, were all true Protestants who had taken the sacramental test, or at least so he proudly reported. Although there was considerable recruitment in Ireland, no Catholic could serve as an officer, and Rawdon, like many other British commanders, required all recruits, even poor Irish Catholic peasants, to take a so-called Protestant Oath and yearly sacrament, making them, in effect, Protestants.

In capitalizing on the popularity of Ireland's patron saint, who certainly belonged to all Ireland, the British had five objectives in mind. They were actively suggesting a new era of good will to rebellious Irish American colonists whose past experiences might have left them with little trust in Britain's words of good will. They were demonstrating to the non-rebelling colonies of Canada that they meant to respect the Quebec Act of 1774 which gave freedom of religion to Catholics. They were showing the Catholic nations of Europe, whose support they wanted, that England might be lessening its anti-Catholic laws. They hoped to keep the Catholics of Ireland loyal, calm, and peaceful during England's overseas troubles. And in New York, they gave the Loyalist Irish Volunteers a chance to show pride in their Irish heritage, often not an easy thing in the British Army.

IRISH SOCIETIES

After the Revolution, and during the first half of the 19th century, Irish organizations typically celebrated St. Patrick's Day not with a huge parade in which all organizations participated, but with banquets. The banquets grew more fancy as the Irish, including the Catholics among them, began to prosper. Each organization usually had its own banquet, which might be accompanied by a small parade, rally, or procession.

Two celebrations developed in Boston. The Charitable Irish Society, originally Protestant but later open to economically comfortable

Catholics, had a very elaborate dinner. The Shamrock Society, its members less well-off and including recently arrived Catholics, had a plainer dinner known as "bone and sinew." In Massachusetts, as elsewhere, the purpose of the Irish societies was not only to have dinners on St. Patrick's Day but to unite their members and to assist with security in a generally anti-Irish environment. The societies sought to help members and other Irish in need of burial insurance, to provide sick benefits and jobs, and to perform a number of charitable functions.

The societies abounded in a number of states, often bearing names that identified their purpose: the Irish Benevolent Society of Lowell, Massachusetts; St. Augustine's Beneficial Society of Philadelphia; the Irish Catholic Benevolent Union of Dayton, Ohio; Father Mathew Total Abstinence Society; the Hibernian Sons of Milwaukee.

In 19th century New York City there were many Irish societies so small that they were confined to local Irish churches and neighborhoods. Others were much larger in scope, such as the Irish Emigrant Society, to which John Calhoun, a United States vice-president, belonged; the Friendly Sons of St. Patrick; the Father Mathew Total Abstinence Society; the Irish Hibernian Society; and the Ancient Order of Hibernians (founded in 1836); the Hibernian Burial Benevolent Society; the Hibernian Universal Benevolent Society; and the Shamrock Society. In myriad service organizations the Irish proclaimed their identity: country and athletic clubs, militia companies, fire-fighting brigades, literary and political groups, charitable societies, veterans' groups.

One cannot omit the organization, perhaps "movement" would be a better word, that brought forth the greatest number of Irish. The Fenian Brotherhood, named and re-named many times in America, had, as its main purpose, the freeing of Ireland from Great Britain. In March 1866, a Fenian rally in New York City drew one hundred thousand to the picnic grounds in the Yorkville section. *(The story of the Fenian Movement in America and Canada is the subject of Chapter 7.)*

AMERICANISM

As the Irish became Americans and moved upwards socially and economically, Irish organizations began to lose their wide popular appeal. Some organizations were no longer as necessary as they had been in the past. Many found their memberships dwindling to first and second generation Irish. All Irish, however, seemed to cling to the 17th of March as the one day on which they must be visible without fail. A parade followed by a Mass became the standard, or vice versa as the parade became longer. The objective was to get all the groups to form one parade on St. Patrick's Day and then, if they wished, to have separate celebrations in the evening.

NEW YORK CITY

As early as the 1820s, the Hibernian Universal Benevolent Society in New York followed its March 17th morning business meeting with a procession to church. In the 1840s, various Irish organizations sponsored similar short processions. Collections were taken for the worthy causes sponsored by these groups.

John Ridge, in *The St. Patrick's Day Parade in New York*, has provided background information on early parades and has given chronological capsule accounts of parades from 1851 to 1987. In 1851, at least seventeen Irish societies, including two from Brooklyn, participated in a single parade in lower Manhattan, but the first great St. Patrick's Day parade in New York under the umbrella of a single organization (the Convention of Irish Societies) was held in 1852 in severe weather. Impressed observers were reported as commenting that they had not realized that there were so many Irish in the city. In 1853, the Ancient Order of Hibernians, which would in time take full responsibility for the parade, marched for the first time. Groups in the City of Brooklyn, which had small local processions since the 1820s, also joined the Manhattan parade. Because of fears of violence from Irish-hating Nativists, the early parades were routed through Irish areas of the city where there would be no attempts at disruption.

In October 1860, Colonel Michael Corcoran and his 69th Regiment refused to parade before and salute the visiting Prince of Wales. Corcoran, who had resigned from the Royal Irish Constabulary and emigrated to America after the Rising of 1848, was ordered court-martialed. His treatment was denounced by the Convention of Irish Societies, who turned the 1861 parade of ten thousand marchers into a tribute to the 69th. Behind the 69th marched a unit of the Fenian Brotherhood, of which Corcoran was a member of the Central Council. (With the beginning of the Civil War, the 69th was pardoned, sent to the battlefields, and took severe punishment in July at Bull Run, where about sixteen percent of its troops died, and Corcoran was taken prisoner. Freed later, Corcoran organized another Irish regiment, fought heroically in many battles, and was killed accidentally in December 1863.)

After the Civil War, the New York parade became a clear symbol of Irish and Catholic power. Politicians courting the vote were quick to associate themselves with the parade. In 1869, Mayor A. Oakley Hall not only wore a shamrock, but also a green suit and tie. In 1870, Hall was the first mayor to join the line of March. Decked again in green, he rode in a barouche and called himself an adopted Hibernian by grace of his initials, "AOH."

In 1876 and 1877, the parade was endangered by hostile publicity concerning a group of Pennsylvania mine workers who belonged both to the Ancient Order of Hibernians and to a labor organization, the Workingmen's Benevolent Association. Stories were spread that the Irish "Molly Maguires," a fictional label created by the mine owners, were members of a secret society connected to the Ancient Order of Hibernians, and that they had pledged to kill all Protestant mine owners and supervisors and to destroy mine property. The pursuit of the "Mollies" was led by an Irish Orangeman, railway president Franklin Gowan. (*See Note 1: Molly Maguires.*)

In the wake of atrocity stories, terror trials, perjured witnesses, hangings of Irishmen, and a rebirth of Know-Nothingism, many New Yorkers were afraid to be seen in the parade in the company of the Ancient Order of Hibernians. Guilt by association could mean loss of jobs, since New York City's bosses would be just as likely as Pennsylvania ones to find excuses to get rid of potential labor union troublemakers. The great parade figure of thirty thousand declined to ten thousand in 1876 and 1877.

At its National Convention in 1877, the Ancient Order of Hibernians, forgetting its motto of "Friendship, Unity, and Christian Charity," tried to save its reputation. It denounced the Molly Maguires and cut off all AOH membership in the Pennsylvania coal regions. This act did not help the New York City parade, which in 1878 hit its lowest record in twenty years (four times the number of marchers participated, however, in the speeches and celebrations at less public Jones Wood).

In the 1880s New York's Mayor Abram Hewitt supported Know Nothingism in its new guise as the Nativist Party. He identified immigrants with the source of the city's problems. Hewitt had run on the Tammany Hall ticket and won by a plurality, defeating Henry George of the Workingmen's Party and Theodore Roosevelt of the Republican Party.

Dissension among the members of the AOH and the Convention of Irish Societies resulted in a split, which led to two parades in 1885. There was a half-hearted reconciliation in 1886, but there were two parades again in 1887. Unlike other politicans who realized that the Irish were still marching to the polls even though not marching in unison, Hewitt believed he could write off the Irish vote.

In 1888, in his second year in office, Mayor Hewitt refused invitations from both organizations to review their parades. Nevertheless, the turnout for the two parades, one uptown, the other downtown, was remarkable (over ten thousand) considering that the city and suburbs were suffering the effects of the famous Blizzard of '88. Beginning on March 11, twenty-one inches of snow fell. On March 12, winds up to eighty-five miles per hour whipped the snowfall into drifts of twenty feet. Transportation was halted, communications were cut, people were stranded, and an estimated two hundred died within the city.

Hewitt also refused to fly Irish flags at City Hall on March 17. The city aldermen promptly passed a bill ordering the flags to be hoisted. Hewitt vetoed it, with some talk about America for Americans. This did not endear him to a large group of voters. Almost thirteen percent of New York's population were Irish-born, and possibly three times that many were at least third or fourth generation Irish, or of part Irish ancestry.

Expediently, in 1888, the leaders of Tammany Hall (the popular name for the city's Democratic Party organization) informed this first mayor in forty years to refuse to review the March 17th parade that he had no chance for re-election. He ran anyway - and lost. His Irish-born successor, William R. Grace, wore a green emblem on St. Patrick's Day and participated in the parades during his term in office. The percentage of people with Irish ancestry in New York gradually decreased, but politicans still must find very good excuses for not being visible on St. Patrick's Day. The parade, which nowadays takes six hours to pass, indicates the rise of the Irish in America to a position of prestige and respect.

OTHER PROBLEMS

Over the years there have sometimes been problems with the Catholic hierarchy. Although most of the participating societies had close ties to the Catholic Church, the parade has never been Church-run. In 1901, Archbishop Michael Corrigan created a precedent by being the first head of the archdiocese to request to review the parade. In 1915, reported historian John Ridge, Cardinal John Farley found himself in the midst of a feud between two factions over the issue of Irish enlistment in the British Army in World War I. One faction, headed by Roderick Kennedy, chairman of the Arrangements Committee and a native of Tipperary, ordered that all bands refrain from playing "It's a Long Way to Tipperary," a London music hall song used by the British in Ireland to recruit young men for the battlefields in France. When the Eccentric Firemen Band, spurred by Mayor John Purroy Mitchel, flouted Kennedy's order and sounded forth with the forbidden song, Kennedy jumped from the reviewing stand where the Cardinal was among the guests, tore an instrument from the hands of one musician, got the attention of the bandmaster, and announced that the band was to leave the parade unless it desisted from playing the banned song. "It's an insult to Tipperary," Kennedy explained, "to associate the county with disreputable streets in London like Leicester Square and Piccadilly. Playing an English marching song in the parade would be a violation of President Wilson's Neutrality Proclamation." The Irish-born Cardinal, after an initial moment of horror at Kennedy's seemingly irrational behavior, reportedly agreed with him.

On another issue, a problem with hierarchy arose in 1983 when Cardinal Cooke did not approve of Michael Flannery as Grand Marshal, even though Flannery had been elected by an almost unanimous vote of the four hundred delegates to the Parade Committee. John Ridge noted that Flannery, an 81-year old native of County Tipperary, was not, in the eyes of the parade committee, the "mindless revolutionary" portrayed by the press and television, which tended to push the Cardinal into the controversy. The committee respected Michael Flannery as a distinguished and thoughtful gentleman who fought in the Irish War of Independence, fought with the Irish Republican Army in the post-Treaty period, was imprisoned by the Irish Free State government for two years, went on a thirty-nine day hunger strike before his release in 1924, emigrated to the United States in 1927, and became active in many causes having to do with justice for both the Irish and the Americans. He was also a leader of the Irish Northern Aid Committee, founded to promote American awareness of British injustices and to provide financial support to families of political prisoners, including I.R.A. As a consequence of that association and of British and even Irish governmental pressure on United States officials and on the Church hierarchy to repudiate the Irish Northern Aid Committee, Flannery's presence on the reviewing stand would be an embarrassment to the Cardinal.

Flannery met with Cardinal Cooke. The meeting was cordial, reported the Cardinal, but Flannery refused to step down as Grand Marshal. The Cardinal, therefore, absented himself from the reviewing stand. Several principals of Catholic high schools withdrew their marching bands and twirlers. The Irish government did not send any representative, nor did the Irish Tourist Board or Aer Lingus officially participate.

Nevertheless, the 1983 parade was an enormous success in terms of the participants and spectators. The spectators, so the press reported, seemed more orderly than they had been in years, and their numbers were estimated to be in the 120,000 range. The absence of the Cardinal and Irish officials was hardly noticeable on the reviewing stand, crammed as it was to overflowing with about five thousand VIPs.

Many Irish and Catholics who had never before attended a parade seemed to be making the point that churchmen should not interfere in matters that were none of their business. They were also, perhaps, refuting the tired stereotype that Irish Catholics are "priest-ridden."

Another issue arose in New York City as women asked for more recognition. Only AOH members are eligible to be grand marshals, and AOH members must be Irish and Catholic and, until recently, male. In 1986, when the Ladies AOH moved from auxiliary to full membership, the women rallied for a turn at Grand Marshal. This would have surprised John Grimes, deceased publisher of the *Irish Echo*, who commented during the Flannery stirup that nobody ever notices the grand marshals unless "their uncles give them a clap."

In 1989, to defuse what should have been a non-issue, two gentlemen with good chances for election asked that their names be withdrawn. These peacemakers were Willie Joe Cunningham of Brooklyn and Joseph Doherty of the Manhattan Correctional Center. (Joe Doherty, honorary Grand Marshal in other towns, had been held in American prisons since June 1983, without charges or trial, at the request of the British government, despite five United States courts having decreed that he was a political refugee who could not be extradited and who should be released.)

In February, with the nominations reduced to two ladies, Dorothy Hayden Cudahy, "the First Lady of Irish Radio," received 256 votes to 233 for educator Mary Holt Moore, and 1989 became the year of the first female Grand Marshal of the New York City St. Patrick's Day parade.

A UNIQUE ACHIEVEMENT

The Irish precedent for an annual parade in New York and elsewhere stimulated other immigrant groups to have their parades, but none has been able to match the enthusiasm and magic of March 17. The feat of the Irish has been to convince Americans of other ethnic origins to celebrate the day with them and to do this without benefit of a government-decreed holiday. The Irish won recognition for their saint and their heritage and they induced others to join with them in the Wearing of the Green. This indeed has been a unique achievement.

MEF

IV
SEEDS THAT GREW
IN AMERICAN SOIL

Chapter 15

HIGHEST STATESMEN:
EIGHTEEN UNITED STATES PRESIDENTS

Among the Uncounted Irish are the eighteen United States presidents who thought of themselves as Irish, at least in part. The early presidents were quick to assert their "Irish" roots, long before the days of Know Nothingism when the term "Scotch Irish" came into popular usage as a way to separate the Protestant Irish from the Catholic Irish whom the Nativists feared. We are especially indebted to Father Kevin O'Neill Shanley of Joliet, Illinois, for his articles on the Irish ancestry of the presidents; to Ronald E. Whealan, Head Librarian of the John F. Kennedy Library in Boston, for providing copies of many documents on John F. Kennedy's lineage; and to Gary Boyd Roberts, Director of Publications at the New England Historic Genealogical Society in Boston, who provided much data from his book, ANCESTORS OF AMERICAN PRESIDENTS *(Carl Boyer III, publisher, Santa Clarita, California, 1989).*

ANDREW JACKSON. Conceived in Ireland but born in the United States, Jackson was the son of Andrew Jackson and Elizabeth Hutchinson of Carrickfergus, County Antrim, who emigrated before 1760-61. His great-grandfather was Thomas Jackson of Ballyregan in Dundonald, County Down.

JAMES KNOX POLK. The family name was originally Pollock, pronounced "Poke" or "Polk." The president's 3rd great grandfather was Captain Robert Pollock/Polk of County Donegal. The president's mother's mother's parents, Thomas and Naomi Gillespie of Rowan

County, North Carolina, may also have had origins in northern Ireland.

JAMES BUCHANAN. His father, James Buchanan, and his grandfather, John Buchanan, were born in Rathmelton, County Donegal. Earlier Buchanan ancestors probably resided in Deroran, County Tyrone. The president's maternal grandparents, James Speer and Mary Patterson, emigrated to Pennsylvania from northern Ireland.

ANDREW JOHNSON. The origin of his father, Jacob Johnson, is unknown, but the father and grandfather of his mother, Mary McDonough, were both named Andrew McDonough (sometimes McDonah or McDonnach). Her father, of Beaufort County, North Carolina, was certainly of northern Irish descent.

ABRAHAM LINCOLN. His immigrant ancestor, Samuel Lincoln, married the probably Irish-born Martha Lyford, whose English-born father, Reverend John Lyford, was a minister at Levalleglish near Loughgall in County Armagh, and in Massachusetts and Virginia.

ULYSSES S. GRANT. His mother, Hannah Simpson Grant, was the great-granddaughter of William Simpson, born in the north of Ireland about 1710. Grant's paternal grandmother was Rachel Kelly, sometimes (and probably mistakenly) called Mrs. Rachel Miller Kelly, likely of Irish stock.

CHESTER ALAN ARTHUR. The birthplace of his father, William Arthur, was Dreen, near Ballymena, County Antrim, now a national landmark in Ireland.

GROVER CLEVELAND. His mother, Anne Neal Cleveland, was the daughter of Irish immigrant Abner Neal, who emigrated in the late 1700s and became a bookseller and publisher of law books in Baltimore. A great-great-grandfather, moreover, was Richard Lamb of Dublin, who died enroute to New England between August 1736 and July 1737.

BENJAMIN HARRISON. His mother, Elizabeth Ramsey Irwin Harrison, was a great-granddaughter of both Archibald Irwin and William McDowell of Franklin County, Pennsylvania, and they were almost certainly from northern Ireland.

WILLIAM McKINLEY. He was a 3rd great-grandson of David McKinley, born in northern Ireland about 1705, who emigrated to York County, Pennsylvania, about 1743. Most of McKinley's other known ancestors - surnames Stevenson, Gray, Rose, Chapman, Allison - also probably emigrated from northern Ireland, although a few may have come from Scotland.

THEODORE ROOSEVELT. Two 3rd great-grandfathers, Robert Barnhill and Daniel Craig of Bucks County, Pennsylvania, were very likely of northern Irish extraction, and so too may be another ancestor, Edmond McVeagh of Lower Dublin, Pennsylvania.

WOODROW WILSON. His paternal grandfather was James Wilson who emigrated from Dergalt, near Strabane, in County Tyrone. The ancestral home is still standing. After arriving in Philadelphia James Wilson married Mary Anne Adams, probably a native of County Antrim or County Down.

JOHN FITZGERALD KENNEDY (1917-1963). He was the most Irish of our presidents. His eight great-grandparents, all of whom were born in Ireland and died in Massachusetts, were:

Patrick Kennedy and Bridget Murphy:
Patrick Kennedy (1823-58), a Boston cooper, born in Dunganstown, County Wexford, son of tenant farmer Patrick Kennedy and Mary Johanna ____; in 1829, married Bridget Murphy (1821-88), the daughter of Richard Murphy and Mary ____; emigrated to Boston about 1848.

James F. Hickey and Margaret (Martha) Field:
James F. Hickey (1837-1900), son of Michael Hickey and Catherine Hassett, emigrated with parents about 1851; married Margaret "Martha" Field (1836-1911), daughter of Patrick Field and Mary Sheehy, in 1857 in Boston. Patrick and Mary, according to one source, were from Coorleigh North townland, County Cork, and were married at either Clonakilty or Rosscarbery in the same county on February 6, 1825. Daughter Margaret/Martha was born January 26, 1835, says the same source.

Thomas Fitzgerald and Rosanna Cox:
Thomas Fitzgerald (1823-85), a grocer of Boston, son of Michael Fitzgerald (d. 1860) and Ellen Wilmouth (1797-1875); emigrated with parents about 1848; married Rosanna "Rose" Cox (1834-79) in Boston in 1857. Rose was the daughter of Philip Cox and Mary ____, according to one record. Another source, Rose Fitzgerald Kennedy, indicates that her paternal grandmother, who was the wife of Thomas Fitzgerald, was Rose Mary Murray. Some say the Fitzgeralds were from the townlands of Lough Gur and nearby Bruff in County Limerick, but the author has not confirmed this.

Michael Hannon and Mary Ann Fitzgerald:
Michael Hannon (1832-1900) married Mary Ann Fitzgerald (1834-1904), who was a niece of Thomas Fitzgerald, above. Michael was born in Lough Gur, County Limerick, according to one source (unconfirmed by author), and was the son of John Hannon (d. July 22, 1835) and Ellen Noonan (1793-1877), who died in Acton, Massachusetts, and whose father was a Daniel Noonan or Newman. Mary Ann Fitzgerald, allegedly of Bruff, County Limerick, was the daughter of Edward (sometimes Edmund on the records) Fitzgerald (1797-1883), a Boston merchant, and Mary Linnehan, who were married in Ireland. Edward was the brother of Michael Fitzgerald, also a great-great grandfather of JFK, and Massachusetts death records, showing parentage, give their parents as James Fitzgerald and Hannah ____. The Irish Genealogical Office claimed in the 1960s that a James Fitzgerald of Skibbereen and spouse Katherine Cadogan were among JFK's direct ancestors (his great-grandparents) but the author has seen no evidence of that.

JFK'S GRANDPARENTS WERE:
   Patrick Joseph Kennedy (1858-1929), known as "P.J.", a Boston saloon keeper and State Senator; in 1887, he married Mary Augusta Hickey (1857-1923).
   John Francis "Honey" Fitzgerald (1863-1950), a mayor of Boston; in 1889, in Concord, Massachusetts, he married his second cousin, Mary Josephine Hannon (1864-1964), daughter of Michael Hannon and Mary Ann Fitzgerald. Mary Josephine lived to see her grandson elected President, but was not told of his assassination.

JFK'S PARENTS WERE:
   Joseph Patrick Kennedy (1888-1969), financier and U.S. Ambassador to England; in 1914, he married Rose Fitzgerald (1890-). Their son John Fitzgerald Kennedy was born in Brookline, Massachusetts, in 1917.

   LYNDON BAINES JOHNSON. Among his 3rd great-grandparents, all southerners, were a McClure, a McCoy, a Butler, and two Jameson sisters. John Jameson, grandfather of the two sisters, was born in County Galway about 1680 and emigrated to York County, Pennsylvania.
   RICHARD NIXON. Always an astute politician fully conscious of the Irish American electorate, President Nixon often sported his Irish roots. His mother was Hannah Milhous Nixon who was descended from Thomas and Elizabeth Milhous, Quakers from Carrickfergus, County Antrim. Their son John moved the family to Timahoe in County Kildare, and John's son Thomas emigrated from Dublin to Chester County, Pennsylvania, in 1729 with his wife Sarah and two children. One of his sons, John Milhous, was the great-great-grandfather of Hannah Milhous Nixon. It is believed that James Nixon, the president's 4th great-grandfather on the paternal side, emigrated from New Ross in County Wexford in 1731.
   GERALD R. FORD. His name at birth was Leslie Lynch King Jr. His great-grandfather, Lynch King, was born in Pennsylvania, according to the death record of Ford's grandfather, and he may well be of Irish descent.
   JAMES EARL CARTER. His father's mother's mother, born Sophronia Cowan in Abbeville County, South Carolina, was a descendant of Cowans, McCulloughs, Brownlees, and Cardwells, all probably from northern Ireland. George Brownlee, a Revolutionary War forebear, is said to have been born in County Antrim about 1757.
   RONALD REAGAN. Among his paternal great-great-grandparents may be Thomas O'Regan, a farm laborer of Doolis, Ballyporeen, County Tipperary, and his wife Margaret Murphy. Their youngest son, Michael O'Regan, born in 1829, may have emigrated to London in 1847 and there married Catherine Mulcahy, dropping the "O" in the name and spelling it Reagan. (The original spelling in Irish is actually "Ó Riagain" or "Ó Réagain.") Michael and Catherine emigrated to

Canada with two sons in 1858, then soon settled in Illinois. Their second son, John Michael Reagan, married Jennie Cusick, daughter of Patrick Cusick and Sarah Higgins (perhaps from Counties Clare and Kerry), and their son, John Edward Reagan, was father of the President.

Additions can probably be made to this list of eighteen. The research of Gary Boyd Roberts indicates that Warren G. Harding, Calvin Coolidge, and Harry Truman may have had ancestors from Ireland. So too George Bush, whose mother's mother's mother, Nannie E. Holliday, was a great-granddaughter of William Holliday, born about 1775, who emigrated from Rathfryland, County Down, to Kentucky, and his son, Joseph Holliday, was born between 1789 and 1792.

NOTE ON A NON-PRESIDENT: *In 1928, Alfred Emanuel Smith, Governor of New York, was the first Catholic candidate of a major party for President of the United States. He has often been described as an "Irish American," but that is not altogether true. He was as much Italian as Irish, according to Matthew and Hannah Josephson in* AL SMITH: HERO OF THE CITIES. *Smith's grandfather was listed on the 1855 New York State Census as Emanuel Smith, age 42, a mariner born in Genoa, Italy, a resident of New York for 30 years and a naturalized citizen. The name "Smith" may have been the work of a customs official with a poor ear for Italian surnames, who therefore assigned the name "Smith" to the young immigrant. Emanuel's spouse was listed on the 1855 census as Magdalena ____, born in Germany, a New York resident for eighteen years. Their children were listed as Alfred, 15, and Teresa, 13, both born in New York. Smith's father was Alfred Emanuel Smith, whose second wife was Catherine Mulvehill. She was the daughter of Thomas Mulvehill and Maria Marsh, both from County Westmeath. Maria was of English stock and a Protestant who accepted the Catholic faith to marry Thomas, earning the disapproval of her parents. She gave birth to the future governor, Alfred Emanuel Smith Jr., on December 30, 1873. Governor Smith, therefore, was a mixture of Italian, German, Irish, and some English strains, a true product of the Melting Pot.*

JAK

Chapter 16

SEEKERS OF JUSTICE:
WOMEN IN THE EARLY LABOR MOVEMENT

In the 19th century, the history of American trade and industrial unions parallels the history of Irish dominance in certain job areas: teamsters, dockworkers, plumbers, plasterers, carpenters, and building trade workers. We honor the memory of many men of Irish birth or parentage who led the struggle for workers' rights from the early days of unionism to the present. Such leaders include Terence Powderly of the Knights of Labor, who in the early 1880s created a precedent for an industrial union by admitting members without regard to race or sex or level of skill in a craft. Honor should also be paid to the less-heralded Irish women who had been organizing all along against overwhelming odds and who took up Powderly's challenge to recruit and organize on equal terms with men. Irish women played leading roles in the drama of the pioneer labor movement.

WORK ETHIC

Some think of the Irish immigrant girl only as the household Bridget, the servant everyone wanted or the subject of a joke. They are surprised to learn that the Irish provided the majority of female leaders for the trade unions during the latter part of the 19th century. This was true for reasons peculiar to the Irish situation at the time, both in Ireland and in America.

What about German, Italian, and Jewish women? Were not they too in the factories organizing the workers one hundred years ago? The answer seems to be no, not until later, for reasons rooted in their own cultures.

For measuring acceptable female behavior, the Irish used standards quite different from Anglo-Protestants and from those of other European immigrant groups.

After the successive failures of the potato crop in the first half of the 19th century, the Irish who survived and did not emigrate no longer sub-divided their land among their sons. With the new inheritance system and land laws, a younger son did not rush into marriage. Having no land on which to support them, he could not afford a wife and children. The result was an abundance of unmarried women who had no option but to emigrate, and emigrate they did in great numbers.

Once they arrived in America, young Irish women often had a better chance of getting steady work than the men. They were especially in demand as domestics. Their culture at that time attached no stigma to such work. Taking care of someone else's home, during the years before they married and began to take care of their own, was perfectly respectable. Nor was domestic work confined only to the single among Irish women. The married woman often supplemented her husband's wages in this way or supported the family totally when her husband was unemployed.

There was no sharp stigma attached to working, even in domestic service, and there was no real stigma attached to remaining single. The majority of Irish women remained single, if not for life, at least until they were in their mid-twenties, and often into their thirties or early forties. Reared as they had been in a famine and post-famine culture that defined a woman's worth in economic terms, they had to choose between marriage and economic aspiration. Those who looked at the poverty and drudgery of their early-married relatives and friends had little trouble postponing marriage. They would, in time, bring to their marriage a sizeable nest-egg. This factor generated some quite business-like, rather than romantic, marriages.

The single Irish American woman often used her disposable income to go to school to get the education she needed to become a teacher or nurse or office worker. An even higher priority for her income was helping her parents back in Ireland, or paying for passage for them and other relatives.

FACTORY WORK

In mid-19th century the majority of Irish American working women were domestics or waitresses. At the end of the century the percentage in those occupations had dropped. At the same time, the number of Irish women in factory work had increased dramatically. These women often brought with them to the mills a keen passion for justice developed under the intolerable conditions of Old World Ireland. In the New World a woman was free to give vent to her convictions. Her culture, with roots in the Heroic Age of the Celts when women fought alongside of the men in battle, placed no sanctions on female assertiveness or aggressiveness.

The Irish Catholic immigrant girl, culturally many miles removed from the working class Anglo-American girl in the factory, did not usually strive to be a model of Victorian prudence and primness who waited for the day when a fairy prince would rescue her and raise her above her class. Anglo-Protestant culture, like that of the German, Italian, and Jew, placed sanctions on female aggressiveness. The Irish acceptance of it explains in large measure why Irish women, far out of proportion to their percentage of the total population, became so heavily involved in the labor movement.

History written from a modern "feminist" perspective focuses on the first women in engineering, science, law, and medicine. It stresses the obstacles encountered by women seeking admission to the professions. It dwells also on allegedly unhappy women bent in bondage to machines and hand-work, full of despair or fatalism, perhaps welcoming the relief of death. This historical stance assumes that the immigrant Irish women in domestic or factory jobs were failures in life, victims of the capitalist system or sex discrimination, or both.

Such a picture is much more false than true. If the typical Irish immigrant woman of the last half of the 19th century could come back to earth today, how surprised she would be to hear of the dismal failure of her life. From the perspective of her own aspirations, not current feminist aspirations, she saw herself as successful. Life was not perfect, but God did not promise perfect happiness on earth. A woman had the opportunity in America to lay the foundation for the greater comfort, and certainly the greater "upward mobility," of her sons and daughters by making a good home for them and instilling in them the important religious and social values. If she had no children of her own, there might be nieces and nephews on whom she could bestow her largesse.

RELIGIOUS LIFE

The Irish woman always had the option, given much prestige in Irish Catholic culture, of joining a religious order and serving God and her fellow man in teaching or nursing or some other fulfilling occupation in which the order was involved. The woman who took this option was a working woman too, and like the others was fulfilling the purpose for which God made her and put her on earth. Some of the enormous contributions of the sisters are covered in Chapter 18, "Torch-Bearers: Religious Leaders and Founders."

LABOR LEADERS

From the beginning women of Irish birth or descent have played an important role in the American labor movement. Those who had the greatest influence in the earliest period of labor unionism fought for their rights in their own women's unions without the direct support of men.

By the late 1850s there were more Irish American women in factories than in domestic service. While Negro slaves were still supplying domestic and fieldhand service in the South, Irish women were in great demand as textile workers in the New England mills that processed the cotton from the South. Jobs were sometimes in short supply, however, especially during recurring periods of depression in the industry. Depression or no, mill owners in those free-swinging, raw capitalist days were not at all slow to exploit immigrant labor. If men went on strike, they would be replaced by women at lower rates of pay dictated by the owners, or by more recently-arrived and even hungrier immigrants.

Women in the mills, no strangers to injustice, were not willing for long to submit to absolute rule and exploitation of their labor. In 1859, one of the first labor strikes by women took place in the textile industry. About five hundred women spinners in three plants in Lowell, Massachusetts, struck against owners who had cut operations and wages. All of the women were immigrants and more than half were Irish. The owners were taken by surprise. They had no doubt looked on the Irish women as similar to the docile Bridgets employed in their mansions. The strike, however, was unsuccessful (the strikers represented no more than five percent of the workers at the mills), but a start had been made. Women of Irish birth and descent showed that they were going to be among the leaders of the American labor movement, even if their co-workers were reluctant or afraid to support them. Brief sketches follow of several of the more prominent women leaders.

LEONORA MARIE KEARNEY BARRY (1849-1930)

Born in Cork, Ireland, Leonora Kearney arrived as a child in New York. She married Patrick (aka William) Barry, but was left a widow at age thirty-two, with three small children to support. On her first day of work at a hosiery factory in Amsterdam, New York, she earned only eleven cents. At the end of the week she found she had earned only sixty-five cents. These starvation wages aroused her to form a union and affiliate with the Knights of Labor, a national organization established by garment workers in Philadelphia in 1869. The Knights advocated equal pay for equal work, opened membership to women in 1881, and denied membership to lawyers, bankers, liquor dealers, and gamblers. Within five years, Leonora headed a local of more than one thousand workers.

Leonora was one of the sixteen women delegates to the Knights of Labor General Assembly and Convention in Virginia in 1886. The same year, she was appointed Knights of Labor investigator for women's conditions, and became a full-time organizer. She is credited with securing in Pennsylvania, in 1889, the first factory inspection act in the nation. After marrying Oliver Lake in 1890, she retired from union leadership but continued to be active as a suffragette.

MARY HARRIS JONES (1830-1930), aka "MOTHER JONES"

Born in Cork, Ireland, Mary was the daughter of Richard Harris, who was considered a labor and economic agitator. In 1835, Richard was forced to emigrate. He did railroad work in Canada and the United States for five years before sending for his wife, daughter Mary, and two sons. Mary studied for both dressmaking and school teaching in Canada. She taught for some years in Maine, Michigan, and Tennessee.

In 1861, Mary married George Jones, an iron molder who had become an organizer in the Iron Molders Union. In 1867, after the death of her husband and four children in an epidemic in Memphis, Mary returned to dressmaking. Soon, she took up her late husband's work, devoting herself full-time to labor crusades, an activity from which she never retired. She was a leader in the strike of the United Mine Workers in the 1890s at the very beginning of that union's struggles. She went to jail with the miners, crossed militia lines, put her hand across the muzzles of the rifles of the guards, and challenged state governors to arrest her. When her 1903 plan for a strike in the Colorado mines was cancelled by UMW president John Mitchell, she quit the UMW and denounced Mitchell violently. From the beginning of her activity in the labor movement, she fought with union leaders. She was less cautious, less diplomatic, more aggressive, and more action-oriented than most of the men.

With daring behavior constantly attracting the media, Mary created a legend for herself as "Mother Jones." She was at the fore of every strike and spoke passionately at any rally, large or small, invited or uninvited. At the age of eighty-three in 1914, she was the most militant leader in Ludlow, Colorado, where the National Guard had brought death to striking miners' wives and children by burning down their tent colony. The miners armed themselves, battled the Guard, burned company property, and seized the mines. More than forty were killed before federal troops arrived and restored order. Adjutant General John Chase of the National Guard blamed Mother Jones for most of the violence and said that she had "to an exceptional

39. Women delegates to the 1886 Knights of Labor Convention. Elizabeth Rodgers is seated in the middle, holding the baby.

40. "Mother Jones" (Mary Harris Jones) on her 100th birthday.

degree the faculty of stirring up and inciting the most ignorant and criminally disposed to deeds of violence and crime." Undaunted, two years later, Mary was working with the International Ladies' Garment Workers Union in New York City.

When she was over ninety, Mother Jones was making speeches at union and political meetings, and letting her sharp criticism and her wrath fall on labor leaders she considered corrupt or with whom she disagreed, just as readily as she had let her denunciations fall on mine operators in the early days.

LEONORA O'REILLY (1870-1927)

Born in New York City of Irish immigrant parents, Leonora O'Reilly became one of the best-known women in labor and women's movements. Her father was Cork-born James O'Reilly, a printer, who died when Leonora was a year old. Her mother was Winifred (Rooney), who emigrated as a child, began work as a nursemaid at age seven, became a needleworker at age eleven, and worked under inhumane conditions for twenty years before marrying at age twenty-seven.

Winifred helped her husband in his grocery store and supplemented the family income by needlework at home. After he died and left her to support infant Leonora, she returned to a factory where she became ardently interested in bettering conditions. Her interest in unionization of workers and in effecting reforms was passed on to Leonora, who started work in a collar factory at age eleven.

At age sixteen, Leonora joined her mother in the Knights of Labor. Just as that organization was reaching its peak of influence, she organized the Working Women's Society.

In 1897, after the Knights had declined, she organized the women's local of the United Garment Workers Union. In 1903, she founded the Women's Trade Union League. From 1902 to 1909, she taught at the Manhattan Trade School for Girls. In 1909, she was a leader of the strike of 20,000 garment workers in New York City. An annuity granted that year by the WTUL made it possible for her to devote the rest of her life to League activities. From a home base in Brooklyn, New York, she travelled throughout the world. In 1915, she was a delegate to the International Congress of Women at The Hague. A suffragist and Socialist Party member, she generated much publicity, but she refused to have her name listed in any *Who's Who*.

MARY KENNEY O'SULLIVAN (1864-1943)

Born in Hannibal, Missouri, Mary was the daughter of Irish immigrants Michael Kenney, a railroad foreman, and Mary Kelly, a railroad cook. Michael was killed in an accident when daughter Mary was in the fourth grade. She left school to work in a bindery to support her sick mother. When she protested against conditions, especially against having to work sixty-five hours a week for only two dollars, she was fired, then blacklisted by other binderies. Not giving up, she moved to Chicago, where she formed and led the Women Book Binders Union. She joined the American Federation of Labor, which was stuggling for dominance over the Knights of Labor, but which previously had not encouraged women workers.

In 1892, Mary persuaded Samuel Gompers, head of the AFL, to appoint her as the first woman general organizer for the union. She worked throughout New York and New England for six months, after which the AFL commended her but said it could no longer afford a full time woman organizer. Mary returned to labor activities in Chicago. In 1893, she moved to Boston again, where she and John F. O'Sullivan worked together to establish more than forty female workers' unions in a single year.

In 1894, Mary married John, who was labor editor of the *Boston Globe*, a former seaman, a former street-car driver, and an activist in the AFL. Except at times when she was confined by her four pregnancies, she remained active as a labor organizer. Widowed while her children were young, she managed real estate to support her family. She also continued her fight for women's rights.

She served as deputy factory inspector in both Massachusetts and Illinois, administered a model tenement for working-class families in Boston, and managed a summer camp for working girls. She was one of the founders of the National Women's Trade Union League and the IWW (International Workers of the World, popularly known as the "Wobblies," one of the most militant trade unions in the history of American labor).

KATE KENNEDY (1827-1890)

Born in County Meath, Ireland, Kate Kennedy was the second oldest of seven children of gentleman farmer Thomas Kennedy and Eliza (King). Having herself received formal schooling, she taught her younger sisters at home when the family's fortunes declined during the devastating famine of 1845-48. In 1849, she emigrated to New York with her older brother and a younger sister. She worked as an embroiderer, went to night school to prepare for teaching, and put aside money for the family in Ireland.

The three Kennedy immigrants saved enough to bring over the rest of the family in 1851. Several years later, all moved to San Francisco, where Kate took a teaching job. Her sisters followed her example by working in trades while attending night school, and three of them became teachers. Kate was always a brilliant leader and activist and led one of the earliest unions of public school teachers.

In 1867, she was appointed principal of a grammar school. Considering it unjust that she be given half of what a man would be paid, she began to fight for equal pay for equal work. Her agitation went on for several years and was primarily responsible for the California legislation in 1874 that mandated "females employed as teachers in the public schools of the state receive the same compensation as is allowed male teachers for like service when holding the same grade certificate."

Kate's five years of experience in the textile industry in New York increased the sympathy she had always felt for downtrodden workers, a sympathy born from her familiarity with the plight of farm workers in Ireland.

In the 1880s, Kate joined the Knights of Labor, helped strikers, and participated in workers' rallies. She became a close friend of Henry George, a reformer who originated the Single Tax Movement. George believed that land is a free gift of nature, that all men should have an equal right to the land, and that it is wrong to allow a relatively small number of landlords to acquire great wealth by possessing land that increases in value. Kate joined George's Land Reform League, and became a regular speaker on workers' rights, unionization, land reform, and the single tax. Her activities did not endear her to the political parties in power, especially when her nomination for State Superintendent of Public Instruction in 1886 by the Labor Party prevented Labor endorsement of the regular Democratic candidate.

In March 1887, on grounds of her unseemly political activities, the Board of Education transferred her to the principalship of a smaller school at a lower salary. Kate refused to accept the demotion and fought for three years in the courts. In 1890, she was vindicated by a State Supreme Court decision that laid the legal foundation for teacher tenure in California. The court ruled that a teacher "cannot be placed in a lower grade or dismissed except for misconduct or incompetence." Unpopular though they might be, political activities could not be classed as misconduct. Kate, whose health had been deteriorating during the court cases, did not live long after her victory.

ELIZABETH FLYNN RODGERS (1847-1939)

Born in Ireland, Elizabeth was the daughter of Robert Flynn and Bridget Campbell. She emigrated as a child with her parents to London, Ontario. She married George Rodgers and moved with him to Chicago, where George, an iron molder, became active in the Knights of Labor.

Encouraged by her husband, Elizabeth combined labor activities with raising children. She was, reportedly, the first woman to join the Knights of Labor and became head of an all-women local organized in September 1881. Active in state and district trades' assemblies, she was the first female to be Master Workman (president) of District Assembly 24, which included almost all of the assemblies of the Knights in Chicago and its suburbs.

In 1886, she was one of the sixteen women delegates to the Knights of Labor Convention in Richmond, Virginia. She attended the convention with her husband, also a delegate, and her two-week old infant child. Nominated for a national office, she declined on the grounds that she had ten children to look after and had time-consuming local union responsibilities. After the Knights waned, she remained active in women's causes and was one of the founders of the Catholic Order of Foresters.

MARGARET HALEY (1861-1939)

Born in Joliet, Illinois, Margaret was the daughter of Michael Haley and Elizabeth (Tiernan). Her father's parents had emigrated from Ireland to Canada, then to the United States. A teacher in Chicago, Margaret became increasingly dissatisfied with working conditions and with the apparently humble acceptance by teachers of their lot. The Teachers' Club was formed in 1893, but that group seemed to her to be concerned mainly with "professionalism" and administration.

In 1897, Margaret and her friend Catherine Goggin, also Irish American, convinced three hundred teachers to form the Chicago Teachers Federation. Membership grew to 2,500 in a year, with Catherine as president and Margaret as vice-president. Their initial move was to demand higher wages by presenting a petition with the signatures of more than 3,500 teachers. The Board of Education agreed to make raises, paid one increase, then announced that it could afford no more because the city lacked the funds.

Pursuing their own investigation, Margaret and Catherine discovered that the city collected no taxes at all from several favored corporations. Claiming that this source could provide money needed for teachers, they submitted their findings to the Board of Education and the irate city fathers. They were ignored, and so they sued. In 1902, they succeeded in getting a writ of mandamus forcing the Board to assess five corporations at full value for the year 1900 and to pay the teachers the increases due since 1898.

Margaret, as a full-time paid business agent of the Chicago Teachers Federation, showed her colleagues that bargaining for more money and better working conditions was not undignified and unladylike.   Chicago teachers saw that they had common cause with all workers, whether glove workers or hod carriers.

AGNES NESTOR (1880/1883-1948)

Agnes Nestor was born in Grand Rapids, Michigan, daughter of Galway-born Thomas Nestor and Anna (McEwen).   Brought to Chicago by her parents, Agnes started work in a glove factory.   She kept a diary describing the miserable conditions under which she toiled for ten hours a day, six days a week.   Glove workers had to pay rent for their machines and buy their own needles.

In 1898, after more than a year's union organization, Agnes and her co-workers at the Eisendrath glove factory went out on strike. The women demanded a union shop, raises for lower paid workers, an end to machine rent, and free oil for their machines.   Agnes quickly became the recognized leader at the daily meetings.   In ten days the strike was won.

The all-male glove cutters union had supported the women, but the female kid glove makers, considered the factory aristocrats, had not.   Agnes admitted that they had ducked one of the kid glove girls in a trough, but she denied that she herself had pushed a policeman into the trough.   In her autobiography she said that the charge was ridiculous because she was barely fifteen years old at the time and "small for my age and frail looking."

Victory in the strike meant that Agnes became president of a newly-formed local, a glovemakers' union separate from the large cutters' union.   Because her organizing and negotiating skills became evident when she represented her local at national conventions, she was often called to other states to help bargain for women's unions. As a paid worker of the Women's Trade Union League, she became a full-time labor activist.

OTHERS

Those whose lives have been sketched are only a few of the many Irish women who were well known in their own times but are usually left uncounted today.   Certainly, one should also count such leaders as Kate Mullany, who organized the laundresses in Troy, New York, in the 1840s and who established a Cooperative Linen, Collar, and Cuff Factory with underwriting by department store millionaire Alexander T. Stewart.   One should also remember Mary O'Reilly, a Rhode Island mill hand, who was one of the sixteen women delegates at the 1886 convention of the Knights of Labor, was first deputy inspector of factories in Pennsylvania in the 1890s, and was labor secretary to Leonora Barry.

A few words should be said about the importance of that 1886 convention of a labor organization that gradually died away. Of 660 delegates, sixteen were women, the first women to participate in labor union business on an equal basis with men. Besides Mary O'Reilly, Leonora Barry, and Elizabeth Rodgers, who have already been mentioned, there were six women shoeworkers, four textile operators, one dressmaker, one ironer, and one salesclerk. The faces of eight of these women have been immortalized in a photo that appears in histories of labor, in histories of women in America, and on walls of union halls. Captured in the photo is Mrs. George Rodgers, holding her new baby.

MEF

Chapter 17

A MUSIC MAKER: BING CROSBY'S IRISH ROOTS

The genealogical record of Bing Crosby's maternal ancestors, the Harrigans, is of historical interest, tracing as it does a migration from County Cork to the Colony of New Brunswick, then to Wisconsin and Minnesota, and finally to the Pacific Northwest. This important route of Irish migration has been discussed in earlier chapters. The chapter that follows is a genealogical exercise.

Bing Crosby had at least a passing interest in his Irish roots. The late Father John Deasy, Parish Priest of Schull in West Cork, told the author that Bing had made some inquiries, but Bing, he said, did not have precise enough information for a successful search.

One problem, it turned out, was that Bing mistakenly thought his grandfather was born in Ireland, whereas he was actually born in the Colony of New Brunswick. This inaccuracy appears on the January 7, 1964, California death certificate of Bing's mother, Catherine Harrigan Crosby. Her father's name is given as Dennis Harrigan, birthplace Ireland. Another problem was that Bing's grandfather and great grandfather both bore the name Dennis Harrigan, usually spelled Horgan on the Irish records.

BING'S GREAT-GREAT GRANDFATHER

Bing Crosby's earliest known ancestor, the "first Harrigan" according to a family tradition, bore the name John. He was born in the mid-1700s but his name appears on no records that have as yet been discovered. The names of several of his children do, however, appear on the records. Two of his sons each named his own first son

290

John and his first daughter Ellen. One of the daughters named her second son John and her second daughter Ellen. The Irish tradition, especially observed by the oldest children, was to name the first four children after the grandparents, paternal first. It is likely then that Bing's earliest known ancestors were John and Ellen Horgan of County Cork who were married in the 1770s and whose five known children - Dennis, Ellen, Ann, Cornelius, John - were born between about 1778 and 1800.

Larry Crosby, Bing's oldest brother, was told that John used two surnames, O'Brien and Harrigan. This was not unusual, writes Irish folklorist Captain Kevin Danaher ("Our Family Names" chapter in *Irish Country People*). To distinguish between cousins bearing the same first and last names, country folk were often identified by the name of the landlord from whom they leased land, or by the name of the townland, or by their trade, or by their "sept" (clan). A natural child raised by a single mother might also be known by the name of both mother and father, if the father were known.

As mentioned earlier *(Chapters 3 and 4)*, the Horgan/Harrigan family were small farmers and carpenters who had weed-cutting rights to Harrigan's Rocks in Toormore Bay. According to a story received and passed along by Larry Crosby, John Harrigan was known as "Organ O'Brien" because he played the organ in the church at Skibbereen, a market town some fifteen miles east of the village of Schull. (Skibbereen did have a chapel, perhaps with an organ, as early as 1816. The foundation for the structure that became the pro-cathedral was laid in 1825 and the new church was dedicated by Bishop Collins in 1830.)

Perhaps the Harrigans were members of the larger O'Brien sept. Irish and New Brunswick records indicate that the Harrigans and their Fitzgerald cousins were neighbors and close friends, most likely kinsmen, of O'Brien families in both Ireland and New Brunswick *(see Chapters 3, 4, and 6)*. It is also possible that "Horgan" and "O'Brien" somehow became "Organ O'Brien" in the oral tradition as it was passed on. "Organ" is also a variant of Horgan, Irish *Ó hArgáin*.

There are records for several of the children of John. They include Ellen, Dennis, and Ann, whose birth years are given variously on United States and Canadian records, from 1778 to 1782; Cornelius, birth year unknown; and John, born about 1800. Ellen married Timothy Lucey; Dennis married Catherine Driscoll; Ann married William Fitzgerald; Cornelius married Elizabeth Sloan in New Brunswick; John married Ellen Murphy in New Brunswick.

GREAT GRANDPARENTS

Bing's great-grandparents were Dennis Harrigan (abt 1781-abt 1867) and Catherine Driscoll (abt 1782-abt 1864). They are probably buried in an unmarked grave by the church of St. Thomas the Apostle at Red Bank, Miramichi, New Brunswick. Dennis and Catherine married about 1808 and had ten children before emigrating in 1831. Their eleventh and last child, the only one born in the New World, was Dennis Jr., born in 1832.

The composition of the family, as put together from Irish and New World records, is as follows (the surname is spelled variously and creatively on early New Brunswick records, for example, *Horigan, Hourigan*):

1. Ellen (abt 1808-1897), married William Sauntry in 1828, Goleen Parish, County Cork.
2. Ann (1811-1857), married Patrick Keys.
3. John William (1813-alive 1871).
4. Catherine (1816-1893), married William Walsh.
5. Michael (abt 1820-1882), married Elizabeth Walsh.
6. Cornelius (abt 1823-alive 1903), unmarried.
7. William (abt 1825-abt 1875), married Jane Gallagher.
8. Jeremiah (abt 1827-1903), married Margaret Murray.
9. Mary (1829-).
10. Patrick (1830-abt 1924), married Catherine Hogan.
11. Dennis (1832-1915), married Catherine Ahearn.

The baptisms of Ann, John, and Catherine are recorded on the register of the Roman Catholic Parish of Schull:

September 16, 1811: Ann Horgan, daughter of Denis and Catherine (Driscoll). Sponsors: Thomas Lancer, Ellen O'Heas.

November 20, 1813: John Horgan, son of Denis and Catherine (Driscoll). Sponsors: Michael Driscoll, Ann Lancer.

May 6, 1816: Catherine Horgan, daughter of Denis and Catherine (Driscoll). Sponsors: James Lucey, Peg Goggin.

The baptisms of two more of their children are recorded on the register of neighboring Goleen Parish (Drinane and Derryleary townlands were on the border of Schull and Goleen parishes):

March 25, 1829: Mary Horgan, daughter of Denis and Catherine (Driscoll). Sponsors: Jerry Murray, Mary Harrington.

March 13, 1830: Patrick Horgan, son of Den[is] and Catherine (Driscoll). Sponsors: Dan Driscoll, Joan Lucey.

The marriage of the oldest daughter, Ellen, to William Sauntry, a poor cottier of Dromkeal townland near the village of Ballydehob, is recorded on the register of Goleen Parish:

February 1828 (exact date not shown on the register): William Sauntry and Ellen Horgan. Witnesses: Denis Sauntry and D. Horgan.

The baptisms of six of the eight children of the William Sauntry and Ellen Horgan marriage are recorded on the Schull register, including that of William Jr., baptized in 1845. (William, future lumber baron of Minnesota, has been mentioned in Chapters 4 and 6.)

NOTE: *Dennis Harrigan Sr.'s sister Ellen married Timothy Lucey before 1810 and the baptisms of two of her children appear on the earliest Schull parish register: Mary, baptized March 20, 1810, sponsors Michael O'Regan and Ellen O'Regan; and Ellen, baptized October 2, 1813, sponsors Cornelius Lucey and Ellen McCarthy. The baptism of her youngest child, John, is recorded on the Goleen parish register, June 2, 1833, sponsors Daniel Foley and Ellen Horgan. Ellen Harrigan Lucey died in Oshkosh, Wisconsin, in 1891, at the reported age of 112. (See photo, Chapter 4.)*

GRANDPARENTS

The baptism of Dennis Jr., the youngest child of Dennis Harrigan and Catherine Driscoll and the only one not born in Ireland, is recorded on the register of St. Patrick's Catholic Church in Nelson-Miramichi, New Brunswick, October 6, 1833, age given as thirteen months, sponsors Patrick Fitzgerald (a first cousin, son of Ann Harrigan Fitzgerald) and Joanne Burchell.

Dennis Harrigan Jr. married Catherine Ahearn (daughter of Irish-born John Ahearn and Ann Meighan, early Miramichi settlers) about 1866. His occupation at the time is given on New Brunswick directories as "brewer" at North Esk Boom. Shortly after the marriage, Dennis and Catherine moved to Stillwater, Minnesota, a sawmill town on the St. Croix River. There, from 1867 to 1880, Dennis pursued the trade of carpenter and building contractor. In 1881, his residence is shown on a St. Paul city directory. But during the years 1881 to 1884 he was living in Knife Falls (now Cloquet) where he was a church trustee and a partner in the construction of the first Catholic Church building. He also erected the first Methodist and Presbyterian churches in this town. He then contracted for some structures in St. Paul, where the family resided at 765 Hawthorne Street (in a house built by Dennis and still standing). Dennis and his oldest son William moved to Tacoma, Washington, in 1888, and the rest of the family followed in 1889. He pursued his career in that state as a building contractor and later as an inspector. He died in Tacoma on September 18, 1915, his obituary noting that he was an

1833

357

B, 186,

Catharine

Fitzgerald

On the sixth of October eighteen hundred *thirty fifth* I have baptised Catharine aged seventeen months of the lawful marriage of William Fitzgerald & Ann Horigan. The Sponsors being Michael Brian & Ann Horigan.

W. Dollard P.P.

B, 187,

Denis

Horigan.

On the sixth of October eighteen hundred thirty three I have baptised Denis aged thirteen months born of the lawful marriage of Denis Horigan and Catharine Driscal. The Sponsors being Patrick Fitzgerald & Joanna Russelle. —

W. Dollard P.P.

41. Baptismal records for Dennis Harrigan, Jr., and his first cousin, Catherine Fitzgerald, October 6, 1833, St. Patrick's Church, Nelson-Miramichi, New Brunswick.

42. Dennis Harrigan, Jr. (1832-1915) and Catherine Ahearn (1836-1918), grandparents of Bing Crosby.

43. Four children of Dennis Harrigan, Jr., and Catherine Ahearn: Ann, Catherine (mother of Bing Crosby), Frank, George. Stillwater, Minnesota, early 1880s.

44. Patrick Harrigan (1830-c1924), son of Dennis Harrigan and Catherine Driscoll, in a long lifetime covered the entire "Northern Migration Route" of the Irish lumbermen and farmers. He was baptized at Goleen, West Cork, on March 13, 1830; brought to Miramichi, New Brunswick, as an infant; there attended the classes of schoolmaster James Evers *(see Chapter 6)*; engaged in farming and logging; in 1858, married Catherine Helen Hogan; in November 1864, entered the United States at Portland, Maine; in 1867, at Oshkosh, Wisconsin, filed Declaration of Intent to become a citizen; farmed and logged with his sons, one of whom (Jack) had three large camps on Lake Manitowish in northern Wisconsin, and another of whom (Bill) went south to found the Scotch Lumber Company of Fulton, Alabama. Patrick was living with the family of his daughter, Alice Neff, at Coos Bay, Oregon, in 1915, and is reported to have died at age 94 in 1924. A grandson recalled that Patrick was "a tremendous reader [who] had a love of fine booze, imbibed freely [and] spouted poetry."

45. The Crosby family, 1963, Catherine Harrigan Crosby cutting the cake at Bing's house. Standing, left to right: June and Bob Crosby; Larry and Elaine Crosby; Mary Rose Crosby Pool; Everett Crosby; Ed Mullin (husband of Catherine); Harry L. "Bing" Crosby; Ted Crosby. Seated, left to right: Catherine Crosby Mullin; Kathryn Crosby, Bing's wife; Catherine Harrigan Crosby; Florence Crosby (Everett's wife).

JOHN ("ORGAN O'BRIEN") HARRIGAN
of Schull (and Skibbereen?), County Cork

- ELLEN 1778-1891
  m Timothy Lucey
  emig 1851 to Littleton,
  ME, d Oshkosh WI

- ANN c1780-1880
  m Wm. Fitzgerald
  emig 1830 to Miramichi,
  NB, d Oshkosh, WI

- DENNIS HARRIGAN 1780-1864
  m Cath. Driscoll
  emig 1831 to Miramichi,
  NB, d Miramichi, NB (11 ch,
  all but Dennis b Co Cork)

- CORNELIUS
  m Eliz. Sloan
  emig c1830 to NB
  d c1851 in NB

- JOHN 1800-
  emig 1830 to NB
  m Ellen Murphy in NB

Children of Dennis Harrigan:

- ELLEN 1809-97
  m Wm. Sauntry,
  Golen, Co Cork;
  emig to NB as
  widow in 1851

- ANN 1811-57
  m Patk. Keyes

- CATHERINE 1816-93
  m Wm. Walsh

- CORNELIUS 1823-f1895
  unmarried

- JEREMIAH 1823-1903
  m Margt. Murray

- DENNIS, JR. 1832-1915
  m Cath. Ahearn
  7 ch.

- JOHN 1813-f1871
  unmarried

- MICHAEL 1820-82
  m Eliz. Walsh

- WILLIAM 1825-77
  m Jane Gallagher

- MARY 1829-

- PATRICK 1830-c1924
  m Cath. Hogan

Next generation:

- WILLIAM 1867-1949
  m Annie T._

- AMBROSE/ALEXANDER 1869-f1915

- EDWARD 1870-1926
  m Dolly Levings

- CATHERINE 1873-1964
  m Harry Crosby
  7 ch

- ANNIE 1875-f1964
  m Ed Walsh

- FRANCIS ALBERT 1876-f1915

- GEORGE L. 1879-c1955
  m Hannah Anderson

THE CROSBYS

- LAWRENCE 1895-1975

- EVERETT 1896-1966

- EDWARD (TED) 1900-73

- HARRY LILLIS (Bing) 1903-77

- CATHERINE 1904-d? m Ed Mullin

- GEO. ROBERT (Bob) 1913- m June Kuhn

- MARY ROSE 1906- m Jim Pool

m/1 Wilma M. Wyatt (Dixie Lee)
ch: Gary, Dennis, Phil, LIndsay
m/2 Olive Grandstaff (Kathryn)
ch: Harry Lillis, Mary Francis, Nathaniel

46. BING'S FAMILY TREE

active member of the Knights of Columbus. His wife, Catherine, passed away in 1918. The children of Dennis Harrigan Jr. and Catherine Ahearn were all born in Minnesota. The baptisms of five of them (asterisked below) appear on the register of St. Michael's Catholic Church in Stillwater:

*1. William John Harrigan (1867-1949), married Anna T. ____.
 2. Alexander Ambrose (abt 1869-alive in 1915).
*3. Edward (1870-1926), married Dolly J. Levings.
*4. Catherine (1873-1964), married Harry Lowe Crosby.
 5. Anne (1875-alive 1964), married Ed. J. Walsh.
*6. Francis Albert (1876-alive in 1915), married ____.
*7. George Leo (1879-abt 1955), married Hannah E. Anderson.

PARENTS

Catherine Harrigan, Bing's mother, was born above the old creamery just north of the Lowell Inn in Stillwater, Minnesota, on February 7, 1873. She was baptized on February 11 at St. Michael's Church, the sponsors being Michael Kinsella and Catherine Mary Dunn. She died on January 7, 1964, at Santa Monica, California.

Catherine Harrigan married Harry Lowe Crosby, a bookkeeper, in 1894, in Tacoma, Washington. Harry, a Protestant with roots going back to a 17th century sea-faring family in New England, converted to Catholicism. The seven children of this marriage are as follows:

1. Laurence Earl, "Larry" (1895-1975), born January 3, 1895.
2. Everett Nathaniel (1896-1966), born April 5, 1896, baptized May 2, St. Leo's, Tacoma.
3. Henry Edward, "Ted" (1900-1973), born July 30, 1900, baptized August 12, St. Patrick's, Tacoma.
4. Harry Lillis, "Bing" (1903-1977), born May 3, 1903, baptized May 31, St. Patrick's, Tacoma. Sponsors: Francis Harrigan, Edith Carley.
5. Catherine Cordelia, born October 3, 1904, now deceased; married Ed Mullin.
6. Mary Rose (1906-), born May 3, 1906, married Jim Pool.
7. George Robert, "Bob" (1913-), born August 25, 1913, Spokane, Washington, baptized September 7, 1913, St. Aloysius, Spokane; married June Kuhn.

The family moved to Spokane in 1913. In 1988, only Bob and Mary Rose were still living.

BING

Bing married Wilma Winifred Wyatt (Dixie Lee) on September 29, 1930, at the Blessed Sacrament Church on Sunset Boulevard, Hollywood, California. The four children of this marriage are:

1.   Gary Evans Crosby, born 1933.
2.   Dennis Michael Crosby, born 1934.
3.   Phillip Lang Crosby, born 1938 (twin).
4.   Lindsay Crosby, born 1938 (twin).

Dixie died of cancer on November 1, 1952, on her forty-first birthday. Five years later, on October 24, 1957, Bing married Olive Grandstaff (Kathryn Grant) at St. Anne's Catholic Church, Las Vegas, Nevada. The three children of this marriage are:

1.   Harry Lillis Crosby Jr., born 1958.
2.   Mary Frances Crosby, born 1959.
3.   Nathaniel Patrick Crosby, born 1961.

It is hoped that these genealogies will clear up much of the misinformation on Bing's Irish roots, some of it distributed by close family members, that has appeared in newspapers, magazines, and biographies.

JAK

Chapter 18

TORCH-BEARERS:
RELIGIOUS LEADERS AND FOUNDERS

Among the Uncounted Irish of America are the extraordinary number of talented, intelligent, creative, and service-oriented men and women who entered the religious life. Their contribution to American society is inestimable, yet they have largely been ignored in the story of America that children receive in the history books used in our schools. Here is a very partial list of such men and women who toiled prior to the 20th century. For much of this data the author is indebted especially to John J. Delaney's DICTIONARY OF AMERICAN CATHOLIC BIOGRAPHY *(1984 ed., Doubleday & Co.). Unfortunately, biographical information on Canadian religious leaders is not so readily available; as a consequence, church builders such as bishops William Dollard and John Sweeny of New Brunswick, John Farrell of Hamilton, Joseph Lynch of Toronto, and Thomas Connolly of Halifax, have not been included.*

ALLEN, Patrick (1853-1926), born Lowell, Massachusetts; named fifth bishop of Mobile, Alabama, 1897; served twenty-nine years; paid particular attention to ministering to blacks in rural areas as Catholic population almost tripled.

BRADLEY, Denis (1846-1903), born Castle Island, County Kerry; first bishop of Diocese of Manchester, Vermont, 1884; built numerous churches and schools; fought Nativism.

BRENNAN, Thomas (1853-1916), born County Tipperary; first bishop of Dallas, Texas, in 1891; founded the *Texas Catholic*, first Catholic newspaper in Texas.

BUTLER, Mother Mary Joseph (1860-1940), educator; born Ballynunnery, County Kilkenny; entered Congregation of the Sacred Heart of Mary in France in 1876; opened Marymount College in New York; established clinics to train students to work among the poor; leader in educating women to participate in world affairs; planned and completed fourteen American schools, including six Marymounts (three

301

of them colleges), and twenty-three foreign institutions in Ireland, Rome, Paris, Canada, England, Spain, and South America.

CARROLL, John (1735-1815), son of Daniel Carroll, an Irish immigrant merchant, and Eleanor Darnall; born Marlboro, Maryland; studied for priesthood in Europe; ordained a Jesuit at Liege, Belgium, 1769; served Catholics in Maryland and Virginia (where Catholic churches were forbidden by law) from 1774; ardent supporter of American Revolution and lifelong friend of Benjamin Franklin, Thomas Jefferson, and George Washington; in 1789, appointed first Catholic bishop in the United States with See at Baltimore; named archbishop in 1809; patron of both religious and public education; planted strong roots for the Roman Catholic Church in America.

CLARKE, Mother Mary Frances (1803-87), foundress; born Dublin; with four companions formed a congregation to give religious education to children; in 1833 they began teaching in Philadelphia, founding the Sisters of Charity of the Blessed Virgin Mary with Mother Mary Frances as the superior; in 1843, founded Clarke College in Dubuque, Iowa; later founded schools all over the United States; by the end of the century more than a thousand members in the congregation.

CONATY, Thomas (1847-1915), born Kilmallough, County Cavan; leader in the temperance movement; appointed second rector of Catholic University in 1897; later appointed bishop of Monterey-Los Angeles, California, where he greatly increased the number of schools and charitable institutions in the diocese and was active in the movement to preserve old Catholic landmarks and missions.

CONNOLLY, John (c1750-1825), born County Meath; joined Dominicans; appointed second bishop of New York in 1814 with only four priests in the diocese; brought the Sisters of Charity into the diocese; laid the basic foundation for his successors in what became the largest diocese in the United States.

CURRAN, John (1859-1936), born Hawley, Pennsylvania; at age seven started working in the coal mines; studied for the priesthood and was ordained in Scranton in 1887; spent the rest of his life ministering to the coal miners as curate and pastor of churches in Carbondale and Wilkes-Barre; famed for his support of John Mitchell, president of the United Mine Workers, and of the miners in the bitter and bloody struggle for better working conditions; achieved national recognition for his role in the anthracite strike of 1902; thanked by President Theodore Roosevelt for his aid in settling the strike.

DEMPSEY, Mary Joseph (1856-1939), hospital administrator; born Salamanca, New York, of Irish immigrant parents; joined Third Order Regular of Congregation of Our Lady of Lourdes, in Minnesota, in 1878; appointed Superintendent of St. Mary's Hospital in Rochester, Minnesota, in 1892, and greatly expanded its facilities, helped by the Mayo Brothers, who later established the Mayo Clinic there; founded St. Mary's School of Nursing in 1906; helped organize the Catholic Hospital Association; known internationally in the medical field.

DRUMGOOLE, John Christopher (1816-88), born Granard, County Longford; arrived in New York in 1824 and supported widowed mother by working as a shoemaker; became world famous for his work with homeless children; built vocational schools and other buildings for the care for two thousand boys annually on Staten Island, New York; helped secure passage of a New York law mandating that homeless children be placed in a home or institution of their own religion.

DUNNE, Edward (1848-1910), born Gortnahoe, County Tipperary; brought to the United States as a child; named second bishop of Dallas, Texas, in 1893; there built a cathedral, an industrial school for blacks, and colleges and sanitariums.

DUNNE, Sarah (1846-1920), Mother Mary Amadeus; born Akron, Ohio; chosen superior of Ursulines in 1874; ministered to Indians in Montana; sent first missionary sisters to Alaska in 1905; joined them in 1910 and became known as "Theresa of the North" and "Great Chief White Woman" during thirty-nine year ministry to Eskimos, Indians, and Army personnel.

ENGLAND, John (1786-1842), born Glanworth Parish, County Cork; ordained in 1808; leader in fight that eventually led to Catholic Emancipation Act of 1829; appointed bishop of Charleston, South Carolina in 1820; in 1826, first Catholic priest to address Congress; encouraged classical learning, establishing a society for its study; founded the Sisters of Our Lady of Mercy in Charleston in 1827; brought the Ursulines into the diocese in 1833; opened a school for free blacks; rendered heroic service ministering to victims of cholera and smallpox epidemics.

FEEHAN, Patrick (1829-1902), born Killenaule, County Tipperary; entered United States in 1850; named bishop of Nashville, Tennessee, 1864; next fifteen years, built up war-ravaged diocese; during the cholera epidemics in Nashville in 1873, 1878, and 1879, won the esteem of his neighbors for his labors among the stricken; transferred to Chicago in 1880, where he increased number of Catholic schools from 88 to 166; noted for charitable works; leader in Catholic social movement.

FITZGERALD, Edward (1833-1907), born County Limerick; arrived United States in 1849; appointed second bishop of Little Rock, Arkansas in 1866; in 1894, dedicated the first Catholic church for blacks in Arkansas; increased number of churches in diocese from four to forty-one, priests from five to sixty, and Catholic congregation from 1,600 to 20,000; in 1869-70, attended Vatican Council I, where he was one of two bishops who voted against the doctrine of papal infallibility, though he accepted it when the doctrine was approved by the Council in 1870.

FITZGIBBON, Mary Irene (1823-96), born Catherine Fitzgibbon in Kensington, England; brought to America at age nine; joined Sisters of Charity at Mount St. Vincent, New York; became superior of Sisters of Charity in 1859; in 1869, opened the Foundling Home for abandoned children (later the New York Foundling Hospital); in 1873, opened the Foundling Hospital and cared for tens of thousands of children during her twenty-seven years as superior; founded St. Ann's Maternity Hospital for homeless and unwed mothers in 1880; founded Hospital of St. John for Children and Nazareth Hospital for convalescent children in 1881 and Seton Hospital for tubercular men (at Spuyten Duyvil, New York) in 1884.

FITZPATRICK, John Bernard (1812-66), born Boston, son of Irish immigrants; Boston's third bishop in 1846; vigorously fought Nativists of the time who destroyed Catholic churches in Bath and Manchester, New Hampshire; in 1854, worked to aid Irish immigrants; staunch supporter of colleges; in 1861 received honorary doctorate in divinity at Harvard, first Catholic to be so honored.

FOLEY, John Samuel (1833-1918), born Baltimore, Maryland, in 1888, appointed fourth bishop of Detroit; provided services for thousands of immigrants drawn to the automobile industry; opened many national churches (Italian, Slovak, Lithuanian, Hungarian, Romanian); increased the number of priests from 100 to 318 in 246 churches and missions.

GALBERRY, Thomas (1833-78), born Naas, County Kildare; brought to United States at age three; joined Augustinians in 1852; president of Villanova University in

1872-75; then served as fourth bishop of Hartford, Connecticut; founded diocesan newspaper *Connecticut Catholic,* renamed *Catholic Transcript.*

GALLAGHER, Hugh Patrick (1815-82), born County Donegal; emigrated 1832; ordained 1840; championed Irish immigrants working in the coal mines; worked as missionary in northern California; founded *Catholic Standard,* first Catholic weekly on the West Coast; travelled in Europe and brought back priests, seminarians, Sisters of Mercy and Presentation sisters; built the first Catholic church in Nevada at Genoa in 1861, and many other churches and schools; involved in civic affairs (his plan to improve Golden Gate Park in San Francisco was adopted in 1869); later, in Detroit, labored to assist immigrants; established colleges, hospitals, retreat houses.

GARRIGAN, Philip (1840-1919), born Whitegate, County Cavan; brought to United States in 1844; ordained 1870; appointed first vice-rector of Catholic University in 1888; helped found Trinity College in Washington, D.C.; in 1902, appointed first bishop of Diocese of Sioux Falls, Iowa, where he doubled the number of schools so that three of every four Catholic children were enrolled in them.

GIBBONS, James (1834-1921), cardinal, born Baltimore, Maryland, but raised in Ireland from age three to thirteen, son of Thomas and Bridget Gibbons; Union chaplain during Civil War; appointed bishop of Richmond in 1873; published enormously popular *The Faith of Our Fathers* (1876) and five other books; Archbishop of Baltimore 1877-1921; made cardinal in 1866; defender of Catholic education and organized labor; instrumental in preventing books of Henry George from being placed on the Index of Forbidden Books in 1887; personal friend and advisor to six American presidents; a champion of social justice and one of the most influential and admired churchmen in the country at the time of his death in Baltimore.

GILLESPIE, Mother Mary of St. Angela (1824-87), born Eliza Maria in Brownsville, Washington County, Pennsylvania; granddaughter of Ulster-born Neal Gillespie and Eleanor Dougherty; daughter of John Purcell Gillespie and Mary Madeleine Meirs; niece of Senator Thomas Ewing of Ohio; became a leading socialite in Washington, D.C.; in 1853, joined Holy Cross Sisters; directress of St. Mary's Academy, South Bend, Ind.; during Civil War organized nuns into a nursing corps and established eight military hospitals and two hospital ships; elected superior and foundress of United States branch of Holy Cross sisters; founded thirty-five schools and other institutions all over the country.

GILLESPIE, Neal Henry (1831-74), brother of Mother Mary Gillespie; educated at Notre Dame, receiving, in 1849, the first degree granted by that institution; joined the Congregation of Holy Cross and was ordained in Rome in 1856; served as vice-president and director of studies at Notre Dame for several years; in 1859, appointed president of St. Mary's of the Lake College in Chicago; later served as editor of *Ave Maria.*

HAYDEN, Mother Mary Bridget (1814-90), born Margaret Hayden in Kilkenny, Ireland; taken by parents to Missouri when she was six; joined Sisters of Loretto in 1841; took charge of new government school for Indians at Osage Mission (later St. Paul), Kansas; expanded the Indian school into St. Ann's Academy, which developed into an outstanding educational institution in the Southwest.

HEALY, James Augustine (1830-1900), son of an Irish immigrant plantation owner and a black slave, born Macon, Georgia; ordained priest in Paris in 1854; appointed chancellor of Boston diocese in 1855; founding pastor in 1866 of St. James Church; second bishop of Portland, Maine, 1875, where he significantly increased the number of parishes (to sixty), missions (to sixty-eight), schools (to eighteen), convents, hospitals, and orphanages in the diocese. His brother Patrick, a Jesuit, was president of Georgetown University (1873-1882).

HENNESSY, John (1825-1900), born Bulgaden, County Limerick; emigrated at age twenty-two; ordained in St. Louis 1850; appointed third bishop of Dubuque, Iowa, 1866; first archbishop in 1893; founded St. Joseph's College and Seminary in 1873; brought in numerous teaching sisters; founded the Sisters of the Holy Ghost in 1890; established 118 new parishes to care for the needs of the many immigrants to Iowa brought by the railroad construction.

HUGHES, John Joseph (1797-1864), born Annaloghan, County Tyrone; son of a farmer, with whom he came to the United States in 1817, settling at Chambersburg, Pennsylvania; in 1829, founded St. Joseph's Orphan Asylum, Philadelphia; in 1833, with Father Michael Hurley, founded *Catholic Herald*; in 1842, appointed bishop of New York; established an independent Catholic school system, to become the most outstanding one in the United States; fought the Nativists and Know-Nothings at the time of anti-Catholic riots in Philadelphia in 1844 by warning the mayor of New York on the planned rally of Nativists in that city that "if a single Catholic church is burned in New York, the city will turn into a Moscow" (alluding to the fires that greeted Napoleon in 1812); opened St. John's College and Seminary (Fordham); laid the cornerstone of St. Patrick's Cathedral, called "Hughes' Folly" because of its location so far out in the country (New York City had eleven Catholic churches in 1841, thirty-two at the time of Hughes' death); generally opposed western colonization schemes proposed by Thomas D'Arcy McGee and the western bishops.

IRELAND, John (1838-1918), born Burnchurch, County Kilkenny; arrived in United States with parents 1848; bishop of St. Paul, 1875; encouraged emigration to the West through his St. Paul Catholic Colonization Society; first archbishop of St. Paul in 1888; headed fight for a national Catholic University; came out strongly for racial equality in 1891 and supported public schools, though he believed Catholic schools were necessary because of Nativist bias in the public schools; in 1885, established St. Thomas Seminary (now College); wrote and published extensively on problems of the church in a democratic and pluralistic society.

IRELAND, Mother Seraphine (1842-1930), sister of Archbishop Ireland; born County Kilkenny; provincial superior of the St. Joseph province of the Sisters of St. Joseph; developed the College of St. Catherine in St. Paul, founded for women; before her retirement in 1921, increased the number of sisters in her province from 116 to 913, the number of schools from 8 to 60; established five hospitals and two orphanages.

KEANE, John (1839-1918), born Ballyshannon, County Donegal; emigrated with parents in 1846; first rector of Catholic University in 1888; archbishop of Dubuque, Iowa, in 1900; active in opening new schools and parishes, and in the temperance movement.

KENRICK, Francis Patrick (1797-1863), born Dublin; ordained in Rome in 1821; taught at seminary at Bardstown, Kentucky, for nine years; labored in the cholera epidemic of 1832 in Philadelphia; helped found the *Catholic Herald* in 1833; appointed bishop of Philadelphia in 1842; helped end the Nativist anti-Catholic riots in 1844 during which St. Michael and St. Augustine churches were burned; re-built churches; dramatically increased number of priests from 35 to 101; appointed archbishop of Baltimore in 1851; considered leading moral theologian of his times (published a four-volume study); wrote commentary on Job and provided a new revision of the Douai Bible in 1849-50.

KENRICK, Peter R. (1806-89), born Dublin, brother of Francis Kenrick, Archbishop of Baltimore; in 1832, ordained at Maynooth; in 1833, became president of St. Charles Borromeo Seminary in Philadelphia; editor of diocesan newspaper, the *Catholic Herald*; rector of cathedral and vicar-general of Philadelphia diocese; bishop of St. Louis in 1843, archbishop in 1847; opposed doctrine of papal infallibility when it was proposed at Vatican Council I in 1869, but submitted when it was promulgated; greatly increased the number of priests and religious, and of churches and other institutions in his huge diocese, which originally included Missouri, Arkansas, and half of Illinois.

LALOR, Theresa (c1769-1846), born Ballyragget, County Kilkenny; entered United States in 1794 and began a religious community in Philadelphia which administered a school for girls; in 1799, opened a school in Washington, D.C., which became Georgetown Academy; took vows in 1816; became first superior of the Order of the Visitation. She expanded the order to Mobile, Alabama; St. Louis, Missouri; Baltimore, Maryland; and Brooklyn, New York.

LARKIN, John (1801-58), born Newcastle-on-Tyne, England, of Irish parents; joined Jesuit order; founder and first president of St. Francix Xavier College in New York City; in 1851, became president of St. John's College (later Fordham University).

LOUGHLIN, John (1817-91), born Drumboneffe, County Down; brought to United States at age six; appointed first bishop of Brooklyn in 1853, serving twelve churches and 15,000 Catholics (by the time of his death there were 125 churches, 93 schools, two colleges, a seminary, numerous charitable institutions, and some 400,000 Catholics); invited Vincentian Fathers to found St. John's College in Brooklyn in 1870.

LYNCH, Patrick N. (1817-82), born Clones, County Monaghan; arrived in South Carolina as a child with his parents, in 1840; educated at St. John the Baptist Seminary in Charleston, and at Rome; in 1858, appointed Charleston's third bishop; in 1864, as representative of the Confederate States of America, presented the Confederacy's case to Pope Pius XI in Rome; helped heal the wounds between North and South during visits to Northern cities to raise funds to re-build the cathedral and other church structures destroyed by the Union army's heavy bombardment and by Sherman's occupation.

MANOGUE, Patrick (1831-95), born Desart, County Kilkenny; ordained in Paris in 1861; worked as missionary among Indians in California and Nevada; founding pastor of St. Mary's-in-the-Mountains Church, Virginia City, Nevada; first bishop of Sacramento in 1886; influential among miners and instrumental in settling disputes between them and mine owners.

McCAFFREY, John Henry (1806-91), born Emmitsburg, Maryland; ordained 1838 from St. Mary's Seminary there, later serving as president for thirty-seven years, building it into a leading seminary; in 1856, prepared a catechism, which became the basis of the famous *Baltimore Catechism*.

McCLOSKEY, John (1810-85), born Brooklyn, New York, of Irish-born parents; appointed first president of St. John's College (Fordham) in 1841; first bishop of Albany, where in seventeen years he established eighty-eight new churches and thirteen schools and built four new orphanages; appointed Archbishop of New York in 1864, Cardinal in 1875, first American of that rank; increased number of schools from fifty-three to ninety-seven; established new hospitals, homes and asylums; rebuilt St. Patrick's Cathedral when it was destroyed by fire in 1866.

McGROARTY, Sister Julia (1827-1901), Susan McGroarty, born Inver, County Donegal; brought to Cincinnati by parents in 1831; named superior of Sisters of Notre Dame de Namur east of Rocky Mountains in 1886, and in 1892 superior of California province; inaugurated new education methods and founded fifteen houses, including Trinity College for Women in Washington, D.C.

McGUIRE, Charles (1768-1833), born Dungannon, County Tyrone; ordained a priest in France; emigrated to United States in 1817; missionary in western Pennsylvania in 1817-20; in 1829, laid the cornerstone of St. Paul's Church in Pittsburgh.

McMULLEN, John (1832-83), born Ballynahinch, County Down; in 1881, first bishop of Davenport, Iowa; founded St. Ambrose College there in 1882.

McQUAID, Bernard John (1823-1909), born New York City, son of Irish immigrants; raised by Sisters of Charity at St. Patrick's Orphanage; first bishop of Rochester in 1868; built outstanding school system, establishing forty elementary schools and many charitable institutions.

MEHEGAN, Mother Mary Xavier (1825-1915), born Skibbereen, County Cork; with two other sisters, opened St. Vincent's Hospital in New York City; founded, with Sr. Mary Catherine Nevin, the New Jersey Sisters of Charity in 1859; worked in hospitals during the Civil War; in 1899, founded the College of St. Elizabeth at Convent Station, New Jersey, the state's first college for women.

MULLANY, Brother Azarias of the Cross (1847?-93), born Killenaule, County Tipperary, as Patrick Francis Mullany; emigrated 1857; joined Christian Brothers; professor of mathematics and literature, and president of Rock Hill College, Ellicott City, Maryland; wrote voluminously on education and literature.

MULLEN, Tobias (1818-1900), born County Tyrone; third bishop of Eric, Pennsylvania, in 1868; inaugurated widespread building program in the diocese.

MURPHY, Margaret Mary Healy (d. 1907), born County Kerry; orphaned as a child; lived in Virginia, Mexico, Texas; married attorney John Murphy in Texas; during Civil War, turned home into clinic and soup kitchen; at Corpus Christi, where her husband served as mayor, helped local inhabitants through yellow fever epidemics and a hurricane; opened "Mrs. Murphy's Hospital for the Poor"; after husband's death, organized Sisters of the Holy Ghost; as their mother superior, made three trips to Ireland, successfully recruiting postulants to staff schools and hospitals.

O'BRIEN, Matthew (1807-71), born Nenagh, County Tipperary; in 1826, settled in Kentucky, where, in 1826, he was ordained as a Dominican; elected provincial of St. Joseph province at Somerset, Ohio, in 1850; opened St. Joseph's College there; except for two years as pastor of St. Peter's Church in [city?] Ontario, Canada, he spent the last years of his life in missionary work.

O'CONNELL, Sister Anthony (1814-97), born County Limerick as Mary O'Connell; brought to United States as a child; joined Sisters of Charity in 1835; founded a home for invalids in Cincinnati; worked as a nurse in military hospitals during the Civil War earning the title "Florence Nightingale of America."

O'CONNOR, James (1823-90), born Queenstown (Cobh), County Cork; as bishop of Omaha, greatly expanded the diocese; built college in 1879, now Creighton University; translated the Mercy Rule into Latin for Mother Catherine McAuley, foundress of Sisters of Mercy in Ireland; guided Mother Katherine Drexel in founding the Sisters of the Blessed Sacrament for black and Indian missions exclusively. The SBS founded Xavier University in New Orleans in 1925, for Negroes.

O'CONNOR, Michael (1810-72), bishop and brother of Bishop James O'Connor of Omaha; born Queenstown (Cobh), County Cork; as bishop of Pittsburgh, actively fought for public funds for parochial schools; sponsored first group of Sisters of Mercy from Ireland to America; founded St. Michael's Seminary, two colleges and the diocesan newspaper, *The Pittsburgh Catholic;* resigned as bishop in 1860 to join the Jesuits, and then taught at Boston College; spent last years as a missionary to American blacks.

O'GORMAN, James (1804-74), born near Nenagh, County Tipperary; titular bishop of Raphanea in 1859, and vicar-apostolic of Nebraska, the Dakotas, Wyoming, and Montana; brought the Sisters of Mercy into the Nebraska Territory in 1864; increased the number of priests from three to nineteen, as the Catholic population swelled from 300 families to over 11,000 over the course of fifteen years.

O'GORMAN, Thomas (1843-21), born Boston; first rector of St. Paul Seminary and, in 1885, appointed president of St. Thomas College in St. Paul; later appointed second bishop of Sioux Falls, South Dakota, where he founded several hospitals and greatly expanded schools and missions as the population doubled before his death.

O'HANLON, John (1821-1905), born Stradbally, Queen's County; emigrated to Missouri with family in 1840; ordained priest for St. Louis Diocese in 1847; witnessed shiploads of Irish escaping from the Great Famine in Ireland and heading up the Mississippi River from New Orleans; consequently, established an immigrant aid station and published the popular *The Irish Emigrant Guide to the United States*, subject of a doctoral dissertation by Edward J. Maguire in 1951, published by Arno Press in 1969.

O'HARA, William (1816-99), born Dungiven, County Derry; first bishop of Scranton, Pennsylvania, in 1868; increased number of priests from 25 to 152, the churches from 50 to 121; built St. Patrick's Orphanage and the House of Good Shepherd; formed the independent Scranton Congregation of the Sisters Servants of the Immaculate Heart of Mary in 1871, and brought other religious orders to teach the school and staff the hospitals and orphanages in his diocese; founded St. Thomas College in Scranton in 1888.

O'REILLY, Bernard (1803-56), born Columkille, County Kilkenny; emigrated 1825; pastor of St. Patrick's Church in Rochester, New York, where from 1832 to 1837 he served laborers building the Erie Canal; in 1850, appointed bishop of Hartford, Connecticut; in 1851, at the height of the Know-Nothing movement, stood up to a mob about to destroy the convent of the Sisters of Mercy; established thirty-four new churches, fourteen new schools and three orphan asylums; died at sea when ship went down with all passengers and crew, returning from Ireland where he had been recruiting religious for his schools.

O'REILLY, Bernard (1820-1907), historian, born County Mayo; emigrated as a young man; joined Jesuits; taught at St. John's College (Fordham); served as chaplain of the Irish Brigade of the Army of the Potomac during Civil War; editorial staff of the *New American Encyclopedia*; wrote several books.

O'REILLY, Patrick Thomas (1833-92), born Kilnaleck, County Cavan; brought to United States by parents who settled in Boston; appointed first bishop of Springfield, Massachusetts, 1870; in twenty-two years, number of priests increased from 43 to 196, parishes from 43 to 96, schools from 2 to 10; expanded charitable facilities.

O'REILLY, Brother Potamian (1847-1917), educator and scientist, born Michael Francis in Baillieborough, County Cavan; emigrated as a child with his parents to New York City; in 1859, at age 12, entered the novitiate of the Christian Brothers in Montreal, Canada; earned his doctorate in science at University of London in 1883 (the first Catholic to do so); professor of physics and first dean of engineering at

Manhattan College; known as a historian of electrical science, published many books and articles; worked with Marconi to develop first apparatus for transmission and reception of wireless radio; spoke five languages.

POWER, Sister Emily (1844-1909), born Ellen Power, Barrettstown, Tramore, County Waterford; raised by parents at Fairplay, Wisconsin; joined Dominicans at Sinsinawa, Wisconsin; elected superior at age twenty-three; order expanded greatly under her charge for over fifty years, opening schools and colleges in the United States staffed today by over 1,200 sisters (at one time over 1,800); insisted on the highest standards for her teachers, encouraging them to get degrees at prestigious universities in the United States and Europe, and invited many intellectuals, including Orestes Brownson, to lecture at Sinsinawa.

PURCELL, John Baptist (1800-83), born Mallow, County Cork; emigrated to United States at age eighteen; appointed bishop of Cincinnati in 1833, archbishop in 1851; in 1853, quelled a Know-Nothing mob that intended to burn the cathedral during a visit by Archbishop Bedini, papal nuncio to Brazil.

QUARTER, William (1806-48), born Killurine, County Wexford; emigrated 1822; pastor of St. Mary's Church in Chicago in 1833; first bishop of Chicago, 1844; built thirty churches, many with his personal funds; active in aiding immigrants.

QUINLAN, John (1826-83), born Cloyne, County Cork; emigrated 1844; appointed second bishop of Mobile, Alabama, in 1859; repaired the damages suffered by the diocese during Civil War; brought in clergy from Ireland, increasing the number of priests from ten to forty-five and the churches and mission stations from eighteen to thirty-six, and rebuilt Spring Hill College in Mobile, which had been destroyed by fire in 1869.

RUSSELL, Mother Mary Baptist (1829-98), born Kate Russell in Killowen, near Newry, County Down; entered Sisters of Mercy at Kinsale in 1848; emigrated to California with eight nuns and novices in 1854; performed valuable work in San Francisco during the cholera epidemic in 1855; founded St. Mary's Hospital, first Catholic hospital on Pacific coast; opened a night school for adults, the House of Mercy for unemployed women in 1855, the Magdalen Asylum in 1861, and established schools for boys and girls and a home for the aged; adamantly spurned the suggestion of the archbishop that her sisters, to obtain public funds, take examinations from public school authorities and dress in lay apparel.

RYAN, Patrick John (1831-1911), born Cloneyharp, near Thurles, County Tipperary; founding pastor of Church of the Annunciation in St. Louis; in 1868, co-adjutor of St. Louis; in 1884, second archbishop of Philadelphia, where he tripled the number of schools and churches and was appointed to the United States Indian Commission by Theodore Roosevelt; famed for his oratory; opened the Republican Party convention in Philadelphia in 1890; lectured widely and helped reduce anti-Catholic feeling in the United States.

SAMMON, Mary Ann (1843-1901), foundress, Dominican Sisters of Blauvelt; born Nenagh, County Tipperary, daughter of Martin Sammon and Esther Kennedy; entered German order of Dominican nuns in 1869; pioneered child-caring institutions in New York City, working with German and Irish immigrants; in 1891, elected prioress of Blauvelt Dominicans at Blauvelt, New York; her sisters staffed scores of parochial schools, colleges, orphanages, hospitals, and asylums; order today is involved in migrant day care centers, schools for the handicapped, and a drug rehabilitation center.

SCANLON, Lawrence (1843-1915), born Ballytarsha, County Tipperary; emigrated to San Francisco in 1868; did missionary work in California and Nevada; in 1873, sent to Utah to administer the diocese; in 1891, appointed first bishop of Salt Lake City; built thirty churches, hospitals, and orphanages, and established All Hallows College; in 1909, dedicated St. Mary Magdalene Cathedral.

SHANAHAN, Jeremiah (1834-86), and his brother John Shanahan (1846-1916) of Silver Lake, Pennsylvania, both bishops. Jeremiah was first bishop of the Diocese of Harrisburg, John its third bishop and one of the founders of the Sisters of St. Casimir, devoted to teaching refugee Lithuanian children.

SHEERIN, James B. (1819-81), chaplain, born Temple Mehill, County Longford; emigrated to Canada in 1831, to the United States in 1833; joined Redemptorists in 1855; sent to New Orleans; became chaplain in Confederate Army, assigned to Army of Northern Virginia; captured by Union forces in Shenandoah Valley in 1864; imprisoned for three months, returned to New Orleans where he ministered to victims of the yellow plague in 1867; while in the Army, kept a diary, a valuable source of information on the Confederate Army and its leaders.

SHIELDS, Thomas (1861-1921), editor and priest; author of autobiography, *The Making and Unmaking of a Dullard*; born in Mendota, Minnesota, the son of Irish immigrants; teased because of his apparent mental retardation; as a farmhand, removed tree stumps, spurring him to invent a grubbing machine; taught himself to read and through self-study gained admission to St. Francis College in Milwaukee and, later, to St. Thomas Seminary; after ordination by Archbishop Ireland, did graduate work and obtained doctorate in biology from Johns Hopkins University; taught psychology at Catholic University in Washington, D.C.; established the first Correspondence School for Catholic Education, and the *Catholic Educational Review*; in 1911, established the Sisters College at Catholic University; as a Dean, organized and staffed the college, and established the Catholic Educational Press to publish textbooks for Catholic schools.

TIERNEY, Michael (1839-1908), born Cahir, County Tipperary; sixth bishop of Hartford, Connecticut, in 1897; built hospitals and charitable institutions; established sixty-nine new parishes and thirty-two new schools.

WARDE, Mary Frances Xavier (1810-84), foundress, born Mountrath, Queen's County (now County Laois); orphaned, raised by an aunt, taught at school for orphans herself; in 1843, emigrated to the United States and with six other Sisters of Mercy opened a hospital and school in Pittsburgh; in 1851, with the aid of Bishop Bernard O'Reilly, warded off an attack in Providence, Rhode Island, by a gang of Nativists about to burn down the convent; later opened foundations, schools, employment agencies for women, and orphanages in the East, Midwest, and West.

WHELAN, Charles (1741-1806), missionary, born Ballycommon, King's County (now County Offaly); joined Capuchins in France in 1770; chaplain in French fleet sent to aid the Americans, but when Admiral de Grasses was defeated by Admiral Rodney in West Indies, was captured and imprisoned for thirteen months in Jamaica, where he ministered to French prisoners; in 1784, went to New York City and helped in the building of that city's first Catholic Church; in 1786, left for Kentucky as a missionary, later ministering to the Catholics in Delaware and Maryland.

WILLIAMS, John (1822-1907), born Boston of Irish immigrant parents; appointed bishop of Boston, 1866, first archbishop, 1875; established St. John's Seminary, 1884; built many schools, churches, and charitable institutions; founded the first conference of the St. Vincent de Paul Society in New England; one of the founders of the North American College in Rome.

This is only a partial list of those who toiled before the present century. It does not include the giants among the church and community builders of this century, such as Cardinal Glennon of St. Louis, Archbishop Harty of Omaha, Cardinal Hayes of New York, Cardinal O'Connell of Boston, and Bishop McDonnell of Brooklyn. Nor does it include a particular Dominican sister who labored for over sixty years as a domestic. We think it fitting she be added to the list with data provided by Dominican archivist Sister Marie Laurence of Sinsinawa, Wisconsin, and from authors' files:

BERNARD, Sister Mary (1849-1932), domestic worker, born Mary Cassin (aka Cashin), near Coolrain, Queen's County, now Laois; daughter of John Cassin and Catherine Brennan who emigrated to Wisconsin when she was a child, leaving her at Derrynaseera, Coolrain, with a Protestant aunt who taught her the Catholic prayers; in 1858, with sister Johanna, joined parents and a married sister, Sarah Smith, in Bovina, Outagamie County, Wisconsin; entered the Dominican order in 1870; served in domestic duties in the order's convents in Illinois, Minnesota, and Wisconsin until 1926; visited by her nephew, Major Charles Martin Fitzgerald, about 1931 shortly before her death, took him by the hand playfully, introduced him to the other aging sisters in the retirement home at Sinsinawa, Wisconsin, and told them little tales about what a mischievous little boy her nephew had been on the farm near Oshkosh sixty years before; her obituary reads, "Sister was a very dear and holy person and she edified and cheered the Sisters by her deep simple piety and her genial disposition."

The bones of this simple, serving woman rest with those of several thousand others in the Sinsinawa Dominican cemetery. Sister Bernard, we think, is representative of the legions of women and men who chose the religious life, making together an enormous contribution to our society, and dying in obscurity, as they wished it. Mary Cassin of Coolrain lived a fruitful life and even a joyful one.

JAK

———

For two additional entries see Notes 1 and 2, Mary A. Cusack ("Nun of Kenmare") and Father John McMahon (Fenian priest), in the "Notes and Selected References" for Chapter 18 (pp. 351-52).

Chapter 19

BIAS: AMERICAN HISTORIANS

The author of this chapter perused four American History textbooks found on the shelves of his community college bookstore. What he wanted to know was whether the textbooks mentioned the enormous contributions of churches and their clergy to building American society. Given the subject of this volume, he was especially interested in items under "Irish" and "Catholic." This chapter summarizes what he found and also contains critiques of two major and perhaps seriously flawed historical studies of the type textbook writers depend on for their information: Merle Curti's THE MAKING OF AN AMERICAN COMMUNITY: A CASE STUDY OF DEMOCRACY IN A FRONTIER COMMUNITY, *and Kerby Miller's* EMIGRANTS AND EXILES: IRELAND AND THE IRISH EXODUS TO NORTH AMERICA.

THE FLAWED TEXTBOOKS

1. John A. Garraty and Robert A. McCaughey, *The American Nation: A History of the United States to 1877,* volume 1, sixth edition, Harper & Row, 1982. Under "Catholic," there is not a single citation. Under "Ireland-immigrants," there are three citations. On p. 69, there is passing mention of the "hordes of Scotch-Irish" in Pennsylvania, who were "mostly Presbyterian." On p. 381 is a reference to the Irish in general who "disliked the blacks," with a confirming quote thrown in for good measure from Irish liberator Daniel O'Connell, testifying that the American Irish were among the "worst enemies of the colored race." This was balanced somewhat by a lament of a contemporary Negro:

Every hour sees us [the Negroes] elbowed out of some employment to make room for some newly-arrived emigrant from the Emerald Isle, whose hunger and color entitle him to special favor.

312

On pp. 295-96 is some really serious misinformation:

> Most of the Irish [after 1815] lacked the means to go west. Aside from the cost of transportation, starting a farm required far more capital than they could raise. Like it or not, they had to settle in the eastern cities and accept any work they could get.

It is distressing that historians not on close terms with primary sources of information are still parroting this nonsense. As mentioned in the authors' preface, the truth is that even as late as 1870, more than a decade after the peak years of Irish immigration, the majority of the Irish were settled outside of substantial urban areas, even if only the Irish-born are counted.

2. David Burner and others, *An American Portrait: A History of the United States,* second edition, volume 1, Charles Scribner's, 1985. Two items under "Catholics" and "Catholicism" are indexed. On p. 294 is mention of anti-Catholicism in the 1830s and 1840s, and on pp. 336-37 a bit more of the same in connection with the Nativist "Know-Nothing" movement. Nothing at all is indexed under "Irish," but there are two full facing pages of pseudo-debate between two of the four authors on "Women and the [American] Revolution," doubtless inserted to appease feminist groups insisting rightfully that women be treated fairly and adequately.

3. Richard Current and others, *American History: A Survey (Since 1865)* seventh edition, volume II, Alfred Knopf, 1987. Several items are indexed under "Irish." On p. 68 is a passing mention of animosity toward the Irish because of *their* historic animosity toward the British. On p. 664 is another passing mention of the Irish, this time as a "disgruntled minority" to whom President Wilson had to answer because of his failure to insert an "independent Ireland" provision in the treaty ending World War I. On p. 526 is an immigration statistic indicating that 30 percent of all immigrants came from Great Britain and Ireland in the last half of the 19th century. On p. 552 is mention of the "Rum, Romanism, and Rebellion" slogan of the 1884 Blaine campaign. On p. 601 is passing mention of the "Social Gospel" of Protestants and Catholics, with a short direct quote by Father John A. Ryan on the rights of labor, spurred by Pope Leo XIII's encyclical of 1893. On p. 693 is a note on Ku Klux Klan terrorization of Catholics and Jews; and on p. 862 is a passing mention of Catholic President Kennedy's opposition to parochial school aid.

4. Robert A. Divine and others, *America Past and Present (Brief Edition),* Scott, Foresman, 1984. Two indexed references to "Ireland," five to "Catholic." On pp. 14-15 is a rather interesting item about Ireland as England's "first colony," with a mention of the brutal treatment of the Irish in the 16th century, including a quote from   Sir

Humphrey Gilbert of Munster [half-brother to Walter Raleigh], who in 1569 during a native rising reported that he had executed "every mane, woman, and childe" that he "could catch." In the same context is an observation that the English transferred their arrogance to the New World in attitudes toward native Americans and toward Irish immigrants. Not bad, but on p. 219 is some predictable mis-information on Irish immigration, 1820-40 period: "Immobilized by poverty and lack of skills required for pioneering in the West, most of [the Irish] remained in the Northeast." On p. 308 is a short paragraph on "religious values" being strong during the 1877-90 period, exemplified by evangelist Dwight Moody and revival meetings, 80 percent of church members being Protestant.

On pp. 313-14 is a passing mention of anti-Catholicism in cities. On p. 364 is a favorable mention of Margaret Sanger, high priestess of planned parenthood and population control. On a facing page, unrelated to the Sanger citation, is a mention of the hordes of Irish and Italian immigrants entering the country. There is no mention that these creatures, together with blacks, were precisely the unfavorably evolved evolutionary specimens whose numbers Margaret Sanger desired to limit. The readers of this text will not learn that Sanger was a spirited racist, advocating the selective breeding of "superior" Aryan types.

On p. 282 are two rather innocuous and vague paragraphs on Spanish "cultural influences" in California.

Using the indexes, nowhere in these texts does the reader find mention of the legions of intelligent, assertive, creative, serving women who chose the religious life; became leaders of their orders; built and/or staffed thousands of schools and colleges, orphanages, and hospitals, healing the sick and teaching millions of the children of immigrants to read and write. Nor does the reader find any references to the legion of giants among the men, the great bishops who built and administered an institution that gave a sense of community and worth to millions of immigrants from Ireland and Italy and eastern Europe who were among the most destitute people on this earth.

These texts tend to confirm the notion that our school history books are still largely WASP and/or "secular" biased, despite some cosmetic festoonings to suggest otherwise, such as a photo or other insert here and there of an Indian chief, a black, or a Margaret Sanger.

SQUEAMISHNESS

The silence in these textbooks about the profound influence of what some academics like to call, pejoratively, "organized" or "institutionalized" religion reflects a major distortion of American history. One reason for the distortion is the squeamishness of textbook writers, publishers, and adopting agencies (school boards) in our pluralistic society. They are already under heavy pressure, and rightfully so, from minorities and women's groups who want their stories told. This pressure, however, can lead to incoherence and even deceit, as in the case of the Sanger citation.

Another reason is the generally "secular humanist" stance of the writers themselves. Academicians are not famous for valuing "organized religion." They may even seem unaware of the larger world beyond the campus cloister. The yellow pages of this author's phone directory (Central Contra Costa County, east of Oakland, and largely suburban) list over four hundred Christian congregations and five synagogues. However, a visiting scholar from, say, the planet Mars would be dismally unaware of the importance of religion to Contra Costans and other average earthlings, if his knowledge came exclusively from the history texts used at the local community college. The man from Mars would remain ignorant of the Hebraic-Christian tradition as a conscience-shaping force.

Nor would he learn much about the crucial and even heroic role of women in passing along this tradition in families. But he would learn much about men in business, politics, and war. That is "history." The contribution of religion, the churches, and women is subtler and harder to write about, even if the historian has the inclination.

MISLEADING STATISTICS

The relative silence in these texts on the presence of the Irish in America, except as poverty pockets in the big cities and as victims of the Know Nothings, is in part explained by some of the reasons cited. But the main reason, as discussed in Chapter 1, that even Catholic Irish historians distort the picture, is the heavy and often sole reliance on the United States censuses of 1850 to 1900 for data on the total number of Irish in America and for their geographical distribution, despite the fact that, until 1880, country of birth of *parents* was not reported on the census. Historians have thus used figures for only the Irish-*born* (*see note on Sister McDonald's study of the Irish in Wisconsin in Chapter 9*), ignoring the far greater number whose families had first settled in Maine and other states and in Canada, raising families there before moving westward.

The historians keep repeating each other, and the distortions find their way into the schools in broad, comprehensive texts prepared by academics who understandably must rely heavily and even exclusively on the prior work of ostensibly reliable specialists working with primary source materials.

MERLE CURTI

One such specialized study, of Trempeauleau County, Wisconsin, was published in 1959 by Merle Curti, then distinguished Frederick Jackson Turner Professor of History at the University of Wisconsin. Entitled *The Making of an American Community: A Case Study of Democracy in a Frontier County*, it has become a classic in its genre, frequently quoted by other historians and textbook writers.

For comparing the performance of various ethnic groups (Scots, English, Norwegians, Irish, Poles, Swiss, Germans, etc.), Curti used for his data base the United States censuses of 1850, 1860, 1870, and 1880, the first three of which did not record the country of birth of the parents. He totally ignored surname and genealogical data.

Stereotypes. Early in his book, Curti reported the opinions of local native Americans in Trempeauleau County with regard to each other and the foreign-born. Curti culled these opinions from old newspapers and from longtime residents. They reflect the worst of the anti-Irish and anti-Catholic prejudices of the Know-Nothing era, but nowhere in his big book did Curti clearly say so. In Trempeauleau, "the reputation of the Scottish [Protestant] settlers for hard work, frugality, and conscientiousness was quickly established." In sharp contrast were the Irish:

. . .accounts of the time would have us believe that the Irish fell into two distinct groups. One was made up of men and women of no book learning, of extremely limited means, and of no great drive or ambition. Such were the firstcomers who took small farms in Trempeauleau in the 1850s. . .The separateness of this group was emphasized by reports of much fighting and contention among them and by the relatively low status of those who came in the early 1870s to work on the railroad construction. [*Curti goes on to describe the "other group," Irishmen of whom Trempeauleau highly approved, including men of some education and culture such as a Protestant druggist, two Protestant farmers (brothers), and a few Catholics.*]

Continuing in this vein, Curti noted that the "Germans, as distinct from the Poles, were respected as industrious and reliable. They were no problem." The Protestant Norwegians got grades almost as high: "The Norwegian communities were not free from quarrels among themselves; but by and large this group established its reputation fairly early as a hard-working, frugal, and law-abiding people." (*Curti's language slips toward acceptance of the stereotypical portraits he is collecting.*)

One must wade very deep into this long and technical book, taking time to decode some puzzling graphs and tables, to find evidence negating the stereotypes. Curti did indeed find the evidence, to his quite obvious surprise. On ownership of property, for example, Curti was surprised to learn the following:

...the record of the Irish farmers on farm values and property values was...good. In view of the general character of the Irish immigration to this country and the low values of property reported by many Irish, especially in 1860, it could not have been predicted *[by Curti, presumably]* that in 1880 the new Irish farmers would almost equal the American-born and the other British-born in median farm value.

Bear in mind that Curti did not consider that many of those American, Canadian, and British born were ethnic Irish in every way. But even despite this omission, Curti "found surprisingly good records among nativity groups traditionally supposed to be low in the socio-economic scale, such as the Irish and the Polish immigrants." Curti would surely have been even more than just surprised if he had inserted surname and genealogical data into his data base, accepting as Irish such household heads as Michael O'Hara and Thomas Whaling of New York, Edward Carney of Canada, Garret Murphy of England, and Thomas Starkey of Massachusetts, to name just a few with fairly obvious Irish roots, easily spotted on a few pages of the 1860 Trempeauleau County census. He might then have concluded that the Irish were the most successful of any ethnic group among the farmers of Trempcauleau County, exceeding the performance of even the English, the Scots, the Norwegians, and other "hardy" Protestants.

Curti was also surprised by evidence of the very high Irish school attendance, but he then proceeds to give the English the credit for it. After noting that the "English-speaking foreign groups" showed the highest school attendance percentages of all, he adds:

...Even the Irish [!] attendance, which we might expect to be low considering the poverty of the country, is on the whole slightly higher than that of native-born Americans, even in the two groups with least property.

He notes further that "of all the groups [including native-born Americans] only the Irish sent [to school] more girls than boys." This emphasis on schooling is, however, no credit at all to *Irish* culture: "The suggestion is strong that we have here a genuine cultural difference, that the tradition of sending children to school was more firmly established and respected among the English-speaking peoples than the others," that is, Belgians, Swedes, Germans, etc.

Curti credited, therefore, the use of the English language for the fact that a people of a culture repressed for centuries, denied formal education by their rulers, their native language largely destroyed, only their religion and allegiance to the Catholic Church remaining intact, could lead all other ethnic groups in Trempeauleau County in sending their children to school. Curti might have found a better answer in the words of historian William Lecky of Trinity College, Dublin:

The passion for knowledge among the Irish poor was extremely strong, and the zeal with which they maintained their hedge schools under pressure of abject poverty, and in the face of prohibitions of the penal code, is one of the most honourable features in their history.

KERBY MILLER

A more recent study, by Kerby A. Miller of the University of Missouri (*Emigrants and Exiles: Ireland and the Irish Exodus to North America*, published in 1985), for which Professor Miller won the Merle Curti Award of the Organization of American Historians for the "most significant contribution in the field of American social history," has also served to reinforce several myths about the Irish in America. He presents the Irish Catholics as possessing a crippling and distinctive world view, a consequence of their forced exile, which left them ill-equipped for life in the New World. They could not adjust to the commercial and industrial revolution. They were overcome with homesickness and self-pity. They fled for security to their pub, their Irish politicans, their priests. A distinctly neurotic lot, indeed.

Miller drew his conclusions from several thousand personal letters of Irish immigrants. His bibliography is awesome, page after page of references to collections of correspondence. One of the problems with his format, however, is the lack of specificity in the text itself and often in the "Bibliography of Manuscript Sources," as to when these letters were written. It is almost never clear as to just how many letters are contained in any item included on the long lists of individual collections, usually identified by family. Two or three letters? One hundred? The bibliography lists the whereabouts of the collections, but one has to guess as to the years and even the century when the letters were written.

Another problem is that the surnames identifying the collections suggest strongly that the greatest bulk of the letters available to Miller were written by Protestants. That should not be surprising, since the bibliography suggests that by far the most fruitful archives for Professor Miller were the Public Records Office for Northern Ireland in Belfast.

Twelve letters are cited to buttress the opinion (p. 252) that Catholics were more fearful than Protestants on the Atlantic voyage. One Protestant voyager wrote scornfully of the "talismans," among other things, that the Catholic Irish carried to protect themselves from shipwreck or disease. More of the same opinion is found on p. 258, thirteen letter writers cited, again bearing names that suggest a Protestant and understandably biased point of view. This is the kind of evidence Miller uses abundantly to prove that Catholic Irish were less self-reliant than Protestant Irish.

Although, as mentioned, it is usually not possible to check Miller's sources of information, certain items that he does *not* include in the body of his work suggest an unbalanced selectivity in the handling of sources. On p. 664, Miller lists as a bibliographical item the "Tyrrell Family Letters," correctly crediting J.A. King as his resource. The collection consists of about a dozen letters, dated 1888 to 1916, to cousins in rural Minnesota from Philadelphians who arrived from County Wexford between 1888 and 1900, as well as some letters from Ireland to Minnesota. Professor Miller was provided with copies of these letters. Those from Ireland tend to be rather downbeat, mostly laments about deaths of the old people and the emigration of the younger ones. The letters from Philadelphia tend to be upbeat. Here is an example:

March 3, 1916. Dear Cousin in Minnesota: I was thinking about all of you out West...It is hard to think of how we are all divided all over the world. Dear cousin, I have raised a big family in this big city. I had twelve, 6 boys, 6 girls. I buried four and have eight living. Five are working and three are going to St. Francis Xavier School. I am buying my home and getting along well. The children are very good to be raised in a big city. I don't think there is any city in the union better than ours. We have churches all over the city and there is no excuse for anyone going bad. Dear cousin, I will expect a long letter from you as I am anxious to know how all the Tyrrells in the West are...I will send you a picture of my youngest daughter, her name is Katie. We call her Kitty. She is just seven years old and as smart as a steel trap. She is in 2nd grade in school [Kitty became Sister Marie Pierre, I.H.M.]. I am your loving cousin./John Tyrrell.

If he could speak today, John Tyrrell, who emigrated to Philadelphia in May of 1888, might be puzzled by the picture of the maladjusted and melancholy Irishman in Exile constructed by Professor Miller. Tyrrell's sentiments clearly do not fit the thesis, and they did not find their way into Miller's text, becoming only an inscrutable, undated citation in the bibliography.

Further evidence that Miller may have been too selective in his choice of letters is in the British *Parliamentary Papers: Third Report from the Select Committee on Colonization* (1848), Appendix X, pp. 122-32. These papers include a few score of 1840s-vintage letters from Irish emigrants to the folks back home in Ireland. Patrick Blessing, for his doctoral dissertation at the University of California at Los Angeles, examined these and many other letters. He concluded that they "were rarely critical of life in the New World." In fact, the avalanche of encouraging letters from the New World to the Old was a major spur to emigration.

One cannot ignore, of course, that the massive evictions of the late 1840s and 1850s were a major cause of the great emigration which, together with famine and fever, reduced the population of Ireland by more than half in less than a generation. Landowners and large leaseholders were clearing the tillage lands for the more profitable grazing. The small tenants had to go. They chose America, and a number of studies have shown their passage was almost always paid with remittances from earlier emigrating relatives in America. It is hard to believe that these remittances and the letters accompanying them came from the alienated, dependent, neurotic, maladjusted, self-pitying, pauperized creatures of Miller's sampling.

Miller believes that Catholic emigrants impeded their own chances of success by their willingness to assist kinsmen who needed passage money. The Catholics, he observes, "retained attitudes toward family and community at marked variance from those displayed by their more individualistic Protestant countrymen." Other scholars, such as Patrick Blessing, have noted the same distinction between the kin-group oriented Irishman and the more "private" Englishman. This difference, however, can just as well be used as evidence to explain the relative success of the Irish in the New World. The strong bonding in large extended families was evidence of a healthy, adaptive, supportive culture. This bonding, it can be argued, was a bulwark against racial and religious discrimination in a land where signs read, "No Irish Need Apply."

The book is full of contradictions. On p. 262: "Many pre-Famine emigrants, especially Catholics, were among the first of their families or neighbors to venture overseas." Is this compatible with Miller's basic conclusion that the Catholics were more "dependent" than the "self-reliant" Protestants? No problem. Miller quotes a Connecticut woolen manufacturer, John Ryan of Kilkenny: "Look to the Yankee as a model for self-improvement and economic progress." Miller concludes that "the incessant, embarrassed repetition of such advice alone indicated that a large number of Catholic emigrants were less prepared than their Protestant countrymen to pass successfully what one Irish-American called their 'second apprenticeship' in a strange land" (p. 269).

Also contributing to Catholic "separateness," says Miller, was the Catholic Church's denunciation of mixed marriages and "godless" public schools (p. 274). This conclusion is also troubling. The opposition to mixed marriages was certainly not distinctly Catholic baggage from Ireland. The penal codes, one of which authorized the death sentence for any clergyman officating at the marriage of a Protestant and a Catholic, were not Catholic law. Further, the creation of Catholic schools in America was not primarily motivated by Catholic exclusiveness or by the godlessness of the public schools, but rather by the fact that Protestant religious indoctrination was the order of the day in most of the "public" schools of America. It was a "Protestant country." The Catholics could not accept the Protestant instruction which was given in the public schools well into the 19th, and even the 20th, century.

Professor Miller knows all this, and indeed he makes a magnificent effort in his book to be fair-minded. Scores and scores of paragraphs contain openers of the "however" and "on the other hand" genre. After evidence is presented of Catholic "dependency," he presents evidence of Catholic "self-reliance." Miller's reader might, therefore, draw the conclusion that the Catholic immigrants can be found on a broad psychological spectrum of dependence-independence, maladjustment-adjustment, ebullience-despair, and so forth, much as Irish, English, and Scots Protestants can be found on a broad spectrum. But pages later Miller seems to ignore, I think, his own considerable *however's* and *on the other hand's* as he relentlessly returns to the interesting and provocative motifs of dependency, alienation, and self-pity. Winning out in Miller's work is a purely intellectual construct: a supposedly more or less typical Irish Catholic immigrant manufactured by a brilliant scholar rationalizing a favored thesis.

Miller's thesis runs counter to studies by scholars such as R.A. Burchell of the University of Manchester. In *The San Francisco Irish 1848-1880*, Burchell failed to find a picture representing much of dislocation, exile, alienation, dependence, despair, failure. On the contrary, most of the Irish in the city of his study (about 25 percent of the total population in 1860) were adjusting quite well. A substantial middle and upper class had emerged among the Irish during the 1850s. Irishmen were firmly ensconced in the financial and political community. The Hibernia Bank, California's oldest banking institution in 1988, was founded by Irishmen in 1859. By 1880, Irish-born males were one-third of the electorate and only 32 percent of them were in unskilled occupations. By 1881, four Irishmen had served as United States senators from California: David Broderick (1857-59), John Conness (1863-69), Eugene Casserly (1869-73), and James Fair (1881-87).

As mentioned in Chapter 12, Burchell credits the uniqueness of the Irish experience in San Francisco not to a crippling personal and world view brought with them from Ireland but rather to the fact that San Francisco in 1850 was a city with "no history" and no long-established Protestant class, clinging as in the eastern cities to their old privileges and advantages. Protestants and Irish Catholics began the race on the same starting line. In such an environment, the culture the Irish brought from the Old Country, especially the traditions of clannishness, hospitality, and "taking care of your own," was a distinct asset. In fact, those aspects of their culture may help to explain why the Irish were able to wrest control from the old Protestant Yankee establishment of so many governmental structures, and so quickly.

To be sure, another story can be told, one of hardship and degradation in the rookeries of the big cities, many of the Irish succumbing to abject poverty, disease, premature death, insanity, and crime. But these problems were not peculiarly Irish. For every Studs Lonergan, the punkish and pathetic son of Irish immigrants and a suicide at age thirty-three, a fictional creature of novelist James T. Farrell, there was a WASP Sister Carrie (Theodore Dreiser's *Sister Carrie*) or a Clyde Griffiths (Dreiser's *An American Tragedy*), and even a black Bigger Thomas (Richard Wright's *Native Son*). They were part of the great movement of all peoples from farm to city. They were all arguably victims of their own inability to adjust satisfactorily to the modern urban world.

The alienation that Kerby Miller underscored certainly did exist among the Irish, no question. But it was, in large measure, alienation from family and community in a Protestant land often hostile to Irish and Catholic immigrants. The evidence is compelling that the great majority of the Irish, far from becoming victims of self-pity and despair, worked very hard to re-establish family and community bonds, and that they were largely successful in doing so. The evidence is in the churches, the schools, the Irish associations, the police and fire departments, the city governments dominated by Irish, the rural Irish settlements which have been the subject of this book, and in the remittances to the Old Country which financed the Irish diaspora in the 19th century. It is hardly a story of inadaptability.

It would be comforting if the textbooks and classroom instruction to which our young people are exposed were to reflect more fully and accurately the real history of the Irish in America. Before that comes to pass, however, many teachers of history will have to pay more attention to the better balanced and more fair-minded accounts of the Irish diaspora that have begun to appear in recent years. A good introduction to the literature is the bibliography by Seamus P. Metress of the University of Toledo, *The Irish-American Experience: A Guide to the Literature.* Another is Dennis Clark's *Hibernia America*, which emphasizes the variety of the Irish experience in America, a refreshing respite from the scores of studies focusing only on the "city Irish."*

JAK

Chapter 20

INHERITOR:
AN IRISH AMERICAN'S RELIGIOUS FAITH

The authors, descendants of Irish emigrants who began arriving in the New World in 1830, are in some measure the product of the heritage and values those ancestors brought with them. Since that Irish heritage is a major theme of this book, it is fitting, we think, to include a personal essay by one of the authors about how those values were challenged and re-shaped by the experience of growing up in 20th century America. The following chapter says something, it is hoped, of the paradoxical simplicity of Faith in a complex world. It first appeared in AMERICA *magazine, December 20, 1986.*

May 14, 1986: This is my 61st birthday, a time for a little reflection. I have been having some thoughts about my Irish Catholic upbringing, what I was taught and what I have come to believe. And some thoughts about life and death.

I was born and raised in Brooklyn, New York, of a Brooklyn-born father and Wisconsin-born mother, both of whose grandparents were Irish-born. I attended St. Jerome's School in the 1930s. There I learned that God was "a spirit infinitely perfect" and that "He made me to know Him, to love Him, to serve Him in this world and to be happy with Him forever in the next." I learned that I should honor my father and mother and avoid certain sins, especially seven very deadly ones called Pride, Covetousness, Lust, Anger, Gluttony, Envy, and Sloth.

I learned that there was something called the Trinity, three Persons in One God - Father, Son and Holy Ghost. It was a concept incomprehensible to mortal man, so the nuns and priests told us, but

323

true nevertheless, to be accepted on faith, part of the revelation that the Son brought to mankind.

God, we knew, was in His Heaven, and He cared for us. If the world was in a mess, with God's help human beings could make it right; and even if we did not succeed in producing a paradise on earth, each of us had an immortal soul. If we led good lives according to God's commandments, an eternal heavenly paradise would be our reward.

So, despite the Great Depression, my father's joblessness for several years, and the anxiety my parents faced trying to feed seven mouths (I was well aware of that), I was as secure as a rock philosophically.

That philosophical security was reinforced at Brooklyn Technical High School, a public institution specializing in engineering, which was then perhaps the best and toughest school of its kind in the nation. There I took chemistry and much physics. I can recall the diagram of the atom in the chemistry text. It had a nucleus firm and indivisible (although there was talk of "splitting it"). Particles called electrons swirled around the nucleus in predictable orbits, like planets around the sun. These electron particles could not be seen, even under the most powerful of microscopes. But they were within the realm of what the imagination could conceive. They could be "pictured."

My sweet and innocent faith in the orderliness of a God-directed universe would be challenged many times after I graduated from high school in January 1943. A few months after graduation, I was in the United States Navy, where I served for three years. One big challenge to my faith occurred during a month-long cruise to the South Pacific on a troop transport. There was plenty of time for reading and reflection. My choice of reading, plucked almost at random from a big carton of Government-printed books, was *A Treasury of Science*, a fat book of essays edited by Harvard mathematician Harlow Shapley. (It was not nearly my first choice. Popular sexy numbers such as *God's Little Acre* and *A Tree Grows in Brooklyn* - those were innocent days - had already been preempted by borrowers.) I was much impressed, even dumbfounded, by the writings of the great modern astronomers such as James Jeans and Arthur Eddington. They described a universe many times more complex than I had ever imagined. It was a universe of countless billions of stars multiplied by many powers, of galaxies and super-galaxies, of stars dying and stars being born in a volatile, ever-expanding universe in which our own sun was just a speck, less than a grain of sand in the Sahara.

These astronomers shook my faith in the simplicity and permanence of things, and in my "illusion of central position." So did the biologists who described the evolution of life forms in a billion-year process of natural selection and survival of the fittest. Things seemed to be happening in this universe that God did not directly or perhaps even indirectly ordain. The simple story of Creation in the Bible did not seem to be in harmony with the observations of the scientists.

I remember being shaken up and sleepless one night after a reading session, as I lay in my bunk, sixth up in the crowded Seabee troop quarters. I climbed down, made my way to the deck, perched myself on the bulkhead, my feet dangling over the sides, as the ship made its way through the waters on a calm and beautiful Pacific night. I was all alone, and the universe was before my eyes. There was a full moon. I could see fish near the surface, and their reflections as some hurled themselves above the surface. In the clear sky were more stars than I had ever seen before and more than I had ever imagined. I felt very small. I was only one among many thousands on one ship among thousands of ships in an ocean that was not quite so big anymore, just part of a very small planet encircling an average-size star that was itself hardly more than a small dot in the vast universe.

Where was God? If He existed at all, could He find me? Did He care?

At the same time I was astonished by the beauty of what I saw and felt. The universe might not be as simple as I had thought, but it was awesome, mysterious and more beautiful than ever. I was *alive* and *aware* of it. Existence itself is a miracle. Consciousness is a miracle. I was, in a sense, the "center" of things. God *did* exist, although His universe was more complex than I had heretofore suspected, and this called for more humility than I had heretofore developed. I went back to my bunk that night, climbing over five bodies to the top tier, and amidst the snoring in many keys, I thought some beautiful thoughts before going soundly to sleep.

Some months later, a few weeks after the Japanese surrender, I was on the first transport carrying troops into Sasebo in southern Japan. That first Sunday there was no Catholic priest yet available to say Mass for the Catholics. Or so we thought, until our Lutheran chaplain located a Japanese priest in town. He asked me if I thought the Catholics in the battalion would attend a Mass said by this Japanese. I was taken aback. A *Japanese* priest, of all things! Attend a Mass said by *him!* Japanese, I had thought, were not Catholic. They were the enemy, buck-toothed, slanty-eyed, cunning, cruel. Would I serve Mass for him? the chaplain asked. I said yes to both questions. The men, I thought, would attend and, yes, I would be the altar boy.

It was a decision I will never regret. The old Japanese priest came to the compound where we were quartered, a warehouse building, and I made a makeshift altar for him in one corner of it. He was nervous too, and so were the forty or so Americans in attendance. But the nervousness disappeared as the Mass began. I knelt, the priest stood, making the Sign of the Cross. *"In nomine Patris et Filii et Spiritus Sancti. Amen,"* followed by *"Introibo ad altare Dei"* ("I go up to the altar of God"), and I responded, the words sort of leaking out, *"Ad Deum qui laetificat juventutem meam"* ("To God who giveth joy to my youth").

The nervousness died. The Mass went on. It was a great healing experience for all of us there. So was the Midnight Mass on Christmas Eve a few months later, when several hundred Catholics in the Japanese community joined a thousand soldiers, sailors and Marines. A chorus of lovely Japanese maidens in flowing gowns in beautiful pastels sang "Silent Night" in Japanese, "Adeste Fideles" in Latin, and another hymn in English. Many tough men wept. I wept. What a healing experience! I was more than Irish, more than Catholic, more than American. Those women in pastels were more than Japanese. We were all persons in the universe together, trying in an imperfect and simplistic way, but perhaps the best way, to exult in the marvelous fact of Existence, the Dance and Song of Life, the Great Mystery of Creation and the promise of Hope in the future.

I think that that experience, one of the most poignant and lasting of my life, prepared me somewhat for the great world of human knowledge I would be exposed to in my college days after the war. I suppose I was a slow learner in the area of philosophy. I never questioned the meaning of words until I entered college and took some courses in semantics and linguistics. Words are not things, I was taught. Words are arbitrary symbols created by man, puffs of air, scribblings on paper. We live in a symbolic world, the only world we can ever know, because when we try to explain what is "out there" or "in here," we are limited to these puffs of air from the throat, these symbols, spoken or written, and then to more symbols to explain the meaning of the symbols. What is the meaning of the meaning of the meaning? If God is a "spirit, infinitely perfect," then what are the meanings of *spirit, infinity, perfection?* The answer to the question "What is God?" given to me by the Baltimore Catechism and Sister Mary Gervase of the Mercy nuns, so many years ago, was not a real answer at all. It just raised many more questions. But I remain grateful to Sister Mary Gervase of the first grade for introducing me to three beautiful new words. Should we not feel sorry today for youngsters using thoroughly disinfected first grade readers with controlled vocabularies? No beautiful words, like *transubstantiation,* need apply.

The academic experience in general, seven years and more of study at several universities earning degrees and over thirty years of teaching at secular colleges and universities, has been a continual challenge to that sweet faith of my childhood. For some years I thought I had lost the faith altogether. It is not popular, and often took more courage and more faith than I could muster, to defend belief in such notions as a Creator, a Redeemer, the immortality of the soul, heaven and the Trinity. One gets smug or amused smiles from colleagues who are quite certain about uncertainty. The only truth is the process of searching for the truth. Shame on the student who obliges the academicians by conducting the search and *finding* truth. He is cheating at the game.

I try to keep up with the major developments in the sciences. I have chatted over the years with my colleagues in physics, chemistry and biology and have a great respect for them, more so perhaps than for colleagues in my own humanities area. The world of the atom is no longer a predictable world of a nucleus with particles swirling neatly around it. The Principle of Indeterminacy reigns. Things happen at random. The electron is a mathematical "point" with no "volume" and occupying no "space," but it also, simultaneously, completely "fills" the space surrounding the nucleus of the atom! How can a mathematical "point" occupying no space and showing no evidence of motion ("angular momentum," in physics jargon) completely fill a finite region of space? There is no answer to that question, say the physicists, but nevertheless "all experimental evidence points to its truth." So speaks a colleague of mine in physics whom I consider something of a theologian, although he might wince at such a title.

So we have a world of the atom where things are not things and where identical conditions do not necessarily produce identical results. At the fundamental level everything is purely random. Matter behaves "statistically" but not "deterministically." Positrons and electrons annihilate each other. Matter turns into light, light into matter. It is a world where words do not mean what they seem to mean. A world of numbers, and what do those numbers mean? A world for which we can draw no pictures, a world where two equals one and one equals two. Quantum mechanics gives at least two answers, seemingly contradictory, to every question. A paradoxical reality. The stuff of priests and poets - and of dreams.

Furthermore, man has a mind that can generate thoughts undreamed of before in his own philosophy or anybody's else's. His mind is creative, evolving, unpredictable, indeterminate. It is truly made "in God's image and likeness," much as I was taught, much as in the awesome physical world of the atom, where "things" behave indeterminately and creatively, and repeated "conditions" do not produce the same results.

Certain physicists and priests are joining hands in this strange world, meeting in such places as the Center for Theology and the

Natural Sciences at Berkeley, California, to discuss Ultimate Questions. They seek one-ness, the unified theory that eluded Einstein, to explain the four known forces in the Universe: gravity, electromagnetism, the "weak" force, and the "strong" force. The latest thinking is that two of these four are really one. Back to a Trinity. A new breed of physicists, known as "Super-Symmetrists," aware that laboratory models to test their hypotheses cannot be built (such models would have to be the size of the solar system itself), look for "symmetry" and "elegance" and "simplicity" to confirm the probability of their formulations. Beauty is truth. They are in the realm of the poet and the priest.

If one can accept "two is one" or "four is one," it is but a small step, I think, to embrace the Trinity as a matter of religious faith. "The Father, the Son and the Holy Spirit, three Persons in One God," is a profound statement about the Creator, the principle behind and in the universe, and, alas, about the limits of human intelligence.

That is why, I think, I remain a Catholic on my 61st birthday, although I have come a distance from the uncomplicated and more innocent faith passed on to me by parents and grandparents and by Sister Mary Gervase of the first grade. I think the answers that were given me in my childhood were pretty good answers after all. Spirit. Infinity. Perfection. Beautiful words to assign to the Supreme Being, the Creator of the universe. "God made me to know Him, to love Him, to serve Him in this world and to be happy with Him forever in the next." Not a bad answer. It suggests that there is a Power in the universe greater than I, and that one should not live primarily for his own pleasure. I am grateful on my 61st birthday for this chance to reflect; for my Catholic upbringing; for Betty (my wife of thirty-one years and a good Presbyterian); and for our four children.

JAK

———————

Notes and Selected References

Chapter 1. Genealogy, History, and Irish Immigration (JAK)

Adams, William Forbes. *Ireland and Irish Emigration to the New World from 1815 to the Famine*. New Haven, 1932.

Akenson, Donald Harman. *Being Had: Historians, Evidence, and the Irish in North America*. Port Credit, Ontario, Canada, 1985.

Byrne, Rev. Stephen. *Irish Emigration to the United States*. New York, 1873.

Duff, John B. *The Irish in the United States*. Belmont, California, 1971.

Hamilton, W.D. *Old North Esk on the Miramichi*. Fredericton, New Brunswick, 1979.

Houston, C.J., and W.J. Smyth. "The Irish Abroad: Better Questions Through a Better Source, the Canadian Census," *Irish Geography*, University of Ulster, Coleraine, County Derry, vol. 13, 1980.

Inglis, Henry D. *A Journey Throughout Ireland During the Spring, Summer, and Autumn of 1834*. London, 1838.

Johnston, James F.W. *Notes on North America*, 2 vols. Edinburgh and London, 1851.

Kennedy, John F. *A Nation of Immigrants*. New York, 1964.

Kennedy, Robert E., Jr. *The Irish: Emigration, Marriage and Fertility*. Berkeley and Los Angeles, 1973, p. 27 and footnote, p. 217, citing statistics on emigration 1817-1844, from *Commission on Emigration*, Statistical Appendix, Table 26, p. 314.

King, Joseph A. "Bing's Family Tree," *Cork Examiner* (Ireland), May 18,1983; also appendix to *The Irish Lumberman-Farmer*, Lafayette, California, 1982.

McDonald, Grace. *History of the Irish in Wisconsin in the Nineteenth Century*. New York, 1976; first published 1954.

Minnesota State Census, Washington County, 1875.

New Brunswick Census, Northumberland County, 1851, 1861, 1871. National Archives of Canada, Ottawa.

Stephenson, Isaac. *Recollections of a Long Life (1829-1915)*. Chicago, 1915.

United States Census, Winnebago County, Wisconsin, 1850, 1860, 1870, 1880.

Chapter 2. A Long Inheritance: The Gael and Genealogy (MEF)

Binchy, Daniel A., editor. *Studies in Early Irish Law*. Dublin, 1936 (and numerous articles from 1936 to 1984).

Bryant, Sophie. *Liberty, Order & Law Under Native Irish Rule: A Study in the Book of the Ancient Laws of Ireland*. Port Washington, New York, 1923, republished 1970.

Caesar, Julius. *The Conquest of Gaul* (trans. by S.A. Handford). New York, 1951.

Chadwick, Nora. *The Celts*. New York, 1970.

Cusack, Mary Frances (Margaret Anna). *The Illustrated History of Ireland from Early Times: 400 A.D.-1800 A.D.* New York, 1987 (first published 1868).

dePaor, Maire, and Liam de Paor. *Early Christian Ireland*. New York, 1958.

Harney, Martin P. *The Legacy of St. Patrick*. Boston, 1972 (includes author's translation of Dr. John Healy's Latin text of St. Patrick's *Confessio*).

Keating, Geoffrey. *The History of Ireland*, edited and translated by D. Comyn and P. Dineen. Ireland and London, 1902-1914.

Kelly, Fergus. *A Guide to Early Irish Law*. Dublin, 1988.

Kinsella, Thomas. *The Táin* (translated from the Irish epic *Táin Bo Cuailnge*). Dublin, 1969.

Lawless, Emily. *The Story of the Nations: Ireland*. New York, 1887.

Lydon, J.F., and Margaret MacCurtain, editors. *Gill History of Ireland*, vols. 1 and 2. Dublin, 1972-75.

Macalister, R.A.S. *The Archaeology of Ireland*. New York, 1977; first published London, 1928, 2nd revised edition, 1949.

MacCana, Proinsias. *Celtic Mythology*. New York, 1970.

MacManus, Seumas. *The Story of the Irish Race*. New York, 1944.

MacNeill, Eóin. *Celtic Ireland*. Dublin, 1921.

_____. *Early Irish Laws and Institutions*. Dublin, 1935, 1937.

_____. *Phases of Irish History*. Dublin, 1919.

Moody, T.W., and F.X. Martin, editors. *The Course of Irish History*. Cork, 1984.

O'Donovan, John, translator and editor, *Annals of the Kingdom of Ireland by the Four Masters from the Earliest Period to the Year 1600*, 7 vols. New York, 1966; first published Dublin, 1848-1851.

O'Rahilly, Thomas F. *Early Irish History and Mythology*. Dublin, 1946; republished 1957, 1984.

Orpen, G.H., editor. *The Song of Dermot and the Earl*. Oxford, 1892.

Raftery, Joseph. *Prehistoric Ireland*. London, 1951.

Rees, Alwyn and Brinley Rees. *Celtic Heritage: Ancient Tradition in Ireland and Wales*. New York, 1961.

Thomas, Charles. *Britain and Ireland in Early Christian Times, A.D. 400-800*. New York, 1971.

Chapter 4. A Parish in West Cork (JAK)

Note 1: Terminology

PLOUGHLAND. Land required for herding 100 cows, among other definitions, which include "the amount of land a single plough could break up in a year." One ploughland equalled perhaps 50 to 120 acres of arable land on the Mizen Peninsula.

GNEEVE. 1/12 of a ploughland, enough for eight cows.

IRISH ACRE. 1.62 English (statute) acres, supposedly the area one man could plough in a day with a pair of yokes; divided into the *rood* (four per acre) and the *perch* (twenty per rood). Holdings shown in *Tithe Applotment Books*, c1825-35, are frequently given in Irish acres (as for Schull and Kilmoe parishes); in *Griffith's Valuations*, c1850, English acres are given.

IRISH MILE. Approximately 1.3 English miles.

TOWNLAND. One or more ploughlands; the unit by which head landlords measured their holdings; sometimes synonymous with ploughland; a shortening of the legal term "town & lands," although many townlands never contained a town.

CIVIL PARISH. An administrative jurisdiction containing many townlands; the Mizen Peninsula parishes were Schull and Kilmoe, the latter including the village and Catholic parish of Goleen. The origin of the civil parish as a geographical division is clouded in uncertainties. It may sometimes correspond with the old Irish *tuath*, the area controlled by a sept or clan. The records indicate that the Normans often used existing Irish land divisions in the re-distribution of land. See Billy Colfer, "Anglo-Norman Settlement in County Wexford," and Henry Goff, "English Conquest of an Irish Barony: the Changing Patterns of Land Ownership in the Barony of Scarawalsh 1540-1640," in *Wexford: History and Society*, edited by Kevin Whelan (Dublin, 1987).

CHURCH PARISH. For the established Church of Ireland, frequently the same boundaries as the civil parish; rarely so for the Roman Catholic parishes. The Catholic parish of Goleen included all of the civil parish of Kilmoe and the western section of the the civil parish of Schull.

DIOCESE. A number of parishes under a bishop; diocese of Cork for the Catholic parishes on the Mizen; diocese of Ross (diocese of Cloyne and Ross after 1835) for the Church of Ireland.

COUNTY. Thirty-two of them in Ireland, each containing many parishes; territory of a count or earl, who sublet to barons, hence:

BARONY. Ancient land division, several in a county and sometimes overlapping county lines, widely used from 16th century onwards for administrative, tax, and regional purposes, its use declining after the 1898 Local Government Act which created a new structure for local government.

PROVINCE. Four in Ireland: *Ulster*, nine counties, including the cities of Belfast and Derry (present "Northern Ireland" contains only six of the Ulster counties); *Leinster*, including the city of Dublin; *Munster*, including the city of Cork; *Connaught*, including the city of Galway.

TITHE. The amount that was assessed by law on land occupiers in Ireland to support the established Church of Ireland; after the reform acts of 1823-24, usually set at 10 percent of what a grain crop would yield in value, averaged for seven years, 1815-21.
POUND. Basic monetary unit, twenty shillings to the pound, twelve pence to the shilling; a *guinea* was worth one pound plus one shilling.

Note 2: Fitzgerald and Harrigan Records. As mentioned in Chapter 3, "Harrigan's Rocks," William Fitzgerald and Ann Harrigan, soon after their marriage, may have settled across Roaring Water Bay near Baltimore and Skibbereen. There, for the civil parish of Tullagh, the *Tithe Applotment Book* for 1828 listed a William and a James Fitzgerald as co-occupiers of a 41-acre farm in Spain Townland (which was later subsumed by Ballymacrown Townland), and they are listed consecutively with O'Briens and Taylors. It is perhaps more than a coincidence that in North Esk Parish, New Brunswick, the William Fitzgerald of this study was also listed consecutively with Taylors and O'Briens on the tax lists for that parish for 1835 to 1837.

Note 3: Over-Encumbered Estates. One interesting case is that of the Lord Audley Estate (see W. Neilson Hancock, *On the Causes of the Distress at Skull [Schull] and Skibbereen during the Famine in Ireland.* Dublin, 1850). The huge estate of Lord Audley included the copper mines at Cosheen, Schull, and eastward to Skibbereen. He inherited the estate in 1818 and by 1837 had run up a debt via mortgages, interest, and legal fees, of 167,300 pounds, on an estate whose rentals through a middleman holding a 99-year lease netted Lord Audley only 577 pounds per year. Furthermore, as the year approached when the lease would fall due (1854), the actual value of the properties decreased. Since the law gave all improvements on the properties to the middleman, or to the receivers in bankruptcy, or to a new bidder and owner, there was less and less incentive for the actual occupiers to make improvements on their holdings. Such improvements would have generated sufficient income for the tenant to produce other kinds of food along with the potatoes. Less reliance on potatoes would have meant less distress when that crop failed.

Note 4: Joint Ownership (Rundale). The acres for Schull Parish, West and East Divisions, are given in the *Tithe Applotment Books (TAB)* for 1827 in Irish acres, a fact that can be confirmed by comparing the *TAB* acreages with the later (circa 1850) *Griffiths Valuations,* which listed the holdings in English acres, allowing for some townlands that "disappeared" (subsumed by other townlands) or were renamed after the Ordnance Survey in the 1840s. Either way, the acreages of the leaseholds listed in the *TAB* for Schull, usually more than 20 acres, sometimes over 300 acres, and rarely less than 10 acres, badly distort the reality of the actual occupiers. The *TAB* indicates much joint ownership: "Joseph Darby and partners" (46 acres), "Timothy Driscoll Sr. and partners" (43 acres). Often, two to five occupiers are listed by name. On the *TAB*, about 450 farm holdings are listed. The parish population was about 14,000, which would mean there were approximately 31 persons per holding. The number of inhabited houses was about 2,300 (2,271 on 1821 census, 2,308 on 1831 census). That would indicate an average of five houses per farm, and six persons per house, a very credible figure for an Irish family.
It is evident that fewer than half of the actual occupiers are given by name on the *TAB* for Schull. The names of only about 1,000 are given for a population of 14,000. This kind of reporting of occupiers was unusual. In most other parishes in Ireland, except in the cities, all occupiers were reported, down to the lowliest cottier whose holding was measured in roods and perches.
Why was Schull an exception? The evidence suggests that the system of rundale, once almost universal among the Irish, still prevailed, more or less, in this rural parish. Under the rundale system, the land was held communally by the *cineadh* or *derbfine*, the Irish extended family consisting of all those with a common great-grandfather. The family lived in the *clachan*, a cluster of huts which included an "infield" of tillage plots (the size of individual plots depending on family tradition and

need) and an "outfield" of common pasturage. The infield holdings had to be regularly adjusted and re-distributed, with deaths, emigrations, and spin-offs of new *cinid-heacha*. Desmond McCourt has noted that the rundale/clachan system still prevailed in areas of the west and south well into the 19th century, despite efforts of the ruling class to impose the English system of leasing to individual householders. (See chart, "Types of Rural Settlement in Ireland: 1831-1841," in *The Rundale System in Ireland: A Study of its Geographical Distribution and Social Relations,* unpublished doctoral dissertation, Queens University, Belfast, Ireland, 1950, p. 112.)

Interestingly, the Fitzgeralds and Harrigans, after they emigrated, seem to have attempted, as far as they were able, to impose rundale/clachan on the lots they occupied and on which they paid taxes for over two decades in Williamstown, New Brunswick. At least that is one explanation for many of them never filing claim for ownership, the lots being passed on to other members of the *derbfine* as older members moved west to Maine and Wisconsin and others arrived newly from Ireland. In any case, the evidence of the *Poor Inquiry* is that the occupiers in Schull Parish thought of their holdings in terms of the gneeve *(see Note 1: Terminology),* not in Irish or English acres. The average holding, it was reported, was 1/8 gneeve, sufficient for grazing one cow. The usual three or four middlemen between the lowliest tenant and the head landlord had to include, so it would seem, senior *derbfine* members. That may be why head landlord Richard Edward Hull, who died at age 96, could boast that he never had to evict a tenant during his long stewardship. The *derbfine* members protected each other.

The author is indebted to the following scholars for valuable critiques of this chapter in its early manuscript form: Reverend James Coombes of Skibbereen; Professor Patrick J. Corish of Maynooth; Reverend Patrick Hickey of Cork City; and Tim Cadogan, archivist of the Cork County Library, Cork City.

Bolster, Evelyn A. *A History of the Diocese of Cork (from the Earliest Times to the Reformation).* Shannon, Ireland, Irish University Press, 1972.

Bowen, Desmond. *The Protestant Crusade in Ireland (1800-1870).* Dublin, 1978, quoted by Hickey, p. 184.

Brady, H.M. *Clerical, Parochial Records of Cork, Cloyne, and Ross*, vol. 2 (1896), pp. 247-48; information on Schull and the rectors Anthony and Robert Trail. Courtesy of Tim Cadogan, Cork County Library. Also vol. I, p. 176 (1863) for information on Reverend W.A. Fisher and the use of famine relief funds to win converts.

Burke, Rev. William P. *The Irish Priests in the Penal Times (1660-1760).* Shannon, Ireland, 1968; first published 1914.

Concannon, Mrs. Thomas (Helena). *Irish Nuns in Penal Days.* London, 1931.

Coombes, Reverend James. "Goleen Parish," *The Fold* (Cork diocesan magazine). Cork, 1967; and letters to J.A. King, 1980-87.

_____. "The O Mahonys of Ivagha," *The O Mahony Journal,* vol. II, Summer 1981.

_____. *A History of Timoleague and Barryroe.* Timoleague, County Cork, 1981.

Corish, Monsignor Patrick J. *The Catholic Community in the Seventeenth and Eighteenth Centuries.* Dublin, 1981.

_____. "Irish Catholics before the Famine: Patterns and Questions," *Journal of the Wexford Historical Society,* no. 11, 1986-87. Also January 1988 letter to J.A. King.

_____. "The Irish Catholics at the End of the Penal Era," *Religion and Identity,* edited by Terrence Murphy and Cyril J. Byrne. St. John's, Newfoundland, 1987.

Cork County Council, Cork City. Addresses of occupiers, Valuations Books, rated occupiers of land in Schull Parish.

Cork Mercantile Chronicle, items cited by Coombes, Hickey, Bowen; also October 8, 1847, report containing Relief Committee statistics on deaths and emigrations, September 1846 to September 1847.

Deady, John, and Elizabeth Doran, "Prehistoric Copper Mines, Mount Gabriel, County Cork," *Journal of the Cork Historical and Archaeological Society,* no. 225, January/June 1972.

A Dictionary of Irish History 1800-1980, ed. by D.J. Hickey and J.E.Doherty. Dublin, 1980. See "Tithes," 561-62.

Donnelly, James S., Jr. *The Land and the People of Nineteenth-Century Cork.* London and Boston, 1975.

Furlong, Nicholas, "The Times and Life of Nicholas Sweetman, Bishop of Ferns," *Journal of the Old Wexford Historical Society,* no. 9, 1983-84.

Hancock, W. Neilson. *On the Causes of the Distress at Skull [Schull] and Skibbereen During the Famine in Ireland.* Dublin, 1850. Courtesy of Tim Cadogan, Cork County Library.

Hickey, Reverend Patrick. *A Study of the Four Peninsular Parishes of West Cork, 1796-1855.* Unpublished master's thesis, University College, Cork, 1980; and letters to J.A. King, 1980-87.

_____. "Fr. Laurence O'Sullivan, P.P., Goleen (1828-48) and *Souper Sullivan* by Eoghan Harris," *The Fold* (Cork diocesan publication), April 1986. Hickey argues that the playwright seriously misrepresented priests L. O'Sullivan and John Murphy by basing his characterizations on inaccurate accounts by P. Somerville-Large and D. Bowen. See also Jim Cluskey, "Controversial TV Series on Famine," *Cork Examiner,* July 15, 1983, and response in that newspaper by Patrick Hickey, August 1983 (undated clipping in author's file).

Holland, Reverend W. *History of West Cork and the Diocese of Ross.* Skibbereen, Cork, 1949.

Keena, Catherine A. "Recollections of Mrs. Mary Blake." Manuscript in Oshkosh (Wisconsin) Public Museum, c1926, 3 pp.

Kennedy, Robert E., Jr. *The Irish: Emigration, Marriage and Fertility.* Berkeley and Los Angeles, 1973. Emigration statistics, 1847-1891, p. 27.

King, Joseph A. *The Irish Lumberman-Farmer,* Lafayette, California, 1982.

Kingston, William J. *The Story of West Carbery.* Waterford, Ireland, 1985.

Lecky, W.E.H. *A History of Ireland in the Eighteenth Century,* abridged with introduction by L.P. Curtis. Chicago, 1972. See Chapter II, "Religion and Society," pp. 37-114.

Lewis, Samuel. *A Topographical Dictionary of Ireland.* London, 1837.

"Living 100 Years is Attainment of an Oshkosh Woman" [Mary Fitzgerald Blake]. *Oshkosh Daily Northwestern,* December (day?) 1925, clipping in J.A. King's file.

McCourt, Desmond. *The Rundale System in Ireland: A Study of Its Geographical Distribution and Social Relations.* Unpublished doctoral dissertation, Queens University, Belfast, Ireland, 1950. McCourt's chart showing rundale patterns of land holding in 19th century Ireland can be found on p. 109 of unpublished doctoral dissertation by Patrick Blessing, *West Among Strangers: Irish Migration to California, 1850-1880,* University of California at Los Angeles, 1977.

McDowell, R.B. *Social Life in Ireland 1800-45.* Cork, 1976.

Merriman, Brian. *Cúirt an Mhean-Oíche, The Midnight Court.* Text and translation by Patrick C. Power, Cork, 1977. Quoted passage is, however, from Frank O'Connor's less literal but more spirited translation in *Penguin Book of Irish Verse,* edited with an introduction by Brendan Kennelly, Middlesex, London, 1970, pp. 91-118.

Moore, John. *Diary of John Moore,* edited by Major-General Sir J.F. Maurice. London, 1904.

Moran, Cardinal Patrick. *The Catholics of Ireland Under the Penal Laws in the Eighteenth Century.* London, 1899. Much information on reports from Ireland to Rome and the continent.

Murphy, Father Denis, S.J. *Our Martyrs.* Dublin, 1896.

New Brunswick Census, Northumberland County, North Esk, Nelson, and Derby parishes, years 1851, 1861, 1871, National Archives of Canada, Ottawa, on film.

Also, *Return of Assessments*, 1830-34, North Esk Parish. Provincial Archives of New Brunswick, Fredericton, New Brunswick, films L95-97.

The O'Mahony Journal, publication of the O'Mahony Records Society, annual, 1971. Cork County Library.

Ó Cruadhlaoich, Diarmuid. *The Oath of Allegiance*, Dublin & London, 1925, pp. 16-17.

Ó Maidin, Padraig. "Leamcon Castle and Leamcon House," *Cork Examiner* (undated clipping in author's file), based on the following articles by Arthur E.J. Went: "Sir William Hull's Losses in 1644," *Journal of the Cork Historical and Archaeological Society*, LII (1947), pp. 55-68; "Pilchards in the South of Ireland," *JCHAS*, LI (1946), pp. 137-57; and "Foreign Fishing Fleets Along the Irish Coast," *JCHAS*, LIV (1949), pp. 17-24.

Ó Murchadha, Diarmuid. *Family Names of County Cork*. Dublin, 1985. Information on (O) Mahony families. See also Holland.

Ordnance Survey Office, Phoenix Park, Dublin. Maps of West Cork and the parishes of Schull and Kilmoe; West Cork 1/2"=1 mi., sheet 24; West Cork 1"=1 mi., sheets 199, 200, 204, 205 (Schull and parts of Kilmoe parishes); West Schull, 6"=1 mi., sheets 131, 139, 140, 148, 1st ed., c1843.

Parish registers, Goleen and Schull, County Cork, National Library of Ireland, Dublin.

The Parliamentary Gazetteer of Ireland. Dublin, 1843-46. Information on tithes, the glebe house, and schools in Schull Parish.

Parliamentary Papers. *Report of Commission inquiring into the condition of the poorer classes in Ireland, 1835 and 1836 (Poor Inquiry)*. National Library of Ireland, Dublin.

"Pioneer Logger [Michael Fitzgerald] Celebrates 99th Birthday," *Oshkosh Daily Northwestern*, November 8, 1924, p. 5.

Reilly, A.J. *Father John Murphy: Famine Priest (1796-1883)*. Dublin and London, 1963. Account of Father Murphy's work in Goleen Parish, winning back "soupers" who had been proselytized by W.A. Fisher.

"Report on the State of Popery in Ireland, 1731," in *Archivium Hibernicum*, vol. I (1912), vol. II (1913), vol. III (1914).

Return of the Commissioners appointed to take up the census of Ireland for the year 1841, pp. 171-72 (504), 1843, XXII, No. 1. National Library of Ireland, Dublin.

Return of the Owners of Land. . .(1876). Information on Richard Edward Hull's land-holdings in 1876. Cork County Library.

Ronan, Myles C. *The Irish Martyrs of the Penal Laws*. London, 1935. Information on 1572-1713 period.

Skibbereen Southern Star, Skibbereen, County Cork, July 3, 1982, account of historic services on the Schull Mass-rock.

Tithe Applotment Books. Schull/Skull and Kilmoe parishes, Barony of West Carbery (West), 1827. National Library of Ireland, Dublin.

Townsend, Rev. Horatio. *A General and Statistical Survey of the County of Cork*, 2nd edition, 2 vols. Cork, 1815, vol. 1, pp. 316-19.

United States Census, Winnebago County, Wisconsin, 1860, 1870, 1880.

Wall, Maureen. *The Penal Laws, 1691-1760*. Dundalk, Ireland, 1967.

Woodham-Smith, Cecil. *The Great Hunger*. London, 1962 and 1970.

Chapter 5. The New Brunswick Irish: Uncovering Their Roots (JAK)

Akenson, Donald H. *Being Had: Historians, Evidence, and the Irish in North America*. Port Credit, Ontario, Canada, 1985.

———. *Small Differences: Irish Catholics and Irish Protestants*. Toronto, 1988.

Doyle, Arthur T. *Heroes of New Brunswick*. Fredericton, 1984, pp. 49-53, "Timothy Warren Anglin."

Fraser, James A. *By Favourable Winds: A History of Chatham, New Brunswick*. Chatham, 1975, pp. 44-51 (Fighting Election).

Gesner, Abraham. *New Brunswick - With Notes for Emigrants.* London, 1847.

Hamilton, W.D. "Early Schools of the Miramichi," *The Moncton Times,* December 19-24, 1977.

_____. *Miramichi Papers.* Fredericton, New Brunswick, 1987.

_____. *Old North Esk on the Miramichi.* Fredericton, 1979 (revised 1988).

Hannay, James. *History of New Brunswick.* Saint John, 1909.

Hansen, Marcus Lee. *The Mingling of the Canadian and American Peoples.* New Haven, 1940.

Huggard, Turner. *An Annotated List of Resource Material on the Irish in New Brunswick.* Fredericton, 1984.

Johnson, Sheriff John M. Report of January 24, 1843, to Provincial Secretary William F. O'Dell, on Fighting Election. Provincial Archives of New Brunswick Document RG2 RS7, vol. 123, pp. 40-47 (Provincial Secretary's Letters), and cited by Spray, item below.

Journal of the House of Assembly of New Brunswick, Minutes, year 1843, February 1, 2, 9, 17, 20, 21, 23; March 11, 24, 25; April 6. The March 24 Minutes record the motion (passed) declaring election of John Williston null and void, and ordering a new election. Provincial Archives of New Brunswick film F-93.

King, Joseph A. *The Irish Lumberman-Farmer.* Lafayette, California, 1982.

_____."Genealogy, History, and Irish Immigration," *The Canadian Journal of Irish Studies,* June, 1984.

_____. "N.B.'s Irish Just Beginning to Uncover Their History," *The Telegraph Journal* (Saint John, New Brunswick), July 19, 1986, p. 23.

Lawrence, Joseph Wilson. *Footprints or Incidents in the Early History of New Brunswick.* Saint John, 1883, pp. 32-34, information on hanging of Patrick Burgan. See also *Judges of New Brunswick and Their Times,* edited by D.G. Bell, Fredericton, 1983, pp. 112-13.

MacNutt, Stewart. *New Brunswick and Its People: The Biography of a Canadian Province.* New Brunswick Travel Bureau, c1980, 44 pp.

Maguire, John Francis. *The Irish in America.* London, 1868; republished 1969.

Mannion, John. *Irish Settlements in Eastern Canada.* Toronto, 1974.

Manny, Louise, and James R. Wilson. *Songs of the Miramichi.* Fredericton, 1968.

O'Driscoll, Robert, and Lorna Reynolds, editors. *The Untold Story: The Irish in Canada,* 2 vols., Toronto, 1988.

Pentland, H. Clare. *Labour and the Development of Industrial Capitalism.* Doctoral thesis for the University of Toronto, 1961; and "The Development of a Capitalistic Labour Market in Canada," *Canadian Journal of Economic and Political Science,* vol. 25, November 1959, pp. 450-61. Both documents cited by Akenson, *op. cit.*

Royal Gazette, Fredericton, February 5 and 26, 1828, items on death sentence and hanging of Patrick Burgan; also *The City Gazette,* February 6 and 27.

Saunders, John Simcoe, letter to son John Saunders, July 12, 1847. Harriet Irving Library collection, University of New Brunswick, Fredericton.

School Inspection Returns, year 1844, in Provincial Archives of New Brunswick, Fredericton, New Brunswick, file RS/MC, 113, item 5/6.

The Shamrock Leaf, Newsletter of the Irish Canadian Cultural Association (109 Roy Avenue, Newcastle, New Brunswick EIV 3N8), November 1987. Information on 1987 provincial election.

Spray, William. "Reception of the Irish in New Brunswick," in *Talamh An Eisc: Canadian and Irish Essays,* edited by Cyril J. Byrne and Margaret Harry, Halifax, 1986.

_____. "The 1842 Election in Northumberland County," *Acadiensis,* publication of the University of New Brunswick, Fredericton, vol. VIII:1, Autumn 1979.

Toner, Peter M. Introduction to *Passengers to New Brunswick: The Custom House Records - 1833, 34, 37 & 38.* Saint John Branch, The New Brunswick Genealogical Society, Saint John, New Brunswick, 1987.

_____. editor. *New Ireland Remembered: Historical Essays on the Irish in New Brunswick.* Fredericton, New Brunswick, 1988.

Wallace, Reverend E.P. "The Beginnings of St. Patrick's Church - South Nelson, New Brunswick," 1936, 13-page manuscript with introduction by Father B.M. Broderick in 1968.

Williston Manuscripts: Local History Scraps, Newcastle, New Brunswick. Films 503,309 and 846,826, Church of Jesus Christ of Latter-day Saints archives, Salt Lake City, Utah.

Chapter 6. The Miramichi Irish (JAK)

Adams, William Forbes. *Ireland and Irish Emigration to the New World: from 1815 to the Famine.* New Haven, 1932.

Arbuckle, Doreen M. *The North West Miramichi.* Ottawa, 1978.

Hamilton, W.D. "Early Schools of the Miramichi," *Moncton Times,* Moncton, New Brunswick, December 22, 1977.

_____. *Old North Esk on the Miramichi.* Fredericton, New Brunswick, 1979.

_____. *Miramichi Papers,* Fredericton, New Brunswick, 1987.

Hoddinott, Reverend D. F. *From Whence We Came.* Newcastle, New Brunswick, 1978.

Johnston, James. *Notes on North America,* 2 vols. London, 1851.

King, Joseph A. "Bing Crosby's Irish Roots: The Harrigan Family of County Cork, New Brunswick, Minnesota, and Washington," *Irish-American Genealogist,* Augustan Society, Torrance, California, vol. VII, nos. 1-4, issue 29-32, 1983.

_____. *The Irish Lumberman-Farmer.* Lafayette, California, 1982.

_____. "Irish Methodists Sunk Deep Roots Along the Miramichi," "The Miramichi Irish: Returning Timber Ships Supported by Migration," and "Williamstown's First Irish Catholic School Master," a series in *The Times-Transcript,* Moncton, New Brunswick, July 15 and 16, 1986.

_____. "Tracing Bing Crosby's Roots to West Cork," *Southern Star,* Skibbereen, County Cork, June 25, 1983.

_____. "When Irish Eyes Are Smiling," *Cork Examiner,* Cork, Ireland, May 18, 1983.

Lawrence, Joseph Wilson, *Judges of New Brunswick and Their Times,* edited by D.G. Bell, Fredericton, New Brunswick, 1983.

National Archives of Canada. *New Brunswick Executive Council, Education, Parish, County and Grammar Schools: Correspondence and Petitions, 1819-1856.* File MG 9 A1, vol. 113, pp. 2004-34. Items on Evers Controversy, including North Esk trustees' report of hearings, letter from John Dunnett, Joseph McLean's petitions. These documents are also available at Provincial Archives of New Brunswick, Fredericton.

New Brunswick Census, Northumberland County, North Esk, Nelson (Northside), Derby, and South Esk parishes, 1851, 1861, 1871, 1881. Nelson (Northside) became Derby Parish, and is so reported on the 1861 census; part of North Esk became South Esk, and is so reported on 1881 census.

Provincial Archives of New Brunswick, Fredericton. *House of Assembly Sessional Records.* Petitions of James Evers and thirteen Williamstown residents, February 4, 1848, RS-24 PE/file 10, 1848; report of school committee, March 15, 1848, FS-24 RE/file 7, 1848; and RS-24/22 files 3 and 5, 1848; Also *Colebrooke Papers,* files RS-345 H8 1848, RS 345-A2 1848, and RS 345-E8 1848; and *Minutes of the Provincial Board of Education,* F-380, May 6, 1848, pp. 5-6 (appointment of three justices of the peace).

Chapter 7. The Fenian Attempt to Establish an Irish Republic (MEF).

Note 1: Terminology. In 1763, the British gained all France's mainland North American territory at Treaty of Paris; in 1774, the British attached Ontario and Quebec; in 1791, the British split Quebec into Lower Canada and Upper Canada; in 1841, Lower Canada and Upper Canada were rejoined and were known as Canada East and Canada West; in 1867, Lower Canada and Upper Canada were divided again at Confederation and became the provinces of Quebec and Ontario. In this chapter, Canada East has been used for present-day Quebec and Canada West for present-day Ontario, because these were the designations at the time of the first Fenian invasions. Actually, all terms remained in popular use.

Note 2: Lynch. Irish-born John Joseph Lynch, C.M. (Vincentian) came to the United States as a missionary. In 1856 he founded Niagara University. In 1859 and 1860 he became successively Coadjutor Bishop and Bishop of Toronto. An ardent Irish nationalist, he was an even more ardent defender of Catholicism.

When D'Arcy McGee tried to exert pressure by creating dissension between him and other members of the hierarchy, Lynch countered by writing directly to Cardinal Cullen of Dublin such things as: "Should these Fenians come here in any force, we are in a very critical position between Fenians on one side and bloodthirsty Orangemen on the other....if we were obliged to denounce the Fenians we could not pass over the iniquity of the oppression of the Poor [in Ireland]....Some would like to see from the hands of Your Grace when this excitement is over, a strong letter on the grievances of Ireland."

Before his death in 1888, Lynch was the target of many anti-Catholic and anti-Irish attacks as he tried to steer a just course between extremes in Canada.

Note 3: O'Neill's Forces. O'Neill later reported "shameful desertion" from the ranks of the approximately eight hundred that he said had assembled on the evening of May 31 for the crossing at Buffalo. Fenians who denied his accusations contributed to divisiveness by holding back support for his invasion plans in 1868, 1869, and 1870, when O'Neill was President of the Fenian Senate.

Note 4: Spear. Spear sent an optimistic report to Mechan at 10:30 A.M. on June 8, in which he said that he had found many patriotic Irishmen in Canada "who will give me all the information in their power; they even loan me horses." He wrote: "Give me men, arms, ammunition, and I will subsist my command sumptuously off the country." Mechan, arrested and under guard, was in no position to comply, but at 11:30 A.M. was able to send a telegram to Spear, in which he congratulated him for his success, and on the basis of his recommendation promoted Captain O'Hara to Brevet-Major.

Meantime, at 6 P.M., Spear had written to Mechan that his position had deteriorated: "Day after day passes, the arms have not arrived....the men *demand* arms and ammunition and beg not to be detained to be slaughtered....in spite of every precaution *officers* from whom I expected much demoralized their own men by inflamtory [*sic*] speeches destructive to our cause." He regretted that two colonels took their men back across the border without notifying him, but that two other colonels will "stick to the last."

Note 5: Prisoners. Major Denison's account of the good conduct of the Fenian soldiers is supported by that of a young Canadian corporal who was taken prisoner. He reported that he was treated very kindly and was bade a courteous farewell with a handshake by O'Neill as the Fenian commander debarked for Buffalo, with the word that he would return some day with stronger forces. *(See W. Ellis reference below.)* The Fenian prisoners seem not to have fared so well. Regarding the approximately sixty stragglers and others taken by the Canadian forces sent ashore from the tugboat *W.T. Robb*, a Canadian railwayman on the scene wrote: "A company of the Brant Battalion of volunteers was called upon to assist in guarding them through the streets to the jail; but even with this additional protection the task was not an easy one, as missiles were thrown over the heads of the guard into the prisoners' ranks." *(See R. Larmour reference below.)*

Note 6: 1870. Some of the prisoners were released on grounds that the Canadians had crossed the border illegally and taken them on American soil. The Canadian officers did not want allegations like those in 1866 when they were accused of pursuing retreating Fenians into Vermont and killing or wounding stragglers.

Amos, Keith. *The Fenians in Australia 1865-1880*. Kensington, New South Wales, 1988.

Archibald, Edith. *Life and Letters of Sir Edward Mortimer Archibald*. Toronto, 1929.

Beach, Thomas M. (aka Henri LeCaron). *Twenty Five Years in the Secret Service: The Recollections of a Spy*. London, 1892; republished East Ardsley, England, 1974.

Campbell, Francis Wayland. *The Fenian Invasions of Canada of 1866 and 1870*. Montreal, 1904.

Casper, Henry, S.J. *History of the Catholic Church in Nebraska*, vol. 3 of *Catholic Chapters in Nebraska Immigration*. Milwaukee, 1966.

Comerford, R.V. *The Fenians in Context*. Dublin, 1985.

Cronin, Sean. *The McGarrity Papers*. Tralee, Ireland, 1972.

D'Arcy, William. *The Fenian Movement in the United States*. Washington, 1947.

Davin, Nicholas. *The Irishman in Canada*. Toronto, 1871; republished Shannon, Ireland, 1968.

Defoe, J.W., "The Fenian Invasion of Quebec, 1866," *Canadian Magazine*, vol. 10, 1898, pp. 339-347.

Denieffe, Joseph. *A Personal Narrative of the Irish Revolutionary Brotherhood*. New York, 1906; republished Shannon, Ireland, 1969.

Denison, George T., Jr. *The Fenian Raid on Fort Erie with an Account of the Battle of Ridgeway, June 1866*. Toronto, 1866; also *Soldiering in Canada*. Toronto, 1900.

Devoy, John. *Recollections of an Irish Rebel*. New York, 1929; republished Shannon, Ireland, 1969.

Dooley, Ann. "D'Arcy McGee, Fenianism, and the Separate School System in Ontario," in O'Driscoll and Reynolds, editors, *The Untold Story: The Irish in Canada*, vol. I, Toronto, 1988.

Ellis, Peter Berresford, "Ridgeway, the Fenian Raids and the Making of Canada," in O'Driscoll and Reynolds, editors, *The Untold Story: The Irish in Canada*, vol. 1, Toronto, 1988; and "The Battle of Ridgeway, 2 June 1866, *The Irish Sword*, vol. xvi, no. 65, Winter 1986; and correspondence between J.A. King and Peter Berresford Ellis, 1988-89.

Ellis, William, "The Adventures of a Prisoner of War," *The Canadian Magazine*, vol. XIII, no. 3, July 1899.

Fitzgerald, Gerald E., unpublished notes in Margaret E. Fitzgerald's files.

Glynn, Anthony. *High Upon the Gallows Tree*. Tralee, Ireland, 1967.

Hassard, Albert W. *Famous Canadian Trials*. Toronto, 1924.

Jenkins, Brian. *Fenians and Anglo-American Relations during Reconstruction*. Ithaca, New York, 1969.

Larmour, Robert, "With Booker's Column: Personal Reminiscences of the Events of the Fenian Raid of June, 1866," *Canadian Magazine*, vol. 10 (1897-98), pp. 228-31.

Langan, Sister Mary M. *General John O'Neill, Soldier, Fenian, and Leader of Irish Catholic Colonization in Nebraska*. Unpublished master's thesis, Notre Dame University, 1937.

Macdonald, Captain John A., *Troublous Times in Canada: A History of the Fenian Raids of 1866 and 1870*. Toronto, 1910.

MacNutt, W.S. *New Brunswick 1784-1867*. Toronto, 1963.

Manning, Helen T. *The Revolt of French Canada*. Toronto, 1962.

McGee, Thomas D'Arcy. *The Irish Position in British and Republican North America*. Toronto, 1866.

McKeown, H.C. *Life and Labors of Most Reverend John Joseph Lynch, First Archbishop of Toronto*. Toronto, 1886.

Metress, Seamus. *The Hunger Strike and the Final Struggle*. Toledo, Ohio, 1983.

Moody, T.W., editor. *The Fenian Movement*. Cork, 1968.

Moran, Patrick F., editor. *The Pastoral Letters and Other Writings of Cardinal Cullen*, 3 vols. Dublin, 1882.

Moynihan, John S., "Fenian Prisoners in Western Australia, *Eire-Ireland*, Summer 1968.
Neidhardt, W. S. *Fenianism in North America*. University Park, Pennsylvania, 1975.
O'Brien, William, and Desmond Ryan, editors. *Devoy's Post Bag, 1871-1928*, 2 vols. Dublin, 1948 and 1953.
O Broin, Leon. *Fenian Fever: An Anglo-American Dilemma*. New York, 1971.
O'Dea, John. *The Story of the Old Faith in Manchester*. London, 1910.
O'Farrell, Patrick. *The Irish in Australia*. Kensington, New South Wales, 1986, pp. 209-215.
O'Hegarty, P.S. *A History of Ireland Under the Union, 1801-1922*. London, 1952.
O'Leary, John. *Recollections of Fenians and Fenianism*, 2 vols. London, 1896, Shannon, Ireland, 1969.
Ó Luing, Sean. *Freemantle Mission*. Kerry, Ireland, 1965.
O'Neill, John. *Official Report of Gen. John O'Neill*. New York, 1870.
Pease, Zephaniah W. *The Catalpa Expedition*. New Bedford, Massachusetts, 1897.
Phelan, Josephine. *The Ardent Exile: The Life and Times of Thomas D'Arcy McGee*. Toronto, 1951.
Quinlivan, Patrick, and Paul Rose. *The Fenians in England 1865-1872*. London and New York, 1982.
Rose, Paul. *The Manchester Martyrs: The Story of a Fenian Tragedy*. London, 1970.
Rossa, Jeremiah O'Donovan. *Rossa's Recollections*. New York, 1898.
Ryan, Desmond. *The Fenian Chief: A Biography of James Stephens*. Dublin, 1967.
Ryan, Mark F. *Fenian Memories*. Dublin, 1945 (completed in 1938 when Dr. Ryan was age 94, and edited by T.F. O'Sullivan).
Senior, Hereward. *The Fenian Movement in Canada*. Toronto, 1978.
Severance, Frank, "The Fenian Raid of 1866," *Buffalo Historical Society Publication*, XXV, 1921.
Skelton, Isabel. *The Life of Thomas D'Arcy McGee*. Gardenvale, Quebec, 1925.
Slattery, T.P. *The Assassination of D'Arcy McGee*. Toronto, 1968.
_____. *They Got to Find Mee [sic] Guilty Yet*. Toronto and Garden City, New York, 1972.
Stortz, Gerald, "The Catholic Church and Irish Nationalism in Toronto 1850-1900," in O'Driscoll and Reynolds, editors, *The Untold Story: The Irish in Canada*, vol. II, Toronto, 1988.
Sullivan, A.M. *New Ireland*. London, 1877, and Philadelphia, 1878.
Sullivan, Timothy D. *Recollections of Troubled Times in Ireland (Irish Politics) 1843-1904*. New York, 1905.
Sweeny, Thomas W. *Official Report of General T.W. Sweeny, Secretary of War, Fenian Brotherhood and Commander-in-Chief of the Irish Republican Army*. New York, September 1866; also printed in *Journal of the American Irish Historical Society*, XXIII, 1924, and in appendix to Denieffe, cited above.
Sweeny, William M., "Brigadier General Thomas W. Sweeny, United States Army," *Journal of the American Irish Historical Society*, XXIII, 1924.
_____. "The Invasion of Canada," *New York Sunday News*, June 18, 1893.
Tansill, Charles. *America and the Fight for Irish Freedom 1866-1922*. New York, 1957.
Waite, P.B. *Life and Times of Confederation 1864-1867*. Toronto, 1962.

Chapter 8. Colonial America: Settlers on the First Frontiers (MEF)
Note 1: Reasons for Myth. A fourth reason *may* be insecure feelings of some that their degrees are not quite as good as those of Oxford or Cambridge, these feelings inducing United States historians to praise all things English and to suppress the idea that any other ethnic group might have had an elevating influence on early American development. Insecurity breeds that kind of arrogance that the establishment historians have displayed toward the few writers who have tried to expose the Scotch-Irish myth and bring this exposure into the mainstream of historical debate. This attitude has a chilling effect on budding scholars who risk being put outside the walls of publish-or-perish academia if they dare to challenge the "conventional wisdom."

Note 2: Ann "Goody" Glover. Ann Glover was a double casualty of the Puritans. As recounted by Cotton Mather, she testified that she and her husband had been sent from Ireland to Barbadoes in the time of Cromwell. After her husband died, she was brought to New England. According to the research of Harold Dijon, Ann related that shortly before the birth of her daughter, her husband was "scored to death and did not give up his religion, which same I hold to." In November 1988 a plaque commemorating Ann Glover as first Catholic martyr of Massachusetts was placed in Our Lady of Victories Church in Boston.

Note 3: Methodists. Irish Methodists in Colonial America are often overlooked because they were not really dissenters. Methodism began in 18th century England under John and Charles Wesley as a revival movement within the Established Church, not as a separate sect. As such, the Irish Methodists built the first Irish church in New York in 1768. Most Anglican clergy and all but one of the official but unordained preachers sent by Wesley to America were Tories who went to Canada or England during or after the Revolution. When the Bishop of London refused to ordain Methodist preachers for the new United States, John Wesley made the break and ordained two men. The Methodist Episcopal Church in America was organized in 1784. The original John Street Methodist Church in New York City was destroyed by fire and a new structure built in 1818. In 1986, when the 1818 structure was being renovated, workmen found bones and artifacts and called in archaeologists of the Landmarks Preservation Commission and the American Indian Community House. There was no conclusion reached as to whether the bones were Methodist or Indian, but the broken clay pipes with elaborately carved patterns and bearded heads have an appearance as much Celtic as Indian.

Note 4: Christopher Plunkett. The extensive research of Fr. Marion Habig indicates that "after the English failed to make a Calvinist preacher out of him [Plunkett], they imprisoned him." Habig wrote that the island where he was imprisoned and where he died may have been in Chesapeake Bay. (The location is speculative, but the island could have been Kent Isle, which was settled by Puritans in 1631.) In a separate article, however, Habig wrote that "very probably . . .this martyr died on the island of Jamaica." (*See Habig items in notes below.*)

Adams, Edmund and Barbara B. O'Keefe. *Catholic Trails West: The Founding Catholic Families of Pennsylvania.* Baltimore, 1988 (compilation of 18th century records).

Bayles, Richard M., editor. *History of Richmond County, Staten Island, New York, from its Discovery to the Present Time,* 2 vols. New York 1887.

Brandow, James C. *Omitted Chapters from Hotten's Original Lists of Persons of Quality. . .and Others Who Went from Great Britain to the American Plantation, 1600-1700.* Baltimore, 1983.

_____. *Genealogies of Barbados Families.* Baltimore, 1983.

Calvert Papers, Maryland Historical Society. Material, much of which was lost when the State of Maryland purchased papers from English Calvert heirs in mid-19th century, is available in various Maryland Historical Society Fund Publications.

Cambrensis, Giraldus. *The Conquest of Ireland,* translation by A.B. Scott and F.X. Martin. Dublin, 1978.

_____. *The History and Topography of Ireland,* edited and translated by John O'Meara. Mountrath, Port Laois, Ireland, 1982.

Curran, Francis X. *Catholics in Colonial Law.* Chicago, 1963.

De Breffny, Brian, "The American Sailor Who Succeeded to an Irish Peerage," *The Irish Ancestor*, vol. IV, no. 1, 1972.

De Courcy. *Manuscripts and Papers.* Manuscript Division, Library of Congress.

deCrevecouer, Hector St. John. *Letters from an American Farmer,* edited by Albert E. Stone Jr. New York, 1963; original edition, Belfast, 1783.

Dijon, Harold, "Goody Glover, an Irish Victim of the Witch Craze, Boston, Mass., 1688," *Journal of the American Irish Historical Society*, vol. V, 1905, pp. 16-22.

Doyle, David Noel. *Ireland, Irishmen, and Revolutionary America: 1760-1820*. Cork, Ireland, 1981.

Dunaway, Wayland F. *The Scotch Irish of Colonial Pennsylvania*. Chapel Hill, North Carolina, 1944.

Dunkak, Harry M. "The Papers of an Unheralded Irish American Historian," *Eire-Ireland*, vol. XXII: 2, Summer 1987.

Eid, Leroy. "The Colonial Scotch-Irish: A View Accepted Too Readily," *Eire-Ireland*, vol. XXI: 4, Winter 1986.

Ellis, Peter Berresford. *Hell or Connaught! The Cromwellian Colonisation of Ireland, 1652-1660*. London, 1975.

Foote, William H. *Sketches of North Carolina*. Philadelphia, 1846-50; republished 1912.

Gallagher, Thomas. *The Doctors' Story*. New York, 1967.

Gwynn, Aubrey, editor, "Documents Relating to the Irish in the West Indies," *Analecta Hibernica*, October, 1932.

Habig, Marion A., O.F.M. *Heroes of the Cross: An American Martyrology*, revised edition. Paterson, New Jersey, 1945, pp. 228-30. Chapter VI, pp. 228-230, "Father Christopher Plunkett." See also Habig's *Heroes of the Cross: The Franciscan Martyrs of North America*, p. 106.

Hanley, Thomas O'Brien. *Their Rights and Liberties*. Westminster, Maryland, 1956; republished Chicago, 1984.

Hening, William W., ed. *The Statutes at Large: Being a Collection of All the Laws of Virginia, 1619-1792*, vol. 1. Richmond, Virginia, 1809.

Hotten, John Camden. *The Original Lists of Persons of Quality; Emigrants; Religious Exiles; Political Rebels; Serving Men Sold for a Term of Years; Apprentices; Children Stolen; Maidens Pressed; and Others Who Went from Great Britain to the American Plantations, 1600-1700*. London, 1874, Baltimore, 1986.

Jones, Maldwyn. "Scotch-Irish," in *Harvard Encyclopedia of American Ethnic Groups*, edited by Stephan Thornstron. Cambridge, Massachusetts, 1980.

MacManus, Seumas. *The Story of the Irish Race*. New York, 1976; first published 1921. See pp. 422-25, for quotations from Oliver Cromwell and Nathaniel Ward.

Mather, Cotton. *Favorable Providences Relating to Witchcraft and Possessions*. Boston 1689.

_____. Mather, Cotton. *Magnalia Christi Americana: or the Ecclesiastical History of New England*, 2 vols. Boston, 1702; republished Hartford, 1853-1855.

Mather, Increase. *An Essay for the Recording of Illustrious Providences*. Boston, 1684, reprinted London, 1890.

McDonald, Forrest, and Grady McWhiney. "The Celtic South," *History Today*, 30 (1980), pp. 179-199.

_____."The South from Self-Sufficiency to Peonage," *American Historical Review*, 85 (1980), pp. 1095-1118.

McDonald, Forrest, and Ellen Shapiro McDonald. "The Ethnic Origins of the American People, 1790," *William and Mary Quarterly*, 37 (1980) 1, 179-199.

Moran, Patrick. *Historical Sketch of the Persecutions Suffered by the Catholics of Ireland Under the Rule of Cromwell and the Puritans*. Dublin, 1862, reprinted 1886.

Newman, Harry W. *The Flowering of the Maryland Palatinate*. Washington, 1961; republished Baltimore, 1984.

_____. *To Maryland from Overseas*. Annapolis, 1982; republished Baltimore, 1984.

O'Brien, Michael J. *A Hidden Phase of American History*. New York, 1919; republished Baltimore, 1973.

_____. *George Washington's Association with the Irish*. New York, 1937.

_____. *In Old New York*. New York, 1928

_____. *The Irish at Bunker Hill*. New York, 1968; posthumously published by Catherine Sullivan.

_____. *Irish Settlers in North America*, 2 vols. Baltimore, 1979, excerpted and printed from articles in *The Journal of the American Irish Historical Society*, 1906-1930.

_____. *Pioneer Irish in New England*. New York, 1937; republished Bowie, Maryland, 1988.

Onderdonk, Henry. *Revolutionary Incidents of Queens County*. New York, 1846 and 1849.

_____. *Queens County in Olden Times*. Jamaica, New York, 1865.

O'Rourke, Timothy J. *Catholic Families of Southern Maryland*. Baltimore, 1985 (compilation of 18th century records).

Prendergast, John P. *The Cromwellian Settlement of Ireland*. London, 1870; 3rd edition reprint, Dublin, 1922.

Riker, James Jr. *Annals of Newtown, Queens Co., N.Y.* New York, 1852; republished Lambertsville, New Jersey, 1982.

Scott, Kenneth. *Early New York Naturalizations*. Baltimore, 1961 (compilation).

Scott, Kenneth, and Kenn Stryker Rodda. *Denizens, Naturalizations, and Oaths of Allegiance in Colonial New York*. Baltimore, 1978 (compilation).

Sewall, Samuel. *Diary*. Massachusetts Historical Society, 1878-82.

Smith, Abbott E. *Colonists in Bondage: White Servitude and Convict Labor in America, 1607-1776*. Gloucester, Massachusetts, 1965.

Van Der Zee, John. *Bound Over: Indentured Servitude and the American Conscience*. New York, 1985.

Chapter 9. Wisconsin: Lumbermen and Farmers (JAK)

Conway, Alan J. *The Welsh in America: Letters from Immigrants*. Minneapolis, 1961. Opinions on Irish passengers on Atlantic voyage.

Curti, Merle. *The Making of an American Community: A Case Study of Democracy in a Frontier County*. Stanford, 1959.

Danky, James P., editor. *Genealogical Research: An Introduction to the Resources of the State Historical Society of Wisconsin*. Madison, State Historical Society of Wisconsin, 1979.

Ginke, Hazel. "Fitzgerald Station and Its Neighborhood," c1926. Oshkosh Public Museum manuscript collection.

Heming, Harry H. *The Catholic Church in Wisconsin*. Milwaukee, 1986.

The History of Jo Daviess County, Illinois. Chicago, 1878; reproduced by Heritage League of Northwest Illinois, Stockton, Illinois, 1973.

Holmes, Fred L. *Old World Wisconsin*. Eau Claire, 1944. Chapter IX.

Humphrey, Desmond J. "Irish Settlers in Milwaukee," *Wisconsin Magazine of History*, XIII (June 1930), pp. 365-374.

Johnston, James. *Notes on North America*, 2 vols. London, 1851.

Kelly, Sister Mary Gilbert, O.P. *Catholic Immigrant Colonization Projects in the U.S. (1815-60)*, monograph (XVII), United States Catholic Historical Society, 1939.

King, Joseph A. *The Irish Lumberman-Farmer*. Lafayette, California, 1982.

_____. "The Tyrrells of Co. Wexford," *Journal of the Old Wexford Society*, 7 (1978-1979).

McDonald, Grace. *History of the Irish in Wisconsin in the Nineteenth Century*. New York, 1976, first published 1954.

Metress, Seamus P. *The Irish-American Experience: A Guide to the Literature.*" Bibliography. Washington, D.C., 1981.

Nelligan, John. *The Life of a Lumberman*. Madison, 1929.

Onahan, William J. "Irish Settlements in Illinois," *Catholic World*, vol. 33 (1881).

Rummel, Leo. *History of the Catholic Church in Wisconsin*. Madison, 1976.

Sinsinawa (Wisconsin) Dominican Archives. Correspondence between J.A. King and archivist Sister Marie Laurence Kortendick, O.P., between 1978 and 1988.

Stephenson, Isaac. *Recollections of a Long Life*. Chicago, 1915, chapter 4.

Strong, M.M. *History of the Territory of Wisconsin (1836-1848)*. Madison, Wisconsin, 1885.

Sweet, James R. *Genealogy and Local History: An Archival and Bibliographical Guide.* Genealogical Associates, Evanston, Illinois, 1962.

Synon, Mary. *Mother Emily.* Milwaukee, 1955.

Titus, William A. "Meeme: A Frontier Settlement that Developed Strong Men," *Wisconsin Magazine of History*, vol. IV, p. 281.

United States Census, Wisconsin (state and territory), data from 1820 to 1880 census enumerations.

"Vinegar Hill Mine and Museum," a handout for tourists at the museum north of Galena, Illinois.

Whelan, Reverend Lincoln. "Then They: The Story of Monches," *Wisconsin Magazine of History*, September 1940.

Wisconsin Territorial Census, 1836 (indexed), 1838, 1842, 1846, 1847.

Chapter 10. Iowa: Pioneers and Sodbusters (MEF)

Note on Sources. Initial source for the story of Wexford, Iowa, was Kenneth Schmitz' work; for the story of the Lizard Settlement, Liam Doyle's article.

Alexander, W.E. *The History of Winneshiek and Allamakee Counties.* Sioux City, Iowa, 1913.

Calkin, Homer L. "The Irish in Iowa," *Palimpsest*, vol. 45, no. 2, 1964.

Carey, S.H. *The Irish Element in Iowa up to 1865.* Master's thesis, Catholic University of America, 1944.

Collections of the State Historical Society of Wisconsin, edited and annotated by Reuben G. Thwaites, vol. XIII, Madison, 1895. Contains the 1836 Wisconsin Territorial Census, maps of the territory, alphabetical index. Film P80-3791, reel 1.

Doyle, Liam. "St. Patrick's on the Lizard," in *Africa: St. Patrick's Missions*, vol. 45, no. 8, November 1983, County Wicklow, Ireland, and Clifford Park, New Jersey.

Hancock, Ellery M. *Past and Present in Allamakee County*, 2 vols. Chicago, 1913.

Hoffman, Matthias M. *Centennial History of the Archdiocese of Dubuque.* Dubuque, 1938.

_____. *The Church Founders of the Northwest.* Milwaukee, 1937.

Kelly, Sister Mary Gilbert, O.P. *Catholic Immigrant Colonization Projects in the United States.* New York, 1939. United States Catholic Historical Society Monograph Series XVIII.

Lokken, Roscoe L. *Iowa Public Land Disposal.* Iowa City, 1942.

Pratt, Harlow M. *History of Fort Dodge and Webster County, Iowa*, 2 vols. Chicago, 1913.

Rohrbough, Malcolm J. *The Land Office Business.* New York, 1968.

Schmitz, Reverend Kenneth P. "Father Thomas Hore and Wexford, Iowa," *The Past* (Ui Cinsealaigh Historical Society), no. 11, 1975-76; also *Wexford, Iowa, 1851-1876*, master's thesis, St. Paul's Seminary, St. Paul, Minnesota, 1959. .

United States Department of Commerce, Bureau of the Census, *Ancestry of the Population by State, 1980: Supplementary Report.* PC80-S1-10, April, 1983.

Chapter 11. Texas: Soldiers, Priests, Empresarios (MEF)

Note 1: Irish. The Irish who fought for Mexico were actually few in number compared to the great number, probably more than half the total troops, who fought for Texas and the United States. Of the enlisted men and regulars, General Winfield Scott wrote: "Truth obliges me to say that, of our Irish soldiers, save for a few who deserted from General Taylor and who had never taken the naturalization oath - not one ever turned his back before the enemy or faltered in advancing to the charge." Among the officers of Irish birth and descent who fought beside Generals Scott and Taylor there were some who would later distinguish themselves as generals on opposing sides in the American Civil War: Philip Kearny, who lost an arm at Churubusco; Thomas Sweeny, who also lost an arm and who later became a Fenian general; Ulysses Simpson Grant, 18th President of the United States; George B. McClellan; George Meade; James Shields; and Thomas (Stonewall) Jackson.

Bancroft, Hubert H. *History of the North Mexican States and Texas*, 2 vols. San Francisco, 1886, 1889.

Bolton, Herbert E. *Exploration in the Southwest 1542-1706*. New York, 1916.

_____. *Texas in the Middle 18th Century: Studies in Spanish Colonial History and Administration*. Austin, 1970.

Castaneda, Carlos E. *Our Catholic Heritage in Texas, 1519-1936*, 7 vols. Austin, 1936.

Cox, Patricia. *Medalla Conmemorativa de Homenaje al Heroico Batallón on de San Patricio*. 24-page pamphlet, Patronato de Homenaje al Heroico Batallón de San Patricio, Mexico City, 1960.

Ericson, Carolyn R. *Residents of Texas, 1782-1835*. Nacogdoches, Texas, 1984. Out-of-print census records from 1782 to 1835. Institute of Texan Cultures has translations of the Spanish-Mexican censuses on three rolls of film, as published by Ericson. Some censuses were destroyed, so records are incomplete. However, Spanish and Mexicans took annual censuses which collected much information. In 1790, the maiden names of wives were listed. The 1809 census inaugurated the listing of names and ages of children; also nativity of individuals, where they were from, when they immigrated, where they lived, what property they inherited and how they inherited it. Ericson, in another work, not listed above (*Citizens and Foreigners of the Nacogdoches District, 1809-1836*, 2 vols., Nacogdoches, Texas, 1985), prints a copy of an unusual Texas record of "Registration of Foreigners." Foreigners who emigrated to Texas before 1809 were required to register and give age, nativity, occupation, religion, and length of residence in area. This was repeated in 1820. Also printed is a copy of those registering under the Colonization Law of 1825, similar information. In 1835, when the last Mexican census was taken in Texas, immigrants had to provide Character Certificates, with not only similar information but also names of local witnesses to their credentials or names of credible witnesses in their homelands. *(See White, below.)*

Flannery, John B. *The Irish Texans*. San Antonio, 1980.

Galloway, Mary Katherine. "The Irish of Staggers Point." Undated manuscript, in collection of library of University of Texas Institute of Texan Cultures, San Antonio.

Heitman, Francis, compiler. *Historical Register and Dictionary of the United States Army from Its Organization, September 29, 1789, to March 2, 1903*, 2 vols. Washington, D.C., Government Printing Office, 1903; republished 1965. Data on enlistments and desertions during Mexican War, vol. II, p. 282.

Hennessy, Maurice. *The Wild Geese*. Old Greenwich, Connecticut, 1973.

Hopkins, G.T., "The San Patricio Battalion in the Mexican War," *Journal of the United States Cavalry Association*, September 1913, 278-290.

Jones, Ann T. "The Texas Irish," *Irish Echo* (New York), July 2, 1983. Interview of author John Flannery.

McBeath, Sister James Joseph. *The Irish Empresarios of Texas*. Master's thesis, Catholic University of America, 1953.

McCornack, Richard B., "The San Patricio Deserters in the Mexican War," *The Americas*, vol. VIII, no. 2, October 1951.

McEniry, Sister Blanche Marie. *American Catholics in the War with Mexico*. Washington, D.C., 1937. See Chapter 5, "The San Patricio Battalion."

Miller, Robert Ryal. *Shamrock and Sword: The Saint Patrick's Battalion in the U.S.-Mexican War*. Norman, Oklahoma, 1989.

Oberste, William H. *Texas Irish Empresarios and Their Colonies*. Austin, 1953.

Potter, George W. *To the Golden Door: The Story of the Irish in Ireland and America*. Boston, 1960.

Power, Walter, "Facets of the Mexican War," *The Recorder*, Journal of the American Irish Historical Society, vol. 36, 1975.

Rice, Bernadine. "The Irish in Texas," *Journal of the American Irish Historical Society,* vol. 30, pp. 60-70, 1932.

Richardson, Rupert H. *Texas: The Lone Star State.* Englewood Cliffs, New Jersey, 1958.

Rives, George L. *The United States and Mexico, 1821-1848,* 2 vols. New York, 1913; republished 1969.

Scott, Winfield. *Memoirs of Lieut.-General Scott, L.L.D, Written by Himself,* 2 vols. New York, 1864.

Semmes, Raphael. *Service Afloat and Ashore during the Mexican War.* Cincinnati, Ohio, 1851. Especially pp. 120-21, 221, 427-28, for battles of Chrurubusco and Chapultepec. An abridged edition of this work was published: *The Campaign of General Scott in the Valley of Mexico.* Cincinnati, 1852.

Shea, John Gilmary. *History of the Catholic Church in the United States,* vol. IV. New York, 1886-1892.

Sweeny, William M., "The Irish Soldier in the War with Mexico," *Journal of the American Irish Historical Society,* vol. XXVI (1927).

Taylor, Virginia H. *The Spanish Archives of the General Land Office of Texas.* Austin, 1955. Appendix contains alphabetical list of settlers who obtained a Spanish land grant in Texas, plus related information, mostly Mexican land grants from 1824 to 1835.

Trigg, Lina. *Father Miguel Muldoon: The Story of an Early Pioneer Priest.* Master's thesis, St. Mary's University, San Antonio, Texas, 1940.

Wallace, Edward S., "Deserters in the Mexican War," *Hispanic American Historical Review,* XV, 374-380.

Wallace, Ernest J., and David M. Vigness. *Documents of Texas History.* Austin, 1963.

Williams, Villamae, editor. *Stephen F. Austin's Register of Families.* Baltimore, 1984.

White, Gifford, editor. *Character Certificates in the General Land Office of Texas.* Baltimore, 1985.

Chapter 12. California: Lure of Gold and Soil (JAK)
Note 1: Donner Party. Surviving intact were Irish-born Catholics Patrick and Margaret Breen and their seven children; and Irish-born Protestant James F. Reed, his wife Margaret, and their four children. The Breens seem to have been more frugal than others in husbanding their limited food resources. Patrick kept a diary of the ordeal, and his entries for February 5 and February 26, 1847, read in part: [Feb. 5] "We have but a little meat left & only part of 3 hides...Murphys folks [family of widow Lavina Murphy of Tennessee] or Keysburgs say they cant eat hide. I wish we had enough of them...[Feb. 26] Mrs. Murphy said here yesterday that [she] thought she would commence on Milt [Elliott] & eat him. I dont think she has done so yet. It is distressing." The four Reed children survived only because they were taken into the Breen cabin. One of them, Virginia, prayed with the Breens every morning and evening, and vowed to become a Catholic if she survived. She kept the vow when she later married John Murphy, son of Martin Murphy of the 1844 Murphy/Stevens Party. (See Virginia Reed Murphy, *Across the Plains with the Donner Party.*) Irish-born Patrick Dolan, age forty and single, achieved the unhappy distinction of being perhaps the first person eaten by Donner Party members.

A plaque in front of Old St. Raymond's Church in Dublin, California, wrongly credits Captain Jeremiah Fallon as being one of the rescuers. The credit should go to Captain William O. "Le Gros" Fallon, a huge and fabled mountain man who led the fourth rescue party. (The literature on the Donner Party is immense. See especially George R. Stewart, *Ordeal by Hunger;* also *Donner Miscellany: 41 Diaries and Documents,* ed. by Carroll D. Hall, which contains on pp. 86-87 a copy of the agreement William Fallon and his partners struck with John Sinclair, guardian of the orphaned children of Jacob Donner, for one-half of any property and money of the Donner brothers that the rescue party recovered.) William Fallon's lurid account of the alleged cannibalism of Lewis Keseberg, widely reported in the press, led to a suit in which Keseberg was awarded nominal damages of $1 after a jury trial at Sutter's Fort.

Nevertheless, a third "Captain Fallon," a native of County Cork, has sometimes been credited with leading the fourth or last rescue party. He was Thomas Fallon of Santa Cruz, San Jose, and San Francisco. His path crossed that of William "LeGros" Fallon at Sutter's Fort, where records of arrivals and departures sometimes confuse the two, and in the California Battalion, in which they both served during the revolt against Mexican Rule. Thomas was elected mayor of San Jose in the 1850s, accumulated much property, and was regularly sued in the courts by a number of people, including two priests (see Bancroft Library file CB 421 Box H, folders 442-448, on film CB 421 mf), two divorced wives, and a mistress. Bernard DeVoto, *The Year of Decision, 1846,* erroneously credits Thomas Fallon as the leader of the fourth rescue, as does Thomas McEnery in the fictionalized biography, *California Cavalier: The Journal of Thomas Fallon.*

Another plaque at Old St. Raymond's Cemetery in Dublin, California, erroneously credits John Martin as a member of one of the rescue missions to the Donners. Actually, it was John's brother Denis Martin, pioneer lumberman of Santa Clara County, who, arriving alone and on snowshoes, performed the heroic rescue of young Moses Schallenberger of the Murphy/Stevens Party of 1844. Two years later, the same Denis Martin rejected an appeal to lead a rescue party to the Donner group, stranded by the same lake. In any case, John Martin of the Dublin community was not a member of any of the rescue parties, the names of all the members being well-documented. (See J. Quinn Thornton, *The California Tragedy,* ed. by Joseph A. Sullivan, pp. 62-63; Moses Schallenberger, *The Opening of the California Trail,* ed. by George R. Stewart; and, for an accurate recording of the members of the Donner Party and of the rescue missions, the appendix by editor William R. Jones to *Across the Plains in the Donner Party* by Virginia Reed Murphy, pp. 56-58.)

Note 2: Amador. Perhaps there was some poetic justice here. Amador, a brutal man by any standards past or present, tells how he invited wild Indians suspected of stealing his horses and other live stock to a feast as his guests, then proceeded to kill about two hundred of them with arrows and shots to the head, after personally baptizing the heathen among them. Before his death at Watsonville in 1883 at the age of eighty-nine, Amador gave an account of the slaughter in his *Memorias,* an unpublished manuscript in Spanish, with a translation into English, in the archives of the Bancroft Library, University of California at Berkeley.

Note 3: Pioneer Families. Information on several of the pioneer Alameda County, California, families (Martin, Lyster, McGrath, Carrell, O'Brien, Murphy, and others) was obtained from papers at the Murray Museum in Dublin, California. Many copies of last wills and testaments, deeds, etc., are among the papers. Newspaper clippings, obituaries, copies of items from local histories and manuscripts are often not identified as to source or date. One valuable and identified item is an Australian immigration document on Lawrence and Sarah Lyster. It notes their departure from Kingstown, Ireland, on the ship *Crusader* on September 1839, their arrival in Australia on January 15, 1840 ("brought out by Government"), their occupations (stonemason and dairywoman), their parents' names and occupations, their county of origin, their religion, names and ages of their children, and more. Source: "Entitlement Certificates for Immigrants arriving on the ship *Crusader,*" AO N.S.W. Ref: 4/4853 (Reel 131), with a further note: "The series Persons on Government Ships, 1840 (4/4781 p. 65 Reel 2668) noted that Laurence Lyster was working in Sydney, wages and conditions unknown." This is an unusually rich genealogical source.

Note 4: Lynch Family. The original of the William Lynch letter is in the manuscript collection of the Bancroft Library, University of California at Berkeley. A sole surviving granddaughter of William Lynch, Viola Lynch Jones, was living in 1989 at age ninety-two in Walnut Creek, California, just a few miles from what once was the site of the Lynch home on Norris Lane, now known as Crow Canyon Road, where she was born and raised. For a reunion in 1987, Mrs. Jones and other members of the family prepared and privately printed an excellent family history, *Memories As I Knew My Family*, which has been drawn upon in this chapter.

Note 4a: Dougherty. The "rugged individualism" of James W. Dougherty was perhaps more a consequence of his Tennessee roots than of any far-back Irish and Protestant roots. In a remarkable study of over seven hundred Protestant families from County Tipperary who emigrated to Canada between 1814 and 1864, Bruce Elliott has shown that they followed a pattern of chain migration based on kinship quite similar to the pattern of Irish Catholic emigration. Elliott's book (*Irish Migrants in the Canadas: A New Approach*, Kingston and Montreal, 1988), which came to the author's attention after this chapter had been prepared for printing, tends to confirm the studies of D.H. Akenson, cited elsewhere.

Note 5: Carrell's Diaries. The excerpts from the diaries of Edward B. Carrell have been taken from copies of pp. 94, 143, and 630 of a typewritten and heavily footnoted manuscript that was found at the Murray Museum in Dublin, California. The author, not identified, had access to the diaries. These diaries cover the years 1846, 1850-51, 1856-58, and 1860-62, according to a note on p. 378 of Hoover, *et al.*, *Historic Spots in California*, 3rd edition revised by William N. Abeloe, Stanford, 1966. In 1966, says Abeloe, the diaries were in the possession of Earle E. Williams, Tracy, California.

Note 6: McGrath Family. There is a tangled web of family relationships. Dominick McGrath was born in Derryshannage, County Longford, on June 6, 1827, son of Peter McGrath and Mary Davis. Bridget Donlon was born in the same county about 1845, daughter of James Donlon, who had four children by each of two wives, names unknown (one possibly McCormack). A product of the first marriage was John Donlon, who married Mary McGovern (McGavin?) and who raised a family in Dublin, California. A product of the second marriage was Bridget Donlon, who married Dominick McGrath in Alameda County, California, in 1867. Therefore John Donlon was half-brother to Bridget and uncle to her children.

John Donlon's oldest son, James, was Assessor for Ventura County in 1888, and therefore a nephew of Bridget Donlon McGrath. Coincidentally, Patrick Murray and Jane Mannion of the Dublin community had a daughter Bridget (baptised at Elphin, County Roscommon, in 1837) and another daughter, June, who served as a witness at the 1867 wedding of Dominick McGrath and Bridget Donlon. More, a "Bridget McGrath" was listed as one of the surviving children of Patrick Murray at the time of his death in 1880. Were there two Bridgets, one the daughter of James Donlon, the other the daughter of Patrick Murray, and did both marry McGraths?

One of Patrick Murray's sons, Luke, married his first cousin, Mary Catherine Fallon, daughter of Jeremiah Fallon and Ellen Murray, suggesting that marriages of close kin were not unknown among these families who emigrated from the neighboring counties of Longford and Roscommon. (For sources researched, see bibliographical items: Bodle, Chancery Archives, Foote, Foxworthy, Heritage Park Museum, Livermore-Amador Valley Historical Society Museum, U.S. Censuses for 1860 1870, 1880, 1900, for Alameda County.)

Note 7: Timothy Murphy. Coolaneck, allegedly the birthplace of Timothy Murphy, was apparently a townland, but it was not among the listings of townlands on the 1851 Irish census. See *General Alphabetical Index to the Townlands and Towns, Parishes and Baronies of Ireland, 1851.* The absence of Coolaneck or similar listing might be a consequence of the fact that many of the old townlands were subsumed by other townlands, or their names changed, in the Ordnance Survey of the 1840s.

Note 8:   Tormey Family.   This chapter regrettably has not included the story of the Tormeys of County Westmeath. John Tormey sailed from Galway with his sister Ann in 1849. In 1854, after mining in the Sierras, John and partners purchased 3,000 acres in Napa County. In 1858, he was joined by his brother Patrick, two sisters, and a third brother from Ireland. In the 1860s, John purchased the 2,000-acre Pinole Grant on San Pablo Bay in Contra Costa County, and soon he and brother Patrick bought another 7,000 acres. The Tormeys' grain and cattle business flourished. John was said to be one of the richest men in Contra Costa County at the time of his death in 1877. He served on the county's Board of Supervisors, as did Patrick (re-elected nine times), who died in 1907. (See article by Nilda Rego, *Contra Costa Times*, March 12, 1987, p. 5a.)

Bennett, Virginia Smith. *Dublin Reflections*. Dublin, California, 1981.

Bisceglia, Louis. *Irish Identity in the Mother Lode: The Hibernian Benevolence Society, Columbia, California, 1857-71.* "Working Papers in Irish Studies," Northeastern University, Boston, Massachusetts, 1986.

_____. "Irish Identity in the Mother Lode: Tuolumne and Calaveras Counties in the 1850's and 1870's," Chispa: The Quarterly of the Tuolumne County Historical Society, Sonora, California, October-December 1985.

Blessing, Patrick, *West Among the Strangers: Irish Migration to California, 1850-1880.* Unpublished doctoral dissertation, University of California at Los Angeles, 1977, on film.

Bodle, Yvonne, "The McGrath Story," Ventura County Historical Society Quarterly, vol. xxii, no. 4, Summer 1977.

Burchell, R.A. *The San Francisco Irish: 1848-1880.* Berkeley and Los Angeles, 1980.

California Territorial Census of 1852, Counties of Santa Clara and Contra Costa (from which present-day Alameda County was formed in 1854). Sutro Library, San Francisco.

Callison, Charles, 2693 Orinda Drive, San Jose, California 95121. Novel in progress, *The Seventy Year Journey.* Mr. Callison engaged in excavations in the Niles Canyon, Alameda County, California, locating what he believes to be the foundation stones of the residence of Joaquin Murrieta and Rosita Feliz. He has also accumulated extensive genealogies on the Murrieta and Feliz families.

Chancery Archives of the Archdiocese of San Francisco, P.O. Box 1799, Colma, California 94014. Baptismal registers for Mission San Jose, 1797-1859. See also *Book of Baptisms*, 1850-53 (sixty-one pages), kept by circuit-riding Father Maximiano Agurto, and *Book of Decedents*, 1852-53 (only fifteen entries), kept by same priest, who sometimes served Dublin, Alameda County, settlers. File B13.7.

Clark, Dennis. *Hibernia America: The Irish and Regional Cultures.* New York, 1986.

Colorful Place Names of Northern California. Wells Fargo Bank pamphlet, 1957.

Davis, Dorothy. *A Pictorial History of Pleasanton* (California). Pleasanton Bicentennial Heritage Committee, 1976.

DeVoto, Bernard, *The Year of Decision: 1846.* Boston, 1943. Devoto mentions "Norris" as one of the companions of J. Quinn Thornton of the Thornton/Boggs Party, which took the Fort Hall route. This could be the Leo Norris who became part of the Dublin-San Ramon community, and it is very possible that Jeremiah Fallon and Michael Murray were also in this party. Complete lists of names of the members of the many parties, often loosely organized, among the approximately 500 wagons with about 2,000 persons who crossed to California in 1846 were never recorded and, except for the more famous groups such as the Donners, are lost to posterity.

Dowling, Patrick J. *California: The Irish Dream*, San Francisco, 1988. This book (the best to date on the California Irish) by the Director of the United Irish Cultural Center Library in San Francisco, came to the author's attention after the chapter was written. Dowling points up the considerable Irish presence in 19th century rural and urban California. See especially Chapter 21 on the Marin County Irish.

Doyle, Leonard. "The Irish of the Old West," *The Irishman* (San Francisco monthly newspaper), December, 1984. Review of McGrath book.

Early Days of San Ramon and Dublin, no author shown, published by Braun and Kauffmann, Inc., 1967. Alameda County Library collection, Dublin Branch.

Foote, H.S., ed. *Pen Pictures from the Garden of the World.* Chicago, 1888. See biographical sketch of Dominick McGrath, pp. 566-67. On film at Sutro Library, San Francisco.

Foxworthy, Donald F., 510 Overbrook Road, Baltimore, Maryland (great-grandson of Jeremiah Fallon). Genealogical data, including Irish records on Fallons and Murrays.

Geiger, Alice McCabe. *County Cavan to California: Edward McCabe (1827-1894) and the "Irish Colony" in the San Joaquin Valley,* edited and printed privately by Robert and Carol DeWolf, 2157 Golden Rain Road #3, Walnut Creek, California.

Giovinco, Joseph. *The Ethnic Dimension of Calaveras County History.* Unpublished paper, undated, N.E.H.-Calaveras Heritage Council, San Andreas, Calaveras County, California, cited by Bisceglia.

Great Register of Voters, for year 1867, Alameda County, California. Copy at Heritage Museum, Dublin, California.

Green, Marion, "Dublin's Old Roads Have Colorful History," *The Valley Times* (Alameda County, California), September 29, 1984. Information on early stage lines.

Gudde, Edwin G. *California Place Names.* Berkeley, California, 1969.

Guinn, J.M. *History of the State of California and Biographical Records of Coast Counties, California.* Chicago, 1904.

Hagemann, Herbert L., Box 28, Livermore, California. A local historian interviewed by Ann Doss, March 14, 1984. Typewritten transcript of the interview is in files of Livermore-Amador Valley Historical Society Museum, Pleasanton. Also letter from Hagemann to King, January 1, 1988, with information on Amador Valley pioneers, including Captain Jack O'Brien, mining, sheepherders.

Hall, Carroll D., editor, *Donner Miscellany: 41 Diaries and Documents.* San Francisco, 1947, pp. 86-87.

Halley, William. *The Centennial Year Book of Alameda County.* Oakland, California, 1876.

Hammond, George P. *The Weber Era in Stockton History.* Friends of the Bancroft Library, University of California, Berkeley, 1982. See Chapter IX for account of Murphy family.

Heritage Park Museum, Dublin, California, and adjoining cemetery - plaques and headstone inscriptions. See note above.

Historical Sites and Landmarks of Alameda County, California, edited by George Tays, under the auspices of the Works Progress Administration. Oakland, California, 1938. See pp. 228-37, "Rancho San Ramon."

History of Alameda County, California. M.W. Wood Publisher, Oakland, 1883. See also Frank C. Merritt, History of Alameda County, California, vol. 1, Chicago, 1928.

History of Contra Costa County. San Francisco, 1882 (no author cited).

History of the Catholic Community in Suisun-Fairfield, 1861-1986. The Centenary Book Committee, 1050 N. Texas St., Box X, Fairfield, California 94533-0624, 1987.

History of Marin County, California. Republished 1972 by Charmaine B. Veronda, Box 505, Petaluma, California 94952. Abstract of deeds, Timothy Murphy; biographies of James Miller, John Lucas, Edward Mahon.

History of Ventura County, California, vol. II. Chicago, 1926. Information on Scarlett/Lyster families, pp. 152-55.

Hoover, Mildred B., H.E. Rensch, and E.G. Rensch. *Historic Spots in California,* 3rd edition revised by William N. Abeloe. Stanford, California, 1966. See pp. 377-78 for information on Edward B. Carrell and Jack O'Brien; also valuable for data on Murphy and Martin families.

Hunt, Rockwell D. *Personal Sketches of California Pioneers I Have Known*. Stockton, California, 1962. See pp. 43-48 for sketch of Virginia Reed of Donner Party, who married John M. Murphy of Murphy-Townsend-Stevens Party.

Keifer, Veronica, *My Grandma Tole [sic] Me*. Unpublished 14-page manuscript by a great-granddaughter of Jeremiah Fallon, September 13, 1956, Twain Harte, California (copy in J.A. King's file).

Keyser, Christine, "St. Pat's Tale: Michael Halloran Meet Michael Halloran Meet. . ." in *Contra Costa Times*, Walnut Creek, California, March 17, 1987, pp. 1-2.

Kolb, H.W., "Dublin's Early History," 3-page manuscript, January 7, 1965, in Heritage Park Museum collection, Dublin, California.

Latta, Frank. *Joaquin Murrieta and His Horse Gangs*. Santa Cruz, California, 1980.

Leonard, Elizabeth, and Yvonne Bodle. *The McGrath Story and Genealogical Chart*, Oxnard, California, 1972, private printing. See also revised version by Yvonne Bodle, "The McGrath Story," *The Ventura County Historical Society Quarterly*, vol. XXII, no. 4, Summer 1977.

Livermore-Amador Valley Historical Society Museum, Pleasanton, California. Records include original Donors' List, Old St. Raymond's Church, Dublin; also list of all headstone inscriptions, Old Dublin Cemetery.

MacManus, Seumas, "Man of Aran," an account of the author's meeting James Concannon, pp. 9-14 in *Chimney Corners: A Journal of Recreation for the Irish Home*, published by Seumas MacManus, vol. 1, no. 12, October 22, 1938, Longford, Ireland.

Mann, Ralph. *After the Gold Rush: Society in Grass Valley and Nevada City, California, 1849-1870*. Stanford, California, 1982.

Mason, Jack, with Helen Van Cleave Park. *Early Marin*, 2nd revised edition. Marin County [California] Historical Society, 1971. See Chapter 4, "The Sons of Erin," pp. 34-46.

McEnery, Thomas. *California Cavalier: The Journal of Captain Thomas Fallon*. Inishfallen Enterprises, Inc., San Jose, California, 1978.

McGrath, Roger D. *Gunfighters, Highwaymen & Vigilantes: Violence on the Frontier*. Berkeley and Los Angeles, 1984.

_____. "The Silver Kings," *American Irish Newsletter*, September 1987.

Murphy, Virginia Reed. *Across the Plains with the Donner Party*, ed. by William R. Jones. Golden, Colorado, 1980.

Official and Historical Atlas Map of Alameda County. Thompson and West, Oakland, 1878. First appearance of name Dublin on a county map. Also contains the 1870 figures on native and foreign-born population by county, p. 165.

Philby, P. William. *A Bibliography of American County Histories*. Baltimore, 1985.

Prendergast, Thomas F. *Forgotten Pioneers: Irish Leaders in Early California*. San Francisco, 1942. This was the best account, before Patrick J. Dowling's work appeared, of early Irish pioneers in California. Prendergast rejects, however, the evidence of traveller William Redmond Ryan *(Personal Adventures in Upper and Lower California)* regarding the liaison of one of the Murphys with an Indian chief's daughter at Murphys Camp, citing minor errors in the Ryan book, published in London in 1852, in an effort to destroy Ryan's credibility. One of the supposed errors is a reference to Mount Diablo being "snow-capped," and another is to Charles Weber's surname being given as "Weaver." However, any resident of Contra Costa County, including this author, can testify that Mount Diablo is indeed snow-capped once or twice almost every winter; and that a popular pronunciation of Weber was WEE-BER, very close to Weaver.

Schallenberger, Moses. *The Opening of the California Trail*, ed. by George R. Stewart. Berkeley, California, 1953.

Several, Robert, "They Were Almost Too Quiet," *Independent* (Alameda County newspaper), March 31, 1982. Charles Dougherty's attempt to have town named after his family. On same subject, see also Chris Anderson, "The Man Who Created the City That Never Was," *Herald and News* (Livermore, Pleasanton, Dublin), July 24, 1967.

Stewart, George R. *Ordeal by Hunger: The Story of the Donner Party,* revised and enlarged. Boston, 1960.

Sullivan, Sister Gabrielle. *Martin Murphy Jr.:California Pioneer 1844-1884.* Stockton, California, 1974.

Thornton, J. Quinn. *The California Tragedy,* ed. by Joseph A. Sullivan. Oakland, 1945, pp. 62-63 for information on Denis Martin.

United States Census, 1860, 1870, 1880, 1900, 1910, for Murray Township, Alameda County; also Township No. 2, Contra Costa County. The Dublin community is on the borderline of the two counties. Also *California State Census* for 1852, Santa Clara and Contra Costa Counties.

Walsh, James P., "The Irish in Early San Francisco," Chapter 2 of *The San Francisco Irish, 1850-76,* edited by James P. Walsh. Irish Literary and Historical Society of San Francisco, 1978.

Chapter 13. Place Names from Ocean to Ocean (MEF and JAK)

Gannett, Henry. *The Origin of Certain Place Names in the United States,* 2nd edition, United States Geological Survey Bulletin #258, 1905; republished Baltimore, 1973, 1977.

Hamilton, W.D. *Old North Esk Revised.* Fredericton, New Brunswick, 1988. See genealogy of the Flynn family.

Hammond Medallion World Atlas. Hammond, Inc., Maplewood, New Jersey, 1973.

Houston, C.J., and W.J. Smyth, "The Irish Abroad: Better Questions Through a Better Source," *Irish Geography* (Derry, Ireland), vol. 13 (1980), pp. 1-19 and footnotes. Data on population of Ontario, 1871.

Jackson, Louise A. *Beulah: A Biography of the Mineral King Valley in California.* Tuczon, Arizona, 1988. The author is indebted to historian Alfred Pietroforte of Visalia, California, for calling this book - and pioneer Harry O'Farrell aka Parole - to his attention.

Mitchell, Brian. *A New Genealogical Atlas of Ireland.* Baltimore, 1986.

Mobil Travel Maps (Rand McNally), 1980. Individual maps of each state.

O'Brien, Michael J. *Irish Settlers in America,* 2 vols. Genealogical Publishing Co., Baltimore, 1979, excerpted from articles in *Journal of the American Irish Historical Society,* 1906-1930.

Pioneer Society of the State of Michigan. *Collections of the Pioneer Society of the State of Michigan,* vol. 18 (1892), pp. 625-26, 694. Data on Charles M. O'Malley, courtesy of Robert Ryal Miller, Professor Emeritus in History, California State University at Hayward.

Rand McNally Road Atlas and Travel Guide: United States. New York, 1978 and 1980.

United States Post Office, *Zip Code Directory,* 1972 edition.

United States Department of Interior Geological Survey maps for Silver Lake, Yosemite National Park, and Sequoia National Park, California.

Special Note. The authors are indebted to the many mayors, county clerks, librarians, historical society officials, and members of the chambers of commerce who took time to respond to requests for information on the origin of Irish-appearing names of their localities.

Chapter 14. St. Patrick's Day Celebrations (MEF)

Note 1: Molly Maguires. Nineteen leaders of the Mollies were convicted of capital crimes and sent to the gallows. In 1979 and 1983, largely as a result of research by legal scholars and historians, the executed Irish labor leaders were granted posthumous pardons. Signing the pardon for John Kehoe in January 1979, Governor Sharp of Pennsylvania commented on the anti-Irish and anti-labor sentiments of the century before, and said: "We can be proud of these men known as the Molly Maguires, because they defiantly faced allegations to make trade unionism a criminal conspiracy. These men gave their lives on behalf of the labor struggle."

Bimba, Anthony. *The Molly Maguires.* New York, 1950.
Condon, Edward O'Meagher. *The Irish Race in America.* New York, 1887; republished New York, 1976.
Cosgrove, J.I. "The Hibernian Society of Charleston, South Carolina," *Journal of the American Irish Historical Society,* 1925-26, pp. 150-158.
Crimmins, John D. *St. Patrick's Day: Its Celebration in New York and Other American Places, 1737-1845.* New York, 1902.
Doyle, David N. *Ireland, Irishmen and Revolutionary America 1760-1820.* Cork, Ireland, 1981.
Fallows, Marjorie. *Irish American Identity and Assimilation.* Englewood Cliffs, New Jersey, 1979.
Gallagher, Thomas. *Paddy's Lament.* New York, 1982.
Maguire, John F. *The Irish in America.* London, 1868, New York, 1969.
McCaffrey, Lawrence. *The Irish Diaspora in America.* Bloomington, 1976.
Nevins, Allan. *Abram S. Hewitt, with Some Account of Peter Cooper.* New York, 1935.
O'Brien, Michael. *A Hidden Phase of American History: Ireland's Part in America's Struggle for Liberty.* New York, 1919, and Baltimore, 1973.
_____. *Irish Settlers in America: A Consolidation of Articles from the Journal of the American Irish Historical Society,* 2 vols. Baltimore, 1979.
Ridge, John. *The St. Patrick's Day Parade in New York.* New York, 1988.
Shannon, William. *The American Irish: A Political and Social Portrait.* New York, 1963.
Wakin, Edward. *Enter the Irish-American.* New York, 1976.

NEWSPAPERS: *Brooklyn Eagle,* and these New York newspapers: *Daily News, Herald, Tribune, Sun, Times, World, Telegram, Irish Echo, Irish People, Irish World.*

Chapter 15. Highest Statesmen: Eighteen United States Presidents (JAK)
Note on Kennedy lineage: Documents provided by the John F. Kennedy Library in Boston on Kennedy/Fitzgerald lineage include: "The Kennedys of Massachusetts" by Edward L. Galvin, from *The Irish in New England* (Boston, 1985); "The American Ancestry of John Fitzgerald Kennedy" by Gary Boyd Roberts, from *The American Genealogist,* 53 (1977); copies of death certificates and obituaries, probate, census, cemetery, marriage, birth, Bible, family, city directory, and tax records, much of this accumulated by Doris Kearns Goodwin in preparation for her work, *The Fitzgeralds and the Kennedys*; family charts of the Hickey, Hannon, and Fitzgerald branches prepared by Harvey Rachlin. Considerable work has been done, the author has been told, by Joseph M. Glynn of the Irish Family History Society of Newton, Massachusetts, but an inquiry to the Society's 173 Tremont Street address has been returned ("moved out, not forwardable"). Father J. F. Brennan's *The Evolution of Everyman (Ancestral Lineage of John F. Kennedy)* (Dundalk, Ireland, 1968) cites James Fitzgerald of Skibbereen and Katherine Cadogan as the parents of JFK's grandfather, John "Honey Fitz" Fitzgerald, which is contrary to all United States records. Brennan cites the conclusions of the Irish Genealogical Office in Dublin as his authority for the Skibbereen origin of JFK's Fitzgeralds.

Bailey, Bernadine. *American Shrines in England.* Cranbury (New Jersey) and London, 1977.
Brennan, Reverend J.F. *The Evolution of Everyman (Ancestral Lineage of John F. Kennedy).* Dundalk, Ireland, 1968. Cites evidence of Irish Genealogical Office, Dublin. See note on Kennedy lineage, above.

Burke's Presidential Families of the United States of America, 2nd edition. London, 1981. See Appendix C, "Ancestral Tables of the Presidents," compiled by David Williams and Gary Boyd Roberts.

Concannon, John J., and Francis E. Cull. *The Irish American Who's Who*. New York, 1984.

Josephson, Matthew, and Hannah Josephson. *Al Smith: Hero of the Cities*. Boston, 1869.

Kennedy, Rose. *Times to Remember*. New York, 1974.

Myers, Albert. *Immigration of the Irish Quakers into Pennsylvania 1682-1750*. Swarthmore, 1902; republished Baltimore, 1969. Data on Milhous family.

Roberts, Gary Boyd. *Ancestors of American Presidents*. Santa Clarita, California, 1989. By far the best source.

Shanley, Reverend Kevin O'Neill. "American Presidents of Irish Descent," *Irish Echo* (weekly newspaper, New York), July 6, 1985.

Chapter 16. Seekers of Justice: Women in the Early Labor Movement (MEF)

Abbott, Edith. *Women in Industry: A Study in American Economic History*. New York, 1910; republished New York, 1969.

Andrews, John, and W.D.P. Bliss. *History of Women in Trade Unions*. Vol. X of *Report on the Conditions of Woman and Child Wage Earners in the United States*, Washington, D.C., 1911 (United States Senate Document No. 645, 61st Congress, 2nd Session, 1911).

Baxandall, Rosalyn and others, compilers and editors. *America's Working Women: A Documentary History, 1600 to the Present*. New York, 1976.

Brandeis, Louis, and Josephine Goldmark. *Women in Industry*. New York, 1908; republished New York, 1969..

Chase, John. *The Military Occupation of the Coal Strike Zone of Colorado by the Colorado National Guard*. Denver, 1914.

DeFord, Miriam. *They Were San Franciscans*. Caldwell, Idaho, 1941.

Diner, Hasia R. *Erin's Daughters in America*. Baltimore, 1983.

Fetherling, Dale. *Mother Jones, the Miners' Angel*. Carbondale, Illinois, 1974.

Foner, Philip S. *Women and the American Labor Movement from Colonial Times to the Eve of World War I*. New York, 1979.

Hand, William. "Chicago's Five Maiden Aunts," *American Magazine*, vol. 62, no. 5, 1906.

Henry, Alice. *The Trade Union Woman*. New York, 1915; republished New York, 1978.

———. *Women and the Labor Movement*. New York, 1923; republished New York, 1971.

James, Edward T., editor. *Notable American Women 1607-1950*, 3 vols. Cambridge, Massachusetts, 1974.

Jones, Mary Harris. *Autobiography of Mother Jones*. Chicago, 1925.

Lynch, Alice. *The Kennedy Clan and Tierra Redonda*. San Francisco, 1935.

Nestor, Agnes. *Woman's Labor Leader*. Rockford, Illinois, 1954.

Reid, Robert L., editor. *Battleground: The Autobiography of Margaret A. Haley*. New York, 1982.

Shannon, William V. *The American Irish: A Political and Social History*. New York, 1974.

Wertheimer, Barbara M. *We Were There: The Story of Working Women in America*. New York, 1977.

Collections:

Catholic University of America, Washington, D.C. Terence V. Powderly Papers, Mary Jones Papers.

Chicago Historical Society, Chicago, Illinois. Agnes Nestor Papers, including diary; Margaret Haley Papers, including autobiographical history of the Chicago Teachers Federation.

Radcliffe College, Cambridge, Massachusetts. Arthur and Elizabeth Schlesinger Library: Leonora O'Reilly Papers, Mary Kenney O'Sullivan Papers, National Women's Trade Union League of America Papers.
Smith College, Northampton, Massachusetts. Leonora M. Barry Lake Folio, in library's Women in Trade Union collection.

Chapter 17. Bing Crosby's Irish Roots (JAK)

Crosby, Bing (as told to Pete Martin). *Call Me Lucky*. New York, 1953. This book contains the misinformation that Bing's mother's parents were born in Ireland.
Danaher, Kevin. *Irish Country People*. Cork, 1966.
Griffith's Valuations, Parish of Schull (Skull), Barony of West Carbery (West Division), County Cork, compiled about 1848, published 1853. Filmed by Church of Jesus Christ of Latter-day Saints, Salt Lake City, Utah.
Hamilton, W. D. *Old North Esk on the Miramichi*. Fredericton, New Brunswick, Canada, 1979.
King, Joseph A. *The Irish Lumberman-Farmer*. Lafayette, California, 1982. Appendix A, Irish Records. See also bibliographical items following Chapter 4, "A Parish in West Cork," in this volume.
New Brunswick Census, Northumberland County, North Esk Parish, 1851, 1861.
O'Connell, Sheldon (with Gord Atkinson). *Bing: A Voice for all Seasons*. Tralee, Kerry, Ireland, 1984.
Records of the Catholic parishes of Schull and Goleen, County Cork, Ireland.
Records of the Catholic Church of St. Patrick's, Nelson-Miramichi, New Brunswick.
Records of the Catholic Church of St. Michael's, Stillwater, Minnesota.
Records of the Bing Crosby Historical Society, P. O. Box 8013, Tacoma, Washington 98408.
Records of Bob and June Crosby of La Jolla, California; and of Margaret Harrigan Kendall of Redmond, Washington.
Tithe Applotment Books, Parish of Schull (West Division), County Cork, Ireland, 1827. Filmed by Church of Jesus Christ of Latter-day Saints, Salt Lake City, Utah.

Chapter 18. Torch-Bearers: Religious Leaders and Founders (JAK)

Note 1: Margaret A. Cusack, "The Nun of Kenmare" (1829-99). Native of Coolock, County Dublin, of Church of Ireland parents; entered Anglican Sellonite Sisterhood in England in 1853; in 1858, accepted Roman Catholicism in London; in 1859, entered Irish Poor Clares as "Mother Mary Francis"; in 1861, opened convent at Kenmare in County Kerry, where began writing books on Irish history and social problems (e.g., *Women's Work in Modern Society*; *The Case of Ireland Stated: A Plea for My People and My Race*); by 1880, achieved fame as the controversial "Nun of Kenmare" (a strong advocate for women's suffrage and equal pay for equal work); founded Congregation of Sisters of St. Joseph of Peace in England in 1884 and sailed for America; opened convent and orphanage at Jersey City, New Jersey, but was frustrated in plans for expansion by Cardinal McCluskey and Archbishop Corrigan of New York, and other hierarchy; lectured widely under Protestant auspices on rights of women and intransigence of Catholic hierarchy; returned to Anglican faith and died at Leamington, England; two province houses in the United States in 1989, at Englewood Cliffs, New Jersey, and Bellevue, Washington, conducting educational, hospital, and social service work. (Information provided by Irene King Mennitt, Associate Member of CSJP and teacher of the blind, Lyndhurst, New Jersey.)

Note 2: Father John McMahon (1821-1872), Fenian Priest. Native of Drumgolat, County Monaghan; ordained by Bishop Crétin of St. Paul in 1855; pastor at Hastings, Minnesota, 1855-1860; was serving as pastor at Anderson, Indiana, in 1866 when he accompanied Fenian unit to Ft. Erie, Canada, serving as the chaplain for the forces under Fenian General O'Neill at the Battles of Ridgeway and Ft. Erie in June 1866; captured and sentenced to die after trial in Toronto that attracted international attention; sentence commuted; served over three years in jails in Toronto and Kingston before release in summer of 1869; lectured on allegedly brutal treatment received in prison, but Toronto Archdiocesan and other records indicate that he was vastly exaggerating and that he was a favored prisoner; parish pastor at Reynolds, Indiana, in 1872 at the time of his death. (See J.A. King, "The Fenian Invasion of Canada and John McMahon: Priest, Saint or Charlatan?" in *Eire-Ireland*, Winter 1988.)

Concannon, John, and Francis Cull, editors.   *The Irish American Who's Who*. New York 1984.

Delaney, John J. *Dictionary of American Catholic Biography*. New York, 1984.

Ellis, John Tracy, editor. *Documents of American Church History*, 2 vols., 3rd edition. Chicago, 1961.

Emerald Society Newsletter (New York City Board of Education), June 1987. Information on Father John Conor O'Hanlon and Father Thomas Shields.

Records of Sinsinawa Dominicans, courtesy of Sister Marie Laurence Kortendick, Sinsinawa, Wisconsin.

Family records on Mary Cassin (Sister Mary Bernard), the authors' great-grandaunt.

Chapter 19. Bias: American Historians (JAK)

Note 1: Virgil Blum, S.J., writing in the *Catholic League Newsletter* (April, 1987) calls attention to the study of Dr. Paul Vitz, professor of psychology at New York University, and his research team. They analyzed ninety popular textbooks. Of 670 items they reviewed in eleven texts used in third and sixth grades, they found that "there is not any story or article in all these books in which the central motivation or major content deals with religion. No character had a primary religious motivation. No informative article dealt with religion as a primary subject worthy of treatment." In a decision almost universally deplored in academia and later struck down by the United States Supreme Court, District Judge W. Brevard Hand, agreeing with Alabama parents who were concerned about such textbooks, observed: "These history books discriminate against the very concept of religion, and theistic religions in particular, by omissions so serious that a student learning history from them would not be apprised of relevant facts about American history."

Note 2: Another provocative analysis of school texts has been done by eleven historians sponsored by the Educational Excellence Network. Their analysis of grade and high school American history texts has been eloquently synthesized by Gilbert T. Sewall in *American History Texts: An Assessment of Quality* (Box 32, Teachers College, Columbia University, New York, New York, 10027), 1987, 78 pp. Sewall reports such problems as "the publishers' growing reluctance to make choices and judgments that might offend some individual or group" (p. 67). He says that "the many-splendored religious sects and movements" may be mentioned in some texts, but "only in a neutral grey zone where they receive little criticism and not too much credit for their achievements" (p. 68). He says that newer American history textbooks "too often [reflect] the declining power of the national history to inflame the imagination and capture the awe of common citizens. This trend may be explained by the sheer narcissism of a culture ignorant of the fact that it stands on the shoulders of giants of civilization long past that have shed much blood and spilled much ink to help create the generally salutary ideas, institutions, and conditions of the American present" (p. 71). A study of six American history textbooks by Nathan Glazer and Reed Ueda, focusing on ethnic history, indicated a tendency to oversimplify the history of ethnics, the old racist myths now having been replaced by new myths hailing the moral superiority of minorities.

Blessing, Patrick J. *West Among Strangers: Irish Migration to California, 1850-1880*. Unpublished doctoral dissertation, University of California at Los Angeles, 1977. Film LD791.9 HGB617.

Burchell, R.A. *The San Francisco Irish 1848-80.* Berkeley and Los Angeles, 1980.

Burner, David, and others. *An American Portrait: A History of the United States,* 2nd edition, vol. 1. New York, Charles Scribner's, 1985, 365 pp.

Clark, Dennis. *Hibernia America.* Westport, Connecticut, 1987.

Current, Richard, *et al. American History: A Survey (Since 1865),* 7th edition, vol II. New York, 1987.

Curti, Merle. *The Making of an American Community: A Case Study of Democracy in a Frontier County.* Stanford, 1959.

Divine, Robert A., and others. *America Past and Present (Brief Edition).* Glenview, Illinois, Scott, Foresman Co., 1984, 544 pp. + appendices.

Doyle, David Noel. "The Regional Bibliography of Irish America," *Irish Historical Studies,* May 1983.

Elliott, Bruce. *Irish Migrants in the Canadas: A New Approach.* Kingston and Montreal, 1988. See "Note 4a: Dougherty" to Chapter 12. Elliott's work casts doubt on Kerby Miller's thesis (*Emigrants and Exiles*) and generally confirms conclusions reached by D.H. Akenson and by Houston and Smyth, cited elsewhere. See critique of Miller on pp. 239-43, 315fn.

Fanning, Samuel J., "A Rebuttal to a Distorted History," *Irish Echo* (New York weekly newspaper), June 6, 1987. A severe criticism of Kerby Miller's *Emigrants and Exiles* by the late emeritus Professor of History, St. John's University, New York. See also Professor Miller's equally heated reply to Professor Fanning in same newspaper, June 27, 1987.

Garraty, John A., and Robert A. McCaughey. *The American Nation: A History of the U.S. to 1887,* 6th edition, vol. 1. New York, Harper & Row, 1987.

Glazer, Nathan, and Reed Ueda. *Ethnic Groups in History Textbooks.* Ethics and Public Policy Center, Lanham, Maryland, 1983.

King, Joseph A. "The Tyrrells of County Wexford," *Journal of the Old Wexford Society," 7* (1978-79).

_____. "Genealogy, History, and Irish Immigration," *The Canadian Journal of Irish Studies,* June 1984.

_____. Personal collection of J.A. King, letters from Ireland, Wisconsin, Minnesota, and Philadelphia, 1874 to 1921. Bolton, Cassin, Tyrrell, Fitzpatrick families.

Metress, Seamus P. *The Irish-American Experience: A Guide to the Literature.* Washington, D.C., 1981.

Miller, Kerby A. *Emigrants and Exiles: Ireland and the Irish Exodus to North America.* Oxford, 1986.

Walsh, Victor A., "Irish Nationalism and Land Reform: The Role of the Irish in America," in P.J. Drudy, ed., *The Irish in America,* Cambridge University Press, 1985. Referring to Kerby Miller's exile thesis, Dr. Walsh writes that "this sense of exile. . .was the wellspring from which Irish-American nationalism flowed" (p. 259).

Index to Persons

Index to Places